HEBES

HEBES

*A Guide to Species, Hybrids,
and Allied Genera*

LAWRIE METCALF

TIMBER PRESS

Published in 2006 by
Timber Press, Inc.
The Haseltine Building
133 S.W. Second Avenue, Suite 450
Portland, Oregon 97204-3527, U.S.A.
www.timberpress.com
For contact information regarding editorial, marketing, sales, and
distribution in the United Kingdom, see www.timberpress.co.uk.

Printed in China

Library of Congress Cataloguing-in-Publication Data

Metcalf, L. J. (Lawrence James), 1928–
    Hebes : a guide to species, hybrids, and allied genera / Lawrie Metcalf.
        p. cm.
    Includes bibliographical references (p.   ) and index.
    ISBN-13: 978-0-88192-773-3
    ISBN-10: 0-88192-773-2
    1. Hebe (Plants) I. Title.
    SB413.H43M48 2006
    635.9'3395—dc22

                                                          2005033503

A catalogue record for this book is also available from the British Library.

To my wife, Lena,
who is so very supportive and
has always been a great friend
and inspiration to me

As wild plants they grow on the sea-coast, in forests and shrubland, on dry or wet rocks, in swamps and bogs, on barren moorland, in the tussock-grasslands, and ascend to the snow-line, forming mossy cushions on the great screes of the Southern Alps, or the scoria of the volcanoes. In the garden there is no place, except the most shady, where one or other of the species will not thrive. The smaller whipcord, and prostrate glaucous veronicas [hebes], are admirable for the alpine garden, while the taller will adorn border or shrubbery.

Leonard Cockayne, *The Cultivation of New Zealand Plants*

Contents

Acknowledgments

In particular I would like to thank Professor Phil Garnock-Jones of Victoria University, Wellington, Michael Bayly of the Museum of New Zealand Te Papa Tongarewa, Wellington, and Shannel Courtney of the Department of Conservation, Nelson, for their unstinting assistance in answering my various requests for information and for sending me copies of relevant scientific papers. They certainly made my task much easier, and nothing seemed to be a trouble to them, even though they were all so very busy with their own projects.

I would like to especially thank the following for their respective contributions to Chapter 2: Neil Bell, community horticulturist at Oregon State University, and his colleague Tom Sauceda, curator of the New Zealand Garden, University of California Santa Cruz Arboretum, United States; Tony Hayter, honorary secretary of the Hebe Society, United Kingdom; Dr. Claudio Cervelli of the C.R.A. Experimental Institute for Floriculture in Sanremo, Italy; and Melanie Kinsey of the Ornamental Plant Conservation Association of Australia. They all willingly agreed to write various sections of the chapter, thus sharing their knowledge and experience as well as increasing the relevance of this book to hebe growers around the world.

My particular thanks must go to Stephen Burton of Annton Nursery, Cambridge, New Zealand, for being so ready to assist with information about various cultivars and for providing descriptive material concerning them. In addition I must mention the assistance of Robyn Smith of the Otari Native Botanic Garden, Wellington, and Jack Hobbs of the Auckland Regional Botanic Gardens, both of whom were most helpful when I was taking photographs of various hebes. Thanks, too, to Joe Cartman for the loan of the photograph of *Hebe ramosissima*.

I would like to thank my agent, Ray Richards, for his helpful suggestions when the project was in its gestation stage and for helping to steer it through its preliminary passage with the publishers. Finally, I must thank Jane Connor of Timber Press for having sufficient confidence in me to offer me the opportunity to write this book about New Zealand's largest and perhaps iconic genus of flowering plants. Also, many thanks to Mindy Fitch, who had, at times, the onerous task of editing the manuscript and coping with my differing opinions. If I have inadvertently forgotten to mention anybody, I trust they will assume my sincere thanks and accept my apology for the omission.

Introduction

When I told a friend I was writing a book on hebes, he said he expected it would be "the last word on this genus." However, I am not at all certain that any book will ever be the last word on any particular topic. There will always be new information and additional research, which means that no book can ever be definitive no matter how the author may try to make it so. In fact, recent developments that occurred during the preparation of this book demonstrated to me just how true that statement is. We have long been accustomed to having *Hebe* and related genera classified in the family Scrophulariaceae; it came as quite a surprise, therefore, to learn that *Hebe* was to be assigned to the Plantaginaceae. Similarly, further research being carried out will result in other major changes to what is perceived by many as the established order. Only time will tell whether those changes will receive general approbation.

My first memory of the shrubs that I later came to know as *Hebe* occurred when I was about four years old. In my parents' garden grew a large shrub that at the time was generally known to belong to *Veronica*, though in later years I learnt that the current name of the genus had actually been *Hebe*. As a child I had admired the numerous spikes of violet-blue flowers that seemed to adorn the shrub for quite long periods. Many years later, after having taken up horticulture as a career, I discovered that the plant was *Hebe* ×*andersonii* 'Andersonii'.

The nursery where I first worked grew quite a number of hebes, but even at that stage I discovered that some were incorrectly named—a not uncommon situation, even today, when we are supposed to be better educated about such things. In my late teens my great love of the back country of the South Island (probably inspired by the distant mountains that formed the backdrop to the Canterbury Plains), my great liking for tramping and climbing, and my enthusiasm for native New Zealand mountain flora, including hebes, led me to join the Canterbury Mountaineering Club.

Quite some years later, the Royal New Zealand Institute of Horticulture appointed me as international registrar of cultivar names for *Hebe* and several other native genera. In addition to being responsible for registering new cultivar names for *Hebe*, I was responsible for compiling a register of all known cultivar names for the genus. What at first appeared to be a relatively easy task eventually proved to be a very lengthy one. The

International Register of Hebe Cultivars was finally published in 2001 and resulted in my gaining an undeserved reputation as an expert on hebes.

Interestingly, most literature dealing with the cultivation of hebes has been written by overseas authors, and none has emanated from New Zealand, the homeland of the genus. Shortly after I began writing this book, an acquaintance commented that it was about time a book about hebes was written by a New Zealander. Accordingly, I hope that my 60 years of experience with the genus will prove helpful to those around the world who desire to know more about this wonderful group of plants.

1

Hebes in New Zealand

If there is one group of garden plants that is really identified with New Zealand, it is the genus *Hebe*. This typically New Zealand group of shrubs has tremendous potential for gardeners and plant breeders. Among the greatest attributes of the genus is the diversity of habit and form among individual species, as Joseph Beattie Armstrong noted in 1880: "If we had only this genus, our flora would be very far from devoid of interest and variety, so different in appearance are many of the various forms which the genus assumes." Leonard Cockayne (1924), one of New Zealand's foremost ecological botanists, also said of hebes, "They are likewise garden plants of the highest value by reason of their many distinct forms, wealth of blossom and ease of cultivation and of propagation." Indeed, it is difficult to find a garden situation for which a suitable hebe cannot be found.

Among New Zealand plants, *Hebe* has the singular honour of having its own society; in fact, this is an honour not lightly accorded to many genera even outside of New Zealand. The Hebe Society was formed in February 1985 and since then has done a great deal to promote knowledge about members of the genus and their cultivation.

Hebe is New Zealand's largest genus of flowering plants and contains more than 100 species and subspecies, and perhaps as many as 120. All hebes were originally placed in the genus *Veronica*; however, in 1921 the genus *Hebe* was established, and *Veronica elliptica* and *V. salicifolia* became *Hebe elliptica* and *H. salicifolia*, respectively. Within a few years, virtually all of the shrubby species had been transferred to *Hebe*. Gardeners, nurserymen, and botanists, particularly those in the northern hemisphere, were slow to accept the change, and it was many years before the new genus was generally recognised in horticultural circles. Interestingly, in spite of the initially slow recognition, "hebe" eventually became adopted as the common name for the whole genus. Since then, various sections of the genus have been split off into other genera, such as *Parahebe*, *Heliohebe*, and *Chionohebe*. Another genus, *Leonohebe*, has been proposed for one group; though not currently accepted, it may yet be resurrected in part. One author published the generic name *Hebejeebie* for a group of New Zealand and Australian species.

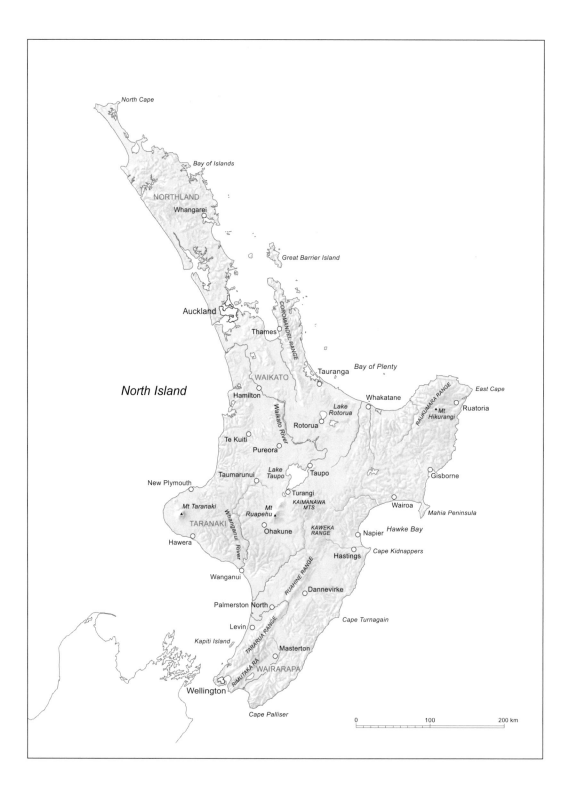

North Cape

Bay of Islands

NORTHLAND

Whangarei

Great Barrier Island

Auckland

Thames

COROMANDEL RANGE

Tauranga

Bay of Plenty

WAIKATO

North Island

Hamilton

Whakatane

RAUKUMARA RANGE

East Cape

▲ Mt Hikurangi

Ruatoria

Waikato River

Lake Rotorua

Rotorua

Te Kuiti

Pureora

New Plymouth

Taumarunui

Lake Taupo

Taupo

Gisborne

Turangi

KAIMANAWA MTS

Wairoa

Mahia Peninsula

Mt Taranaki ▲

Mt Ruapehu ▲

TARANAKI

Whanganui River

Ohakune

KAWEKA RANGE

Napier

Hawke Bay

Hawera

Cape Kidnappers

Hastings

Wanganui

RUAHINE RANGE

Dannevirke

Palmerston North

Cape Turnagain

Levin

TARARUA RANGE

Kapiti Island

Masterton

RIMUTAKA RA

WAIRARAPA

Wellington

Cape Palliser

0   100   200 km

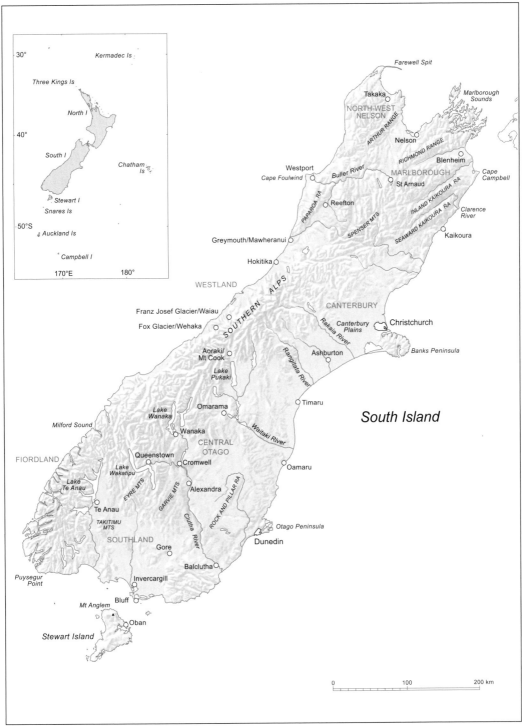

Inset map labels:

30°
Kermadec Is
Three Kings Is
North I
40°
South I
Chatham Is
Stewart I
Snares Is
50°S
Auckland Is
Campbell I
170°E   180°

Main map labels:

Farewell Spit
Takaka
Marlborough Sounds
NORTH-WEST NELSON
ARTHUR RANGE
Nelson
RICHMOND RANGE
Blenheim
Westport
Cape Foulwind
Buller River
MARLBOROUGH
Cape Campbell
PAPAROA RA
St Arnaud
Reefton
INLAND KAIKOURA RA
Clarence River
SPENSER MTS
SEAWARD KAIKOURA RA
Greymouth/Mawheranui
Kaikoura
Hokitika
WESTLAND
SOUTHERN ALPS
CANTERBURY
Franz Josef Glacier/Waiau
Rakaia River
Christchurch
Fox Glacier/Wehaka
Canterbury Plains
Aoraki/Mt Cook
Ashburton
Banks Peninsula
Lake Pukaki
Rangitata River
Milford Sound
Lake Wanaka
Omarama
Timaru
Wanaka
South Island
CENTRAL OTAGO
Waitaki River
FIORDLAND
Queenstown
Cromwell
Oamaru
Lake Wakatipu
EYRE MTS
GARVIE MTS
Alexandra
Lake Te Anau
ROCK AND PILLAR RA
Te Anau
TAKITIMU MTS
Clutha River
Otago Peninsula
SOUTHLAND
Gore
Dunedin
Puysegur Point
Balclutha
Invercargill
Mt Anglem
Bluff
Oban
Stewart Island

0   100   200 km

Chris Edkins

New Zealand's Climate

New Zealand's climate varies from subtropical in the far north to warm-temperate over much of the country and more temperate in the far south. Being an insular country that lies athwart the westerly weather systems, continually encircling the higher latitudes of the southern hemisphere, New Zealand can be subject to frequent and sudden changes of weather, with anti-cyclones arriving from the west and depressions frequently coming up from Antarctica. Occasionally, tropical cyclones also come down from the north. New Zealand can be said to have an oceanic climate because the nearest large land-mass is Australia, some 1800 km to the west.

Within New Zealand the climate can be quite variable mainly because of the nature and shape of its topography. No part of New Zealand lies more than 130 km from the sea. A chain of high mountains extends along most of the country, from south-west to north-east, and acts as a significant barrier to the prevailing westerly winds, particularly in the South Island. These mountains produce a föhn effect, causing high rainfalls on the western side of the main divide and warm, dry conditions in the rain-shadow areas on the eastern side. In the North Island the föhn effect is not quite as pronounced but still exists, especially in the south-eastern part of the island.

Generally the climate is fairly windy, the winds tending to increase in strength from north to south. In some areas, especially in the mountains, winds often cause a high evapo-transpiration rate, which can have a distinct effect on plant growth. Cook Strait separates both main islands and, being the only significant gap in the mountain chain, acts as a wind funnel. The strait and the land about it is a particularly windy area, with the westerlies frequently being exceptionally strong. Foveaux Strait in the far south acts as another wind funnel and has a pronounced effect on coastal Southland.

Unlike some northern hemisphere countries, where wind can bring freezing conditions, in New Zealand it almost never freezes if there is wind or air movement of some kind. This can be especially so in the river gorges of mountain regions where there is frequently some kind of air movement down the gorge. This is one reason why many New Zealand plants, including some hebes, are not always hardy in northern hemisphere countries. Although they grow in supposedly rigorous conditions, they seldom if ever experience the severe conditions that can occur in the northern hemisphere.

Over a large part of the country the rainfall is fairly equable, but there are great local variations. For example, in Central Otago, the closest thing in New Zealand to a continental climate, very arid desert-like conditions occur and the annual rainfall can be as little 325 mm. Meanwhile, 150 km to the west at Milford Sound, rainfall may be in excess of 7500 mm, with individual falls up to 600 mm occasionally occurring over a 24-hour period. In eastern areas from Marlborough down through Canterbury to Central Otago, conditions are usually very dry. In fact, Central Otago and North Otago are the nearest thing to semi-desert of any part of New Zealand. In the North Island the driest areas receive an annual rainfall of 825–1000 mm, while over quite a large part of the North Island the annual rainfall is over 2500 mm.

Frosts may occur over most of the South Island, although there are frost-free microclimates. A similar situation exists for much of the North Island, where there can be great variations in the occurrence or absence of frosts. In general, however, winters over much of the North Island are mild.

Snow is not nearly as common as might be imagined, and in the North Island, apart from the Central Volcanic Plateau area, it rarely descends to below 600 m, even in winter. In eastern coastal districts of the South Island, from about Christchurch southwards, snow may occur over a few days during winter but seldom stays long. In summer the snowline on the Southern Alps averages about 2100 m.

Annual sunshine rates are at their lowest in the far south. Southland experiences about 1600 hours of sunshine per annum, but the number of hours of bright sunshine increases markedly from south to north. Much of the country receives at least 2000 hours, while areas such as Marlborough, Nelson, and the eastern Bay of Plenty may receive in excess of 2400 hours per annum.

Where Hebes Are Found

"Anyone exploring the mountains of these islands cannot fail to be impressed by the remarkable characters of these plants," wrote Joseph Beattie Armstrong in 1880 of *Hebe* and its relatives, all placed in *Veronica* at that time. "They abound in all situations; on the lower grassy slopes, in the beds of the numerous mountain torrents, on the steep shingly slopes of the higher peaks and even on the most barren looking rocks, these hardy Veronicas will be found struggling to maintain an existence and to beautify the scene. Many of them are indeed most beautiful garden plants; from the tiny [*Veronica*] *canescens* [*Parahebe canescens*], a little trailing plant forming matted patches less than one inch high, to the stately *V. arborea* [*Hebe parviflora*] with a trunk three feet in diameter, there is not one but is worthy of the most careful cultivation."

New Zealand is considered to be the headquarters of the genus *Hebe*, with most species confined to mainland New Zealand, which includes the North, South, and Stewart islands. The greatest variety of species occurs in the South Island, but most of the larger-leaved species occur in the North Island. While it is possible to find hebes in most parts of New Zealand, there are actually very few locations where a great assortment of species may be seen at any one time. For such a large genus this may seem strange, but in general many of the different species have rather scattered, localised distributions, with no more than three or four occurring in any one locality. Considering how many species exist, it is amazing how far one may travel in New Zealand without observing a single hebe in the wild.

Some species are a little more ubiquitous, with *Hebe elliptica* growing around much of the South Island coast, particularly along the western and southern coasts. This species also extends far south to the subantarctic Auckland Islands and Campbell Island, the latter being the southern limit for woody plants in this part of the world. Another species, *H. odora*, also occurs on the Auckland Islands and is the only other mainland species to occur in that region. The lovely bluish-flowered *H. benthamii* is endemic to both the Auckland Islands and Campbell Island and is regarded as one of the gems of that far southern flora; unfortunately, however, it has the reputation of being difficult to maintain in cultivation.

Three endemic species (*Hebe chathamica, H. barkeri,* and *H. dieffenbachii*) occur on the Chatham Islands, some 700 km east of the South Island. A further island-dwelling species, *H. insularis,* is confined to the Three Kings Islands, about 53 km north of Cape Maria van Diemen. Similarly, *H. breviracemosa* is endemic to New Zealand's subtropical Kermadec Islands, about 800 km north-east of the North Island; this hebe was thought to have been made extinct by wild goats until a plant was re-discovered in 1983 on a cliff where marauding goats had been unable to browse it.

The only *Hebe* species to occur outside of the New Zealand botanical region are *H. rapensis, H. salicifolia,* and *H. elliptica. Hebe rapensis* is endemic to the tiny island of Rapa (also known as Rapa Iti) in southernmost French Polynesia, about 3000 km north-east of the Chatham Islands, and has the distinction of being the only *Hebe* endemic outside of the New Zealand botanical region. Apparently its nearest relatives are the Chatham Islands species, with *H. barkeri* stated as being rather similar. *Hebe elliptica* is distributed far across the South Pacific Ocean to southern South America and even as far as the Falkland Islands in the southern Atlantic, extending the range of the genus to almost halfway around the southern hemisphere. *Hebe salicifolia* also occurs in southern Chile. It is believed that seeds of both *H. salicifolia* and *H. elliptica* may have been carried to South America from New Zealand, possibly by albatrosses, or, less possibly, on a driftwood log from New Zealand.

It used to be thought that the genus *Hebe* also extended to eastern Australia and Papua New Guinea, but the Australian plants are now classified in the genus *Derwentia,* while those occurring in Papua New Guinea are referred to *Parahebe* and *Detzneria.*

Throughout New Zealand, hebes occur in all shapes and sizes and in all habitats. Around the coasts grow tough species such as *Hebe elliptica,* admirably suited to with- stand the brunt of the ocean gales that frequently sweep in from the sea. In fact, in some areas *H. elliptica* forms the first line of defence to provide other plants with valuable shel- ter. In somewhat more sheltered areas, especially around the North Island and the Marl- borough Sounds area of the South Island, *H. stricta* or one of its varieties may form a prominent part of coastal scrub. It may also be common on road banks. Some species inhabit swampy areas, while species such as *H. gracillima* and *H. diosmifolia* can be found inside open, lowland forest.

Moving inland, *Hebe pareora* and its allies grow on the cliffs of rocky river gorges, while other hebes, especially in the South Island, favour streamsides and the terrace lands of the large river valleys that pierce deep into the mountain ranges. This latter habitat is a favourite of species such as *H. brachysiphon*, *H. odora*, *H. traversii*, and *H. subalpina*. In the alpine grasslands at least one of the unique whipcord hebes, such as *H. lycopodioides*, may be seen. Whipcord hebes are those species with very small, scale-like leaves closely appressed to their stems so that the stems resemble a piece of plaited whipcord. Rocky, high-alpine habitats may also be home to one or another species in the *Hebe* informal group "Semiflagriformes" (semi-whipcord). In the subalpine scrub, above the tree line of the North Island mountains, *H. evenosa* and *H. venustula* may be typical. *Hebe vernicosa* may be a common component on the floor of the *Nothofagus* forests of the Nelson area and north Canterbury.

Some of the grey-leaved species, such as *Hebe pinguifolia*, occur on the dry eastern ranges of the northern half of the South Island. Further south, *H. pinguifolia* may be replaced by *H. buchananii*. *Hebe decumbens*, with distinctively red-margined green leaves, is another species restricted to the dry north-eastern part of the South Island. This area, extending as far south as mid Canterbury, is also home to one or another of the species of *Heliohebe*. Most notable is *Heliohebe hulkeana*, which from October to November enlivens many areas of Marlborough and north Canterbury with its showy flowers.

Beyond the subalpine scrub is snow tussock–grassland, followed by a region of tussock grassland and mixed shrubland. The higher-rainfall areas are where *Hebe macrantha* occurs, adorning the landscape in mid summer with its large, chalice-shaped, white flowers—the largest flowers of the genus. Beyond the tussock grassland–mixed shrubland, the vegetation becomes sparser, with more rock showing between plants. This is the fellfield, and it accommodates relatively few species of *Hebe*, although one might discover an occasional plant of *H. tetrasticha* or *H. tumida*. They are diminutive species, with branchlets much more like those of a conifer than might be expected of a hebe. Both species are more common higher up on rocky bluffs and rock outcrops. On rocks and the more stable shingle screes, it may be possible to observe *H. epacridea* or *H. haastii* and one or another species of *Parahebe*. Parahebes often occur along mountain streams, where they favour moist, shady rock faces.

Hebe tetragona, a whipcord species, occurs on the Central Volcanic Plateau and other North Island high-country areas. There, in southern areas, whipcord species *H. subsimilis* may also be found. Whipcord hebes that are quite common in cultivation may be rare in the wild and seldom seen. Two such species, *H. armstrongii* and *H. cupressoides*, are both classified as endangered.

The far north of the North Island is home to *Hebe diosmifolia*, a forest-dwelling species, while *H. obtusata* occurs in coastal scrub along the wild sea coast west of Auckland. *Hebe macrocarpa* is found in Auckland Province, particularly the northern half. *Hebe speciosa*, the species most used as a parent for the production of hybrids and cultivars, is now quite uncommon as a wild plant, with few locations where it can be observed growing naturally; but then it was probably always a rather rare plant.

What Constitutes a Hebe?

Hebe is very closely related to *Veronica* but can be differentiated in a few ways. If the plant in question is a shrublet, shrub, or small tree, it is most likely a hebe; if it is a herb or herbaceous plant, chances are it is a veronica. These are the most obvious differences between the two genera. However, one of the main characters by which hebes may be distinguished from veronicas is by the structure of their seed capsules.

Members of both genera have seed capsules comprising two hollow compartments, or locules, separated by a partition or cross-wall technically referred to as a septum. With *Hebe*, its usually pointed capsule is flattened, and the septum extends across the broad diameter, although there are species on which the capsule may appear to be more rounded and twinned, with both parts having a similar shape. In some instances the septum may extend across the narrow diameter instead of the broad diameter. The capsule of a hebe generally splits open along the septum. On the other hand, the capsule of a veronica opens by splitting along the outer wall of each compartment of the capsule.

Hebes can also be identified by their woody nature. They may vary from small shrublets about 15 by 6 cm to veritable trees up to more than 7 m tall with quite substantial trunks. Their branchlets may be smooth and glabrous, or pubescent. Some species have hairs in two opposite rows (bifarious pubescence). When viewed from the tip of the branchlet, the leaves are in opposite pairs in four ranks or rows, so that they have the form of a cross. All of these characters assist with the identification of different species.

One of the characters most commonly used to help identify *Hebe* species is the vegetative leaf bud at the tip of each stem or branchlet. This bud is generally closed to protect the delicate young leaves inside it from adverse conditions. On the buds of some species the margins of the leaves are joined for their full length. With others, particularly if the leaf has a distinct petiole, there will be a small gap at the bases of the two leaves where the margins do not quite join. This gap is known as a sinus, and depending upon its shape, it enables species that have similar sinuses to be separated from those in which the leaf bud may be quite different.

Hebe cheesemanii and three other species, *H. ciliolata*, *H. tetrasticha*, and *H. tumida*, belong to the informal group "Semiflagriformes." They differ from other hebes not only in their generally diminutive habit but also in having dioecious flowers. They are mostly, though not always, unisexual.

Hebe is a relatively young genus still in an active stage of evolution; thus, although it is currently thought that it may contain as many as 120 species and subspecies, new species may be expected to arise. Species previously considered to be of uncertain status are now recognised as valid entities, and no doubt others will follow.

Although *Hebe* used to be placed in the Scrophulariaceae, DNA sequences have shown that it does not readily fit in with this family and is more suited to the Plantaginaceae, or plantain family, where it is now placed.

In 1987, Michael J. Heads proposed the creation of a new genus, *Leonohebe*, which included virtually all the whipcord species and one or two other species. The main character for *Leonohebe* was the connate leaf bases of most whipcord species but it also included the *Hebe odora* group. The genus also included *Chionohebe densifolia*. Heads's more widely embracing original *Leonohebe* never gained general acceptance by New Zealand botanists and is now mentioned mainly only in literature. Some botanists now accept a more limited definition of the genus, which includes only *L. cheesemanii*, *L. ciliolata*, *L. cupressoides*, *L. tetrasticha*, and *L. tumida*.

The genus *Hebe* is named after the daughter of Zeus and Hera (or in Roman mythology, Jupiter and Juno). Perpetually fair and youthful, Hebe was known as the goddess of youth. Her mother made her cupbearer to all of the gods. Hers is a fitting name for a genus whose members are frequently fair of aspect and often seem to be in the bloom of youth. The genus *Veronica*, to which these plants were originally assigned, is said to have been named to commemorate St. Veronica.

Heliohebe

In 1993, five species of *Hebe* were placed into a new genus, *Heliohebe*, a name which translates to "sun hebe" (*helios*, "sun," plus the name of the parent genus) in allusion to the tendency of these plants to grow in sunny places. All five species had been members of the *Hebe* informal group "Paniculatae" because of the terminal, compound, branching inflorescences arising from the tips of their branchlets. The inflorescences are paniculate, particularly on *Heliohebe hulkeana*. Heliohebes are confined to Marlborough and Canterbury provinces to as far south as the Rakaia River gorge in mid Canterbury. They are further differentiated in not having the terminal growth buds so typical of *Hebe* species.

×Heohebe

This putative hybrid genus originated in New Zealand and is believed to be the result of crossing *Heliohebe hulkeana* with *Hebe diosmifolia*. The generic name is a combination of *helio* and *hebe*. To date, only two cultivars of ×*Heohebe* have been produced: ×*H. hortensis* 'Spring Monarch' and ×*H. hortensis* 'Waikanae'. Both are rather similar, resembling *Heliohebe hulkeana* more than *Hebe diosmifolia*. ×*Heohebe hortensis* 'Waikanae' appears to be the more robust of the two. Not a great deal appears to be known about the origin of this hybrid genus except that it appears that it originated in New Zealand and may have occurred, on two separate occasions, at probably two different nurseries.

Parahebe

This is a genus of small subshrubs, usually of a prostrate or semi-prostrate habit, with woody or semi-woody stems. It is mostly in its flowers that *Parahebe* demonstrates its affinity with *Veronica*. Whereas the flowers of *Hebe* have a distinct tube before expanding to the corolla lobes, those of *Parahebe* have virtually no tube and abruptly expand into a salverform or flattened corolla. The flowers of *Parahebe* are often coloured and prettily marked with an eye of yellow, and have a coloured ring of pink or magenta lines radiating from around the ocular ring.

In New Zealand, *Parahebe* contains 17 species and a number of cultivars. The genus has recently been revised, with a number of new species being recognised. The generic name derives from the Greek *para* ("beside"), signifying that *Parahebe* and *Hebe* are closely related and alluding to the fact that *Parahebe* species were once included in the genus *Hebe*.

Parahebe contains some very attractive species and cultivars for the garden. Unfortunately, as a genus it has been very much overshadowed by *Hebe*, and the contribution that *Parahebe* can make towards the garden flora has been greatly overlooked.

Chionohebe

The high-alpine plants of the genus *Chionohebe* are not widely grown, even in New Zealand, where most species occur. Accordingly, in this book this genus is dealt with in a more cursory manner. Two species extend into the mountains of Tasmania and eastern Australia.

The Discovery of Hebes

Plants of *Hebe*—or *Veronica*, as the genus was originally known—were discovered in 1769 by Joseph Banks and Daniel Solander, the two scientists who accompanied Captain James Cook on his first voyage to New Zealand, between 1769 and 1771. They discovered both *H. pubescens* and *H. stricta* around the shores of the North Island. Although Banks and Solander collected large numbers of specimens, the work they prepared remained in manuscript form and was never actually published. Consequently, the fact that they were the first to discover the New Zealand "veronicas" was overlooked for some years.

During Captain Cook's second voyage to New Zealand, between 1772 and 1775, expedition botanists Johann and Georg Forster (father and son) discovered two further species: *Hebe elliptica* and *H. salicifolia*, both from around the coast of the South Island. The Forsters recognised that the New Zealand plants had a strong affinity with the northern hemisphere veronicas and accordingly classified them under *Veronica*.

Interestingly, the first *Hebe* species brought into cultivation was *H. elliptica* (then known as *H. decussata*) from the Falkland Islands. It was taken to England about 1776 by a Dr. Fothergill. The lovely *H. speciosa* was first collected by Richard Cunningham from the mouth of the Hokianga Harbour in 1833, but it was not introduced into cultivation in England until 1841. The years in which *H. salicifolia* and *H. stricta* were first introduced into cultivation are not known; however, since the early days of European exploration, both species have tended to be confused in cultivation.

Hebe tetragona was the first whipcord hebe collected by a botanist, namely John Carne Bidwill, on Mount Ngauruhoe in 1839. Bidwill's specimen was sent to W. J. Hooker at the Royal Botanic Gardens, Kew. Before Bidwill's specimen arrived, Hooker received a flowerless specimen of the same species, collected by surgeon-naturalist Ernst Dieffenbach. Hooker had a drawing prepared of Dieffenbach's specimen, which he provisionally named *Podocarpus dieffenbachii* in the mistaken belief that it was a species of conifer. Fortunately, Bidwill's specimen arrived just in time for Hooker to realise that the plant belonged to *Veronica* (*Hebe*) and was not a conifer. He was able to prevent the publication of the name but not the plate illustrating the hebe.

In 1840 the French corvette *L'Aube* arrived in Akaroa Harbour with naval surgeon and botanist Etienne Raoul on board. Raoul extensively botanised around the Akaroa area and also briefly ventured onto the Canterbury Plains. On the hilltops above Akaroa he discovered what is now called *Heliohebe lavaudiana*, becoming not only the first person to find this very beautiful little plant but also the first person to observe any shrub of the genus now known as *Heliohebe*.

From about the 1860s onwards an increasing number of local collectors in New Zealand began sending *Hebe* seeds to contacts in the United Kingdom and other overseas destinations, and before too long many species were represented in northern hemisphere gardens. Unfortunately, some of the seed thus collected was of hybrid origin, and this contributed towards the confusion over the identification of hebes that can still be found in northern hemisphere gardens.

Early Plant Breeding with Hebes

Gardeners in the United Kingdom were very quick to realise the possibilities for plant breeding when they saw the first hebes brought into cultivation. The first artificial hybrid was probably produced in 1845 by John Oates, gardener to Sir J. Rowley of Tendring Hall, Suffolk, England. It appears that his hybrid, *Hebe speciosa* var. *rosea*, was produced by open pollination rather than by a deliberate cross. Oates continued producing seedlings of various hybrid hebes until 1856 or thereafter, but it is not known whether any were named and, if so, what the names were.

In the British Isles, the name most associated with the production of *Hebe* hybrids is

Isaac Anderson-Henry of Maryfield, Scotland, near Edinburgh. In addition to being the first person to produce an artificial hybrid between two New Zealand species, Anderson-Henry made a tremendous contribution towards popularising hebes with British gardeners, continuing his plant breeding work until about 1880. His best-known hybrid is *H. ×andersonii* 'Andersonii', which he produced sometime prior to 1849 using *H. speciosa* and *H. stricta*. At that time the form of *H. stricta* that he used was known as *Veronica lindleyana* and was believed to be a separate species. Subsequently, it was discovered to be a form of *H. stricta*. Whether Anderson-Henry's hybrid pre-dates John Oates's hybrid will probably never be known.

Another Anderson-Henry hybrid was the very well known *Hebe ×franciscana* 'Lobelioides', which, along with its various congeners, has had an enormous influence on plantings in northern hemisphere maritime areas. This fine cultivar was produced by crossing *H. elliptica* with *H. speciosa*.

An important but little-known breeder of the 1850s was John Luscombe of Devon, England, who wrote gardening periodicals under the nom de plume "A Devonian." In 1850 Luscombe felt that a "distinct race might be originated between [*Veronica*] *speciosa* and *V. decussata* [*Hebe elliptica*]" (Heenan 1993). Accordingly, he set about trying to hybridise these two species and eventually, in 1856, raised several plants he considered worthy of naming. For many years one of these plants was mistakenly known as *H*. 'Blue Gem' or *H. ×franciscana* 'Blue Gem'. It was only in 1994 that Peter Heenan, a researcher working on *Hebe* cultivars, discovered that the name 'Blue Gem' belonged to quite a different cultivar and accordingly bestowed 'Combe Royal' on Luscombe's plant.

During the latter part of the 19th century, several French nurserymen took up hybridising hebes. Those principally involved were Lemoine, Boucharlat, and Rozain; one or two others were also involved, but little is known of them. In total they produced some very fine cultivars, although few remain in cultivation. Among the cultivars they produced are 'Arc-en-ciel', 'Conquête', 'Reine des Blanches', and 'La Perle'.

There has been little systematic breeding of *Hebe* cultivars since the beginning of the 20th century. Most have been of chance origin, appearing as spontaneous seedlings in somebody's garden or nursery. This has even been the situation in New Zealand, where all of the material needed is available on our very doorstep. Whether this has been due to laziness is difficult to say, but it is true that if we only wait, sooner or later, a worthwhile chance seedling occurs. Likewise, little breeding has occurred in the northern hemisphere. Perhaps gardeners there have been distracted by the large numbers of other interesting plants being introduced from around the world.

One of the few northern hemisphere horticulturists to have undertaken any breeding of hebes during the past few decades is Graham Hutchins of County Park Nursery in Essex, England. Hutchins has made several plant-collecting trips to New Zealand and for many years maintained an extensive collection of *Hebe* species and cultivars at his nursery. He has introduced many new cultivars of his own breeding and has also been responsible for introducing British gardeners to a number of species that were either not represented or were represented by incorrectly named material. Only some of his breeding resulted from a structured programme, much of it occurring spontaneously.

Even with the resurgence of interest in hebes, about the only person in New Zealand who has undertaken a properly structured breeding programme is Jack Hobbs of the Auckland Regional Botanic Gardens, whose programme commenced in 1982 and continued until the late 1990s. Hobbs aimed to produce a race of hebes that was relatively disease-resistant, with improved flower production and floral appearance, and attractive foliage and habit of growth. This breeding programme naturally took due cognizance of the fact that the greatest percentage of New Zealand's gardeners live in the upper North Island. All of the cultivars that were produced bear the prefix "Wiri." Altogether, some 17 cultivars were produced, including 'Wiri Charm' and 'Wiri Gem', both outstanding garden plants.

Unfortunately, in New Zealand, the home of hebes, most gardeners now almost exclusively grow cultivars. Admittedly, there are some very fine garden plants among them, but this trend diverts attention away from the species. As a result, many *Hebe* species are now very difficult to locate in cultivation, regardless of whatever fine horticultural qualities they may have. In Chapter 2, Tony Hayter alludes to a similar problem in the United Kingdom with regard to older cultivars.

Hebe Classification

The following synoptic key assigns the species of *Hebe* to various sections or groups and is provided as an aid to identification. It was originally devised by Lucy Moore in *Flora of New Zealand* (Allan 1961, p. 887) but has been brought up to date with the inclusion of new species and various nomenclatural requirements. It is not a technical key as most botanical keys are. The various sections are not necessarily sections of a botanical nature and are generally referred to as informal groups.

Most recognised species are listed in this key. While it would be possible to assign some cultivars to a respective section of the key, others whose parent species come from different sections would not easily fit into any one section. Consequently, no attempt has been made to fit cultivars into the key.

As previously mentioned, one character that helps distinguish between members of the various sections is the presence or absence of a sinus in the leaf bud. It must be remembered that the size and shape of the sinus can alter according to the development of the leaf bud. When using this synoptic key, examine only fully developed leaf buds. It is also advisable to examine leaf buds from more than one part of the plant, because one bud may not always give a good indication of the shape.

The leaf margins of most hebes are entire, but the margins of one or two species may have small incisions or teeth. Some *Parahebe* leaves are quite distinctly toothed. A further point to consider is the stem or branchlet. Again, those of some species are quite smooth and glabrous, while others are bifariously pubescent or occasionally entirely pubescent. The colour of the branchlet may also be important, whether it is green, purplish, reddish, brownish, or in some instances almost black. Furthermore, the position and form of the flower racemes sometimes help with identification. Are they simple and unbranched or are they branched? Do the racemes arise from just below the growing tip or from farther down the stem?

Synopsis of the Informal Groups of *Hebe* Species

Capsules compressed along their backs; septum across their widest diameter

A. "Subdistichae." Inflorescences lateral. Leaf bud with a narrow, pointed sinus. Bracts sometimes but not usually opposite. Rather closely branched. Usually small shrubs with smallish leaves tending to a distichous arrangement

  (a) Inflorescences corymbose; bracts small: pedicels sometimes long: *diosmifolia, divaricata*

  (b) Lowest inflorescences often tripartite; pedicels short or absent: *colensoi, insularis, rigidula, rupicola, scopulorum, venustula*

  (c) Inflorescences simple (very occasionally tripartite): pedicels short, bracts small: *arganthera, bishopiana, brachysiphon, canterburiensis, cockayneana, crenulata, cryptomorpha, dilatata, societatis, vernicosa*

B. "Apertae." Inflorescences lateral. Leaf bud with broad, more or less square sinus. Bracts not opposite, small. Flowers pedicellate. Many-branched shrubs, leaves medium to large: *corriganii, elliptica, gracillima, paludosa, pubescens, salicifolia, speciosa, townsonii*

C. "Occlusae." Inflorescences lateral. Leaf bud without a sinus. Bracts not opposite, mostly small. Flowers pedicellate. Many-branched shrubs, occasionally small trees

  (a) Leaves mostly larger than 3 by 1 cm: *acutiflora, adamsii, barkeri, bollonsii, brevifolia, breviracemosa, calcicola, chathamica, dieffenbachii, ligustrifolia, macrocarpa, obtusata, perbella, rapensis, stricta,* "Swamp," *tairawhiti*

  (b) Leaves either less than 8 mm wide or less than 3 cm long: *evenosa, fruticeti, glaucophylla, murrellii, parviflora, rakaiensis, stenophylla, strictissima, subalpina, topiaria, traversii, truncatula, urvilleana*

D. "Subcarnosae." Inflorescences lateral. Leaf bud without a sinus. Bracts often opposite. Flowers mostly sessile or only shortly pedicellate, giving compact inflorescences. Capsule often turgid. Mostly more or less decumbent, rather woody shrubs with leaves more or less fleshy and/or glaucous

(a) Flowers shortly pedicellate; bracts not opposite, mostly shorter than the calyx lobes: *albicans, brockiei, decumbens, matthewsii, pareora, recurva, treadwellii*

(b) Flowers sessile; lowest bracts opposite, equalling the calyx lobes: *amplexicaulis, biggarii, buchananii, carnosula, gibbsii, pimeleoides, pinguifolia*

E. "Buxifoliatae." Inflorescences lateral or terminal or both. Leaf bud with a heart-shaped or shield-shaped sinus. Bracts opposite, the lowest large and leaf-like in texture. Flowers sessile. Small shrubs with small, stiff leaves and strict, usually erect twigs: *masoniae, mooreae, odora, pauciflora, pauciramosa*

F. "Flagriformes." Inflorescences terminal, simple. Leaf bases connate. Bracts opposite, often slightly less than the leaves. Flowers sessile. Shrubs usually low-growing, with twigs of whipcord form

(a) Nodal joint well marked: anterior calyx lobes free except near the base: *hectori* (including subspecies *coarctata, demissa, laingii, subsimilis,* and *subulata*), *imbricata* (including subspecies *poppelwellii*), *lycopodioides* (including subspecies *patula*), *propinqua, tetragona*

(b) Nodal joint obscure, anterior calyx lobes almost completely fused: *annulata, armstrongii, ochracea, salicornioides*

(c) Capsule laterally compressed and more or less in two similar parts, very small: *cupressoides*

G. "Connatae." Inflorescences terminal, sometimes lateral, also forming a compact head. Leaf bases connate. Bracts opposite and more or less leaf-like. Flowers sessile. Low-growing to decumbent shrubs with ascending tips, leaves usually imbricated: *benthamii, epacridea, haastii, macrocalyx, petriei, ramosissima*

H. "Paniculatae." Inflorescences terminal and usually compound. Leaves all petiolate, members of a pair diverging early in bud. Flowers mostly sessile. Capsule turgid, more or less in two similar parts. Seed narrow, spindle-shaped: *acuta, hulkeana, lavaudiana, pentasepala, raoulii* [these species are now included in the genus *Heliohebe*]

Capsules compressed laterally, especially towards their tips; septum across the narrow diameter. Inflorescences lateral, few-flowered. Foliage almost black when dry

I. "Grandiflorae." Leaves large, toothed, petiolate, members of a pair diverging early in bud. Flowers very large. Short woody shrub with leafy twigs: *macrantha*

J. "Semiflagriformes." Leaves small, margins ciliate, bases connate. Flowers small, unisexual, plants usually dioecious. Much-branched, very low shrubs from a stout woody base, twigs of semi-whipcord form with close-set leaves almost or quite hiding the very slender stem: *cheesemanii, ciliolata, tetrasticha, tumida*

2
Hebes Around the World

United Kingdom

TONY HAYTER

Hebes have always been popular in the United Kingdom. Walk down any street in June or July and you will see quite a few in flower. They are regularly used in landscaping schemes. The attractions of hebes are many and obvious: a neat evergreen bush, free-flowering over a good period, with a wide range of foliage, habit, and flower colour. Also, hebes survive wind and salt spray, and grow well on chalk soils. Several varieties, such as *Hebe* 'Sapphire', have intensely purple foliage in winter. Moreover, people are beginning to realise that hebes attract butterflies to gardens.

Hardiness was the big issue in the past, but not so much now. For many years hebes carried the stigma of not being hardy. Due to changes in the climate, including hotter, drier summers (giving better ripening of branches) and milder, wetter winters, we can attempt to grow all but the tender *Hebe speciosa* and its varieties.

It should not be forgotten that the United Kingdom has a wide variety of climates, from the mild south coast to the colder areas of the Pennines and Scottish glens, and from the high-rainfall areas of Wales and Cumbria to the semi-deserts of East Anglia. In their homeland of New Zealand, hebes grow in an even wider range of climates, so there is a hebe for every situation in the United Kingdom.

Among other cultural issues are drought, especially in our eastern regions, and wind scorch, which can affect new growth in exposed gardens. Sometimes hebes do not flower as well as might be expected. Hebes also have a tendency to legginess; this is not helped by books saying that they do not need pruning, when they would benefit from a trim after flowering. Gardens in the United Kingdom can have a problem with rabbits, or even deer in some places. Septoria leaf spot and downy mildew are the main problems when it comes to disease.

In 1980 the information available on hebes was thinly distributed throughout various books published in the United Kingdom and New Zealand. Since 1988 four books have been published on hebes, three from the United Kingdom and one from New Zealand. Douglas Chalk's *Hebes and Parahebes* (United Kingdom, 1988) is a horticultural guide. Graham Hutchins's *Hebes Here and There* (United Kingdom, 1997) is a horticultural and botanical guide. Lawrie Metcalf's *International Register of Hebe Cultivars* (New Zealand, 2001) is a summary of all known *Hebe* cultivars, including some that have fallen by the wayside. Chris and Valerie Wheeler's *Gardening with Hebes* (United Kingdom, 2002) is a colourful and valuable introduction to growing hebes.

In 1985, with the support of the Royal Horticultural Society (RHS), a band of hebe enthusiasts formed the Hebe Society, which publishes a quarterly magazine, *Hebe News*, exhibits at horticultural shows, and runs a cuttings exchange. In 1994 the Hebe Society established a national reference collection at the Duchy College, Rosewarne, Cornwall. There are several other collections throughout the United Kingdom and Channel Islands, some of which are national collections. In 1996 the society developed a Web site, which has gradually expanded, and which provides a more international window on the society's activities.

Each year new hebe cultivars are marketed. Most originate from the United Kingdom, Netherlands, and New Zealand, but Denmark and Australia are also active in the field. The most noteworthy hebes are those in the "Wiri" series, introduced in the 1990s from New Zealand and bred for the Auckland climate. One worry is that the flood of new, untried hebes with snappy names might displace older, better cultivars. On the Hebe Society display at an RHS show in the summer of 2003, visitors greatly admired flowering plants of *Hebe* 'Spender's Seedling'. This late-flowering cultivar is at least 50 years old and is rarely offered for sale. This underlines the need for conservation of old cultivars in *Hebe* collections. They would then be available for reintroduction into gardens.

In terms of the number of hebes available for sale, we in the United Kingdom have never had it so good. However, some unnamed or poorly named hebes are being offered very cheaply, which creates confusion among gardeners and results in queries to the Hebe Society. Many new cultivars may have poor resistance to diseases, especially downy mildew. Hebes are shallow-rooted and therefore vulnerable to drought in dry summers, particularly in the eastern, low-rainfall counties.

Currently, herbaceous plants are in fashion in the United Kingdom, but these are labour-intensive and offer little ornament to the garden in winter, which is especially important in the average small garden. Hopefully the pendulum will swing back again, and gardeners will appreciate the usefulness of shrubs that are less demanding of time, especially evergreen shrubs that work hard throughout the year and look good in winter.

North America

NEIL BELL and TOM SAUCEDA

Hebes are grown in North America primarily as a landscape plant. Because of the intolerance of most hebes for excessively hot or cold weather, cultivation of these plants in North America is almost entirely limited to west of the Cascade or Sierra Nevada mountains in the Pacific Northwest and California. Elsewhere in North America the climate is generally too cold or hot, or both, to allow for outdoor cultivation, although dedicated enthusiasts have been successful with some varieties in many other areas. In addition, the European practice of growing hebes as potted flowering plants occurs to a limited extent in many areas of the continent. The differences in climate and growing conditions between California, the Pacific Northwest, and the remainder of North America mean that each of these areas can best be discussed individually.

California

California is a large state with a complex topography. As a result there are many different climates, some more amenable to the culture of hebes than others. The state is bordered on the west by the Pacific Ocean and on the east by the Sierra Nevada and Cascade mountain ranges. Between these, the Coast Ranges north and south of the San Francisco Bay area separate the Central Valley from the ocean. Southern California is another distinct area, being separated from the Central Valley by the Transverse Ranges and from the Mojave Desert by the Peninsular Ranges. The best climate for the cultivation of hebes occurs in the coastal region, particularly in northern and central California. Most of this area remains relatively cool in summer and avoids severe freezes in winter. As with many areas of California, summer drought is an issue, and hebes will do better with some summer irrigation, even in coastal areas. In the Central Valley and southern California, summer heat becomes a limiting factor for the cultivation of hebes.

In central and coastal California, hebes are grown as ornamental shrubs, and their use is increasing as new varieties become available. In coastal situations, including the immediate coast and areas up to a couple of miles inland, hebes perform marvellously, adapted as they are to salt-laden winds, relatively mild winter temperatures, and dry summers. Some of the most tender hebes, such as *Hebe speciosa*, *H. ×franciscana*, *H. stricta*, and *H. ×andersonii*, are well suited to this environment. In the residential landscape of coastal communities up and down California, hebes are being used to a greater extent. Several are grown (or should be grown) as a ground cover, including *H. pinguifolia* 'Pagei', *H.* 'County Park', *H.* 'Hartii', and *H. macrocarpa* var. *brevifolia* (*H. brevifolia*). In the central coastal area there seems to be a group of landscapers, gardeners, and designers who regularly use these hebes in their gardens. Among the more popular "newer" varieties are *H.* 'Wiri Spears', *H.* 'Wiri Blush', and *H.* 'Wiri Gem'. Some of the variegated hebes are also quite popular, including *H.* ×*andersonii* 'Andersonii Variegata', *H.* 'Tricolor', and *H.* ×*andersonii* 'Andersonii Aurea'. These plants are relatively stable and thus are good candidates for the garden, especially as foliage plants.

In other parts of California, conditions are not as ideal for hebe cultivation, and so the range of cultivars grown is reduced. Coastal mountain conditions are different from those of the immediate coast—there is less light available due to the forested slopes, the winters are colder and wetter, summer temperatures are higher, and the varieties mentioned previously can become leggy, show more frost damage, and do not flower as regularly. However, other varieties do perform well in these conditions, such as *Hebe macrantha*, *H.* 'Hartii', and *H. decumbens*.

In the Central Valley of California, hebes are not commonly grown as landscape plants, and this may be due to the hot, dry summers and cold, foggy winters. Hebes can be grown in southern California, particularly near the ocean, but the plants tend to be short-lived, often becoming leggy and requiring replacement after four or five years. Whipcord types in general do not do well in this region. However, a number of varieties are grown, including *Hebe* 'Nicola's Blush', *H.* 'Oratia Beauty', *H.* 'Otari Delight', *H.* 'Great Orme', *H.* 'Blue Elf', and *H. albicans*. More trialling needs to be done in these areas to see which of the many varieties perform well.

Although whipcord species are challenged by the hot summers in many areas of California, several species are good for growing in containers. *Hebe cupressoides*, *H. ochracea* 'James Stirling', and *H. tetragona* make wonderful container plants and are also great in a rock garden. Also worth mentioning for a rock garden are *H. topiaria*, *H. venustula*, and *H. decumbens*, so long as drainage is good and the plants receive plenty of sun.

Among the non-climate factors affecting the growing of hebes are the deer, rabbits, and ground squirrels that like to eat them. This can be a challenge, as hebes have no defence against these mammalian herbivores. Deer can do a lot of damage as they browse on foliage and flowers. One strategy is to protect the plant by placing a protective wire cage around it, which will also guard against rabbits and squirrels. Young hebes planted in the garden are particularly vulnerable to rabbits. Older, taller plants are generally safe from rabbits, as the leaves are usually out of reach; however, they do nibble on the stems, and this can cause scarring.

One major source of new cultivar introductions in California has been the University of California Santa Cruz Arboretum, which has been growing hebes for more than 20 years. Over this time more than 100 species, varieties, and cultivars have been evaluated in the New Zealand section of the arboretum. Although not conceived of as a trial, it is essentially just that. The arboretum imports hebes from New Zealand, grows them to see which perform best, selects those that do well, propagates them, and sells them to the general public. Local nurseries have become involved, and as a result, more promising cultivars have been added to the plant palette in many areas of the state.

Pacific Northwest

This region can be considered as extending from southern Oregon to southwestern British Columbia, west of the Cascade Mountains. It is an area strongly influenced by the Pacific Ocean, which moderates temperatures throughout the year and creates generally good conditions for growing a wide range of hebes. The climate changes dramatically to a continental climate on the east side of the Cascades, with conditions too harsh to allow unprotected growth of hebes.

As is the case with California, within the Pacific Northwest the climate changes from north to south and east to west. This is partly a function of both latitude and topography. The entire region has a pseudo-Mediterranean climate, with warm to hot, dry summers and cool, wet winters. This Mediterranean pattern becomes less pronounced the farther one travels north, so that southern Vancouver Island could be considered its northernmost terminus. In general, seasonal temperatures and the length of the summer dry period decrease as one goes north in the region.

As expected, the coastal areas within the Pacific Northwest experience year-round mild temperatures, and those areas are distinctly different from the remainder of the region. The coast lies, for the most part, in USDA (United States Department of Agriculture) hardiness zone 9. Precipitation is generally 130–150 cm per year and is supplemented by frequent summer fog. Winters are cool and cloudy, with intermittent wind and rain. The coastal strip is separated from the interior valleys in much of the Pacific Northwest by the Coast Range. The interior valleys, including the Rogue and Illinois valleys in southern Oregon, the Willamette Valley to the north in Oregon, and the Puget Sound region in Washington, are bound on the west by the Coast Ranges and on the east by the Cascade Mountains. For the most part, these valleys are in USDA hardiness zone 8. They are warmer in summer and drier than coastal areas, and are where the majority of the population resides. The southwest corner of British Columbia, including the Fraser River valley, Vancouver, the Gulf Islands, and southern Vancouver Island, enjoys a similar mild, dry summer climate.

The climate in both coastal and valley areas has generally been amenable to the culture of a wide range of hebes, and so the cultivars available have been embraced by gardeners and even to some extent by commercial landscapers. Hebes are typically sold in 1- or 4-gallon pots through retail garden centres or in some cases through mail-order suppliers for home gardens. More than 75 cultivars in the region were available in 2004 from these sources, but many were only offered by a single source. The principal hebes sold in the Pacific Northwest are *Hebe* 'Alicia Amherst', *H.* 'Autumn Glory', *H.* 'Blue Mist', *H.* 'Patty's Purple', *H. buxifolia* (*H. odora*), and *H.* 'Tricolor'. As in many areas of the world,

Hebe nomenclature is a problem, and in some cases some of these names are widely used but invalid or confused.

Wholesale nurseries are another source of hebes for the landscape trade, and so these plants have been used to a limited extent in public landscapes. The plants seem to do well in both the clay soils characteristic of most parts of Oregon and the alluvial soils of the Puget Sound region. Although they are often referred to as drought-tolerant, almost all available hebes do better with regular summer water, especially in warmer areas.

Hebes can be grown in the Pacific Northwest, as in California, with few pest or disease problems. Insect problems in the landscape are minor and often involve earwigs feeding on and distorting the clasped leaves at shoot tips. Disease problems can be more severe. Downy mildew is not a problem in the landscape as it is in the United Kingdom, but it can be problematic in nurseries. The major foliage disease is septoria leaf spot, which causes small lesions to form on the leaves of susceptible varieties. Affected leaves often fall off, producing a leggy growth habit. The other major disease problem is phytophthora root rot, which causes major dieback and death of infected plants.

The limiting factor for the cultivation of any particular cultivar in the Pacific Northwest is winter cold. The region is subject to an occasional severe freeze, often referred to as an Arctic Express, which brings cold air, wind, and clear skies for a period of several days. Temperatures dipped as low as −12°C during events in December 1972 and December 1990, although less severe freezes have occurred sporadically. In each case, significant damage has been done to numerous *Hebe* varieties. The effect of these events has been to give the genus a reputation for lack of hardiness in the Pacific Northwest. This reputation is unfortunate and is primarily a reflection of the limited range of *Hebe* cultivars that have become established in the trade in the region. Some of the most popular cultivars, such as 'Alicia Amherst', 'Patty's Purple', and 'Tricolor', are very showy but are among the least hardy. The key to growing these tender cultivars is to provide a protected location near a house or nearby plant. Despite this, many hebes, like *H.* 'Emerald Gem', *H. carnosula*, and *H. cupressoides* 'Boughton Dome', never suffer winter damage.

In recent years, interest in hebes has increased and so has the range of available varieties. Much of the interest is undoubtedly due to the initiative of individual enthusiasts and innovative growers, in which this region abounds. Virtually all of the newer varieties have come from the United Kingdom or New Zealand. However, two new varieties, 'Oswego' and 'Alameda', were selected and introduced by Stuart Fraser of Portland, Oregon, a long-time member of the Hebe Society. There has also been an increase in hebe-related articles and information in regional newspapers, magazines, and Web sites. All of this has led to a better understanding of the range of ornamental attributes the genus offers.

A trial of *Hebe* varieties at Oregon State University, begun in 2000, has also contributed to the availability of varieties and information on their landscape adaptability.

This trial contains approximately 150 varieties, each evaluated for cold hardiness and other landscape attributes.

Other Parts of North America

In other areas of North America the climate almost entirely excludes the use of hebes as landscape plants, and so the genus tends to be unknown to most gardeners and landscapers. Excessive summer heat and humidity preclude widespread use in the southern United States, while in midwestern, mountain, and northern areas, cold winters are a problem. There is some production of hebes as potted flowering plants, in some cases using Danish varieties specifically developed for this trade. This is still an embryonic industry, however, and it remains rare to see hebes sold as potted plants in nurseries or supermarkets.

In the landscape there are few areas where hebes can be counted on to survive consistently through the winter. Some enthusiasts have enjoyed success in parts of the continent that receive good snow cover, such as around the Great Lakes. Under these conditions, lower-growing hardy selections, such as some whipcords, *Hebe odora*, or *H. subalpina*, can be made to survive. Parts of eastern Canada are actually more suitable than many other areas, especially coastal areas of Newfoundland around St. John's and near Halifax, Nova Scotia. The climate of the immediate coast is moderated by the ocean, and so winters are somewhat mild, while during the summer there are relatively few excessively hot and humid days compared with coastal areas in the eastern United States. Even in this area, cultivation is restricted to enthusiasts, and only in the immediate coastal strip; the climate becomes too cold for hebes even a short distance inland. However, some particularly tough species and selections have persisted, including *H. pinguifolia* 'Pagei' and *H. epacridea*. Hebes such as *H.* 'Youngii' may be grown but are inevitably killed if cold temperatures occur without protective snow cover.

Europe

CLAUDIO CERVELLI

In Europe hebes are grown in a variety of climates, from cool-temperate (Central Europe) to warm-temperate (Mediterranean) regions. The choice of cultivars, the modalities of cultivation, and the articles produced are largely affected by differences in climatic conditions, above all temperature and solar radiation intensity.

Hebe falls roughly into two major groups, the first one represented by the hardy hebes (whipcord and small-leaved species). In this group, two different kinds of production can be distinguished. Nursery production, with plants grown in the open air for one or more years in 9–17 cm pots, represents most of the traditional Dutch hebe assortment of the Boskoop area, where the largest concentration of nurseries in Europe is located. Pot plant production is more typical of Danish floriculture, with plants grown for about a year in little pots (usually 9 cm) and maintained in greenhouses during the frost period to allow for better quality and faster growth; in this case only species and cultivars with compact habit and ornamental foliage (often coloured) are used, because the little plants are sold without flowers (for example, *H. albicans*, *H. buxifolia* [*H. odora*], *H. rakaiensis*, *H. topiaria*, *H.* 'Green Globe' [*H.* 'Emerald Gem'], *H. ochracea* 'James Stirling', *H. odora* 'New Zealand Gold', *H. pinguifolia* 'Pagei', *H.* 'Pluto', *H.* 'Red Edge'). On the whole, hardy hebes are available year-round, even if pots are sold only beginning in spring. Often, little pots are available on the market in a mixed assortment.

The second group of hebes includes the foliage and flowering species and cultivars, with medium to large leaves. Some cultivars of this group, like *Hebe* 'Amy', *H.* 'Autumn Glory', *H.* 'Mrs. Winder', *H.* ×*franciscana* 'Variegata' (*H.* 'Silver Queen'), and *H.* ×*andersonii* hybrids, are common in nursery catalogues across Europe and are among the best-known hebes. Some have been produced more and more in the last decades as pot plants, mainly in Denmark. At the beginning of the 1960s, growers began producing *H.* ×*franciscana* 'Variegata' in Denmark, and it remained the main cultivar for many years. Since about the 1980s a continuous introduction of new cultivars has expanded the selection of hebes on the market and allowed an increase in the number of pot plants produced (more than two million in 2002). Plants with different colours of foliage or flowers are now readily available. Among the more common cultivars are 'Blue Star', 'Grethe', 'Helena', 'Karna', 'Linda', 'Lisa', 'Louise', 'Maria', 'Mette', 'Nanna', 'Paula', 'Pinocchio', 'Tricolor', 'Variegata', and 'White Lady'.

In Central Europe and other areas where temperatures drop below zero for several months, such as northern Italy, cultivation is carried out in greenhouses during the cold season. Propagation is usually done in late summer or autumn (October–December), and plants are maintained in a greenhouse with a minimum temperature of 2°C–8°C until there is no risk of frost (May–June in Central Europe); plants are then transferred into the open air until the flowering period commences. The usual production scheme includes repotting once or twice and pinching out the growing tips, once, soon after the rooting of the cuttings; the final pot is larger than for hardy hebes, usually 12–17 cm in diameter but sometimes up to 24 cm. One or two plants are grown in 12–17 cm pots, depending on vigour and the branching capability of each cultivar. Artificial lighting (to obtain at least a 14-hour photoperiod by night interruption) is used during growth in greenhouses to obtain an earlier flowering. Slow-release fertilisers are commonly used. Flowering pot plants are available from August to the end of October, but several cultivars with showy foliage (variegated or coloured) are sold without flowers beginning in July. Plants that flower all summer are obtained by shifting the period of propagation or by a further pinching.

Climatic conditions of Central Europe, with cold winters and wet summers, are good for hardy hebes and allow them, when established, to have a massive flowering in June–July. This climate also provides suitable conditions for flowering during the entire summer period for other species of *Hebe*.

In the Mediterranean climate, where winters are mild and summers are hot, the growth of hardy hebes is not as good as in cooler climates, and their flowering is sporadic or absent; for this reason, the cultivation of these hebes is not common. As frosts are rare in winter in this climate (with minimum temperatures a few degrees below zero), cultivation of foliage and flowering hebes is possible in the open air year-round; caution must be taken only for the hybrids of *Hebe speciosa*, the most tender of hebes. The best climatic conditions for plant growth occur in spring and autumn; in summer, temperatures may be too high (reaching 32°C or more in July and August, with night temperatures sometimes over 25°C), with shoot growth decreasing or stopping on the hottest days. High temperatures determine strong transpiration from the leaves, favouring dehydration of foliage and fading of flowers if abundant and frequent irrigation is not supplied. Root problems may be caused by direct solar radiation on pot walls: during summer, temperatures inside a pot can reach more than 40°C, with root death easily occurring in cases of long exposure. Non-black pots may limit the temperature, but shading of plants is also necessary. Using plastic nets from late spring to the end of summer to achieve a 50% reduction of light is the best way to prevent serious decreases in flower production. High temperatures accelerate the release of nutrients from controlled-release fertilizers. This is especially so regarding the optimum temperatures governing the release of nutrients (about 20°C). Such fertilizers should be evaluated in order to ascertain their effectiveness regarding the optimum release temperature for specific climatic conditions. The protection of pots from strong solar radiation is also important.

Cultivation in open air allows a higher branching of plants after pinching and a better winter flowering than is possible in a greenhouse. Root mass development is higher in the open air, so that more care than usual is necessary to avoid root penetration into the soil; plastic mulching and gravel beds are more suitable than the sand beds used in Central Europe, and larger pots are preferable. Effectively, the standard pot for hebes in the Mediterranean area is 18–20 cm in diameter: plants in such containers can be produced in eight to ten months, taking advantage of favourable climatic conditions that allow a continuous growth during the year.

Like vegetative growth, flower growth is affected by temperatures in a Mediterranean climate. The flowering period of most cultivars is June–July (main flowering) and the first half of autumn; when the first flowering is suppressed for any reason, the second flowering occurs a little earlier and is more abundant. Some cultivars have a single flowering period in the year; this usually occurs June–July, as with *Hebe ×franciscana* 'Variegata' (*H.* 'Silver Queen'), *H.* 'Autumn Glory', *H.* 'Midsummer Beauty', and *H.* 'Wiri Image', but sometimes it begins at the end of winter (February–March) and lasts about two months, as with *H.* 'Headfortii' and *H.* 'Inspiration'. Some cultivars, such as *H.* 'Amy', *H.* 'Grethe', *H.* 'Karna', *H.* 'Maria', *H.* 'Nanna', and *H.* 'Paula', show the possibility of an abundant flowering in full winter. The phases of pot plant production and cultivation duration are similar to those of the Central European climate; nevertheless, the possibility of both plant growth in the open air and flowering in different seasons allows for the production of saleable plants year-round by the use of specific cultivars and a suitable production scheme. For each cultivar it is important to know the response in terms of the flowering period in natural conditions with reference to the propagation dates. For instance, *H.* 'Malene' can flower in the summer even when plants are small (propagated till April of the same year), while *H.* ×*franciscana* 'Variegata' remains non-flowering during the current year if not propagated before February. Such information allows production to be scheduled for obtaining high-quality pot plants in a suitable size.

In the *Hebe* floriculture industry of Central Europe, located mainly in Holland and Demark but also present in Germany and Belgium, attention has been focussed on the quality of plant material for propagation. A continuous selection of the best clones is carried out on the basis of the number of branches and flowers, as well as on uniformity of flowering. This involves taking special care of the mother plants, with regard to cutting, picking, and control of sanitary conditions (especially for fusarium wilt). Such activity results in a product of high quality, identifiable in the market when trademarks are set up.

Hardy hebes produced in nurseries are traditionally used for landscaping and garden maintenance in cool climates; the small plants are useful for rocky garden decoration. Pot plants of this group represent the new trend for borders and are suitable as tub or terrace plants. The foliage and flowering hebes are used for patios, balconies, and flower beds; they are also ideal for low or tall hedges (depending on the cultivar) and can eventually be clipped into regular shapes. The tenderness of many cultivars heavily affects their use in cool climates, forcing a yearly renewal of plants. Maintenance of plants in the Mediterranean climate mainly involves providing suitable irrigation during summer. Cultivars with large foliage and big inflorescences are particularly appreciated for the decoration of gardens and public green areas, growing safely year-round and often carrying flowers in full winter. They are used in coastal regions and can be joined with subtropical plants like palms, aloes, and yuccas. A growing site with light shade is required, whereas a sunny position is better in cooler climates.

Australia

MELANIE KINSEY

Hebes have enjoyed popularity in Australian gardens for many years. They are widely grown in the more temperate (southern) parts of the country, particularly Victoria and New South Wales, where they seem to do best. Even though the name of the genus changed in 1926, many Australians, especially the older generation, still refer to these plants as veronicas.

According to the *Aussie Plant Finder* (Hibbert 2004), *H. buxifolia* (*Hebe odora*) and *H.* 'Inspiration' vie with each other as the most widely propagated hebes, with *H.* 'Emerald Green' (*H.* 'Emerald Gem') and *H.* 'Wiri Image' close behind. There are many more cultivars available than species, and it seems the showier the flower the better.

The hardiness of hebes has long been recognised by the landscaping fraternity, and cultivars can be seen in municipal spaces, fast food outlets, shopping centre car parks, and industrial sites. Their popularity has grown to such an extent that the genus rates an entire section to itself at many plant nurseries alongside roses, perennials, and annuals. Hebes have long been planted in the home garden in mixed garden beds, and we have begun to see hebes planted en masse or as a replacement for *Buxus sempervirens* when a hedge is needed.

Southern Advanced Plants (SAP), located on the Mornington Peninsula in Southern Victoria, is among Australia's largest growers of hebes. They import many new varieties from Ian Ashton of Lowaters Nursery in the United Kingdom and Stephen Burton of Annton Nursery in New Zealand, among others. SAP is responsible for the release onto the market of the "Southern" series of hebes, all of which were chance seedlings. This series consists of about eight cultivars, of which the best is *Hebe* 'Southern Sunrise', a hot pink, prolific, repeat-flowering variety that is self-cleaning and resistant to downy mildew. This is a cross between *H.* 'Oratia Beauty' and probably *H.* 'Wiri Joy' and is protected by Plant Breeder's Rights (PBR). Annton Nursery has picked up the entire "Southern" series.

Stephen Membrey is nursery manager at SAP, where hebes have been grown for ten years. According to Membrey, the following cultivars continue to sell well: *Hebe* 'Wiri Blush', *H.* 'Wiri Vision', *H.* 'Emerald Green' (*H.* 'Emerald Gem'), *H.* 'Mrs. Winder' (though it goes in and out of fashion), *H.* 'Sandra Joy', *H.* 'Snowdrift', and a white sport of *H.* 'Blue Gem' (*H.* ×*franciscana* 'Lobelioides') called *H.* 'Southern Gem'. The following are poor sellers: *H. pagei* (*H. pinguifolia* 'Pagei'), *H. albicans*, 'Pink Elephant' (too slow-growing), and *H.* 'Red Edge'. When it comes to variegated hebes, those with cream and green variegation sell better in Australia than those with yellow and green variegation, especially if flushed pink; for example, *H.* ×*franciscana* 'Waireka' (*H.* 'Silver Queen') sells well, as does

H. 'Orphan Annie'. 'Gold Beauty', a yellow-variegated sport from 'Oratia Beauty', has gone to the United Kingdom, and interest has been expressed from South Africa. SAP has a lot of variegated sports waiting in the wings, and their informal breeding programme has had some success to date. They have imported 'Lowaters Blue' from the United Kingdom and are crossing that with the goal of obtaining plants with good disease resistance. Some promising plants have come from that crossing, and one of these has been crossed with 'Rosie' to produce an improved version of that cultivar. SAP has also crossed 'Wiri Splash' with 'Snowdrift', and they are getting better, tighter plants with good foliage and good disease resistance.

In Sydney and northern New South Wales, the humidity and high rainfall prevent many hebes from doing well; they grow and flower but never as well as they do in Victoria. According to Membrey it is the smaller-leaved forms that do better in this area— for example, *Hebe* 'Heebie Jeebies' (*H.* 'Inspiration' × *H. buxifolia* [*H. odora*]), *H.* 'Lowaters Blue', *H.* 'Inspiration', *H.* 'Snowdrift', and *H. headfortii* 'Purple Haze' (*H.* 'Purple Haze'). Sydney growers have to use a lot more chemicals than Victorian growers to control the two worst enemies, downy mildew and septoria leaf spot. In Perth, Western Australia, Canning Plant Farm is the largest grower of hebes, and they find that the following lines sell best in Perth's dry heat: 'Emerald Green' ('Emerald Gem'), 'Inspiration', 'Southern Gem', 'Wiri Charm', and 'Marie Antoinette' ('Mary Antoinette').

When it comes to growing hebes, SAP has found that their plants do better when calcium is added to the potting mix. Membrey found that when they started using a commercial potting mix made especially for lavenders, they noticed big improvements. The added calcium also appeared to stop many varieties from snapping off at ground level in high winds. SAP uses only a controlled-release fertiliser, and there is no liquid feeding. Watering of the stock is by overhead sprinklers; they recognise that this is not ideal, however, so they water early in the evening to make sure the leaves have all night to dry out. The only major pesticide used is copper spray, which is applied in winter as a preventative and at other times of the year, with some varieties needing fortnightly spraying to control downy mildew. SAP has decided to pursue only those hebes that don't need spraying; in fact, this has become the number one factor when choosing to grow a particular variety.

SAP is particularly happy with a few noteworthy cultivars, including the following:

Hebe 'Great Inspiration' (*H.* 'Inspiration' × *H.* 'Blue Gem' [*H.* ×*franciscana* 'Lobeli-oides']). Doesn't require trimming or spraying, holds its foliage well, and doesn't mind being hedged. Its purple flowers, the size of those of *H.* ×*franciscana* 'Lobeli-oides', fade to white, and it retains one flush of flowers from spring to summer.

Hebe 'Heebie Jeebies'. A compact shrub with bluish-mauve flowers. It flowers profusely from late winter to mid spring and spot flowers throughout the rest of the year. It is also very disease-resistant and tolerant of frost, heat, and coastal conditions.

Hebe 'Mauve Magic'. Flowers prolifically in autumn and spring, handles pruning very well, and in winter the stems turn an attractive black.

Hebe 'Moorillah Melody'. From Moorillah Nursery in the Grampians, Victoria. It has pink variegation and dark magenta or purple flowers. It needs spraying in pots, although it's okay in the garden.

Hebe 'Ohakea'. From Greenhills Propagation. Its leaves are like those of *H. diosmifolia*. Pale pink/mauve flowers appear in spring.

Hebe 'Pink Cloud' and *H.* 'Magenta Cloud'. Imported from the Netherlands. Both are good cultivars, the hot magenta–pink 'Magenta Cloud' appearing to be the better of the two.

Hebe 'Purple Shamrock'. Imported from Ian Ashton and probably originating in the Netherlands. A variegated plant with vibrant dark pink new growth in winter, and pale purple flowers. It doesn't revert too badly and can be cut hard back.

Species and cultivars of *Heliohebe* are not readily available in Australia, although *H. hulkeana* occasionally pops up at rare-plant nurseries or markets and *H.* 'Hagley Park' is sometimes available. *Heliohebe* does not rate a mention in the *Aussie Plant Finder* (Hibbert 2004). SAP tried a few cultivars of *Heliohebe* from the United Kingdom and New Zealand, but they didn't perform and didn't sell, and are no longer stocked.

3

Growing Hebes and Their Relatives

As a matter of generality most hebes are not difficult to grow in the average garden and, in fact, are really quite easy, but therein lies a trap for the unwary gardener, since a few species may have special requirements. The majority, however, have no special requirements and are like any other garden shrub, needing adequate drainage, without becoming excessively dry, a soil that is reasonably friable, and, of course, for the best results it is usually necessary to devote a little more attention to their culture.

Many gardeners, especially those in New Zealand, tend to regard hebes as "bulletproof." In other words they are simply planted and left to their own devices and are then expected to grow well and remain in good condition forever more. While hebes will tolerate a wide range of soils and conditions, a little attention to the basics will reward the gardener with far better plants that will remain in good condition for much longer. A number of hebes, soon after planting out, assume a most attractive ball-like habit of growth that lulls many gardeners into a sense of false security. Anyone who has seen hebes in the wild will realise that with age they gradually begin to lose that ball-like appearance. The lower foliage commences to fall off, the lower branchlets may begin to die, and ultimately the main stems become exposed, resulting in the plant having a very leggy appearance. A few winter snows will cause the stems to splay out, which spells the end of what was once a most attractive and symmetrical shrub.

In the garden it is no different, apart from the fact that winter snows (southern and inland parts of New Zealand excepted) may not occur to wreak havoc with those overmature hebes. While hebes will tolerate poorer soils, better results will always be obtained if the soil is of reasonable quality. The use of compost or some other soil conditioner will certainly repay the effort of incorporating it into the soil. The next requirement is that the plant is intended to remain in the garden, and in the best possible condition, for the longest possible time. An annual dressing of a suitable fertiliser, applied just before growth commences, will do a great deal to promote healthy growth. Alternatively, if you like to avoid artificial fertilisers, a good, rich compost should be as good.

In *Hebes Here and There* (1997), Graham Hutchins states that "the majority of *Hebe* species are hardy enough to take an average winter in the southern part of England or the warmer areas further north. It is often the larger and more showy hebes that are tender and the condition of the plant is important when the cold weather strikes." This is difficult for most New Zealand gardeners to imagine, because the majority of hebes are regarded as hardy throughout the country, and it is only some of the far northern species such as *H. brevifolia* that may be frost-tender. Most hebes grown in the United States are hardy in USDA zone 8 and above, although a few may be hardy in zone 7.

The place in which a species of *Hebe* naturally grows is not always a good guide to its hardiness. For example, *H. macrocarpa* var. *latisepala* grows in the far north, but in spite of that, it is actually hardy in most lowland areas of New Zealand. On the other hand, the coastal *H. speciosa* is inclined to be damaged by severe frosts in southern lowland areas.

Drainage

Drainage is most important because most hebes will not tolerate poorly drained soils. If there have been exceptional rains, hebes will withstand a few days of wet soil conditions, but not for too long. If soil drainage cannot be improved sufficiently to prevent the plants from having continually "wet feet," it is preferable to seek a site with better soil. One solution is to construct raised beds, which allow for good drainage and prevent hebes from having continually wet feet. In such a case it may be well to install some drainage under the bed so as to ensure that any surplus water is taken away. A raised bed also allows for substantial improvements to the soil and can be ideal for growing a number of the smaller hebes, particularly as more plants can be grown in a relatively small area. Raised beds are also ideal for elderly gardeners because they obviate the need to bend down or stoop as far to view or tend the plants.

As well as having main roots that penetrate quite deeply into the soil, hebes have a mass of fine feeding roots that come right up to the surface of the soil. In this respect, these plants are rather like rhododendrons, camellias, kalmias, and similar shrubs. They appreciate having a mulch applied around them.

A mulch will prevent the soil from drying out and keep the surface roots moist. It will also help to prevent weed growth, and as the mulch gradually decomposes it will supply nutrients to the soil. Mulches help protect soil from erosion and keep soil warmer in winter and cooler in summer. Generally a mulch should be sufficiently thick that weeds do not easily grow up through it, usually 7–10 cm deep. With hebes it should be spread right under the bush so as to keep the surface roots moist. The type of mulching material will depend upon what is most commonly used and available in each country, but may include shredded bark, peat moss, pine needles, or straw of various kinds (pea straw, for example). Pebbles may also be used but, unlike other mulching materials, are mainly for appearance and do not add anything to the soil.

Position in the Garden

Most hebes will tolerate sun or shade, providing the shade is indirect and not overhead. In fact, some may even grow better if planted on the shady side of a building or fence. The only disadvantage with planting in the shade is that flowering may not be as prolific, but if flowers are not a consideration, that may not be a problem.

Pruning

Regular pruning is essential for many hebes if they are to be kept in good condition. This is especially true for those with a ball-like habit of growth. In general they should be pruned immediately after flowering so that they have time to make new growth that will produce the next crop of flowers. With hebes it pays to remember that they always produce flowers on young growth. For many, a light clipping with a pair of hedge clippers or a mechanical trimmer, so as to remove the tip growths that have flowered, will be sufficient to make the bush tidy and promote the production of young growth. If the use of hedge clippers is not a practical option it will usually be necessary to use secateurs. Secateurs make it possible to remove the slightly longer pieces of growth, thus encouraging more new growth to come from nearer the base of the shrub. They also make it possible to preserve a good shape so that the bush does not obviously appear to have been pruned.

For bushes that are normally trimmed only with hedge clippers, it is a good idea to provide a really good thinning every two or three years. This requires the removal of some of the older growth so as to encourage the production of healthy new growth from inside the base of the plant. Thinning involves pruning out whole branchlet systems as close to the base as possible. If there are indications of young growth buds at the base of the old wood, so much the better. If not, as long as there is plenty of green growth on the bush, it should eventually produce new basal growth. Initially such pruning will leave the bush with quite an open appearance, but it is amazing just how quickly the new growth thickens. Naturally, such pruning should be carried out only during the growing season so that there is plenty of time for the new growth to mature before colder conditions bring growth to a halt.

Hebes in Containers

Many of the smaller hebes in particular are highly suitable for growing in containers, and there are quite a number of reasons for this. In towns and cities where there may not be sufficient space for a proper garden, plants in containers may be the ideal solution.

Some hebes have quite a long flowering season and will provide colour and interest over a long period. When spent flowers are removed quickly, some cultivars soon produce new flowers to give an extended flowering season. Being evergreen, some hebes are attractive right through the year, especially those with coloured young foliage or variegation. Some variegated varieties also have attractive flowers that make the display even more prolonged.

Always try to choose a variety of hebe to suit the particular container, especially as regards the container's shape and colour. Dwarf hebes are ideal for smaller containers and can also be grown in trough gardens. Some of the smaller hebes such as *Hebe tetrasticha* are well suited for container culture in an alpine house.

Containers come in all shapes and sizes, and some provide exciting possibilities. In addition to the traditional terracotta, concrete, and plastic containers are glazed earthenware containers, available in a variety of colours and designs. It must be said, however, that some designs are quite impractical, owing more to the designer's imagination than to his or her desire to create a container that not only looks good but also meets the practical requirements of the grower.

The main requirement with any container is that it has at least one good drainage hole. With plants such as hebes, once they are well established in the container the main problem is not making certain that surplus water will drain out, but ensuring that the root ball does not dry out too much. The drainage hole should be well covered with some large pieces of crock or potsherds so as to prevent potting mix from filtering down and blocking it. Those first, large crocks should then be covered with a layer of finer crocks, over which is placed a layer of dead but unrotted oak leaves or something similar. This will ensure that the potting mix is unlikely to block the drainage.

Earthworms are sometimes a problem in containers. They have a remarkable capacity to turn over some of the drainage material and completely block drainage holes. To overcome this problem some growers place pieces of fine wire gauze inside the container and over the drainage holes before the crocks are put into place. This should at least prevent most earthworms from entering via drainage holes.

Correct and regular maintenance of the container is essential if your plant is to thrive, and to that end, watering is most important. Because hebes very quickly fill a container with roots, they can easily become too dry; therefore, it is essential to regularly check the moisture content of the potting mix. If there is to be a number of containers it may be worth installing an irrigation system.

Plants in containers also need to be regularly fed. Using a slow-release fertiliser is probably the easiest solution. Slow-release fertilisers only work well when the air temperature is above about 16°C–21°C, and consequently there is little or no benefit to be gained when temperatures are cooler. A regular grooming by removing all spent flowers and perhaps some light pruning to maintain a good shape will do much to ensure that the plant remains in good condition. Finally, about once a year the plant should be taken out of the container to have its roots pruned, reducing the root ball to about one-third; afterward it should be replaced in the container using fresh potting mix. If it is not feasible to remove the whole plant, the alternative is to remove as much as possible of the old potting mix and replace it with new potting mix. When refurbishing established plants it is also a good idea to add some extra fertiliser to the potting mix rather than relying on the amount incorporated in a standard mix. The ideal time for this is either in the spring or at the beginning of the growing season.

Planting in the Open Ground

Generally, planting is a fairly straightforward operation, though some authors have managed to make it appear to be unnecessarily complicated. There are also a few myths and fallacies that need to be laid to rest. Reference books tend to describe the need for a good, deep, loamy soil that is well cultivated and well drained. This may be the ideal, but then how many of us have gardens with ideal soil? The soil may not always be as good as might be desired, but it is what is available, and so it is up to the gardener to make a better soil if necessary. Most plants are actually quite resilient and will grow surprisingly well in soils that are less than ideal. In any case, the addition of some compost not only improves the soil but also helps provide necessary nutrients. A suitable fertiliser will also provide nutrients that may be lacking, but apart from that it will do nothing to improve the physical condition of the soil.

One important point to bear in mind when planting: if there is a clay subsoil, the planting holes should not be dug down into the clay. It is better to finish the bottom of the hole at the clay, even if it leaves the hole a little shallow, rather than to dig into it. By digging into the clay you risk creating a sump hole that will hold water and create problems for the plant's root system later on.

Hebe plants should have a healthy appearance and be well furnished with foliage. Do not choose those on which the leaves are yellowing and the main stems are becoming bare and woody at the base. This is usually a sign that they have been too long in the nursery. Such plants may grow quite well after planting, but they usually take much longer to become established and commence making good growth. Size is immaterial as long as the plant has a good, healthy appearance.

The first step before planting is to make certain the root ball is well moistened. The easiest means of doing this is to soak the plant in a bucket of water, making sure the root ball is completely immersed. When no more air bubbles make their way out of the root ball, it is properly saturated. If the soil has been well cultivated, it will not be necessary to dig a large hole. As long as the root ball fits comfortably into it, that is all that is necessary. If the soil has not been well cultivated, the hole should be dug somewhat larger.

The hole should be deep enough so that the top of the root ball can be covered by about 2–2.5 cm of soil. There is a very good reason for this. After planting, the soil usually consolidates, and if the hebe is planted so that the top of the root ball is right at the surface, as is advised by some authors, it will then be left sitting quite exposed and liable to dry out. By planting a little deeper, that possibility will be avoided. Most plants will tolerate being planted slightly deeper without detriment to themselves.

Before planting, use a sharp stick or something similar to scratch around the outside of the root ball and loosen some of the roots. This will encourage the plant to more quickly root into the surrounding soil. Should the root ball be very hard and tight, cut its lower half in the form of a cross; this enables each quarter to be slightly spread open so that the plant quickly produces new roots. While it might appear to be a rather drastic treatment, it in no way materially affects the plant or causes any great damage.

While some authors advocate placing fertiliser in the base of the hole before planting, to me this seems to be a waste. Most of a plant's feeding roots are nearer to the surface, and by the time any roots grow down far enough to reach the fertiliser, the fertiliser is likely to have been leached away. Therefore, it makes far more sense to work the fertiliser into the soil around the plant, where it is more readily available and less likely to be lost. In normal gardening practice, fertiliser would never be buried up to 20 cm or more deep in the soil; it would always be spread on the surface and then worked in so that it soon becomes available to the plant.

Once the hebe has been correctly positioned, the hole may then be back-filled. Using the heel of one foot, firm the soil around the root ball into place. This is to make certain there is good contact between the garden soil and the root ball, as well as to ensure that the plant is firmly in position and unlikely to be rocked and loosened by strong winds. If necessary, provide a short stake for support.

If conditions are inclined to be dry, the plant should be given a good watering, but watering should not be necessary if rain is imminent. For a week or two after planting it may be necessary to check that the plant does not become dry. This can easily happen while the plant is still reliant on what is available in the old root ball. Once it makes new roots that penetrate into the surrounding soil, the plant will be able to derive its own moisture and sustenance from the soil and be well on its way to independence.

4

Propagation of Hebes

Hebes may be propagated from seed, by cuttings, or by grafting, but the most generally adopted method is by cuttings.

Seed

The main disadvantage of growing hebes from seed is the fact that they cross-pollinate so readily with each other. If growing in proximity to other hebes, the resultant progeny may not be at all true to type. If the seed is from a known source, there may be no problem; if not, there can be no guarantees as to what the result may be.

Hebe seeds are quite small and flat and usually germinate quite easily. While they are probably better if sown when fresh, they do store well, and no great harm will be done if they are not sown for a few months. They can be held in dry storage or cool-moist stratified; there appears to be little difference.

To sow the seeds, prepare a container (a pot or something similar) with a seed-sowing mix. A suitable mix is usually equal parts peat and sand (pumice or perlite are also suitable). Add a small quantity of slow-release fertiliser. Thinly scatter the seeds over the surface and then sift some seed-sowing mix over them so that they are barely covered. (Alternatively, you could cover the surface of the seed-sowing mix with a layer of 8 mm stone chips and then scatter the seeds so that they fall among the stone chips.) Place the container in a greenhouse or cold frame until germination occurs. Germination usually takes place within 10–30 days, and a good percentage of the seeds should germinate. Once the seeds have germinated, maintain a close watch for damping-off fungi and, if necessary, use a suitable fungicide to control it. The seedlings grow quite rapidly and will soon need to be pricked out or transplanted into another container. Until they are large enough to pot individually, it may be more convenient to prick them out into a larger container where they will have a little more room to grow.

Cuttings

Semi-hardwood cuttings are the usual, and they often root well at various times of the year, with the optimum period occurring between late summer and early autumn. Semi-hardwood cuttings are made from the current season's growth before the wood has ceased growing and become hard but after it has lost the sappiness of spring growth. Cuttings taken during the optimum period usually root fairly quickly, the ambient air temperature ensuring root growth before colder autumn conditions cause a general slowing down of growth. Such cuttings often produce roots within about four to six weeks and can then be potted for growing-on. The one time of the year when cuttings may not be so successful is during the spring, when many hebes are in active growth. Cuttings taken during the winter may root, but they will probably be very, very slow. Low light and low night temperatures are not very conducive to root initiation.

Cutting material should be taken from the parent plant using secateurs or a suitable pair of scissors. Scissors are actually very easy and convenient to use and can also be used for trimming the cuttings. The length of the cutting will depend upon the variety being propagated. Generally a length of 10–15 cm is desirable, but with smaller varieties such as 'Youngii' or 'Emerald Gem' the cuttings need to be only about 4–5 cm long.

It is usually preferable to take shorter and sturdier lateral growths rather than the more vigorous, sappier terminal growths. With the laterals the internodal spaces are usually shorter and the cutting will root more readily, whereas with the more vigorous terminal growths the internodal spaces are much longer so that the growing tips are usually very soft, sappy, and inclined to wilt easily. Of course, to a degree this can be overcome by removing the growing tips.

Once the cuttings have been gathered from the bush they should be prepared as soon as possible. Some of the lower leaves should be removed. Propagators normally retain a third to a half of the leaves on the cutting. They can usually be stripped by holding the growing tip in one hand and running the fingers of the other hand slowly down the stem so that the leaves cleanly break off. On some hebes this method may not be very successful, and it may be necessary to cut off the unwanted leaves with secateurs or scissors.

The leaves of most whipcord hebes do not strip very readily, and so it is less damaging to leave them on rather than trying to remove them. When making cuttings of the larger-leaved hebes it is often necessary to reduce the size of the remaining leaves in order to prevent unnecessary moisture loss; reducing the size of the leaves also makes the cuttings easier to handle. While handling cuttings, it is important to remember that they should be kept moist at all times.

Once the cuttings have been made they can be treated with one of the proprietary rooting hormones. Rooting hormones generally help the cuttings produce a better root system and root more quickly; however, they are not a substitute for good propagation practices. These hormones are available in powder form or as a liquid (usually concentrated). The powder-based hormones are the easiest and most convenient to use, as it is simply a matter of dipping the moistened ends of the cuttings into the powder. When treating cuttings, it always pays to tip a small quantity of the powder into a convenient second container so that the main batch of hormone is not contaminated. At the end of the day any left-over powder should be discarded.

Liquid rooting hormone is not quite so convenient to use because it has to be diluted to the desired strength, after which the ends of the cuttings are soaked in it for up to 24 hours. There is also a quick-dip method in which the bases of the cuttings are dipped into a much stronger solution for no longer than three to five seconds. When not in use, the hormones (both powder and liquid) should be kept in a refrigerator in order to prolong their life.

Rooting Cuttings

If there is only a small quantity of semi-hardwood cuttings, they can be quite easily inserted into a flower pot for rooting, but for larger quantities a nursery tray is probably more convenient.

Rooting media may vary somewhat, but the usual media are peat or peat moss, sand, pumice, or perlite. Although sand can be quite suitable, it has a tendency to produce rather long and brittle roots, whereas pumice and perlite produce more compact root systems. Generally the rooting medium should be made from peat or peat moss and pumice or perlite. About equal parts of each ingredient will usually provide good results. The cuttings should be inserted into the rooting medium so that all of the bare stem is covered and the lowest leaves are just free of the medium. They should be well firmed into place and then watered in. Finally, each batch of cuttings should be labelled with the correct name and date when they were made.

If a greenhouse is available, the cuttings can be placed in it until they root. Much better and quicker results will be obtained if the container is covered with a sheet of polythene film that is tucked in around the edges. Cuttings should also be shaded from direct sunlight. At least once a week, remove the polythene film and allow the cuttings to ventilate for a few minutes. While they are ventilating, spray them with water from an atomising spray bottle. After about four weeks or so, lift one or two cuttings to see whether they have begun making roots. If not, or if root formation is only just beginning, put them back and check again in 10–14 days. Once they have produced good roots they should be put into small pots for growing-on.

When only a few cuttings are to be made, a greenhouse is not necessary, and it is amazing just what can be done with only very basic facilities. It can be easy to root a pot of cuttings by placing the pot inside a clear plastic bag. Open the top of the bag and place the pot inside. Loosely gather the opened top and hold it partially closed with a rubber band or something similar. If a finger cannot be inserted into the bag, the mouth is too tightly closed, which means the cuttings will not receive adequate ventilation. Place the bag and pot in a well-lit situation, though not in direct sunlight, and check it weekly for ventilation and watering.

For whipcord hebes, mound-layering is a useful method of producing a few new plants. This involves mounding around the base of the plant with a suitable medium (for example, potting mix modified with sand or fine grit) so that the bases of the stems are covered to a depth of about 10 or 15 cm. After several months the bases of the stems should be inspected. If any have produced roots, they can be removed and put into individual containers to grow-on for planting out.

Hebes as Standards

There is considerable interest in growing many different plants as standard specimens, and not the least among them are hebes. A standard is a plant trained so that it has an upright stem free of branches or branchlets and a small, bushy top or head. Hebes may be trained as full standards (usually about 80–90 cm tall) or half standards (about 45–55 cm tall). Not all hebes are appropriate for this treatment, but those that are can be very effective. Varieties with small foliage and more compact growth are particularly suitable. The following are examples of hebes appropriate for training into standards:

Hebe diosmifolia. The smaller, spring-flowering form of this species makes quite a good standard and is capable of being formed into a compact head. It is less vigorous than the later-flowering H. diosmifolia 'Wairua Beauty' and will produce masses of heliotrope flowers that soon fade to white.

Hebe 'Hartii'. Eminently suited for training as a standard because it has a naturally trailing habit. It has dainty foliage and flowers very freely in spring. The violet-blue flowers often almost hide the leaves.

Hebe obtusata. A more vigorous species, with shining, deep green leaves and inflorescences of mauve flowers up to 10 cm long. It is inclined to be frost-tender and is not recommended unless it can be protected over the winter.

Hebe rigidula. Another species with fairly compact growth that makes an ideal standard. It is particularly good because of its profuse flowering.

Hebe topiaria. The fairly compact growth and grey or grey-green foliage of this species make it ideal as a standard.

There are two ways of producing hebes as standards. The first is to take a young plant and progressively train it until it attains the desired height. The second is to root a cutting of a vigorous hebe, train it to the desired height, and then graft a piece of the required variety onto it. Both methods have merit.

To turn a young plant into a standard it is necessary to begin with a plant that is making good vigorous growth. As it produces side branchlets, the lowermost branchlets are progressively removed, thus encouraging the top to continue to grow upwards. During this process, the side branchlets should not be removed too quickly if a strong main stem is to be produced; in fact it is worthwhile leaving them in place as long as possible.

A good practice is to leave the side branchlets attached but to pinch out their growing tips in order to prevent them from growing too much outwards. Their presence will enable the main stem to become much sturdier than it would be if the side branchlets were removed too quickly. After several months the lowermost branchlets can be removed. As the young plant grows it will need to be moved into a larger pot so as to prevent it from becoming root-bound. It should also be staked with a bamboo cane to keep the top from flopping over and breaking the stem. Once the main stem has reached the desired height, pinch out the growing tip to encourage the standard to produce a good head. A shapely head can be produced by carrying out some general pruning and persevering with pinching out the growing tips as required.

Grafting Standards

For this it is necessary to have a rootstock that makes sturdy, rapid growth and scion material of the variety that is to be grafted onto the stock. *Hebe barkeri* is particularly suitable as a rootstock because it has strong, erect growth and will quickly produce a stem; once the rooted cutting of *H. barkeri* has grown to the desired height, it will be ready for grafting. A side graft appears to be the most suitable and easiest graft to make. This involves grafting a shoot of the desired variety onto the side of the rootstock. Once the graft has taken, the top is cut off of the rootstock, and it is then just a matter of training and shaping the head of the standard.

5
Hebes in the Garden

As a general rule, hebes will grow in many different garden situations, and some will even thrive under quite hostile conditions. However, it is still necessary to understand the particular growing conditions preferred by some species. For example, *Hebe odora* and *H. pauciramosa* both naturally grow in moist conditions, and while they will tolerate drier environments, they do best if grown in a good, average soil that maintains adequate moisture. On the other hand, although *H. pauciramosa* often grows in not just moist but actually quite boggy conditions, this is not to say that it needs a boggy environment in the garden. Quite the contrary, in fact. Accordingly, it is necessary to understand some of the factors that influence the growth of native New Zealand plants.

New Zealand's windy climate has a distinct influence on the way in which native plants evolve and grow. In many areas, particularly mountain areas, the influence of wind means that there is a high evapo-transpiration rate. Thus a plant may grow in a region with very high rainfall or quite moist soils, but because of the wind factor it may actually have to tolerate high rates of evaporation and transpiration.

This means that over the years, despite living in a high-rainfall environment, these plants have evolved to cope with what are actually drier growing conditions. Various adaptations, such as hard leaves with protective coatings, or leaves shaped so that only a small portion of their surfaces are exposed to the wind at any one time, help them withstand the rigours of their habitat. Leaves that are dramatically reduced in size and tightly appressed against the stem are designed to protect the plant against excessive transpiration. *Hebe pinguifolia*, with its waxy, glaucous leaves, and *H. speciosa*, whose leaves have a thickened, shiny cuticle, are good examples of plants with protective coverings. The former species inhabits drier mountain areas, while the latter is a coastal species designed to withstand salt-laden winds.

Hebe epacridea has hard leaves that are so closely placed on the stem that they not only protect each other against the effects of wind but leave virtually only the leaf margins exposed to the wind. The various species of whipcord hebe all show a dramatic reduction in leaf size (*H. cupressoides* having the smallest leaves) and have upper leaf surfaces tightly appressed against the stem so that only the undersurfaces are actually exposed to the elements.

Therefore, to properly understand New Zealand's native plants, it is necessary to realise that while many live in areas of high rainfall, these same plants exhibit character-istics of a somewhat xerophytic nature. The reverse is also true, with many plants of the drier eastern mountain ranges of the South Island receiving more moisture than their habitat suggests. On most evenings, the tops of these ranges are shrouded in a thick mist that wets everything it touches. By dawn most plants have innumerable droplets of water clinging to every part. They have several hours to take up this water, with much of the surplus running off and soaking in around the plants' roots, before the mist clears and everything dries off under the alpine sun. The mist usually clears from the tops by about 9 a.m., by which time the plants are quite refreshed and ready for another day. Even though there may be no rain for several weeks, most of the alpine plants do not appear to show any distress.

As previously mentioned, hebes such as *Hebe pauciramosa* grow in wet soils but also exhibit some xerophytic characteristics. While they may grow in an apparent abundance of moisture, boggy conditions ensure that much of the soil water is not readily available to them. Therefore, they compensate by adopting some of the characteristics of plants that grow in drier conditions. Some of the whipcord species also tend to grow in rather wet soils, and so their general form makes them ideally suited for their environment.

Plants for Special Purposes

One of the great strengths of the genus *Hebe* is the variety of foliage and form that can be found among its members. There are leafy shrubs with different sizes and shapes of foliage as well as different leaf colours. There is a considerable range of flower colours, shapes, and sizes. The whipcord hebes, which could easily be mistaken for conifers, pro-vide a completely different dimension. Finally, to cap it all, hebes range in size from dwarf shrubs to small trees.

Depending upon the variety, hebes may be grown as single specimens, planted in groups of three or more, or used as ground cover or hedging. They will mix in with a wide variety of other plants but can also be planted on their own.

Hedges

Hebes can be used for more formal clipped hedges or for informal hedges; however, because of the wide-spreading nature of some varieties, an informal hedge can take a great deal of space. Perhaps the most suitable location for an informal hedge is in a coastal area, where shelter is required and space may not be critical.

Before planting a formal hedge, it is necessary to decide how tall the hedge should be, because to a degree this will influence the choice of species or variety. For hedges 1.5 m tall or more, one of the taller hebes can be considered. Another point to take into account is leaf size. Larger-leaved hebes such as *Hebe ×andersonii* are not so suitable, because every time the hedge is clipped its large leaves show the effects of the clipping, and it takes quite a long time for new foliage to hide the clipped leaves. Smaller-leaved hebes such as *H. stenophylla* are far more suitable. *Hebe stenophylla* also has a rather erect growth habit, which can be an advantage.

Gardeners often fail to adequately prepare the ground before planting a hedge. Keep in mind that the hedge will be there for many years; if anything, the soil should receive at least the same preparation as would be given when planting a prized tree or shrub. Ensure that the soil is thoroughly cultivated and, if possible, incorporate plenty of compost or other suitable organic matter into it. The site should be well drained, but it should also be remembered that hebes prefer a reasonably moisture-retentive soil. The site preparation should be carried out some weeks before the hedge is to be planted.

Planting distance varies according to the intended height of the hedge and how quickly an effect is required. It also depends upon which variety is used and whether the hedge is to be formal or informal. For taller hedges the usual planting distance is 75–90 cm, although very bushy varieties for use in informal hedges may be 1–1.2 m apart. For medium hedges the distance between plants is usually 45–60 cm. For low hedges the distance is 20–30 cm unless using hardwood cuttings, a method described at the end of the section on low hedges.

Immediately after planting, apply a dressing of fertiliser around each plant to help initiate good growth. About three or four months after planting, apply a further side dressing of fertiliser to help maintain the momentum of growth so that the plants can be shaped into a good hedge.

Annual maintenance is important for hedges, and this is an area where many gardeners fail. Once a hedge has been planted, it is often expected to happily grow year after year without any further attention beyond a regular clipping. An annual side dressing with compost or fertiliser helps prevent the soil from becoming too impoverished and keeps the hedge in good health.

The following hebes are suitable for hedges 1.5–1.8 m tall:

Hebe 'Combe Royal'. Features medium-sized, deep green foliage and rather compact racemes of reddish violet-purple flowers that appear over a long period. Often has repeated flushes of flowers.

Hebe diosmifolia 'Wairua Beauty'. A rather robust form of this species that will grow to 2 m or more. The largish corymbs of flowers are heliotrope but fade to white. It flowers in early summer.

Hebe divaricata. A fairly tall species that will grow to 3 m. Its white flowers are in corymbs, similar to those of *H. diosmifolia*, and it is quite free-flowering.

Hebe elliptica. A hardy species very suitable for coastal areas. Rather small leaves and large flowers that may be white or mauve to pale violet.

Hebe ×franciscana 'Lobelioides'. A well-tried and proven variety particularly suitable for coastal areas. It has dense growth and violet-blue flowers in compact racemes. It often produces flowers over a long period.

Hebe 'Spender's Seedling'. Not dissimilar to some forms of *H. stenophylla*. It has long, narrow leaves. Its flowers are white, on racemes of medium length, and are produced over quite a long period.

Hebe stenophylla. Its long, narrow leaves are often yellowish-green. It flowers after mid summer and has medium racemes of white flowers. Its growth tends to be erect.

Hebe 'Waikiki'. Particularly during the colder months of the year, the young foliage is purplish-bronze. Its racemes are longer than the leaves and its flowers are violet.

The following hebes are suitable for hedges 75–90 cm tall:

Hebe canterburiensis. This species has smallish, somewhat rounded, shining green leaves and short, densely flowered racemes of white flowers.

Hebe odora 'Purpurea'. Features small deep green leaves and distinct purplish-red young growing tips. Flowering is inclined to be sparse, with white flowers borne towards the tips of the branchlets.

Hebe rigidula. Ideal for hedging because of its compact growth. Smothers itself with white flowers, which are produced on inflorescences similar to those of *H. diosmifolia*.

Hebe topiaria. A densely branched species with grey or grey-green foliage and white flowers on short racemes. It does not always flower profusely but will make a compact hedge.

Hebe venustula. Features small, rounded, deep green leaves and white flowers on simple or branched inflorescences. Can be very free-flowering.

The following hebes are suitable for hedges 15–45 cm tall:

Hebe pinguifolia 'Sutherlandii'. Its rounded, grey-green leaves are crowded on short branchlets that are decumbent at their bases. Flowering is inclined to be sparse.

Hebe odora. Leaves are rounded to oval, dark green, and shining. Tolerates clipping well and is ideal for low hedging. Its white flowers are not always freely produced.

Hebe pauciramosa. Resembles a smaller form of *H. odora*. Quite small foliage with a fairly compact habit of growth. Ideal for low hedging.

Hebe rakaiensis. Small, bright green leaves are closely placed along the branchlets. White flowers in short racemes. This species makes a compact hedge.

Hebe rigidula. Compact growth makes this hebe ideal for low hedging. Smothers itself with white flowers, which are produced on inflorescences similar to those of *H. diosmifolia.*

Hebe topiaria. A densely branched habit makes this species ideal for low hedging. The grey or grey-green foliage is unusual and stands clipping very well.

Hebe venustula. When not in flower, it has a superficial resemblance to *H. odora.* Its small foliage makes it ideal for a small hedging plant. It also has the advantage of being able to flower in shade.

While some of the species recommended for low hedging will actually grow much larger in the open garden, they are recommended because they have small leaves, a dense habit of growth, and are able to withstand the frequent, close clipping necessary to maintain these plants at the required size. Some of these hebes make a suitable substitute for the ubiquitous box (*Buxus*) still so fashionable in some gardens; a low hedge of hebe along a pathway or at the front of a border can be so much more attractive and interesting.

The best and most satisfactory way to plant a low hedge is to use a large number of hardwood cuttings and adopt the following method. Firstly, along the line where the hedge is to be planted, cut out a narrow trench deep enough to ensure that each cutting has about three-quarters of its length in the ground. Place the cuttings about 2–3 cm apart and then back-fill the trench. Make certain the cuttings are well firmed into place. Alternatively, low hedges can be planted using larger plants, in which case the plants should be spaced 20–30 cm apart. At such spacings the hedge may take a little longer to thicken up.

Depending upon the severity of the winters, such a hedge would normally be planted in late winter or early spring. After a time, existing hedges will ultimately reach the stage where they need to be renovated. This involves lifting the old plants and putting in new cuttings. From the old plants it should be possible to tear off a sufficient number of self-rooted pieces to replant the hedge. Obviously, this is less trouble than having to start from completely unrooted cuttings. After planting the hedge, lightly clip the tips of the cuttings to make them even and encourage branching. Once the hedge commences to grow, all that is required is normal maintenance.

Rock Gardens, Trough Gardens, and Raised Beds

Many of the smaller hebes are very well suited for cultivation in rock gardens, trough gardens, or raised beds. Trough gardens are sometimes referred to as sink gardens, although sink gardens are generally smaller. Raised beds are, in effect, really a form of rock garden, except that, not infrequently, they may be more formal and constructed in the form of a rectangle.

Combining hebes with other plants often comes down to a matter of personal taste and finding plants that appear to be in harmony with each other. For larger rock gardens, some of the medium-sized hebes may add a bit of extra dimension without being too large. The habit, foliage, and flowers of most hebes harmonise well with most rock garden plants, and the smaller whipcord species, with their conifer-like appearance, are also excellent for rock gardens and will complement most plants. Larger and bolder hebes can be used on their own as specimen or feature plants.

Smaller hebes such as *Hebe buchananii*, *H.* 'Emerald Gem', *H. odora* 'Prostrata', *H. pinguifolia* 'Pagei', *H. propinqua* 'Minor', *H.* 'Wingletye', and *H.* 'Youngii' are suitable for rock gardens or raised beds. Heliohebes such as *Heliohebe lavaudiana*, *H. raoulii*, and *H. raoulii* subsp. *maccaskillii* are also eminently suitable, as are a number of parahebes, including *Parahebe* 'Baby Blue', *P. decora*, *P. hookeriana*, *P. hookeriana* 'Olsenii', and *P. lyallii*.

For trough gardens there are some delightful and charming little hebes, such as *Hebe buchananii* 'Fenwickii', *H. ciliolata*, *H. haastii*, *H. tetrasticha*, and *H. tumida*. All of these are probably more easily maintained in a trough garden than in the open ground of a rock garden. Being in raised containers, they are also much more easily viewed, without having to get down on hands and knees to so do.

Another point to keep in mind with smaller hebes is that they can be quite sensitive to dry conditions. A number of these species inhabit moister situations such as occur on the cooler southern slopes of mountains, or grow in areas with a somewhat higher rainfall. Rock gardens are generally constructed to provide exceptionally good drainage, and so with some of the very dwarf hebes, care has to be taken that they do not become too dry at their roots. In fact, it is probably wise to plant them in pockets of a more moisture-retentive soil on the lower parts of the rock garden.

Ground Cover

When people talk of ground cover they normally think of low-growing plants, generally no taller than 10–30 cm, but in actual fact ground cover may include any plant, regardless of how tall it grows. The main purposes of ground cover are to cover the ground, to prevent the growth of weeds, and to a lesser degree to protect the soil against excessive transpiration. For most gardens, the lower-growing hebes are obviously the most useful for these purposes; however, where space permits, some larger hebes are also quite suitable.

Ground cover hebes can be planted as a complete block of a single variety or as multiple blocks of individual varieties so that the differing forms, leaves, and flowers contrast with each other to make an harmonious picture. Some hebes with variegated foliage can be very effective when used in contrast with non-variegated varieties. However, some gardeners do not fancy variegated plants and prefer to garden with non-variegated plants.

By using some of the hebes with a ball-like or hemispherical habit, some interesting effects can be obtained. Their somewhat billowing masses often appear to have been sculpted, an effect not easily found in other plants. Suitable hebes of this nature are *Hebe brachysiphon*, *H. canterburiensis*, *H. evenosa*, *H. odora*, *H. rakaiensis*, *H. topiaria*, and *H. venustula*.

Of course, these hebes do not retain their attractive habit forever; with age they become leggy and tend to lose their attractive ball-like form. Some judicious pruning before they get to that stage will help to keep them in good condition.

Some hebes have a prostrate or almost prostrate habit of growth. Some form a good, dense ground cover, while the growth of others may be more open. One or two are quite vigorous and may cover a wide area, but others are not as wide-spreading. The following are examples of useful wide-spreading hebes:

Hebe albicans 'Sussex Carpet'. A wide-spreading, prostrate cultivar with very attractive grey leaves and short racemes of white flowers in summer. It may grow to about 2 m across and is ideal for growing on banks.

Hebe obtusata. A very handsome species and an excellent plant for growing on banks or over low walls. Displays its flowers well, over a long period. Inclined to be somewhat frost-tender.

Hebe pinguifolia 'Pagei'. A rather more robust cultivar than *H. pinguifolia* 'Sutherlandii', with larger leaves margined with reddish-purple and perhaps of a better grey colour. Usually about 30 cm high. White flowers are rather freely produced.

Hebe pinguifolia 'Sutherlandii'. Features smaller foliage than *H. pinguifolia* 'Pagei' but is a very useful plant nonetheless. Branchlets have a spreading habit and their tips grow upwards. Usually about 30–37 cm high. In time it will cover up to a square metre or more. Its leaves have a good grey colour.

Hebe propinqua 'Minor'. A very neat and useful whipcord hebe with lovely yellowish-green branchlets. Grows to about 30 cm high and forms attractive masses that appear to have been sculpted.

Hebe 'Youngii'. A fine and useful cultivar either for the rock garden or as a ground cover in a small garden plot. It has medium green leaves on dark purplish branchlets and usually grows to 15–23 cm high. Violet flowers are quite freely produced during early summer.

It goes without saying that hebes planted for ground cover should be out in the open where they can receive plenty of sunshine, especially during the winter. They should not be planted under or close to deciduous trees, particularly those with large leaves, as falling autumn leaves will clog and smother the hebes.

As with any shrub, some pruning will be required in order to remove spent flowering stems, promote the growth of new wood, and keep the bushes shapely. One of the main objects of pruning is to try to encourage the regeneration of new wood from inside the base of the shrub, which is essential if it is not to become leggy or open at its centre. Not all hebes become leggy with age, however; some, such as *Hebe* 'Combe Royal' and *H. ×franciscana* 'Lobelioides', require very little pruning and can essentially be left to their own devices.

Planting distances vary according to which species or variety is being planted. Taller varieties (those growing to 1.8 m or more) can be planted a bit farther apart, although they still need to be reasonably close in order to obtain a quick coverage. Usually about 1.5 m will be a suitable distance, but if a quicker coverage is required, plants could be placed about 1 m apart. For medium ground cover (up to 90 cm tall), plants should be 80 cm–1 m apart; generally, 1 m is quite adequate, but if a quicker effect is desired, they can be planted 80 cm apart. When planting low ground cover (up to 50 cm high), place the taller varieties about 50 cm apart and the dwarfer ones as close as 25–30 cm apart.

With their great variation of foliage, hebes give the gardener free rein to explore his or her artistic temperament when planting ground cover. Firstly are the various greens, grey-greens, greys, and blue-greys, secondly the variegation. Then there are the numerous leaf shapes and sizes. With such a palette, the artistically minded gardener should be able to put together a picture that will please the eye of even the most discerning observer.

Specimen Plants

Some hebes make excellent individual specimen plants, particularly the medium to larger shrubs. One well-grown plant of, say, *Hebe* 'Wiri Spears' can be most effective when in full bloom, and it is just as valuable when not in flower on account of its handsome foliage. One of the larger species of whipcord hebe can also be quite eye-catching, such as *H. cupressoides*, with its various lovely greens, from the fresh young green of the young branchlets to the deeper green of the older branchlets. Even *H. ochracea*, with its distinctive colour and broad, flat-topped appearance, can attain enough size with age to make an impact as an individual specimen shrub.

Mixed Plantings

Using hebes in mixed plantings presents all kinds of artistic possibilities. Instead of planting a group of all one species or cultivar, try experimenting with a variety of hebes, either contrasting one with another or selecting plants that complement each other. Considering the range of available hebes and the fact that flowers can be seen on one or another plant throughout the year (depending on climate), the effects that can be obtained by planting a range of hebes are virtually limitless.

Plants for Different Situations

Dry Places

Most hebes will tolerate varying degrees of dryness, but some will not tolerate much at all. Many of the whipcord species in particular are rather drought-intolerant, despite their appearance; while they will tolerate the desiccating effects of drying winds, they are definitely not happy when it comes to drought conditions in the soil. One of the best drought-tolerant species is *Hebe topiaria*, which in my own garden has withstood up to seven months of extremely dry conditions without showing signs of distress. *Hebe stenophylla* is also well used to prolonged dry periods, as are *H. albicans*, *H. amplexicaulis*, *H. diosmifolia*, *H. macrocarpa* var. *latisepala*, *H. strictissima*, and *H. treadwellii*. Cultivars such as *H.* 'Lavender Lace' and *H.* 'Wiri Mist' will also tolerate periods of drought.

When planting hebes in dry situations, it is a mistake to imagine that because a particular species is described as drought-tolerant that it will behave this way right from the moment it is planted. Nothing could be further from the truth. Once established, the plant may be drought-tolerant, but firstly it needs to be nurtured and given the same treatment that any other new garden plant would receive. This means regular watering, which will allow the plant to make a good root system. If it is continually under stress because of a shortage of soil water, it will certainly not become well established to the stage where it will be able to tolerate quite dry conditions. It is also necessary to make certain the new plant has sufficient nutrients to make good growth, at least for the first 12 months. One important point to remember is that the soils of dry places are often inherently poor, in which case every effort should be made to improve them before planting. After about 12–18 months (some plants may take even longer) the new plant should be sufficiently well established that it will be able to withstand more rigorous conditions.

Shady Places

Shady places are among the most difficult places in the garden, particularly when it comes to shrubs such as hebes, and especially if the shade is more or less perpetual. Shade falls into two categories. The first is indirect shade, which results from the presence of fences or walls, buildings, or adjacent tall trees. Places with indirect shade may receive sunlight for part of the day, either early in the morning or late in the afternoon, or occasionally during the middle of the day, while at other times they receive no sunlight at all. The second kind of shade is the heavy shade found under trees; in these places, there is little point in even contemplating the planting of hebes.

Some hebes tolerate indirect shade fairly well. One or two forest-dwelling species are suitable for such places, and some others are sufficiently shade-tolerant to also be suitable. Among the forest dwellers are *Hebe diosmifolia*, *H. evenosa*, *H. gracillima*, *H. venustula*, and *H. vernicosa*. Species such as *H. salicifolia* and *H. stricta* frequently dwell at the margins of forests and consequently may also be suitable. Even *H. speciosa* will tolerate a certain amount of shade. It may not flower very freely but could be worth growing for its handsome foliage and occasional flowers.

Coastal Plantings

When discussing coastal planting it is important to distinguish between hebes suitable for very exposed places, where plants may be lashed by salt-laden winds and salt spray, and hebes appropriate for more sheltered coastal gardens, where they may only occasionally suffer from the influence of strong winds or salt.

The biggest problem with exposed coastal areas is the need to provide shelter from strong sea breezes, behind which other plants will thrive. For such situations, a few hebes immediately spring to mind as being eminently suitable: *Hebe elliptica*, *H.* 'Combe Royal', and *H. ×franciscana* 'Lobelioides'. They are hardy in severe coastal conditions, able to withstand strong salt-laden winds without suffering damage. *Hebe elliptica* occurs on the Falkland Islands and the remote subantarctic islands of New Zealand, and in both locations it endures extreme conditions, particularly the Antarctic gales that continually buffet those regions. Both *H.* 'Combe Royal' and *H. ×franciscana* 'Lobelioides' have *H. elliptica* as one parent, and they have certainly inherited its tolerance of extreme coastal conditions; in both cases the other parent is *H. speciosa*, a coastal species, though unfortunately rather frost-tender. Consequently, while they are very hardy in coastal conditions, they are not always reliably hardy to freezing conditions.

Such hebes are quick to provide important initial shelter from sea breezes. *Hebe* 'Combe Royal' and *H. ×franciscana* 'Lobelioides' are particularly good for this purpose, as both have dense growth and are quite wide-spreading. When planting in highly exposed areas it is often important to provide some kind of temporary artificial shelter, in the lee of which the hebes can be planted. This might include wind-cloth fencing, an earthen bank, bales of straw, or anything else suitable. Impatience and a desire for quick results often lead gardeners to use large plants in these situations. Quite often there is little benefit to be gained from this, however, because of the difficulty and extra time it takes for the plants to become established. It is generally better to use smaller plants, which will experience less of a transplanting shock and more quickly become established.

As with any shrub planting, the ground should be thoroughly prepared beforehand. Make sure the planting sites have been well cultivated, incorporating compost into the soil if necessary. Before planting it is important to make certain that any perennial weeds have been removed. If left, they may grow into the hebe's root system and become a problem to remove later. For this initial planting, the shrubs should be quite closely placed so that they will soon grow together and begin to provide some shelter. A rather thick mulch around each plant will also help them become established. Use stakes to support the plants until they are capable of withstanding strong winds. Keep in mind that establishing shelter areas is sometimes quite a slow process, and a certain amount of patience may be required until the shrubs are sufficiently well grown to enable further planting to take place in their lee.

Where extreme conditions do not prevail and there is a reasonable degree of shelter, a much greater range of hebes may be planted, particularly if conditions are milder and only light frosts occur. Any hybrid with *Hebe speciosa* in its breeding is generally suitable, especially those mentioned in the preceding paragraphs. Similarly, any member of the

H. ×andersonii group, such as 'Mauvena', 'Midsummer Beauty', and 'Miss Fittall', is useful, as are 'Alicia Amherst' and 'Eveline'. Where there is more shelter, a greater range of hebes can be planted, especially smaller varieties.

Damp Places

Most gardens contain areas where the soil is perpetually damp and at certain times of the year may even be quite wet. There is often the added complication that such places may be quite shady and consequently also quite cold. Some hebes will tolerate these conditions quite well. When such areas are discussed, it must not be thought that the soil is necessarily wet and ill-drained; it may simply be that it is always damp and seldom dries out.

Because they are accustomed to sometimes growing in boggy conditions, *Hebe odora* and *H. pauciramosa* are two obvious candidates for quite damp soils. Similarly, *H. subalpina* and *H. rakaiensis*, which may be found growing along stream banks, are both suitable. *Hebe glaucophylla*, which often grows on scrubby banks and in gullies in tussock grassland, is another possibility. Other species will undoubtedly prove to be tolerant of damp situations, and some cultivars may also prove to be suitable.

6
Pests and Problems

Fortunately, unlike some other plants, hebes are not afflicted by many problems, and only one or two can be really troublesome. This chapter covers the main problems likely to be encountered, although it should be noted that the occurrence of certain pests and diseases may vary from country to country.

When dealing with pests and other problems, the main object is to adopt preventive measures rather than waiting for the problem to occur and then finding that control can be very difficult if not impossible. Quite often, once a disease occurs the most a gardener can do is hold it in check rather than completely control it.

One thing to keep in mind is that good culture or nurture and a plant's ability to withstand a pest or some other problem usually go hand in hand. A plant that is healthy and growing well is less likely to succumb to a pest, disease, or some other problem than a plant that is under stress because of poor growing conditions. Some species also have an inherent resistance to certain problems. For example, *Hebe albicans* appears to be fairly universally resistant to downy mildew, while the various species of *Heliohebe* can be almost guaranteed to attract downy mildew when humid conditions prevail. Making sure to avoid the overcrowding of mildew-susceptible species and ensuring that there is good air circulation around each plant can do much towards preventing the incidence of this disease.

Garden hygiene is another very important, though often neglected, preventive measure. This involves keeping weeds under control, which may harbour or act as hosts for certain pests and diseases. As far as is practicable, all dead wood should be removed from hebes, thus avoiding any possibility that it may cause trouble. Diseased wood should also be removed and destroyed as soon as it is noticed so as to prevent the disease from spreading to healthy growth or uninfected bushes.

The old axiom that prevention is better than cure is well worth remembering. The little bit of time and effort spent on preventive measures will certainly pay off should it be necessary to bring a severe attack of a pest or disease under control.

Pests

Aphids or Plant Lice

These small, soft-bodied insects are well known to most gardeners. They are popularly known as green-fly, although at certain stages of their growth they may be reddish rather than green, and some species may be black or darker-coloured. Aphids are more often most prevalent during the spring when plants are making soft, sappy growth. They are also liable to attack plants that are under stress because of dry conditions or some other cause. They mainly attack the undersides of young leaves, young shoots, and leaf buds, and symptoms of their presence are usually a curling and distortion of young leaves or shoots. When the attack is severe, premature leaf fall may also occur. Sometimes these pests particularly attack the flower racemes, which may affect the plant's flowering. A close inspection of the inflorescences will reveal numerous aphids clustered along their rachises and on the pedicels.

The main damage these pests cause in hebes comes from their sap-sucking activities, which may affect the plant's growth. At the same time they exude a honeydew that tends to make the attacked parts of the plant sticky and may encourage the growth of an unsightly sooty mould. If the attack is particularly severe, before spraying the bush with a suitable insecticide, prune off and destroy the most heavily affected shoots. For less severe attacks, a spray with an insecticide will be sufficient, taking particular care to also direct the spray at the undersides of the leaves. Aphids have not only males and egg-laying females but also females that are capable of giving birth to live young without having mated. Therefore, it is prudent to apply a second spray a few days later so as to kill any further aphids that may have hatched in the meantime.

Meadow Spittle Bug

This insect is a more unsightly than a damaging pest, although at times it can cause distortion and damage to the young growths of hebes. It is also known as the frog hopper because of the appearance of the nymphs, which are greenish at first, becoming darker as they mature. Adult spittle bugs are 5–6 mm long and have a short, blunt head with prominent eyes. They occur around most of the northern hemisphere and were accidentally introduced into New Zealand in 1960. They are most prevalent in mid to late spring, when frothy blobs of a spittle-like substance may be noticed on the young leaves and young stems of some hebes (see Plate 4). This "spittle" is produced by the young nymphs as they suck the sap of the host plant. They surround themselves with it as protection against desiccation. The nymphs mature towards mid summer and lay their eggs in autumn so that they are ready to hatch the following spring.

Meadow spittle bugs are fairly easy to wash off plants with a high-pressure hose, but the nymphs will soon crawl back onto the plants. The spittle also protects them against insecticides, and so the most effective control is to more gently wash off the spittle without disturbing the nymphs and then follow up with a quick application of insecticide. After mid summer they mainly disappear.

Leaf-Rolling and Leaf-Tying Caterpillars

These are larvae of several species of tortricid moths that sometimes cause considerable damage to the leaf buds and young leaves of hebes (see Plate 5). They are quite common in New Zealand and parts of Australia, but comparable damage may be caused in other countries by the caterpillars of similar moths. The first generation of caterpillars hatches from overwintering pupae, and they either chew their way into the young leaf buds of many hebes or roll the young leaves and join them together with webbing during their feeding activities. In particular, the growing tips of the shoots may be attacked and destroyed so that the plant is severely checked. During summer the moths lay their eggs, which hatch very quickly. The resulting caterpillars immediately begin to feed on the foliage, and when they mature they pupate. When the next generation emerges, they lay their eggs to commence the cycle all over again. There may be two or more generations over the summer months.

The attacks of these caterpillars often become quite severe during dry summers and autumns when many hebes may be under stress. About the only satisfactory method of control involves spraying the bushes with a stomach poison that the caterpillars will ingest as they feed. Several successive sprayings may be necessary to control each generation. Attention to garden hygiene also helps. Clearing away fallen dead leaves during winter will help to eliminate overwintering pupae, thus reducing the amount of infestation early the following summer.

Hebe (Veronica) Gallery Fly

This pest is apparently confined to New Zealand, although there is always the chance that it might be accidentally introduced elsewhere. The larvae of this small fly (*Agromyza flavocentralis*) tunnel into the leaves of some species of *Hebe*, particularly some of the larger-leaved species, to form long, narrow galleries with parallel margins except where they widen and become scalloped. Their course is normally irregular or serpentine, and sometimes they run so close together that they form blotches. These mines or galleries are usually obvious on the upper surfaces of the leaves but obscure beneath. The adult flies also appear to be responsible for making small puncture marks that disfigure the young foliage. Attacks by this insect can seriously affect both the young growth and the later flowering of hebes. It appears to mainly attack *H. salicifolia*, *H. speciosa*, and various other large-leaved cultivars. Spraying with a contact insecticide during the late spring and throughout the summer should control it.

Diseases

Downy Mildew

Without doubt, downy mildew (*Peronospora grisea*) is the most serious and most universal disease affecting hebes around the world. It can affect a wide range of species and varieties, seriously debilitating them to the extent that they may eventually die. Leaves and young shoots become distorted and discoloured, eventually turning black, and in severe attacks dying. On the undersides of the leaves the greyish or buff-coloured conidiophores of this fungus appear as a fuzzy patch of growth. Whole branchlets may be attacked. Downy mildew is liable to appear at any time between autumn and spring, and if moist or humid conditions prevail during the summer it will also appear then. Hebes grown indoors are also susceptible.

The best way to combat this disease is to remove and destroy affected growth the moment it is noticed. Afterward, thoroughly spray the plant with a suitable fungicide. Spraying should be continued every two to three weeks for as long as the downy mildew continues to appear. Of course, if humid conditions are severe or very protracted, trying to control mildew can be extremely difficult if not impossible. The situation in the garden can also influence the incidence of downy mildew: make sure susceptible hebes are planted in an open situation with good air circulation and not crowded by other plants. The various species of *Heliohebe* are particularly susceptible to this disease, and it can be quite devastating to them.

Garden hygiene is particularly important. All mildew-affected material should be burned or, if that is not practicable, disposed of in such a way that it will not infect other hebes. It has been suggested that some of the weedy species of European *Veronica*, such as *V. arvensis* or *V. persica*, may act as overwintering hosts for this disease.

Fusarium Wilt

This fungus disease can affect hebes in certain areas. It causes wilting and dieback of branchlets or whole branches. Sometimes it only causes the dieback of individual branches, but at other times it spreads quite rapidly so that all or most of the bush dies. If the infection does not appear to be too severe, prune out and destroy the infected branches, then spray the bush with a suitable fungicide three times at two-weekly intervals. If the infection does seem to be very severe it may be prudent to dig out the bush and destroy it.

Phytophthora Root Rot

The several species of the fungus *Phytophthora* are collectively known as collar rot or root rot because they frequently attack plants around their stems, at soil level, or through their roots (see Plate 6). On other plants these fungi do cause other symptoms, but where hebes are concerned the main symptoms are a wilting and turning brown followed by an eventual dieback of whole branches or even the whole bush. On whipcord hebes, branchlets or branches turn brown or black and then die. If only individual branches are attacked it may be possible to prune out and destroy the affected branches and hope for the best. With severe attacks, virtually the whole bush is killed fairly quickly, and when this happens the only course of action is to dig it out and destroy it. Needless to say, another hebe should not be planted in the same soil. It is preferable to remove the soil from where the infected hebe grew and replace it with fresh soil.

Phytophthora may be present in most soils, but attacks are only triggered when certain conditions prevail. Hebes growing in poorly drained or shallow soils may be more vulnerable than those growing in better-quality soils. A combination of cold temperatures and overwet soil, as may occur in late winter and early spring, also favours root rot. By the time the symptoms become obvious, usually later in the spring or even early summer, it is too late to do anything: the damage has been done.

Septoria Leaf Spot

Caused by the fungus *Septoria exotica*, septoria leaf spot can be very disfiguring, particularly on some of the larger-leaved hebes (see Plate 7). Affected plants typically develop numerous dark purple or blackish-purple spots of various sizes on the upper surfaces of the leaves. With more severe infections, some of the spots may coalesce to form larger areas of discolouration. Septoria leaf spot mainly occurs during very wet weather marked by frequent rain, grey skies, and cool temperatures. At times it may be merely disfiguring, but with severe and more persistent attacks it can cause the shrub to lose vigour and may cause the death of some branches.

The disease is probably carried over from season to season either in the soil or on decaying foliage from the infected shrub. Spores may be carried from plant to plant by wind, rain, insects, or human beings, but infection may also be spread by compost from the compost heap.

Control measures involve clearing away and destroying all refuse from beneath infected bushes. The most heavily infected branches should also be removed and destroyed. Spray infected plants with a copper spray or suitable substitute at about 10- to 14-day intervals until spots no longer appear on new leaves. In some districts, septoria leaf spot can be extremely troublesome.

Other Problems

Drought

While most hebes are fairly tolerant of dry conditions, some will exhibit typical drought symptoms when such conditions occur, and plants in containers that are not regularly and properly watered will also exhibit such symptoms. On the smaller-leaved hebes, symptoms generally begin as a yellowing of the lower leaves on the branchlets; within a short time the leaves commence to fall off, with the yellowing and leaf fall continuing to progress along the branchlet (see Plate 8). On larger-leaved hebes, the first sign that the plant is under stress from moisture loss is often leaf wilt; leaves will then quickly yellow and either fall off or turn brown and remain attached to the branchlet.

As soon as these symptoms are noticed, the affected plant should be thoroughly watered to ensure that the root ball is well moistened. A regular re-application of mulch around the root area will also help. It can be more difficult to wet the root balls of container-grown plants. If at all practicable, they should be soaked in a container of water until all air bubbles cease to rise from the root ball. Otherwise it will be necessary to water them repeatedly until their root balls appear to be thoroughly moistened.

Frost Damage

Frost damage can be quite a problem with certain hebes, especially in parts of the northern hemisphere (although it can also occur in the southern hemisphere). The main damage does not occur because of freezing but is usually the result of rapid thawing when the early morning sun strikes the frozen plants and causes a sudden rise in temperature. Hebes that are protected from the rising sun will usually endure a greater degree of freezing, without damage, than those that are not. The most obvious sign of frost damage is when the bark of the stems splits open and exposes the underlying wood. In addition to the stems, leaves may also be damaged by severe frosts. Frost damage may result in the death of individual branches or, in severe instances, of the whole plant. Mounding around the base of a hebe with about 10–15 cm of a suitable mulch may protect enough of the basal wood to enable new growth to sprout from it the following spring.

In areas where freezing is prolonged for several days at a time, it is quite possible for plants to suffer and die from drought because their moisture supplies are locked up in the frozen soil. In areas where such conditions may occur at frequent intervals, mulching and use of protective cloth may be necessary to ensure the survival of the more susceptible hebes. The alternative may be to treat them as annuals and overwinter them as rooted cuttings taken in the autumn.

Poor Flowering

Growers of hebes sometimes complain about the poor flowering of some species and cultivars. The one thing that should be borne in mind, with regard to that, is that some species and cultivars may need a degree of maturity before they will flower freely. For example, Hebe topiaria collected as cuttings from a wild source in 1994, and since grown in my garden, only commenced flowering more freely after being grown for approximately ten years. Originally the plants did not flower at all, and only after five or six years did they manage to produce a few racemes of flowers. *Hebe cupressoides* may grow for many years without producing any flowers, or at the most will produce just a few. Some of the larger-growing hebes in particular, such as *H. salicifolia*, *H. gracillima*, *H. stricta*, and *H. ×franciscana* 'Lobelioides', must be reasonably mature before they will become quite floriferous.

There may be other factors affecting the flowering of hebes. Experiments on container plants cultivated indoors indicate that temperature and day length may have a strong influence on flowering. For example, a case study (Noack 1991) found that "seven species and cultivars from the subtropical lowland climate of New Zealand will flower freely after a 6–12 week 15.5/9.5 or 9/3°C (day/night) treatment (*H. diosmifolia* [summer-flowering], *H. elliptica* var. *elliptica*, *H. corriganii*, *H. obtusata*, *H. macrocarpa*, *H.* 'Icing Sugar', and *H. ×franciscana* 'Variegata'), while the one variety of *H. diosmifolia* [spring-flowering] flowered only 25%–50% after the low temperature treatments." Additionally, "subtropical species native to the outlying islands of New Zealand needed no low temperature as the two species flowered 75%–100% independently of treatments (*H. pubescens* and *H. breviracemosa*), whereas *H. dieffenbachii* from a coastal temperate climate did not flower independently of treatments."

Flowering appeared to be promoted by chilling, followed by warmth; a period of about 12 weeks of this appears to be critical. Photoperiodicity also appeared to be essential. Thus it seems there may be a number of reasons for poor flowering, and the answers are perhaps not always straightforward.

Wind Scorch

Wind scorch rarely occurs in countries of the southern hemisphere but can be a problem in some parts of the northern hemisphere. It mainly occurs when near-freezing air masses come down from the north and desiccate the leaves of certain *Hebe* species and cultivars. There is not a great deal that can be done about it apart from trying to protect vulnerable plants. Hebes known to be rather tender can be sheltered with wind cloth or some other protective material, such as the cloth sold for frost protection.

Rabbits, Hares, Deer

Except for those districts where rabbits, hares, and deer occur in close proximity to garden areas, these pests are not usually a problem. If any of them do cause problems, local wildlife laws and regulations may frustrate a gardener anxious to protect his or her precious plants. Paying attention to adequate fencing and using suitable repellents are probably all that can be done. In countries where such laws and regulations do not exist, gardeners are free to resort to other more practical measures of control.

Rabbits browse on the young growth of hebes, and small plants may be so severely browsed as to render their future uncertain. Hares are in some respects worse than rabbits; they seem to have a mischievous nature and often cleanly bite off the tops of young plants without showing any indication they have eaten anything. Of course, deer browse anything that takes their fancy, and they have the ability to jump quite high fences.

In New Zealand, feral deer, rabbits, and hares are all introduced pests, and there are no restrictions on their hunting. However, rabbits are likely to be the only common pest in gardens, and then only in rural or semi-rural areas.

7

Hebe Species and Their Cultivars

This chapter covers all known species of *Hebe* and their most popular cultivars. Flowering times and months given apply to the southern hemisphere unless otherwise stated. Seasonal equivalents are provided where there may be doubt. For example, a plant that blooms in December in New Zealand is said to bloom in early summer. More newly recognised species that I have not yet seen or grown myself are marked by an asterisk (*).

Hebe acutiflora (PLATE 9)

This interesting shrub is distinguished by its flowers having acute corolla lobes, something shared only by *Hebe townsonii*, *H. adamsii*, and possibly one or two others. It also has a very restricted distribution and the distinction of being among the few *Hebe* species officially listed as endangered, although its situation is better than it once was. It usually forms a rather open, spreading shrub to 1 m tall. The quite narrow leaves may be spreading or arcuate and taper to a long, narrow tip that appears to be sharply pointed but that on closer examination is actually blunt. The open placement of the flowers and their pointed corolla lobes give the shrub a dainty appearance when in flower.

The form from the Waima Forest has an erect habit of growth compared with the bushy, spreading habit of the form from the Kerikeri Falls, and its flowers are more closely placed on the rachis so that the inflorescence has a denser appearance. Its flowers open a pale mauve, similar to the Kerikeri Falls form, but soon fade to almost white or white. The anthers are also a lovely shade of bluish-violet. *Hebe acutiflora* is easily grown, but although it will tolerate considerable drought, it grows much better when given moister growing conditions. It usually flowers just after mid summer. The specific epithet refers to the acute corolla lobes.

Originally this species was thought to be confined to the Kerikeri Falls, Northland, where it was discovered by Allan Cunningham in 1838, but it has since been found in two other localities. Its total population is estimated to be several hundred plants.

DESCRIPTION: A spreading shrub to 1 m tall. Branchlets glabrous to minutely pubescent, length of internodes four to seven times the diameter. Leaf bud without a sinus. Leaves spreading to arcuate, 4–13 cm long by 4–7 mm wide, linear-lanceolate, glabrous or possibly with minute hairs on the margin near the base of the midrib, coriaceous, gradually tapering to a narrow, obtuse tip. Inflorescence lateral, simple, usually

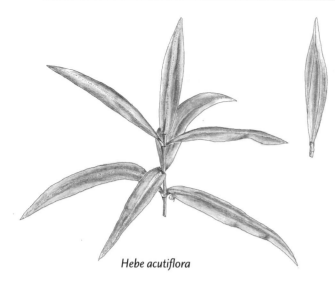

Hebe acutiflora

longer than the leaves, peduncle 1–2 cm long; bracts up to 3 mm long, minutely pubescent. Corolla white to pale mauve, tube slightly flared, calyx lobes longer than the tube, acute, pubescent and ciliolate. Capsule 3 by 2.5 mm, broadly rounded.

DISTRIBUTION: North Island, where it was for many years known only from under the falls at Kerikeri. Sometime before 1981 it was discovered in the Puketi Forest and several years later was found in the Waima Forest. Both locations are within a radius of about 50 km from the Kerikeri Falls site.

Hebe adamsii (PLATE 10)

A species that for a long time was regarded as being of hybrid origin. First collected in January 1896, it was not again collected until about 1986, when it was considered to be an unnamed species and given the tag name *Hebe* "Unuwhao." It is confined to a restricted area of Northland near Cape Reinga. *Hebe adamsii* is named after James Adams, headmaster of the Thames High School, who accompanied Thomas Frederick Cheeseman on his 1896 expedition to North Cape, where the species was discovered. At the time only a few flowering twigs were collected by Cheeseman and Adams.

Hebe adamsii is said to be similar to *H. macrocarpa* var. *macrocarpa* but can be differentiated by its low, spreading habit (it grows to 1 m tall), distant flowers, pointed flower buds, and smaller, bronze-green leaves (although on specimens that I have seen the leaves have been a definite yellow-green to green). Its leaf bud usually has a small, rounded sinus. The flowers are described as pale pinkish-mauve; however, the flowers on cultivated plants vary from whitish to pale mauve without any hint of pink. The corolla lobes are acute, rather wide-spreading, and the flowers are quite widely spaced on the rachis. This species is said to differ from *H. ligustrifolia* in its thicker, larger leaves, its low, spreading habit, its sinus in the leaf bud, its glabrous or minutely pubescent stems, and its larger flowers and fruits.

DISTRIBUTION: North Island. Unuwhao Ridge, The Pinnacle, Pinnacle Ridge, and Tarure Hill in the Te Paki area. Also originally recorded from Kapowairua to Tom Bowling Bay (formerly Tom Bowline's Bay) and North Cape. Grows on steep, conglomerate cliffs covered with *Astelia banksii*.

Hebe albicans (PLATE 11)

This handsome, most striking hebe is very reliable in the garden. In the wild it exhibits considerable variation but is generally easily recognised by its stout, compact growth; bold, glaucous, usually rather crowded foliage; and short, compact, slightly dumpy-looking inflorescences. It is related to *Hebe amplexicaulis* and *H. pareora*, both of which have sessile flowers and glabrous branchlets, and may be distinguished from those species by its pedicellate flowers and usually bifariously pubescent branchlets (although on some forms of *H. albicans* the branchlets are sometimes almost glabrous). Generally the leaves of *H. albicans* are also narrower than those of *H. amplexicaulis* and *H. pareora*. The calyx is usually slightly pinkish so that as the flowers begin to open there is the impression that they are pink in the bud. The anthers are purple and stand out prominently against the white corolla.

As a garden plant, *Hebe albicans* may be regarded as one of the best, particularly as it has a very neat habit at all times. Its compact growth also means that it seldom needs to be pruned. While it is capable of making larger growth, in cultivation it usually makes a bush 45–75 cm tall and up to a metre across. There is a certain amount of variation, depending upon where the plant was collected. This plant has very handsome grey foliage and at flowering time often covers itself with flowers. Flowering usually commences in January (mid summer) and continues until late February (late summer). This species is generally quite hardy except in the coldest areas and will tolerate full sun, although it is also quite happy in indirect shade. It was apparently first collected by F. G. Gibbs, either on Mount Cobb or Mount Arthur, in the early part of the 20th century. Its specific name means "whitish" and refers to the colour of the leaves and possibly the flowers.

Hebe albicans 'Cobb' is a bushy form, 60–75 cm tall, with pale green branchlets that are pubescent all around; it originated from seed collected from the Cobb Reservoir in 1990. 'Cranleigh Gem' is another shrubby form that appears to be little different from commonly cultivated forms of the species. According to Graham Hutchins (1997), 'Snow Mound' is the most commonly cultivated form of the species in Britain; it was given its cultivar name, by Hutchins, to distinguish it from the others. 'Snow Cover' is another prostrate form.

DESCRIPTION: A usually low, rather spreading, much-branched shrub 40 cm–1.2 m tall. Branchlets stout, terete, usually bifariously pubescent with rather long hairs, length of internodes one to two times the diameter, green becoming dark brown with age. Leaves spreading or more or less ascending, somewhat overlapping, 1.7–3.2 cm long by 8–16 mm wide, sessile with a broad and sometimes almost cordate base. Leaf blade broad-ovate to oblong, obtuse to subacute, thick and coriaceous, and glaucous on both surfaces, midrib usually evident. Leaf bud without a sinus. Inflorescences lateral, simple, crowded near the tips of the branchlets and greatly exceeding the leaves. Peduncle hairy, up to 2 cm long. Flowers white, densely placed and hiding the rachis, pedicels pubescent, bracts narrow, ciliolate, about equalling the pedicels. Calyx glabrous, lobes about 2 mm long, narrow-ovate, subacute, ciliolate; corolla tube longer than the calyx lobes, pubescent within, lobes spreading, short, rounded. Stamens exserted, longer than the lobes, anthers purple. Capsule erect, twice as long as the calyx lobes, ovoid, glabrous.

DISTRIBUTION: South Island in the mountains of Nelson Province, particularly the north-western ranges. Usually grows in subalpine scrub and rocky places at 1000–1370 m.

Hebe albicans 'Silver Dollar' (PLATE 12). A fairly new variegated form that appears to be confined to cultivation in the United Kingdom. Nothing much is known of its origin. Its leaves have irregular margins of creamy-yellow that eventually become less distinguishable as the plant ages. The most striking feature is the colour of the young foliage: the variegated margins are suffused with a bright rosy-red before eventually changing to their normal creamy-yellow.

Hebe albicans '**Sussex Carpet**'. This is a fine and very useful cultivar. It has a prostrate and rather wide-spreading habit and will eventually cover an area up to 1.5 by 1.5 m. It makes an excellent ground cover and is very drought-tolerant. In time it mounds up to 25 or 30 cm tall but retains a prostrate habit of growth. About the only pruning it might need will be to restrain its spread should it take too much space. This cultivar very likely originated from around the Cobb Reservoir in north-western Nelson, where similar forms are not uncommon.

Hebe amplexicaulis (PLATE 13)

This small shrub may be wide-spreading or trailing or, in some forms, erect and bushy. The more spreading forms grow to about 1 m in diameter and 25 cm in height. The main distinguishing characters are the almost glabrous stems (except on *Hebe amplexicaulis* f. *hirta*), the leaves being strongly amplexicaul at their broad bases, the hairy peduncles, and the sessile flowers. The rather narrow corolla lobes are also distinctive. Its leaves are quite closely placed on the branchlets and are pale grey-green to glaucous. Generally their apexes are blunt and rounded, although on some forms they may be subacute. *Hebe amplexicaulis* is a characteristic plant of rocky places, usually growing on exposed rock outcrops, sheer rock walls, or windswept ridges where the basement rock is exposed, and on the faces of stony terraces in open tussock grassland. It occurs in eastern South Canterbury, usually at low altitudes of 1200–1400 m.

This is a fairly hardy species and is quite drought-tolerant. If given sufficient space it will grow in a mostly uniform manner, forming an evenly circular plant. In the garden it is ideal because it requires virtually no pruning and appears to be affected by few problems. Flowers usually appear between late spring and early summer. This species was discovered in 1869 by John Francis Armstrong in the upper Rangitata River. The name *amplexicaulis* means "stem clasping" and refers to the way by which the bases of the leaves clasp the stems.

DESCRIPTION: A small to medium shrub 15–60 cm tall. Branchlets may be more or less trailing or decumbent to erect, naked for much of their length (on wild plants) and sparingly branched, glabrous (hairy in *Hebe amplexicaulis* f. *hirta*) or sometimes with a few hairs near the leaf bases. Leaves wide-spreading, 1.5–2 cm long by 8–15 mm wide, oblong, apex obtuse or rarely subacute, amplexicaul at their broad bases, margins yellowish to reddish. Inflo-

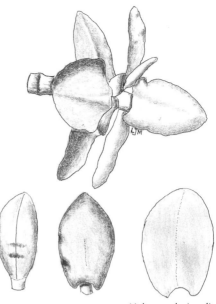

Hebe amplexicaulis

rescence lateral, simple (occasionally thrice-branched), rather short or compact; peduncle 2–2.5 cm long, hairy. Flowers white, sessile, densely placed, bracts and calyx lobes about equal, 2–2.5 mm long, ciliate or pubescent. Corolla tube narrow, slightly longer than the calyx; lobes narrow and wide-spreading, about equalling the calyx. Anthers purplish. Capsule ovoid, rounded at the apex, pubescent.

DISTRIBUTION: Occurs in scattered locations in eastern South Canterbury, from Mount Somers to near the Rangitata River gorge, Four Peaks Range, Mount Peel, and the Orari River gorge.

Hebe amplexicaulis f. *hirta* (PLATE 14)

Formerly known as *Hebe allanii*, this hebe is now classified as a form of *H. amplexicaulis*, which is a somewhat variable species. It is distinguished by an overall hairiness that at once serves to identify it, and its leaves are narrower and more pointed than those of non-hairy forms of *H. amplexicaulis*. With its hairy grey foliage and reddish margins, this is quite a handsome plant and a fine little shrub for use along the front of a garden border or in a rock garden. It is usually a low shrub and has proved to be very hardy in the United Kingdom. It should be planted in a rather dry, sunny situation. This plant was discovered in a rock crevice near a waterfall in the upper gorge of the Lynn Stream, Mount Peel, South Canterbury, in 1919 by H. H. Allan. The name *hirta* means "hairy" and refers to the leaves.

DESCRIPTION: A low shrub seldom more than 30 cm tall with spreading branches. Branchlets stout and covered with dense, rather long pubescence. Length of internodes

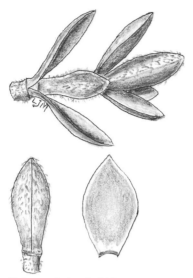

Hebe amplexicaulis f. *hirta*

two to three times the diameter of the branchlets. Leaves spreading, about 18 by 8 mm, oblong to elliptic-oblong, thick and glaucous, both surfaces covered with dense, hairy pubescence. Inflorescence lateral, simple and compact, 1.5–2 cm long, projecting well beyond the leaves on villous peduncles. Flowers sessile, bracts and calyx lobes about 3 by 2 mm, pubescent all over. Corolla white, tube narrow, slightly longer than the calyx.

DISTRIBUTION: Confined to Mount Peel, Canterbury, where it grows in tussock grassland and on rock outcrops, usually at 300–1200 m.

Hebe annulata (PLATE 15)

While not a well-known species, this little hebe is particularly delightful in gardens. It belongs to the whipcord group and is eminently suitable for rock gardens, small gardens, or trough gardens. It usually forms small, tight mounds of numerous branchlets that are densely branched on their upper sides. The branchlets are yellowish-green to bright green (usually bright green on cultivated plants) and quite distinct. As with many whipcord species, *Hebe annulata* may not be as drought-tolerant as might be imagined. Its original habitat is on the drier north face of the Takitimu Mountains, but since this area is subject to frequent mists and a relatively high rainfall, the plants that grow there do not have to endure very dry conditions. *Hebe annulata* is usually grown for its form rather than its flowers.

Earlier botanists tended to liken this species to *Hebe armstrongii*, and when it was originally collected, *H. annulata* was actually named *H. armstrongii* var. *annulata*. Apart from its much smaller size, *H. annulata* is distinguished from *H. armstrongii* by its profuse mass of small branchlets and by the tips of its leaves being truncate or obtusely rounded, as opposed to those of *H. armstrongii*, which are sharply or acutely pointed. There remains some doubt as to whether *H. annulata* is sufficiently distinct from *H. armstrongii*. *Hebe salicornioides* is also somewhat similar but differs in its much larger size (up to 1 m tall) and looser habit of growth. Additionally, the leaves of *H. salicornioides* form a sheathing collar around the branchlet for at least half their length, while those of *H. annulata* form a sheathing collar for only a third to half their length. The name *annulata* refers to the appearance of the nodal rings on the branchlets. This hebe was discovered in 1912 by Leonard Cockayne at an altitude of 900 m.

DESCRIPTION: A low-spreading shrub 10–15 cm high. Sometimes rather open and of straggling growth, branches mainly decumbent or arching (cultivated plants always quite dense and compact), densely branched along the upper sides of the branchlets, sometimes erect and plumose. Ultimate branchlets close-set, 2–3 cm long by 1.5–2 mm in diameter, terete, softly flexible when fresh, yellow-green (bright green on cultivated plants), internodes 1–1.5 mm long and partly exposed; nodal joint obscure except on older stems. Leaves 0.75–1 mm long, joined for a third to half their length to form a short sheathing collar, appressed and thinly fleshy when fresh, rounded and convex on the outer surface, apex truncate or slightly rounded. Spikes four- to ten-flowered. Bracts about 1 mm long, obtuse or truncate. Calyx 2–2.5 mm long, anterior lobes completely fused into a broad-oblong, truncate or emarginate segment. Corolla tube more or less equalling the calyx.

DISTRIBUTION: Found only in Southland on the Takitimu Mountains, where it is confined to a rock face at 900 m altitude, and in three other localities as far north as the southern end of the Pisa Range, including Wye Creek near Lake Wakatipu, where it grows on rocky, well-drained sites at 1000–1300 m.

Hebe arganthera *

Hebe arganthera has some comparisons with *H. cockayneana*, *H. rupicola*, and *H. subalpina*. It was first collected in 1952 by W. R. B. Oliver in Takahe Valley in the Murchison Mountains. Subsequently it has been found in two other widely separated locations in Fiordland and, as with the first locality in Takahe Valley, always on limestone or marble outcrops. Its specific name refers to its distinctive white anthers, a feature that is rather unusual in the genus.

Hebe arganthera superficially resembles *H. cockayneana* but differs in having larger, dull green leaves of a uniform colour, short stem pubescence, and very short hairs on the leaf margins. It differs from *H. subalpina* in having dull leaves, no leaf bud sinus, some inflorescences with one or two branches at the base, and white anthers. It is distinguished from *H. rupicola* by having dull green rather than glaucous leaves, a hairier inflorescence, obtuse corolla lobes, white anthers, shorter, broader, thicker, paler fruits, and much smaller seeds. In the wild it is usually less than 1 m tall, often prostrate and hanging over ledges.

DESCRIPTION: A shrub that is often spreading or rounded and up to 50 cm tall. Branches ascending or erect, brown. Branchlets green, internodes 4–8 mm long, bifariously pubescent, leaf scars prominent. Leaf bud with a narrow, acute sinus. Leaves more or less spreading to spreading, 1.5–3 cm long by 6–11 mm wide, oblong to elliptic, coriaceous, M-shaped in transverse section, upper surface green or yellowish-green, dull, hairy along the midrib, undersurface pale green, dull, apex subacute and mucronate, base cuneate, margins entire, translucent, bevelled or rounded, minutely papillate or denticulate, petiole 3–4 mm long. Inflorescences lateral, simple or with one to two branches from near the base, 4–5 cm long, peduncle up to 1 cm long, pubescent, bracts opposite, ciliolate, linear to lanceolate, sometimes becoming alternate above, subacute to acute. Flowers all hermaphrodite, calyx rounded at the base, four-lobed and equally divided, lobes all similar, lanceolate to elliptic, ciliolate, margins scarious. Corolla white, tube glabrous, 1–2 mm long, longer than the calyx, lobes glabrous, longer than the tube, lobes elliptic or ovate, obtuse, more or less spreading. Filaments white, anthers white. Capsule 3–4 mm long by 2.5–3.5 mm wide, dark brown.

DISTRIBUTION: South Island. Known from only three locations in Fiordland: Wapiti Lakes in the southern Stuart Mountains, Takahe Valley in the Murchison Mountains, and Lake Monk in the Cameron Mountains in southern Fiordland. Occurs in subalpine scrub among rocky bluffs near the tree line, mainly on rock ledges, in fissures, around sinkholes, and in small debris fans and boulder screes. Always grows on limestone or marble.

Hebe armstrongii

For general garden use, *Hebe armstrongii* may be regarded as one of the best in the whipcord group. It is very handsome at any time, but its yellow-green to golden branchlets make it especially attractive during the winter months, when its colour contrasts nicely with other evergreens. Its rounded habit and conifer-like appearance make it a shrub with a great deal of appeal—truly, no garden should be without it. It usually grows to about 80 cm tall and can be suitable for larger rock gardens as well as the shrub border. In the northern hemisphere there appears to be a considerable amount of confusion as to what constitutes this species and whether the material is true to name. *Hebe ochracea* seems to be one species with which it is confused.

If *Hebe armstrongii* has a fault, it is its propensity to suddenly die back during the summer. G. R. Williams and D. R. Given mention this in *The Red Data Book of New Zealand* (1981), where they describe this plant as "commonly grown in rock gardens, particularly in New Zealand, although prone to severe dieback in the summer." The cause of this dieback is unknown, although it could possibly be one of the soil-borne fungi such as *Phytophthora* or *Rhizoctonia*. Overseas literature does not mention this problem occurring in the United States, British Isles, or Europe, and so perhaps it is more peculiar to New Zealand. New Zealand gardeners tend to plant whipcord hebes in relatively dry situations in the belief that they are drought-tolerant and prefer such conditions; however, as anyone who is familiar with these plants in the wild can attest, they are seldom seen in very dry situations. Perhaps northern hemisphere gardeners grow their whipcord hebes in moister conditions and therefore avoid such problems.

Hebe armstrongii was originally collected at the headwaters of the Rangitata River in 1869 by John Francis Armstrong and W. Grey. It has never been common, however, and at one stage Leonard Cockayne and H. H. Allan doubted its occurrence as a wild plant. In more recent years, a population of about four plants was discovered growing in the Castle Hill area of the Waimakariri River basin, and the species is now regarded as endangered. Nursery-grown plants bred from this wild population are being planted to enhance the wild population. This hebe associates with *Halocarpus bidwillii* (a species of the Podocarpaceae), and the two plants are almost indistinguishable when *H. armstrongii* is not in flower (Williams and Given 1981).

Hebe armstrongii is distinguished from related species by its leaves having a small, sharp tip, by its lack of glossiness, and by its nodal joint being weakly marked or obscure. The related *H. ochracea* has glossy branchlets and thick, keeled leaves. *Hebe annulata* is much smaller, with blunt leaves, and *H. salicornioides* has terete branchlets, the internodes exposed for most of their length, and leaves that do not at all overlap. *Hebe armstrongii* was named by John Francis Armstrong in honour of his son Joseph Beattie Armstrong.

DESCRIPTION: Usually a rounded, much-branched shrub 30–90 cm tall. Branches stout, erect to somewhat spreading, roughened with the old leaf scars. Branchlets rather crowded, terete, 1.5–2 mm in diameter including the leaves, yellow-green, internodes 1–1.5 mm long. Leaves about 1 mm long, joined together for about one- to two-thirds their length, apex truncate or rounded, abruptly tapering to a slightly keeled, acute tip, margins yellowish. Spikes about two- to six-flowered. Bracts 1–1.5 mm long, obtuse or with a small acute tip. Calyx 2–2.5 mm long, outer lobes completely fused into a broad, obtuse segment, sometimes with a short secondary split. Corolla tube more or less equalling the calyx, lobes white or pale mauve.

DISTRIBUTION: Confined to a few plants near Castle Hill in the Waimakariri River basin, and a population in the valley of the Esk River, both localities in north Canterbury. Though originally collected at the headwaters of the Rangitata River, this species has never since been found there. Most other herbarium records refer to other species of whipcord hebe.

Hebe barkeri (PLATE 16)

This is one of several species that grow on the remote Chatham Islands. It is distinguished by its strong, erect growth and by its leaves being covered with extremely fine but rather sparse pubescence, especially when young. The leaf buds also have a distinctly rectangular appearance when viewed in cross section. This species appears to be relatively drought-tolerant and will happily grow in quite dry situations where other hebes may not be so well suited. In cultivation it grows to 2 or even 3 m tall and is quite a good plant for the back of a border, where it can be seen towering above lower-growing hebes. *Hebe barkeri* is listed as a vulnerable species, the reasons for its decline being the destruction of its habitat and the grazing of young plants by livestock. In the absence of livestock, reproduction in the wild is good. It is thought to have once been an important constituent of lowland and tableland forests on the Chatham Islands, where it was probably more common.

Hebe barkeri can be quite reluctant to flower, at least in its young stages, and may need a few years' maturity before much can be expected. Strangely, *Flora of New Zealand* (Allan 1961, p. 910) does not describe the flower colour, while the *Manual of the New Zea-*

land Flora (Cheeseman 1925, p. 786) says the flowers are pale lilac. In cultivated specimens, I have seen only white flowers, which suggests that there may be some variation. In general appearance this species can be rather similar to *H. dieffenbachii*, except that *H. dieffenbachii* is a lower-growing, more sprawling plant without very fine pubescence on its leaves. *Hebe barkeri* was discovered in 1898 by S. D. Barker, after whom it was named.

DESCRIPTION: An erect shrub, occasionally up to 7 m tall, with stout branches. Branches terete, greenish to brownish, internodes about 1 cm long. Leaf bud with a sinus. Leaves spreading, about 5 cm long by 1.2 mm wide, lanceolate to oblong-lanceolate, either one or both surfaces covered with very fine, sparse pubescence when young, upper surface pale green, paler beneath, apex subacute, base of leaf inclined to be slightly wider than the branchlet. Inflorescences lateral, simple, usually about equalling the leaves. Flowers white or mauve, crowded, bracts subulate, acute; calyx lobes 3–3.5 mm long, acute, ciliolate. Corolla tube and lobes about equalling the calyx, style quite pubescent. Capsules about 5 by 4 mm, ovate, almost twice the size of the calyx.

DISTRIBUTION: Chatham, Southeast, and Pitt islands, where it occurs in mixed broadleaf forests as an occasional canopy tree.

Hebe benthamii (PLATE 17)

This hebe from the subantarctic Auckland and Campbell islands is generally rated as one of the gems of the New Zealand flora. Most authors describe the flower colour as a lovely bright blue, but few have actually seen the plant and are simply reiterating what others have written. In actual fact, the flowers are not a true blue at all but a most attractive violet-blue.

In nature *Hebe benthamii* is frequently a low-growing shrub, generally reaching about 30 or 40 cm tall and spreading to about 50 cm or more. Its deep green leaves are oblong to obovate-oblong, upper surfaces shining, with their margins conspicuously whitened with soft, fine hairs. The flowers, which are relatively large for the size of the plant, are borne in terminal, leafy racemes that are rather crowded. It is named in honour of George Bentham, a systematic botanist of the 19th century. *Hebe benthamii* was discovered on the Auckland Islands by J. D. Hooker in 1840 while on Sir James Clark Ross's Antarctic expedition.

This is not an easy species to cultivate, and certainly in my own experience (as well as the experience of others) it is not easy to maintain in cultivation. It usually lasts about two years before gradually beginning to languish. On the subantarctic islands, its native habitat, there is no soil as such, only great depths of peat. The islands also experience average summertime temperatures of 6°–7°C, frequent winds, and up to six cold fronts per day. It is no wonder, then, that plants from these islands are not easily managed in cultivation. Aphids also have a great fondness for this species and soon cause the plant to become sickly and debilitated. In the end, while *Hebe benthamii* is a very desirable species, it is not one for the tyro. Additionally, it is quite difficult to obtain live material of this species, and so I am afraid it will have to be admired only by those fortunate enough to visit its homeland. In general it flowers from November (early summer) till about January (mid summer).

DESCRIPTION: A generally stout shrub, 15 cm–1 m tall. Branches about 5 mm in diameter, quite leafy towards their tips. Branchlets ranging from having wide, bifariously pubescent bands to almost glabrous, length of internodes usually less than the diameter. Leaves spreading to more or less deflexed, crowded towards the tips of the branchlets, sessile and connate at their very bases, narrowly elliptic-oblong, coriaceous, 1.5–3 cm long by 7–10 mm wide; the characters on the one stem may vary in size and shape according to the plant's habitat. Upper leaf surface bright to deep green and somewhat shining, apex obtuse, margins rounded, more or less bluntly toothed, conspicuously whitened with a fringe of soft white hairs. Inflorescences terminal, leafy racemes that are usually simple, at first short but lengthening with maturity to become up to 10 cm long. Flowers crowded, violet-blue; calyx lobes about 8 by 4 mm, spathulate, obtuse, edged with white pubescence, lobes of both calyx and corolla often five or six. Capsules erect, about 8 by 4 mm, pointed, glabrous.

DISTRIBUTION: Confined to the Auckland and Campbell islands, where it may be common in rocky places among low grasses and also other low vegetation.

Hebe biggarii (PLATE 18)

Hebe biggarii has some resemblance to *H. pinguifolia* but is usually easily recognised. It is usually a small, rather decumbent shrub, no more than about 15 cm tall and with greyish, red-margined leaves that are often tinged reddish, particularly when young. Its flowers are white, on inflorescences no more than about 3 cm long. In the garden it seems to prefer a well-drained, sunny situation. It is an interesting species but is not to be compared with the best forms of *H. pinguifolia*. It was collected by D. L. Poppelwell from the Eyre Mountains in the early part of the 20th century and is named after a Mr. Biggar.

DESCRIPTION: A decumbent or prostrate, small shrub of a rather spreading habit. Branchlets rather stiff and usually densely leafy, up to about 20–24 cm long, internodes quite short. Leaf bud without a sinus. Leaves ovate or oblong to oblong-ovate, 12–18 mm long by 6–8 mm wide, apexes rounded to subacute, bases almost sessile. Inflorescences lateral, simple, about 3 cm long, peduncles 2 cm long; calyx lobes about 1 mm long, obtuse, ciliolate; bracts, like the calyx lobes, usually fleshy, obtuse, short; pedicels mostly 1.5–2.5 mm long, the lowest occasionally longer than the flowers; corolla tube 1.5 mm long, lobes about 3 by 2 mm. Capsule 4 mm long, acute, glabrous.

DISTRIBUTION: Appears to be confined to northern, central Southland, where it occurs on the Eyre, Garvie, and Thomson mountains. Grows on subalpine rocks at 1200–1450 m.

Hebe bishopiana (PLATE 19)

After its discovery this species was generally considered to be of hybrid origin, possibly a cross between *Hebe obtusata* and *H. stricta* var. *stricta*; however, it has now been accepted as a valid species. It is easily recognised and unlikely to be confused with any other hebe. It forms a rather open, spreading shrub to about a metre in height, and the upper surfaces of its leaves are shining and are a very deep, almost blackish-green. The stems are also dark purplish, as are the leaf buds, which may be quite purplish on the undersides of their leaves. The flowers are a light purple but soon fade to white and are produced on slightly drooping racemes about 8–12 cm long. This is a useful shrub in the garden because its dark-coloured, shining leaves provide a useful contrast against hebes with lighter foliage. Flowering generally occurs from about mid summer until autumn, with occasional flowers appearing in early winter. It was first collected in 1924 by J. J. Bishop of Titirangi and his companions. Specimens in the Auckland Regional Botanic Gardens proudly display an interpretive sign that proclaims "Nowhere else in the world," thus highlighting the fact that this species grows only in a very restricted area.

DESCRIPTION: A rather low, straggling, widely branched shrub (more bushy in cultivation) that reaches 50–90 cm tall. Stems rather slender, reddish-purple and puberulous when young, becoming green and glabrescent with age, length of internodes four to six times the diameter. Leaf bud reddish-purple, with a small, very narrow sinus. Leaves 5–7.5 cm long by 1.2–2 cm wide, narrow, lanceolate-elliptic, glabrous, upper surface deep green and shining, less so beneath, fine pubescence at the base of the midrib on the upper surface, margins minutely pubescent, apex obtuse, base abruptly tapering to a broad, short petiole. Inflorescences to 10 cm long, flowers more or less hiding the rachis; peduncle about 1.5 cm long, pubescent, rachis and pedicels pubescent, bracts narrow, ciliolate, acute, about equalling or longer than the pedicels; calyx lobes ovate-lanceolate, ciliolate on their hyaline, purple margins, obtuse; corolla tube flaring, about equalling or shorter than the lobes, white; corolla lobes subacute to obtuse, pale mauve to white. Anthers pale violet, filaments white. Style pale mauve. Capsule ovoid, acute, pubescent.

DISTRIBUTION: North Island. Apparently confined to rocky knobs between Huia Hill and Little Huia, near the Manukau Heads in the Waitakere Range

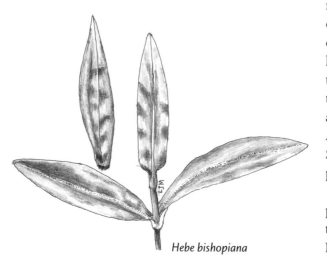

Hebe bishopiana

west of Auckland City. It occurs in moist places near streamsides, along seepages, and on exposed igneous outcroppings and shaded cliff faces.

Hebe bollonsii (PLATE 20)

This is a coastal species that occurs only on some of the offshore islands that lie around the eastern coastline of Northland. Even so, it has proved to be relatively hardy in the United Kingdom, surviving all but the harshest winters, and although it does suffer damage from severe conditions, it usually produces new basal growth the following spring. Generally it is an erect or slightly spreading shrub, up to 2 m tall, with shining leaves and quite long racemes of white or pale mauve flowers. It is ideal for the back of a border or similar situation, especially in coastal gardens, and normally has quite strong growth.

    Hebe bollonsii has been used in the breeding of some of the "Wiri" series of hebe. It was discovered on the Poor Knights Islands in the early part of the 20th century and named in honour of Captain J. Bollons, master of the government steamer *Hinemoa* around that time.

    DESCRIPTION: An erect shrub 1–2 m tall. Branchlets green and finely pubescent, length of internodes six to ten times the diameter. Leaf bud without a sinus. Leaves more or less erect to rather spreading, 4–8 cm long by 1.5–3 cm wide, broad-elliptic and rather coriaceous, upper surface shining to glossy, apex acute to shortly acuminate, base gradually narrowed to the branchlet, glabrous except for some minute pubescence along the upper surface of the midrib; margins entire. Inflorescence lateral, simple, usually 5–10 cm long including the peduncle, many-flowered but the flowers somewhat laxly placed; bracts, rachis, and pedicels densely pubescent; pedicels 3–4 mm long, equalling or longer than the narrow, ciliolate bracts. Calyx lobes broad-ovate, acute to subacute. Corolla white to pale mauve, rather large, tube narrow, lobes almost as long as the tube. Capsule about 4 by 3 mm, subacute, glabrous.

    DISTRIBUTION: Confined to the Poor Knights Islands, Mokohinau Island, Hen and Chickens Islands, and Ponui Island in the Hauraki Gulf, where it attains its southernmost limit. Grows in coastal scrub.

Hebe brachysiphon (PLATES 2 AND 21)

Hebe brachysiphon forms a rounded shrub to about 1 m tall with shining, light green to medium green foliage. Its occasionally branched inflorescences are usually produced in profusion, which makes it a very good garden shrub. The specific name *brachysiphon* means "short-tubed" and refers to the corolla tube; however, there is nothing about the length of the corolla tube that would readily distinguish this species from others with similar corolla tubes. It is quite a hardy species and usually flowers from just after mid summer until late summer or even later. Numerous bushes of *H. brachysiphon* present a wonderful sight when in full flower during January (mid summer) in the upper Wairau Valley, Marlborough. This species quite literally covers itself with a sheet of white so that it is not possible to see a single leaf poking through.

In the northern hemisphere there has been some confusion over the identity of this species. J. D. Hooker originally described and illustrated it as *Hebe traversii* in the *Botanical Magazine* in 1878. It was not until 1927 that V. S. Summerhayes of the Royal Botanic Gardens, Kew, formally determined the true identity of this species and named it *H. brachysiphon*. *Hebe traversii* is a distinct species, quite unrelated to *H. brachysiphon*, and was named and described by Hooker some 14 years before he applied the name *traversii* to the species that is now known as *H. brachysiphon*. Not only does *H. brachysiphon* differ in its leaf shape, it also differs in its leaf bud having a long, narrow sinus and may be further distinguished by the inflorescence sometimes being twice- or thrice-branched. It is, in fact, quite closely related to *H. venustula*.

DESCRIPTION: A rounded, bushy shrub to about 1 m tall. Branchlets very finely pubescent, length of internodes one to three times the diameter. Leaf bud with a long, narrow sinus. Leaves more or less spreading, or sometimes deflexed, 1.5–2.5 cm long by 4–6 mm wide, elliptic to lanceolate, upper surface light to medium green, shining, paler beneath, base gradually narrowed to a short, winged petiole, apex acute, glabrous except for minute and fine pubescence on the slightly bevelled margin. Inflorescences lateral, simple to occasionally bi- or tripartite, about 2–4 cm long. Peduncle shorter than the upper leaves, pubescent; bracts narrow, ciliolate, lowest acute, upper obtuse, mostly shorter than the pedicels, which decrease from 2.5 mm at the base of the raceme to less than 1 mm near to its tip. Calyx lobes about 1.5 mm long, obtuse to subacute on the same flower, ciliolate. Corolla white, tube about 3 mm long, rather broad, lobes equalling the tube. Capsule erect, about 4 by 3 mm, glabrous.

DISTRIBUTION: South Island. Found in subalpine scrub of the Canterbury and Amuri districts, including the upper Wairau River valley, and possibly extending to the nearby mountains of Nelson.

Hebe brevifolia (PLATE 22)

This hebe was formerly regarded as a variety of *Hebe macrocarpa* but is now recognised as a distinct species. It is a somewhat low-growing, rather sprawling shrub and in cultivation seldom attains a height of more than about 60 cm, whereas *H. macrocarpa* and *H. macrocarpa* var. *latisepala* both attain heights of up to 2.4 m or more. *Hebe brevifolia* has handsome foliage at all times of the year, and its flower colour is rather variable, ranging from crimson or magenta to rose-pink or even violet-purple. Closer examination will reveal that the corolla tube is white or pinkish and that only the corolla lobes are brightly coloured. It is quite distinct from any other hebe. This hebe is still not overly common in cultivation, although it is becoming more so. New Zealand nurseries have begun to market it as *H*. "Ruby" in what appears to be another case of failing to identify a plant and then giving it a cultivar name meant to appeal to the public.

In the wild *Hebe brevifolia* is confined to a relatively small area around North Cape, at the northernmost tip of the North Island. Coming from the subtropical north of New Zealand and having regard for its coastal habitat, it is, as might be expected, rather frost-tender. In northern hemisphere countries it is really only suited for outdoor culture in mild areas. Given suitable conditions it will produce flowers from early summer (November) until late winter (August). In more humid climates its leaves are quite susceptible to septoria leaf spot. The epithet *brevifolia* was adopted by Thomas Frederick Cheeseman in 1906 and refers to its smaller, narrower leaves that distinguish this plant from *H. speciosa*, to which *H. brevifolia* was, at that time, considered to belong as a variety. *Hebe brevifolia* was discovered by Cheeseman in 1896 at North Cape.

DESCRIPTION: A low-growing, often rather sprawling shrub of open growth, up to 60 cm tall or more. Branchlets greenish, length of internodes two to five times the diameter. Leaf bud without a sinus. Leaves spreading, up to about 10 cm long by 1.2–2 cm wide, elliptic-oblong, apex acute, gradually tapering to the almost sessile base, upper surface deep green and shining, paler beneath. Inflorescences shorter than or equalling the leaves. Flowers quite widely spaced and not hiding the rachis, reddish-purple, calyx glabrous, lobes broad-oblong, obtuse or sometimes somewhat acute, ciliolate; corolla tube broad and open, white or pinkish, lobes ascending and not very wide-spreading. Stamens far exserted, filaments purple; style purple.

DISTRIBUTION: North Island. Found only in a small area, within a few kilometres, around North Cape, including the Surville Cliffs and adjoining plateau area. Usually found growing on weathered serpentine and related ferricrete soils. It apparently attains its greatest abundance on the Surville Cliffs.

Hebe breviracemosa

This now rare species has had a rather chequered career since it was originally observed on the Kermadec Islands in 1888 by Thomas Frederick Cheeseman, who noted that it was then fairly plentiful. Cheeseman originally identified it as *Hebe salicifolia* but commented that it may be a distinct species. When W. R. B. Oliver visited the islands in 1908 he found few specimens, which were then mainly confined to cliffs and other places inaccessible to goats. During the middle of the 19th century, goats had been introduced to the islands as a source of food for shipwrecked mariners. As usually happens with such introductions, the goats soon decimated the indigenous plant population, including *H. breviracemosa*. Noted naturalist H. Guthrie-Smith commented in 1936 that "goats had eaten every scrap of a certain rare *Veronica* [*H. breviracemosa*]." Hopes remained that it may have survived on the steep cliffs, but these were gradually diminished as more sites were investigated and nothing was found.

The main island, Raoul Island, had been the site of a meteorological and radio station, but the station was abandoned after severe volcanic activity threatened the safety if its inhabitants. Following that, the islands were visited only by occasional parties of scientists. By 1981 *Hebe breviracemosa* was officially considered to be extinct. However, in 1983 a member of the team charged with the task of exterminating the last of the goat population was tracking a lone goat across a bluff when he discovered a single plant of *H. breviracemosa* that had escaped the attention of the goats. This miraculous discovery enabled cuttings to be taken, and the species was brought into cultivation, thus ensuring its survival. In fact, that single plant is the source of all cultivated material of the species. In 1998, after intensive searching, a further 50 plants were found. Since then it has been discovered that introduced rats may also be responsible for devouring young seedlings and thus preventing the re-establishment of *H. breviracemosa* on the island.

It should be noted that while Oliver was responsible for naming *Hebe breviracemosa* as a distinct species in 1910, Cheeseman was the first to discover it.

Hebe breviracemosa is a rather loosely branched shrub to 2 m tall and, as already noted, has similarities with *H. salicifolia*. Its racemes are usually 5–7.5 cm long and shorter than the leaves, while its flowers are lilac to pale lavender. Being a subtropical hebe, it is rather tender and needs to be grown in a protected environment. It is very uncommon in cultivation, and as yet only a few growers have it, such as Graham Hutchins of County Park Nursery, United Kingdom, and several growers in Auckland, New Zealand. Those who are familiar with it do not rate it very highly as a hebe, and it will probably appeal only to the connoisseur. Its specific name refers to its inflorescences being shorter than its leaves.

DESCRIPTION: A laxly branched shrub 1–2 m tall. Branchlets green, finely pubescent, length of internodes two to five times the diameter. Leaf bud without a sinus. Leaves spreading, 5–11 cm long by 2–3 cm wide, elliptic to oblong-lanceolate, upper surface somewhat shining, sessile, apex subacute, margins entire but finely ciliate at the very base and with some fine pubescence on both surfaces of the midrib near the base. Inflorescences lateral, simple, usually shorter than the leaves; peduncle 1–2 cm long, pubescent. Flowers crowded, pedicels 2–3 mm long; bracts about 5 mm long by 1 mm wide, narrow-acuminate, ciliolate. Calyx lobes about 4 mm long, narrow-acuminate, ciliolate. Corolla white to pale lilac, tube about 1.5 mm long, lobes about 3 mm long, ovate, acute. Capsule erect, about 5 mm long by 2.5 mm wide, acute, glabrous.

DISTRIBUTION: Raoul Island (formerly Sunday Island) of the Kermadec Islands. Originally distributed mainly on cliffs on the eastern coast and inland.

Hebe brockiei

This hebe is somewhat of an enigma. It appears to be a distinct species but has only ever been found in the one locality where it was first discovered. It has been suggested that it may be a hybrid, but available evidence does not lend credence to that. In some respects (leaf margins, colour, inflorescences, and flowers) it closely resembles *Hebe subalpina*, but in others (habit, leaf shape) it resembles *H. pinguifolia*. Regardless of whether it is a hybrid or a valid species, it is an attractive and worthwhile garden plant. It forms a spreading shrub to 20–30 cm tall, although usually no more than half that height. Eventually it will grow to about 30–45 cm across. Its leaves are light green, closely placed on the branchlets, wider towards their tips, and distinctively spoon-shaped or concave. Its white flowers are crowded on short inflorescences 2–4 cm long. In the garden, if used in quantity, it makes a useful ground cover. *Hebe brockiei* was discovered by W. B. Brockie on the Amuri Pass at the head of the Doubtful River in the early 1940s.

DESCRIPTION: A much-branched, spreading shrub 20–30 cm tall. Branchlets rather stout, bifariously pubescent, dark brown, length of internodes two to three times the diameter, leaf scars rough. Leaf bud without a sinus. Leaves rather closely imbricated, 1–1.5 cm long by 7–10 mm wide, broad-ovate, deeply concave, broadly obtuse towards their apexes, gradually narrowed at their bases, margins smooth, yellowish, cartilaginous. Inflorescences lateral, simple, 2–4 cm long, peduncle 5–15 mm long. Flowers white, crowded, pedicels very short, bracts 1–2 mm long, ovate-lanceolate, acute, ciliolate; corolla tube about equalling the calyx, corolla lobes no longer than the tube. Capsule erect, about 4 by 3 mm, glabrous, broadly ovate, acute.

DISTRIBUTION: South Island. Found in north Canterbury on the hills between the Amuri Pass and Lake Man, at the head of the Doubtful River. Usually plentiful in grassland at 1200–1500 m.

Hebe buchananii (PLATE 23)

This is an attractive but quite variable species, with some forms forming small shrubs up to 30 cm tall and others forming diminutive ground cover no more than 3 cm tall. Its usually quite small size means that it can be very useful for rock gardens or trough gardens. When some forms are grown in full sun, their leaves become quite glaucous; otherwise they are of a more greyish-green. The larger forms of this species usually flower quite profusely, but the smaller forms are often not very free-flowering at all. Flowering is usually from November (early summer) to March (early autumn). In the United Kingdom *Hebe buchananii* is rated as being very hardy. It is named in honour of John Buchanan, draughtsman and botanist to the Geological Survey of Otago Province. It was discovered in the Otago Lakes District by Buchanan and James Hector, probably in the early 1860s.

Hebe buchananii 'Fenwickii' and *H. buchananii* 'Minor' are probably the most commonly grown cultivars. One or two similar selections are also grown in the United Kingdom, but it is difficult to say whether they are very distinct from 'Fenwickii' and 'Minor'. Also grown in the United Kingdom are 'Christchurch', 'Mount White', 'Ohau', 'Otago', and 'Wanaka'. 'Christchurch' was obtained from the Christchurch Botanic Gardens; the other three were collected from the areas indicated by their cultivar names.

DESCRIPTION: A small, much-branched, decumbent to erect shrub 10–30 cm tall. Branches stout, tortuous, more or less black, old leaf scars very close together. Branchlets bifariously pubescent, internodes very short. Leaf bud without a sinus. Leaves spreading 3–7 mm in length and about the same in width, sessile. Leaf blade broadovate, more or less concave, gradually tapering to a broad base, apex subacute, thick and coriaceous, dull and rather dark green above, paler beneath, margins entire. Inflorescence lateral, simple, up to 1.6 cm long, peduncle pubescent, up to 1.2 cm long but usually hidden. Flowers white, densely placed, erect, sessile, bracts ovate, acute to subacute, ciliate, shorter than the calyx lobes. Calyx lobes similar to the bracts but broader, ciliate, corolla tube short and about equalling the calyx lobes. Corolla lobes spreading, ovate to oblong-ovate, obtuse. Stamens exserted, style pubescent.

DISTRIBUTION: South Island. Occurs in low- to high-alpine areas of Canterbury from about the Godley Valley then southwards to Central Otago and the Lakes District. Found in the drier eastern ranges from about 900 to 2100 m. Often grows in gravelly and rocky situations, especially in highly exposed sites in cushion vegetation and fellfield.

Hebe buchananii 'Fenwickii'. This very diminutive hebe forms a small, bun-shaped shrublet no more than 5–7 cm tall and about 15–20 cm wide. It is especially suitable for small rock gardens and trough gardens. It rarely flowers. For many years it was known to gardeners as *H. buchananii* 'Sir George Fenwick', but this name has proved to be nothing more than a synonym. This cultivar was named for George (later Sir George) Fenwick, who was editor of the *Otago Daily Times* in the late 19th and early 20th centuries, and a keen amateur botanist. *Hebe buchananii* 'Fenwickii' was discovered about 1907 on Mount Earnslaw by H. J. Matthews.

Hebe buchananii 'Minor'. Smaller and more compact than the larger forms of *H. buchananii*, although not as small as 'Fenwickii'. It is densely branched and usually forms a low, spreading shrub to 15 cm tall and 45–60 cm wide. Its leaves are 4–5 mm long by 3 mm wide. In New Zealand it is probably the most widely grown form of *H. buchananii* and is very useful for the front of a border. If planted in quantity it also makes a very good ground cover.

Hebe calcicola *

Hebe calcicola is a newly described species from north-western Nelson, where it grows on marble outcroppings. It was first recognised and collected by A. P. Druce in 1975, who found it at the Salisbury Hut on the Mount Arthur Tableland at 1000 m. It was not formally named *H. calcicola* until 2001. It belongs to the informal group "Occlusae," and, as such, its leaf bud does not have a sinus. This species is apparently very closely related to *H. rakaiensis*, from which it differs in having longer leaves and corolla lobes with glabrous margins, unlike those of *H. rakaiensis*, which are often sparsely or densely ciliolate. It also has similarities with *H. subalpina*, *H. truncatula*, *H. traversii*, and *H. strictissima*. This species has not yet made its way into general cultivation. The specific name *calcicola* is Latin and refers to this plant's apparent preference for growing on calcium-rich rocks.

DESCRIPTION: A shrub to 1.4 m tall. Branches erect, old stems mottled grey or brown. Branchlets brown to red-brown or green, internodes short, uniformly bifariously pubescent. Leaf bud without a sinus. Leaves more or less erect to spreading or recurved, oblong-elliptic to lanceolate or oblanceolate, usually about 2–3.8 mm long by 3.5–9 mm wide, apex subacute or obtuse, base cuneate, margins not thickened, light green or yellowish-green, bevelled, glabrous or ciliolate, entire, upper surface dark green, glossy, undersurface dull green and densely covered with stomata, glabrous or sometimes covered with minute glandular hairs when young. Inflorescences lateral, simple, 2.5–7 cm long, longer than the leaves just below them, peduncle usually 1–2 cm long, pubescent with a mixture of glandular and eglandular hairs, bracts alternate, obtuse to acute, ciliate with both eglandular and glandular hairs, deltoid or ovate; pedicels varying in length, longer than to shorter than the bracts; calyx about 1.5–2.5 mm long, usually four-lobed but occasionally five-lobed, lobes oblong or lanceolate, obtuse or more rarely subacute; flowers white, tube hairy inside, 0.7–1.2 mm long, shorter than the calyx, lobes longer than the corolla tube, posterior lobe elliptic or ovate to obovate, obtuse, erect to recurved, lateral lobes suberect or spreading. Stamen filaments white, 3.5–5 mm long, anthers obtuse, magenta. Capsule 2–3.5 mm long by 2.5–3 mm thick.

DISTRIBUTION: South Island. Endemic to north-western Nelson, where it is known only from the Peel, Lockett, Douglas, and Arthur ranges. It is known to occur on only marble outcropping rock.

Hebe canterburiensis (PLATE 24)

This species usually forms a ball-shaped shrub to about 1 m tall. Its glossy green leaves are 7–17 mm long, more or less distichously arranged on the branchlets, and blunt at their apexes. The leaf bud has a long, narrow sinus. This species flowers profusely and is therefore very useful in the garden. The flowers, usually white, are produced on short spikes. After flowering, which generally occurs around mid summer, this shrub should be given a light clipping to remove the old flower spikes and to keep the plant compact. *Hebe canterburiensis* was discovered in 1879 at Arthur's Pass and in other parts of Canterbury by Joseph Beattie Armstrong, who accordingly named it *Veronica canterburiense*.

DESCRIPTION: A low-growing shrub to 1 m tall. Branchlets usually minutely pubescent, length of internodes one to two times the diameter. Leaf bud with a long, narrow sinus. Leaves partly imbricated and also more or less distichously arranged, 7–17 mm long by about 4–6 mm wide, shortly petioled; blade more or less obovate, rather coriaceous, apex blunt, upper surface shining green; margin, petiole, and sometimes the upper surface of the midrib minutely pubescent. Inflorescence lateral, simple, 3–5 cm long, peduncle short and pubescent. Flowers usually white, pedicels short, longer than the short ciliolate bracts. Calyx lobes about 2.5 mm long, subacute, ciliolate along their membranous margins, corolla tube about equalling the calyx or slightly longer. Capsule erect, acuminate, glabrous, barely twice as long as the calyx.

DISTRIBUTION: In the North Island from near Mount Holdsworth in the Tararua Range, and in the South Island in the mountains of Nelson and western Marlborough southwards to Arthur's Pass. Usually occurs in scrubland, tussock grassland, snow tussock–herbfield, and to a lesser extent in subalpine scrub, at 900–1400 m.

Hebe carnosula

For many years *Hebe carnosula* was a problem for both botanists and horticulturists. The question of whether it existed, as a distinct species, or whether forms of the closely related *H. pinguifolia* were being treated as *H. carnosula* was something nobody seemed able to answer. The position has now been clarified, and the existence of *H. carnosula* as a distinct species is beyond doubt.

Hebe carnosula is rather similar to some forms of *H. pinguifolia*, which may also have a small sinus in their leaf buds, but true *H. carnosula* may be distinguished by having an always prominent sinus, a usually more erect, though low-growing habit, and darker green leaves with a glaucous bloom. It also has smaller, sometimes alternate bracts, and its capsules are more acute and glabrous. It is possible that true *H. carnosula* is not in general cultivation overseas, but it does appear to be cultivated in New Zealand. *Carnosula* means "somewhat fleshy" and refers to the rather fleshy nature of the leaves. The species was apparently discovered on Mount Morse in the Nelson area by John Carne Bidwill before 1854.

DESCRIPTION: A shrub much-branched to erect, 15–25 cm tall. Branches stout and spreading, ringed with the scars of the fallen leaves. Branchlets pubescent towards their tips, internodes short. Leaf bud with a distinct and prominent sinus. Leaves closely imbricating, spreading to more or less erect, 9–12 mm long by 6–7 mm wide, broadly obovate, thick and coriaceous, dark green under a glaucous bloom; apex obtuse. Inflorescences lateral, crowded near the tips of the branchlets, up to 2.5 cm long, often appearing to form a dense terminal head. Peduncle up to 1 cm long, pubescent; pedicels less than 1 mm long, bracts 2–2.5 mm long, narrow and ciliolate; calyx lobes 2–2.5 mm long, rather broad, obtuse, ciliolate. Corolla white, tube slightly longer than the calyx, lobes longer. Capsule erect, 5 by 2.5 mm, rather acute and glabrous.

DISTRIBUTION: Occurs on the ultramafic areas of the Red Hills Ridge and on the Bryant Range in Nelson Province. Forms of *Hebe pinguifolia* from the St. Arnaud Range, which sometimes have a small sinus in their leaf buds, have often been misidentified as *H. carnosula*.

Hebe chathamica (PLATE 25)

Among the few *Hebe* species from the Chatham Islands, *H. chathamica* may easily be recognised by its prostrate, spreading habit of growth and rather small, elliptic leaves that usually spread out from the branchlet in the one plane. The flower racemes are fairly compact and usually have a dumpy appearance. Flowers are generally violet and fade to white soon after opening. This hebe is reasonably hardy in all except the more rigorous northern hemisphere climates and is an excellent plant for growing in seaside localities. It is an excellent shrub for trailing over low walls or for use as a low ground cover. It was possibly discovered by H. H. Travers before 1865.

In its homeland this plant grows in coastal locations, where it may frequently be splashed by salt water. Flowers may appear from November (early summer) to March (autumn). The plant that I originally grew only flowered rather sparsely, and it was not until I received new material from Douglas Chalk, of England, that I discovered how well it could flower. It is a very nice little hebe and well worth growing.

DESCRIPTION: A prostrate to trailing shrub 60 cm–1.2 m across. Branchlets bifariously pubescent to almost glabrous, length of internodes short or four to five times the diameter, greenish. Leaf bud without a sinus. Leaves spreading and usually inclined in the one plane, 1.2–3.2 cm long by 7–12 mm wide, sessile. Leaf blade elliptic to elliptic-oblong or obovate-oblong, obtuse to subacute, the base slightly wider than the branchlet, rather thick and fleshy, upper surface green to pale green and dull or somewhat shining, lower surface paler; margins entire, cartilaginous. Inflorescences lateral, simple, exceeding the leaves, up to 4 cm long, peduncle up to about 2.1 cm long, puberulous. Pedicels about 3 mm long, puberulous, usually exceeding the linear-lanceolate, ciliolate bracts; calyx glabrous, lobes about 3 mm long, acute, ciliolate. Flowers white and pale to medium violet, closely placed and hiding the rachis, corolla tube exceeding the calyx lobes, pubescent inside, lobes wide-spreading, rather rounded and obtuse. Stamens exserted and longer than the tube. Capsule about 5 mm long, ovate, subacute.

DISTRIBUTION: Confined to the Chatham Islands, where it mainly occurs on steep and remote, rocky coasts.

Hebe cheesemanii (PLATE 26)

This species seldom attains more than 20 cm in height. It belongs to the informal group "Semiflagriformes" and is quite distinct. Along with the other members of the group, its branchlets are squarish when viewed in cross section. Its twigs are distinctly greyish-green, while stiff, short, white hairs are quite obvious along the leaf margins of the younger branchlets. One distinguishing character is the relatively smooth outline that the closely appressed leaves give to the twigs.

Hebe cheesemanii is an excellent plant for trough gardens or as a potted specimen in an alpine house. It is not too difficult to grow and makes an attractive, bun-shaped shrublet. In the rock garden it is particularly attractive when planted in a rock crevice. It should have a gritty, well-drained soil and a situation in full sun. If not grown in full light it tends to lose its distinctive character and its growth becomes too loose. It also flowers quite well in cultivation, from October (mid spring) to November (early summer). In the wild, flowering usually occurs from December (summer) to January (mid summer). This plant was named after Thomas Frederick Cheeseman, one of New Zealand's foremost early botanists, and was discovered by John Buchanan on Mount Alta, Otago, prior to 1882.

DESCRIPTION: A low, spreading shrub 10–20 cm tall, usually forming a rounded, bun-shaped plant 10–20 cm or more across. Branchlets numerous, distinctly tetragonous; when viewed from the side, the angles are bluntly and shallowly toothed in outline because of the slightly projecting leaf tips. Leaves tightly appressed, about 2 by 2 mm, broadly triangular, apex obtuse to subacute, margins ciliolate with white hairs. Inflorescences lateral from just under the tip of the branchlet and overtopping it, up to 1 cm long; flowers white, closely placed, perfect or male and female on separate plants.

DISTRIBUTION: South Island. Occurs in low- to high-alpine areas of the drier mountains east of the main divide from Marlborough to Canterbury, but rare south of Canterbury, at 1100–1700 m.

Hebe ciliolata

Another species in the informal group "Semiflagriformes." *Hebe ciliolata* is easily recognised by its angular branchlets, which are distinctly cross-shaped when viewed from end on. Its forward-pointing leaves are more widely spaced than other species of the group, circular in outline, with blunt tips and scattered hairs along their margins, while the leaf bases are widened and trough-shaped. In the wild it tends to form a rather straggling shrub, but cultivated plants are a bit better behaved, being usually well shaped and attractive. Its leaves are a lovely bright green to deep green and contrast well with the white flowers. As with *H. cheesemanii*, this is also good as a containerised specimen.

Hebe ciliolata has enjoyed a few name changes. In 1867 J. D. Hooker named it *Logania ciliolata*, in 1882 John Buchanan named it *Mitrasacme hookeri*, in 1896 Thomas Kirk named it *Veronica gilliesiana*, and in 1926 Leonard Cockayne and H. H. Allan placed it into the genus *Hebe* and gave it its present name. The specific epithet refers to the tooth-like cilia along the margins of its leaves. It was discovered on the slopes of Browning Pass by Julius Haast prior to 1864.

DESCRIPTION: A low-growing, usually straggling shrub forming a loose plant 10–30 cm tall and up to 20 cm across. Main stems prostrate or decumbent, branchlets numerous, erect or spreading, 2.5–7 mm in diameter, strongly tetragonous and distinctly cross-shaped when viewed from end on. Leaves forward-pointing, spreading and not closely appressed to the branchlet, becoming wider-spreading with age, about 4 by 1 mm, upper portion more or less rounded in outline and swollen at the tip, widening to a broad trough-shaped base, margins with scattered tooth-like cilia, apex blunt. Inflorescences about 6 mm long, sometimes hiding the tips of the branchlets; flowers white, in one to three pairs, sessile.

DISTRIBUTION: South Island. In low- to high-alpine areas of the wetter mountains from Nelson southwards. Usually found along or close to the main divide, at least as far south as Otago. Most common on rock ledges and in clefts, especially in fellfield, but may also occur on moraine and exposed rocky sites in snow tussock–herbfield. Grows at 1000–2000 m.

Hebe cockayneana (PLATE 27)

This is a species of the wetter mountain regions of the south-western part of the South Island. It forms an erect shrub to 1 m tall and is distinguished by its numerous stout branches, which are very rough with the old leaf scars. Its leaf bud also has a narrow sinus. The upper surfaces of its leaves are shining, and the undersurfaces are glaucous except for the prominent midribs. Its white flowers are on rather short racemes, about 2.5 cm long. It is quite hardy, but as Graham Hutchins points out in *Hebes Here and There* (1997, p. 50), it is very shy of flowering, possibly because it is accustomed to a much higher rainfall than it would receive in the United Kingdom. Fiordland in particular receives extremely high rainfalls—the rain being measured in metres, not just millimetres or centimetres. Of course, other factors such as degree of insolation may play a role. This species was named after Leonard Cockayne, one of New Zealand's foremost botanists and ecologists, who discovered it on the Humboldt Mountains near Lake Wakatipu in 1897.

DESCRIPTION: An erect, much-branched shrub to 1 m tall. Branches numerous, stout, very rough because of old leaf scars. Branchlets bifariously pubescent with harsh, sometimes golden hairs, internodes usually a little longer than broad. Leaf bud with a narrow sinus. Leaves suberect to spreading, sometimes distichous, 1–1.7 cm long by 5–8 mm wide, elliptic-oblong, thick and leathery, upper surface shining, lower surface glaucous except on the prominent midrib and the rounded, slightly thickened margins, apex subacute, margins entire, petiole very short and winged to its rather broad base. Inflorescence lateral, simple, up to 2.5 cm long, peduncle short, hairy-pubescent. Flowers shortly pedicellate, bracts short and ciliolate. Calyx lobes about 2 mm long, subacute and ciliolate. Corolla white, tube not quite equalling the calyx, lobes much longer, rounded. Capsule to 5 mm long, erect, acuminate, glabrous and dark.

DISTRIBUTION: South Island. Found in subalpine to low-alpine areas of the wet mountain regions of western Otago, Southland, and Fiordland. Its habitat is similar to that of *Hebe odora*, with which it may occur. Grows at 800–1500 m.

Hebe colensoi

This very attractive hebe has been much confused in northern hemisphere gardens. Over the years a variety of species and hybrids have masqueraded as *Hebe colensoi*, each serving to further increase the confusion as to which was the true species. Fortunately, material of the true *H. colensoi* is now in cultivation. It is recognised by its attractive greyish foliage, which is glaucous on both surfaces, by the small incisions or toothing around its leaf margins, and by the narrow sinus on its leaf bud. It is further distinguished by the lowermost pairs of racemes often being thrice-branched. The species is named after William Colenso, a missionary-printer who was also a very active botanist, particularly in the central North Island. Colenso discovered this hebe on the Ruahine Mountains around the mid 1840s.

This low-growing shrub reaches up to 60–75 cm tall, although often less than that, and spreads a bit wider. When in flower its 2 cm racemes of white flowers contrast most attractively against its grey foliage. Contrary to general supposition, the possession of grey foliage is not necessarily an indication that a particular plant prefers to grow in sunny situations. Some grey-foliaged plants are much happier when growing in a shaded or semi-shaded situation. *Hebe colensoi* is a case in point. In its natural habitat it grows along the steep banks of mountain streams, where it grows in cracks and crevices on cliff-like sites (Hutchins 1997, p. 48). While it will grow in full sun, it often appears to be more at home in a shady or semi-shady situation. The shade effect is particularly enhanced if there has been recent rain and the leaves are bejewelled with droplets of water. According to Graham Hutchins, in cultivation it freely produces flowers throughout the summer, while during winter in the United Kingdom it needs some protection from frosts. Both *H. colensoi* var. *colensoi*, the typical form, and *H. colensoi* var. *hillii* flower from early spring to early summer.

DESCRIPTION: A low-growing shrub to 75 cm tall but usually 40–60 cm tall. Branchlets glabrous, glaucous, length of internodes one to two or occasionally three times the diameter. Leaf bud with a narrow sinus. Leaves more or less obovate to elliptic, rarely to 2.5 cm long by 1 cm wide, glabrous, glaucous above and below, apex subacute, basal portion extending as a diminishing wing almost to the leaf base; margins almost to quite entire or sometimes with a few small incisions, slightly revolute. Inflorescences lateral and occasionally terminal, the lowest pairs or two pairs often tripartite, usually longer than the leaves and extending beyond the growing tip; peduncle glabrous, 1–2 cm long. Flowers white, almost sessile; bracts about 2 mm long, narrow, subacute to acute, quite glabrous. Calyx lobes very similar to the bracts; corolla tube not longer than the calyx lobes, narrow, subacute. Capsule glabrous, less than twice the length of the calyx.

DISTRIBUTION: North Island. From the head of the Taruarau River in the inland Patea region eastwards to the face of the northern Ruahine and Kaweka ranges and the

Moawhango River. Grows along the cliffs and steep banks of river valleys, particularly in rocky cracks and crevices, at 400–900 m.

Hebe colensoi var. *hillii*

Distinguished mainly by its larger leaves, which have several pairs of small but distinct marginal incisions. Named in honour of H. Hill, who presumably discovered it.

DESCRIPTION: Leaves more or less 3 cm long by 11 mm wide, elliptic, with three to ten pairs of marginal incisions. Leaves on plants in exposed places are linear-oblong, more or less 1.9 cm long by 6 mm wide, with 0–2 pairs of marginal incisions.

DISTRIBUTION: North Island. Found in a few localities, from the Ngaruroro River near the inland Patea Road to the Taruarau Razorback and the eastern face of the Kaweka Range. Usually grows on the cliffs of river valleys.

Hebe corriganii

A species confined to the eastern middle half of the North Island. *Hebe corriganii* is close to *H. salicifolia*, but its leaves do not show the sudden narrowing below their acuminate tips that is so characteristic of *H. salicifolia*. It also differs in having shinier, stiffer, more coriaceous leaves. The flowers of *H. corriganii* have a longer tube with less acute, usually shorter and broader lobes, while its capsule is also quite different, being acute and glabrous. It is named in honour of D. H. L. Corrigan, who discovered it at McLarens Falls near Tauranga.

According to Graham Hutchins (1997, p. 84), this hebe is not particularly hardy in the United Kingdom but is useful for shady situations in mild areas. A forest-dwelling species, it is among the few hebes ideal for shade, although it probably does not flower as freely as when grown in a more open situation. In the United Kingdom, flowering occurs in autumn and again in spring.

DESCRIPTION: A shrub to about 2 m tall. Branchlets stout, usually glabrous, length of internodes several times the diameter. Leaf bud with a distinct sinus. Leaves usually 8–15 cm long by 1–2.5 cm wide but occasionally larger, linear-lanceolate, more or less coriaceous, narrowed rather abruptly to a short petiole and evenly tapered to a narrow, subacute tip; glabrous except for some minute pubescence on the margins and sometimes remotely denticulate in the upper half. Inflorescences lateral, simple, equalling or longer than the leaves, peduncle long. Pedicels 2–3 mm long, equalling or longer than the narrow ciliolate bracts. Calyx lobes about 2 mm long, obtuse to subacute, ciliolate on their pale, membranous margins. Corolla white or pale mauve, tube up to twice as long as the calyx, rather wide, lobes equalling or shorter than the tube. Capsule more or less erect to spreading, acute, glabrous.

DISTRIBUTION: North Island. Occurs in the central portion from near Tauranga to the Mount Pirongia area, the Kaimai Range, and then southwards to Mount Taranaki and about the northern Ruahine Range, except for Mounts Ruapehu and Tongariro.

Hebe crenulata *

This species is described as being similar to *Hebe cockayneana* and *H. cryptomorpha*, another recently described species. From the former it differs in having coarse pubescence along the midribs and upper surfaces of its leaves, leaves that are oblanceolate, and leaf margins that are sometimes crenulate. It can be distinguished from *H. cryptomorpha* by the longest leaves on the individual plants being 1.4–2.2 cm long or occasionally longer. It also differs in having a combination of 7–18 ovules per locule on hermaphrodite plants. Previously this species was included with *H. cockayneana*, which occurs in Fiordland and South Westland. *Hebe crenulata* and *H. cryptomorpha* are morphologically very similar, and the decision to recognise them as distinct species was made largely on the basis of their flavonoid chemistry. The specific name *crenulata* refers to the fine notches around the leaf margins.

DESCRIPTION: A low, spreading shrub to about 1 m tall. Branchlets brown, red-brown, or green, internodes 2–6 mm long, leaf scars prominent, bifariously pubescent. Leaf bud with a broad, acute sinus. Leaves more or less spreading to erect, obovate or oblanceolate to elliptic, 7 mm–1.55 cm long (occasionally smaller or longer) by 5.3–6.9 mm wide, upper surface green, dull or slightly glossy, lower surface glaucous to glaucescent or light green, coriaceous, concave, apex obtuse to acute, base cuneate, margins usually slightly thickened, rounded or often slightly squarish, entire or crenate (may vary on the one plant), petiole 1–2.5 mm long. Inflorescences lateral, simple, occasionally compound with one or two branches at their bases, 1–3 cm long. Flowers white, either hermaphrodite or female on individual plants, tube glabrous, 1.8–3 mm long and more or less equalling the calyx, lobes ovate to elliptic, obtuse. Stamen filaments white, anthers magenta. Capsule subacute or obtuse, 3.2–4 mm long by 2.5–3.2 mm wide.

DISTRIBUTION: South Island. Mountains of western and central areas of the northern South Island between the Douglas Range in the north-west and the Poplars Range in the south-east. Grows in subalpine shrubland and tussock grassland, often on rocky sites.

Hebe cryptomorpha *

Hebe cryptomorpha is very similar to *H. cockayneana* and *H. crenulata*. From the former it differs in the size and shape of its leaves, which are generally somewhat larger; from the latter it differs mainly in having 15–33 ovules per ovary locule, although it may also have larger leaves. The specific name *cryptomorpha* is from the Greek *crypto* ("hidden") and *morphus* ("shape"), a reference to the obscurity of the morphological differences between this species and *H. crenulata*.

DESCRIPTION: A shrub or rounded shrub up to 1.2 m tall with erect branches. Branchlets usually brown or green, leaf scars prominent, pubescence bifarious. Leaf bud with a broad, acute sinus. Leaves decussate, somewhat erect to spreading, 1.3–2.8 cm long by 4–8 mm wide, oblanceolate to lanceolate or elliptic, fleshy or slightly thin, upper surface green, dull or slightly glossy, lower surface light green or glaucous or glaucescent, apex acute or subacute, base cuneate, margins not thickened, rounded or squarish, almost always entire or with minute teeth only sometimes present. Inflorescences simple, racemose and usually unbranched, or compound with one or two branches near the base, 1.2–3.7 cm long, peduncle 3–6 mm long, pubescent, rachis pubescent, bracts almost always opposite and decussate, usually free but sometimes very shortly connate, acute or subacute, ciliolate. Flowers white, either hermaphrodite or female on individual plants, calyx 2.4–3 mm long, three- to four-lobed; corolla tube glabrous, 1.5–3 mm long, equalling or slightly longer than the calyx, lobes longer than the tube, ovate to elliptic, obtuse. Stamen filaments white, anthers dark pink or purplish-mauve. Capsule obtuse to subacute, 3–4 mm long by 2.4–2.8 mm wide.

DISTRIBUTION: South Island. Occurs in Marlborough and Nelson provinces, mainly on the mountains of the Wairau River catchment, especially the Richmond, Raglan, St. Arnaud, and Crimea ranges, and extending westwards to Mount Robert and eastwards to Mount Severn and the upper Saxton Valley.

Hebe cupressoides (PLATE 28)

Once more common, and locally distributed from Marlborough to Otago, this species is now listed as vulnerable and has a very restricted distribution. At present it is confined to the Broken River basin in north Canterbury, Lake Pukaki, and the Lake Ohau area. It is estimated that only several hundred plants exist, most of them in the Lake Ohau population. Of its rarity there is no question; in all my wanderings I have only ever seen a single wild plant, growing in subalpine scrub near the summit of Jacks Pass, above Hanmer Springs. Burning-off and stock grazing have contributed to its scarcity. This species was probably discovered by James Hector and John Buchanan, possibly in the Lindis Pass area. The name *cupressoides* alludes to the plant's cypress-like appearance.

This distinct and remarkable species is recognised by its green, cypress-like foliage and by the rather distant placement of the small, scale-like leaves on its thin branchlets. No other hebe quite resembles it. In New Zealand the most commonly grown form has quite a fresh, green appearance, but, especially overseas, there is at least one other form that may be somewhat more glaucous. Additionally, several other cultivars are listed. Because of the differences between this and other species of *Hebe*, it is quite possible that *H. cupressoides*, along with four other members of the informal group "Semiflagriformes," will be placed in the genus *Leonohebe*.

Hebe cupressoides looks like a plant that will tolerate quite dry conditions, but its appearance is deceptive. Like many New Zealand plants, it has evolved to withstand the desiccation of the winds to which New Zealand, particularly in mountainous areas, is frequently subjected. While its branches, with their very small, tightly appressed leaves, will tolerate such conditions, this plant is not always so tolerant of dry soil conditions around its roots. In the garden it is usually much happier if planted in a soil that retains moisture reasonably well. It usually forms a rounded, ball-shaped shrub to a metre tall or more and is worth growing for its foliage and form alone. It does not always flower well, but when it does the whole bush becomes covered with a soft violet-blue haze. Unlike other whipcord species, its flower spikes frequently have fewer than eight flowers. An annual pruning is usually necessary to stimulate the production of new wood and prevent the bush from becoming leggy.

DESCRIPTION: A usually densely branched, rounded shrub 1–1.5 m tall. Ultimate branchlets erect, very close-set and more or less 1 mm in diameter, flexible, medium green and more or less glaucous, internodes 2–4 mm long, exposed, nodal joint obvious. Leaves 1–1.5 mm long, scarcely connate, narrowly triangular, subacute to acute, rounded on their backs, fleshy and appressed when fresh. Inflorescences about six- to eight-flowered, flowers all sessile or the lower ones subsessile, usually not tightly crowded; rachis glabrous; bracts similar to the leaves. Calyx 1–1.5 mm long, anterior lobes subacute, fused for all or most of their length; posterior lobes entirely fused into a single obtuse or emarginate segment. Corolla about 3 mm in diameter, tube slightly exceeding the calyx. Capsule about 2 by 1 mm, narrowly oblong, somewhat laterally compressed.

DISTRIBUTION: South Island. Found in subalpine to low-alpine areas, formerly common along the eastern side of the island from Marlborough to the Otago Lakes District but now confined to a small population near Lake Pukaki, a larger population around Lake Ohau, and a population of just a few individuals in the Broken River basin of the Waimakariri River catchment. Usually grows on river flats and terraces among tussock grassland or in subalpine scrub at 600–1400 m.

Hebe cupressoides '**Boughton Dome**'. This dwarf form grows to about 45 cm tall, has a compact, dome-shaped habit, and rarely flowers. Young plants often have a fair proportion of juvenile foliage. According to Graham Hutchins (1997, p. 198), plants usually change to adult foliage after a few years. Thomas Frederick Cheeseman (1925, p. 820) observed that juvenile leaves are sometimes produced by reversion on the branches of old ones. Perhaps this accounts for the character of this cultivar. 'Boughton Dome' is said to have originated as a branch sport that occurred in Scotland around 1970. It was distributed by Lady Scott (Valerie Finnis), who named it after the dome of Boughton House in Northamptonshire, England.

Hebe cupressoides '**Glauca**'. This cultivar is not grown in New Zealand, but Graham Hutchins (1997, p. 198) of the United Kingdom maintains that it grows to a height of about 2 m and has branchlets that are more greyish, foliage with a more distinct fragrance, and inflorescences with as many as ten flowers.

Hebe cupressoides 'Nana'. According to Graham Hutchins (1997, p. 197), this is the form most commonly cultivated in New Zealand and the United Kingdom, although, as far as New Zealand is concerned, that is not strictly correct. All older New Zealand material does not exhibit any dwarf characters whatsoever. In the United Kingdom, *H. cupressoides* 'Nana' does not appear to have been cultivated much before 1959, and its presence in New Zealand is obviously much more recent than that. As Hutchins so rightly states, its name is misleading because it will eventually grow into a shrub up to 1.3 m tall. *Hebe cupressoides* 'Nana' begins as a shrub of distinctly dwarf habit, and while it will eventually grow larger, it takes some time to do so.

Hebe decumbens (PLATE 29)

Hebe decumbens is a handsome species that is very easily recognised by its purplish-black stems, red-margined leaves, and almost sessile flowers. In cultivation it usually forms a low, spreading bush 30–45 cm tall and sometimes 90 cm or more in diameter. The specific name *decumbens* means "to lie along the ground with the tip ascending"; however, most cultivated material grows as a spreading shrub and is not decumbent. In some areas completely decumbent forms of this species do occur, but as yet none has been generally cultivated. These decumbent plants usually grow in crevices and on ledges on rock faces, while the more shrubby forms occur in open tussock grassland or exposed rocky places. *Hebe decumbens* was discovered near the Rutherford Bridge, over the Waiau River, Nelson, by Joseph Beattie Armstrong in 1869.

This hebe is useful for growing in the front of a border and similar places in the garden, and can even be used in a larger rock garden. It is very drought-tolerant and will withstand quite dry conditions with no apparent ill effects. In this respect it is an excellent little shrub. It produces short racemes of white flowers from late November (early summer) to mid December (summer). While it usually prefers a sunny situation, it will also tolerate some light shade, particularly if it receives sun during the morning and later afternoon. While it is represented in cultivation by just one or two clones, in some localities, such as Hell's Gates on the upper Wairau River, some interesting variations occur that would well repay collection.

DESCRIPTION: A small, often decumbent, much-branched shrub 30–50 cm tall, occasionally taller. Branchlets dark, blackish-purple, stout to rather slender, bifariously pubescent, length of internodes two to eight times the diameter. Leaf bud without a sinus. Leaves spreading to slightly ascending, 8–20 mm long by 5–8 mm wide, elliptic to broad-elliptic, apex subacute to somewhat obtuse, coriaceous, upper surface pale to yellowish-green or dark green, lower surface similar, shortly petioled, flat or somewhat concave, margins usually red, minutely pubescent. Inflorescences lateral, simple, equalling or just exceeding the leaves, 2–2.5 cm long, peduncle very short, minutely puberulous. Flowers white, closely placed and hiding the rachis, rather erect, lower flowers on very short

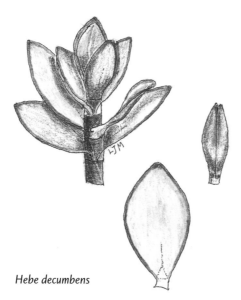

Hebe decumbens

pedicels, upper flowers almost sessile; bracts very narrow, acute, much shorter than the calyx; calyx lobes acute, margins minutely ciliolate, much shorter than the corolla tube; corolla tube up to 5 mm long, lobes spreading, ovate, obtuse. Stamens exserted, anthers purple. Capsule erect, about 4 mm long, ovate, acute, glabrous.

DISTRIBUTION: South Island. Found in subalpine to low-alpine locations in the mountains of Marlborough, eastern Nelson, and north Canterbury, where it is confined to the drier areas. Usually grows on rocky sites in grassland or low scrub, though also on rock faces and bluffs, at 900–1500 m.

Hebe decumbens 'Gina Marie'. Originated from Westbay Propagation, near Westport, New Zealand. Flower buds are pinkish. There appears to be little to distinguish this from the commonly grown bushy forms of the species. Regardless, it is a very fine plant.

Hebe decumbens 'Southey'. From a plant collected by Graham Hutchins (1997, p. 101) on Mount Southey near Lake Tennyson in north Canterbury. Hutchins describes it as "an open-branched, sprawling shrub, wide-spreading but usually more than 30 cm tall."

Hebe dieffenbachii (PLATE 30)

Hebe dieffenbachii is a low-growing shrub, seldom more than 60 cm–1.2 m tall, with wide-spreading branches. There is apparently some confusion in northern hemisphere countries as to what constitutes this species, which is variable. The problem is further compounded by the fact that gardeners tend to regard a single cultivated clone as typical of the species and are often not prepared to accept the variation that can mark so many *Hebe* species in the wild. By all accounts this species can be quite variable in its natural habitat, and, particularly with the genus *Hebe*, such variation can be quite a normal character. On the Chatham Islands *H. dieffenbachii* grows on limestone cliffs and rocks, especially around the Te Whanga Lagoon or Great Lagoon, and it is the commonest hebe on the Chathams. In some coastal areas its branches are said to spread laterally or hang downwards, although according to Leonard Cockayne this character, which is quite noticeable in cultivated plants, is not so noticeable in wild plants.

The foliage of *Hebe dieffenbachii* is light to medium green and has quite a pleasing appearance. This plant does not commonly flower, but when it does, flowers are a light mauve, fading to white, with a white corolla tube. It is easily grown but is not reliably hardy and may be damaged by winter frosts. *Hebe dieffenbachii* is named to commemorate Ernst Dieffenbach, surgeon-naturalist for the New Zealand Company, who botanised the Chatham Islands from 1840 to 1841 and discovered this species.

DESCRIPTION: A rather stout, low-growing shrub 60 cm–1.2 m tall with sometimes very wide-spreading branches. Branchlets glabrous to bifariously pubescent or hoary, terete, pale green, length of internodes two to four times the diameter. Leaf bud without a sinus. Leaves spreading to slightly ascending, 5–11.2 cm long by 1.2–3.2 cm wide, elliptic to elliptic-oblong, apex obtuse, glabrous except for fine pubescence on the upper surface of the midrib, upper surface dull, paler beneath, sessile with the broad base more or less clasping the stem, margins entire and with a narrow cartilaginous border. Flowers purplish to white, densely placed, hiding the rachis, pedicels spreading, longer than the small bracts. Calyx lobes ovate, acute, ciliolate; corolla tube rather broad, longer than the calyx lobes; corolla lobes approximately equalling the tube, rounded. Capsule 5–7 mm long, more than twice the length of the calyx, ovate, acute, glabrous or with a few hairs.

DISTRIBUTION: Chatham Islands.

Hebe dilatata

Lucy Moore in *Flora of New Zealand* (Allan 1961, p. 947) regarded this Southland hebe as being of doubtful status, but it has since been definitely recognised as a species. *Hebe dilatata* is known from the Garvie Mountains, where it was originally collected at the Blue Lake by botanists George Simpson and John Scott Thomson during the early 1940s. Whether this species remains in cultivation is open to conjecture.

For more than 50 years I have been associated with what I believe may be *Hebe dilatata*, but as the plant has never flowered, I have never been able to verify its identity. Certainly, its general characters are similar to those given for this species, but without flowers it is difficult to say. One plant of it grew in the rock garden in the Christchurch Botanic Gardens, while the other grew in the alpine garden in Queen's Park, Invercargill. Both were in climatically different locations, the first with a low rainfall (625 mm) and the second with a much higher rainfall (1200 mm). Both plants grew well, forming attractive, compact, cushion-like plants up to 60 cm or so in diameter. However, in all the time that I knew these two plants I never observed any indication of flowers on them. I now have several plants propagated from the Invercargill plant, but in more than 12 years in my garden in Nelson Province, they have failed to flower. The habit of the flowers aborting may be the reason why *H. dilatata* is so shy of flowering. The plant in the Christchurch Botanic Gardens could well have come from Simpson and Thomson, who used to send some of their collections to both Christchurch and Dunedin botanic gardens.

Hebe crawii, a more recently described species from the Eyre, Garvie, and Takitimu mountains of Southland, has now been merged with *H. dilatata* on the grounds that, although often a little larger, it generally does not appear to be sufficiently distinct to warrant being regarded as a distinct species.

DESCRIPTION: A prostrate, much-branched shrub that may spread to form close mats up to 1 m or so across. Branchlets purplish, sparingly bifariously pubescent. Leaves obovate-oblong, spreading or recurved, usually 1–1.5 cm long by 5–6 mm wide, coriaceous to almost fleshy, pale green. Leaf bud with a narrow sinus. Inflorescences lateral, simple, few, longer than the leaves, apparently poorly developed, with many aborting in the leaf axils on both wild-collected specimens and those in cultivation.

DISTRIBUTION: South Island. Grows on debris slopes around the Blue Lake on the Garvie Mountains, and in the Eyre and Takitimu mountains, in Southland at 1370 m.

Hebe diosmifolia

A very attractive and distinct species that was discovered in the Bay of Islands area by Richard Cunningham, possibly around 1833. Cunningham obviously collected it from more than one locality, as his specimens include material from near the source of the Waikare River, the cataracts of the Kerikeri River, and possibly the South Hokianga Head. *Hebe diosmifolia* is easily recognised by having small, narrow leaves that are more or less inclined in the one plane, leaf margins marked by small teeth or incisions, and much-branched racemes that appear to be terminal because of the way they overtop the growing tip. It rather closely resembles *H. divaricata*, which may be recognised by its leaves not having notches or incisions around their margins; additionally, *H. divaricata* is well separated geographically from the northern *H. diosmifolia*.

Hebe diosmifolia is a handsome species that has a fine appearance even when not in flower. It usually flowers very well and produces an impressive display. Being a forest-dwelling species, it will tolerate some shade and still make a reasonable bush that flowers quite well; on the other hand, it will also thrive in an open situation in full sun.

Hebe diosmifolia is quite a variable species, and it has sometimes been suggested that it may comprise two separate species. There is one form that has been in cultivation in New Zealand for many years. It usually forms a rather low-growing shrub, 70 cm–1 m tall, although under some conditions and with age it may attain 2 m. It is a very distinct plant and may be recognised by its branching pattern, which tends to range from spreading to more or less horizontal; by its deep green leaves, which are 1.2–2 cm long by 3–4 mm wide, usually with notched margins; and by its flowers, which are heliotrope in the bud but soon fading to white. This form usually produces flowers over quite a long period, from mid August (late winter) until late November (early summer). It is often referred to as the spring-flowering form of the species. Nothing appears to be known of its origin.

Other, quite different forms have subsequently been collected from various wild habitats. In general they are taller and more erect, forming quite substantial shrubs 2–3 m or more in height. These plants are usually referred to as the summer-flowering form.

Their leaves are often green to yellowish-green, and their margins are often inconspicuously notched, as opposed to the slightly more obvious notches of the so-called spring-flowering form. Flowering is from November (early summer) or December (summer) to early January (mid summer). Some plants even flower as late as February (late summer). There appears to be nothing that would indicate that the spring-flowering and summer-flowering forms are sufficiently distinct to warrant splitting them into two different species.

When growing in some of the Northland forest habitats, *Hebe diosmifolia* will become very tall, attaining heights of several metres, perhaps as much as 6 m, but when cultivated in more open situations it may not grow as tall. In New Zealand *H.*

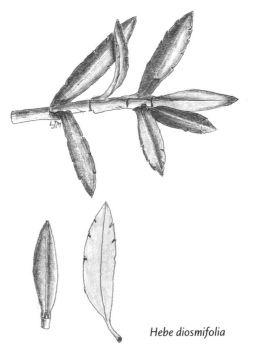

Hebe diosmifolia

diosmifolia is quite hardy around all parts of the country, but in the United Kingdom (and no doubt other northern hemisphere countries) it is not regarded as particularly hardy. The derivation of the specific name is not certain, but it is thought that in 1836, when this plant was originally named, it must have been thought to resemble a species that then comprised the genus *Diosma*.

DESCRIPTION: A much-branched shrub 60 cm–2 m or more in height, sometimes even up to 6 m. Branchlets usually rather slender, yellow-green to brownish or even reddish, puberulous and with conspicuous bifarious pubescence, length of internodes two to four times the diameter. Leaf bud with a conspicuous, long, narrow sinus. Leaves suberect to spreading, almost distichous, 1.2–2.8 cm long by 3–7 mm wide, lanceolate to obovate-oblong, apex acute, base cuneate and shortly petiolate, upper surface green to dark green, paler beneath, margin ciliolate and slightly thickened, with one to several (usually paired) small incisions. Inflorescences lateral, compound, crowded near the tips of the branchlets and usually overtopping the leaves to form flat-topped corymbose heads. Peduncle usually shorter than the leaves, puberulous. Flowers usually mauve or heliotrope but may also be white, densely placed, pedicels pubescent, bracts ciliolate, equalling or slightly shorter than the pedicels. Calyx lobes about 1.5 mm long, ovate-obtuse, ciliolate; corolla tube 1.5–2 mm long, about equal to the calyx lobes, corolla lobes ascending. Stamens equalling the lobes, filaments white or coloured. Capsule 4 mm long, ovate to more or less orbicular, acute to subacute.

DISTRIBUTION: North Island. Occurs in Northland from Cape Reinga to Woodhill Forest just north of Waimauku, a few kilometres north of Auckland City. Usually grows in lowland scrub and around forest margins, but is not always common.

Hebe diosmifolia 'Garden Beauty'. A loosely upright shrub to 80 cm or 1.2 m tall. Its branchlets are pale reddish-brown and contrast well against its deep green foliage. The flowers open to lavender and gradually fade to white. Generally this hebe flowers from September (early spring) to November (early summer). It was discovered as a branch sport on a specimen of *H. diosmifolia* 'Wairua Beauty' growing in the Auckland Regional Botanic Gardens.

Hebe diosmifolia 'Marie'. Said to be more vigorous than the smaller-growing form of the species. Its leaves are slightly larger and with fewer incisions. Its anthers are also said to be greyish-white. It originated from a plant given to Graham Hutchins by Marie Turnbull of Rangiora, New Zealand.

Hebe diosmifolia 'Wairua Beauty'. This cultivar has larger corymbs of heliotrope flowers and is quite spectacular when in full bloom. It appears to have a shorter flowering season, about four weeks, although it may have a longer season in other parts of the country. It is a fine garden plant for areas where this species is sufficiently hardy. This cultivar originated at the Wairua Falls, Titoki, near Whangarei. It belongs to what is commonly known as the summer-flowering form of *H. diosmifolia*.

Hebe divaricata

This very showy, floriferous species deserves to be better known. It is not common in cultivation but nonetheless is worth the effort of trying to acquire it. When it flowers, between December (summer) and February (late summer), the whole bush becomes a foamy mass of white flowers. It is quite closely related to *Hebe diosmifolia* but differs in not having small incisions around the margins of its leaves and in its flowers being pure white, usually without a trace of any colour. It appears to be quite hardy in the United Kingdom and will grow in full sun or tolerate the light shade of trees. It has very neat foliage and makes a compact shrub, usually growing to about a metre tall.

In the wild, *Hebe divaricata* grows in a variety of habitats, including *Nothofagus* forest and the subalpine zone above the tree line. It can also be seen in forests close to the shoreline around parts of the Marlborough Sounds, although not where it is liable to be splashed by salt water. When growing in a forest habitat it can be drawn up to a height of 3 m, but in open situations in subalpine areas it is usually less than half that height. In north-western Nelson, where it can be quite plentiful in localities such as the Cobb Ridge, it can be variable with regard to form and quantity of flowers. It is possible to select some very good forms. Some may be very floriferous with quite large inflorescences, others less so. Habit of growth may also vary. The leaf bud sinus is usually described as long and narrow but is sometimes somewhat shorter and broader.

The specific name *divaricata* means "to diverge from" or "to spread widely," but this plant is not as divaricating as a number of other New Zealand shrubs commonly referred to in this way. *Hebe divaricata* was discovered in the Rai Valley, Nelson, by J. H. McMahon, probably in the early part of the 20th century.

DESCRIPTION: An erect to spreading, much-branched shrub 1–3 m tall. Branchlets rather slender, bifariously pubescent, yellow-green, length of internodes two to four times the diameter. Leaf bud with a long, narrow (though sometimes shorter and broader) sinus. Leaves spreading to slightly deflexed, 2–3.2 cm long by 3–5 mm wide, narrow-lanceolate, glabrous, upper surface mid green and more or less shining, paler beneath, margins entire and usually with minute hairs towards the base, apex acute, base narrowed to a short petiole about 2 mm long. Inflorescences lateral, usually much-branched, crowded towards the tips of the branchlets and hiding the terminal growth; peduncle much shorter than the leaves, fulvous, pubescent. Flowers white, rather loosely placed and not hiding the rachis, pedicels ascending, up to about 2 mm long or slightly longer than the narrow, ciliolate bracts, pubescent; calyx more or less glabrous, lobes about 2 mm long, obtuse to subacute, ciliolate; corolla tube longer than the calyx lobes, corolla lobes spreading, slightly shorter than the tube, ovate, obtuse to subacute. Stamens exserted, little longer than the lobes, anthers violet. Capsule about 4 mm long, acute, glabrous.

DISTRIBUTION: South Island. Found in Marlborough and Nelson provinces in forests, along streamsides, on rocks, and in subalpine grassland-scrubland, from sea level to 1500 m.

Hebe elliptica (PLATE 31)
kokomuka

This is a distinct and somewhat variable species, and it is also one of three species that extend or occur outside of the New Zealand botanical region. It also occurs around the coast of southern South America and on the Falkland Islands, in this instance being the only hebe to extend its range into the southern Atlantic Ocean. In New Zealand it occurs along part of the western coastline of the North Island (var. *crassifolia*), around most of the coastline of the South Island, Stewart Island, and southwards to the subantarctic islands. The specific name refers to the elliptic leaves.

Hebe elliptica is a particularly hardy shrub as far as coastal conditions are concerned. It grows close to the water's edge (within a metre or so of the high-water mark) and may frequently be splashed with salt spray and lashed by the Antarctic gales that occur around the South Island's southern coast and its more southerly habitats. In the northern hemisphere it has proved to be not completely hardy and may be damaged by severe frosts. In New Zealand it is hardy throughout the country, and I have never known it to suffer from frost damage. Its flowers are among the largest in the genus; generally they are white, but forms with varying amounts of mauve or pale violet occur. This is an excellent shrub for coastal gardens and is also useful for hedging. In cultivation it will form a bush 1.8–2.4 m tall and will grow in almost any soil or situation. Although young plants will flower, the best flowering usually does not occur until this hebe has attained a degree of maturity. Flowering usually occurs from November (early summer) to March (autumn).

A number of forms have been selected and brought into cultivation. 'Anatoki', 'Charleston', 'Donaldii', and 'Stewart' are cultivars from New Zealand's *Hebe elliptica*. With the exception of 'Donaldii', all were named by Graham Hutchins of County Park Nursery in Essex, England. 'Bleaker', 'Pebble', 'Port Howard', 'Sea Front', and 'Stanley' are all from the Falkland Islands. They too were named by Hutchins, who received them from Patrick Roper. According to Hutchins (1997, p.55), the Falkland cultivars all differ in some ways from each other but do not have any distinct differences as compared with the New Zealand plants.

Hebe elliptica was discovered by Johann or Georg Forster (father and son), who accompanied Captain James Cook on his second voyage to New Zealand between 1772 and 1774. The type locality is given only as New Zealand, but it was probably Dusky Sound, where the Forsters spent some time collecting.

DESCRIPTION: A much-branched, erect to spreading shrub or small tree 1.5–5 m tall. Branchlets usually bifariously pubescent, length of internodes one to six times the diameter, young branchlets usually green. Leaf bud with a distinctive sinus. Leaves spreading, often more or less facing in the one plane, 1.2–4 cm long by 7–16 mm wide, elliptic to elliptic-oblong, sometimes obovate-oblong, apex apiculate to mucronate, base tapering to a short erect petiole, coriaceous to somewhat fleshy, upper surface green to deep green, paler beneath, glabrous except for a white pubescent margin. Inflorescences lateral, simple, crowded towards the tips of the branchlets and little longer than the leaves, 4- to 14-flowered, peduncle short, puberulous. Flowers white to pale violet, rather loosely placed and not completely hiding the rachis; pedicels more or less spreading, up to 4 mm long, elongating in fruit, puberulous, exceeding the narrow ciliolate bracts. Calyx glabrous, lobes up to 3 mm long, broad-ovate, acute, margins pale and ciliolate; corolla up to 1.4 cm in diameter, tube equalling the calyx lobes, corolla lobes wide-spreading, up to 8 mm long, ovate to broad-ovate, subacute to acute. Stamens exserted but not as long as the lobes. Capsule about 7 mm long, broad-ovate, acute, twice as long as the calyx lobes.

DISTRIBUTION: South Island, at Totaranui (in Golden Bay) and then westwards along the whole coastline to southern Fiordland, the southern coast of Southland, and northwards up the eastern coastline of Otago. Common on Stewart Island, the Snares

Islands, the Auckland Islands, and Campbell Island. Absent from the Canterbury and eastern Marlborough coasts as well as the Marlborough Sounds. Also found around southern South America, Tierra del Fuego, and the Falkland Islands.

Hebe elliptica 'Anatoki'. From the Anatoki River in north-western Nelson. Hutchins considers this to be the hardiest form, and it is very free-flowering. It differs from 'Charleston' in having more or less purplish internodes. It has bluish flowers with as many as 20 flowers on each raceme. The flowers are also slightly fragrant.

Hebe elliptica 'Bleaker'. Collected on Bleaker Island in the Falklands. Branchlets with bifarious pubescence. Flowers white.

Hebe elliptica 'Charleston'. Similar to the typical form. It is fairly hardy and free-flowering even while young. Collected from Charleston, near Westport.

Hebe elliptica 'Donaldii' (PLATE 32). A variegated cultivar that was discovered as a branch sport on the *H. elliptica* that grows wild on Bluff Hill, Southland, by Invercargill nurseryman F. J. Saunders. Its green and grey-green leaves are broadly margined with cream. Branching is usually rather erect, and it tends to remain a smaller and more compact plant than the common *H. elliptica*. It appears to be more suited to cooler climates and does not always thrive in warmer areas.

Hebe elliptica 'Pebble'. Collected from Pebble Island in the Falklands. Branchlets pubescent all around, leaf margins pubescent. Flowers white.

Hebe elliptica 'Port Howard'. Branchlets with bifarious pubescence, leaves subacute, margins nearly glabrous. Flowers white. Collected in the Falklands.

Hebe elliptica 'Sea Front'. Came from the sea front at Stanley in the Falklands. Branchlets with bifarious pubescence. Leaves almost rounded, flowers pale bluish, 1.8 cm in diameter.

Hebe elliptica 'Stanley'. Branchlets with bifarious pubescence, leaves with a distinct excurrent tip, flowers not seen. Collected from the Falklands.

Hebe elliptica 'Stewart'. This form is said to come from Stewart Island. It has dark purplish internodes and leaves 2–3 cm long. Hutchins states that it is not as hardy and says that although he has had it for 18 years it has never flowered for him.

Hebe elliptica **var.** *crassifolia* (PLATE 33)

This variety is quite distinct and may be recognised by its larger, rounder leaves and larger flowers. Although its flowers are usually said to be white, those that I have seen are a lovely strong medium violet. The parent of these particular plants originated from Titahi Bay, on the western coast of the North Island, to north of the city of Wellington. The varietal name refers to the thickened leaves: *crassus* ("thick") and *folium* ("a leaf").

DESCRIPTION: Differs in having branchlets that are very stout and leaves that are 2.7 by 1.5 cm long, more or less broad-obovate, almost fleshy, pale green to medium green. Flowers white or violet, corolla to 2 cm in diameter, the lobes all broad-ovate.

DISTRIBUTION: North Island. The south-western coast from Cape Egmont to Titahi Bay and Kapiti Island.

Hebe elliptica var. *crassifolia* 'Kapiti'. A form collected from Kapiti Island by Graham Hutchins. It has white flowers.

Hebe epacridea (PLATE 34)

Hebe epacridea is an easily recognised species because of its trailing or sprawling habit and its distinctively leafy stems, with hard little leaves joined together at their bases so that when viewed from end on they give the branchlets a very square appearance. Generally this plant is no more than a few centimetres high and may be up to 40 cm across. Its specific name refers to the fact that it resembles *Epacris*, a southern hemisphere genus of heath-like shrubs related to *Erica*. *Hebe epacridea* was discovered in 1861 in the Tarndale area by Andrew Sinclair.

This species is really only suited for rock gardens, trough gardens, or containers. When well grown it is very interesting and can be quite attractive. Its compact inflorescences can be quite showy, and they hide the growing tips of the branchlets. Its leaf colour varies from yellowish-green to deep green, according to the situation and growth of the plant. Because it is a plant of rocky areas and stable scree slopes, this hebe needs to be planted in a free-draining, gritty soil, preferably in full sun. It will also grow in a small amount of indirect shade.

DESCRIPTION: A low-growing to decumbent shrub to 40 cm across. Stems rather stiff, internodes short and usually hidden by the leaves. Leaves spreading and usually rigidly recurving, about 5–7 by 4–6 mm, broadly ovate-oblong, widened bases joined together around the stem, strongly keeled, glabrous, coriaceous, with cartilaginously thickened margins. Inflorescences compact, about 1.5 by 1.2 cm, subterminal; flowers white, only the lowest two to four on each spikelet fully developed. Flowers on individual plants either hermaphrodite or female.

DISTRIBUTION: South Island. Widespread in high-alpine areas from north-western

Nelson and Marlborough along the main divide to Southland. Usually about and east of the divide and more common on the drier eastern ranges. Mainly occurs on rocks, open areas of rock debris, or stable scree slopes, at 1000–2900 m. *Hebe epacridea* (together with *Parahebe birleyi* and *Ranunculus grahamii*) ascends to the highest altitudes for any species of vascular plant in New Zealand.

Hebe evenosa (PLATE 35)

This is one of the "box-leaved" hebes, so called because of their resemblance to the European *Buxus* or box. It is confined to the Tararua Range in the southern half of the North Island, where it was discovered in 1908 by Donald Petrie. It is a distinct shrub with a rather wide-spreading habit that can be recognised by its flat and rather thin, elliptic leaves with acute tips. A shrub of forest margins, in the wild it very likely becomes drawn up by overhanging and surrounding trees and may attain a height of up to 2 m. In the garden it is more likely to average about 1 m. The specific name *evenosa* refers to the fact that it appears to have no veins showing on its leaves. In *Hebes Here and There* (1997, p. 94), Graham Hutchins noted that although he had cultivated this plant since 1978 it had not yet flowered for him.

DESCRIPTION: A shrub to 2 m in height with widely spreading main branches, usually much-branched below their leafy tips. Branchlets rather stout, bifariously to fully pubescent, length of internodes two to three times the diameter. Leaf bud without a sinus. Leaves more or less spreading, 1.5–2 cm long by 6–8 mm wide, obovate-oblong, broadest towards their blunt thickened tips, glabrous except for minute pubescence on the margins, somewhat coriaceous, upper surface dull to shining green. Inflorescences lateral, simple, 2.5–3 cm long; peduncle short and hidden, pubescent. Flowers crowded. Bracts about equalling the short pedicels, obtuse, ciliolate; calyx lobes about 1.5 mm long, broad, obtuse, ciliolate. Corolla white, tube about 2 mm long, lobes slightly longer, rounded. Capsule erect, about 4 mm long by 2.5 mm, obtuse, glabrous.

DISTRIBUTION: North Island. Confined to the Tararua Range, where it grows around the edges of the forest belt at 800–900 m. Originally found on Mount Holdsworth.

Hebe fruticeti

A species of very restricted habitat, found only at the head of the Estuary Burn, Lake Wanaka. It is virtually unknown in cultivation and is likely to be found only in the gardens of a few enthusiasts. It is closely related to *Hebe subalpina*, which mainly differs from *H. fruticeti* in having larger, wider leaves, acute calyx lobes, and a corolla tube that is more than 5 mm long. The specific name *fruticeti* probably refers to the fact that this plant grows in bushy places. It was discovered by George Simpson and John Scott Thomson in the early 1940s.

DESCRIPTION: A closely branched, rather spreading shrub 1–1.5 m tall. Branchlets slender, glabrous, length of internodes three to six times the diameter. Leaf bud without a sinus. Leaves more or less spreading, about 2.5–3 cm long by about 5 mm wide, linear-lanceolate, slightly narrowed to the base, apex subacute, upper surface rather pale green, shining, lower surface less so, rather coriaceous, margins entire and very smooth. Inflorescences lateral, simple, up to 5–6 cm long, peduncle short; bracts narrow, ciliolate, equalling or shorter than the pedicels; calyx lobes about 1.5 mm long, subacute with a narrow, pale border. Corolla white, tube shorter than the calyx, lobes about 2 mm long. Capsule erect, about 4 by 2.5 mm.

DISTRIBUTION: South Island. Known only from the head of the Estuary Burn at Lake Wanaka. Occurs in subalpine scrub at 1000–1500 m.

Hebe gibbsii (PLATE 36)

This species has a very restricted distribution in the Nelson area. It is closely related to *Hebe amplexicaulis* f. *hirta*, which differs in having whitish hairs on one or both leaf surfaces, whereas *H. gibbsii* only has distinctly whitish hairs forming a fringe around its leaves, bracts, and calyx lobes. In colder weather the leaf bud is often purplish, and cultivated plants are often more robust than wild plants. Plants seen in cultivation in the United Kingdom have more of a decumbent habit than cultivated material in New Zealand, which can be quite erect. This hebe is named after F. G. Gibbs, a botanist of local repute, who discovered it in the Nelson area during the late 19th century. He particularly botanised on the local Nelson mountains and discovered *H. gibbsii* on Mount Rintoul, probably in the early 1890s.

Hebe gibbsii is quite distinct and easily recognised. Its sometimes small size and lovely, very glaucous leaves, usually with reddish margins, are usually sufficient to identify it. Mostly it has a distinct reddish margin, but on some forms the red is lacking and the margins are pale. It grows in rocky places, often where there is shattered rock containing many crevices in which it can put down its roots. It is ideal for growing in a rock garden or trough garden and would be a handsome plant for growing in a pot. A gritty soil and a position in full sun suit it best.

DESCRIPTION: A sparingly branched small shrub 10–30 cm high. Branchlets rather stout, glabrous, roughened with the old leaf scars, length of internodes about equalling the diameter, Leaf bud without a sinus. Leaves loosely imbricated, spreading or deflexed, 1–1.8 cm long by 6–12 mm wide, elliptic to ovate, thick and strongly glaucous, margins usually more or less red, base broad but not cordate, apex subacute to obtuse, margins entire, glabrous except for a fringe of long, silky hairs. Inflorescences lateral, simple, peduncle villous, usually shorter than the leaves, spike broad, about 1.5 cm long. Flowers sessile, bracts and calyx lobes about 3 mm long, narrow-triangular, acute, fringed with long cilia, in some plants pubescent on the outer surface. Corolla white, tube narrow, usually longer than the calyx, equalling the narrow spreading lobes. Capsule not greatly compressed, narrowed to a subacute tip, dark, glabrous to slightly pubescent.

DISTRIBUTION: South Island. Confined to Mounts Rintoul, Ben Nevis, and Patriarch on the Richmond Range near Nelson. Usually grows in rocky places, especially on shattered rock, at 900–1220 m.

Hebe glaucophylla (PLATE 37)

Overseas there has been much confusion as to what constitutes *Hebe glaucophylla*. In the United Kingdom, various hebes have been known by the name *glaucophylla*, and the true species has sometimes been improbably labelled *H. colensoi* and even *H. darwiniana*, the latter seeming to be a bit of a catch-all name. The correct *H. glaucophylla* is now in cultivation in England thanks to Graham Hutchins (1997, p. 99), who collected it on one of his trips to New Zealand. He has given it a cultivar name, *H. glaucophylla* 'Clarence', as he says, "to separate this species from hebes incorrectly but commonly known in gardens as *H.* 'Glaucophylla' including the variegated form *H.* 'Glaucophylla Variegata'." As he further states, "These hebes are probably hybrids and should be given cultivar names."

Hebe glaucophylla is an attractive species, but if a glaucous hebe is required, there are much more desirable choices, such as *H. albicans* or one of the better forms of *H. topiaria*. This hebe forms a rounded, ball-shaped shrub to about a metre tall, with greyish leaves and white or sometimes pinkish flowers. It flowers during January (mid summer) and February (late summer). The specific name refers to the leaves, which are grey-green or bluish-green. It was discovered in 1902 in the Craigieburn Mountains, Canterbury.

DESCRIPTION: A rounded, bushy shrub to 1 m tall. Branchlets rather slender, usually very finely bifariously pubescent, length of internodes several times the diameter. Leaf bud without a sinus. Leaves spreading, 1.3–1.6 cm long by 5–6 mm wide, lanceolate, glaucous, drying dark brown but not black, stomata numerous on both surfaces, gradually narrowed to a subacute to acute tip, margins entire, glabrous except for some microscopic pubescence on the more or less bevelled margin. Inflorescences lateral, simple, two to three times the length of the leaves; peduncle short, finely pubescent. Bracts less than 1 mm long, ciliolate, shorter than the pedicels. Calyx lobes 1–1.5 mm long, broad, obtuse, ciliolate on a pale membranous border. Corolla white or sometimes pinkish, tube barely equalling the calyx, hairy in the throat, lobes longer than the tube, about 2.5 mm long, rounded, spreading. Style and ovary with fine, sparse pubescence. Capsule to about 5 by 4 mm, less than twice the length of the calyx, narrowly to broadly ovate, subacute, pubescent.

DISTRIBUTION: South Island. Found from southern Marlborough to mid Canterbury, where it grows on scrubby banks and in gullies in tussock grassland at 900–1400 m.

Hebe gracillima (PLATE 38)

This seldom-grown species is likely to be seen only in the gardens of a few discerning collectors. It certainly does not appear to be in cultivation in the United Kingdom. It is an interesting species in that it mainly appears to inhabit damp forests where conditions can be quite shady—an indication of the kind of growing conditions it prefers. When growing in its natural habitat, its branching is often rather sprawling in nature, but in more open situations, or in the garden, the branching tends to be more erect. Similarly, on cultivated plants the inflorescences may diverge from the branchlet almost at right angles. The specific name *gracillima* means "most graceful" and may refer to the appearance of the shrub when in flower. It was discovered near Westport by a Dr. Gaze, sometime during the late 19th century.

Hebe gracillima is easily grown, and despite being a plant of shady, moist situations, it is quite drought-tolerant and will grow in open situations without any ill effects. In cultivation it grows to 2.5–3 m tall and flowers from January (mid summer) to February (late summer).

DESCRIPTION: An erectly branched to spreading shrub 2–3 m tall. Branchlets uniformly covered with fine pubescence, green to yellowish-green, length of internodes up to three times the diameter. Leaf bud with a small sinus. Leaves spreading to reflexing and often arcuate, 2.5–5.5 cm long by 6–10 mm wide, upper surface yellowish-green to darkish green, very finely pubescent above, on the margins, and extending to the very short petiole. Inflorescence simple, diverging at an angle or sometimes extending at right angles to the branchlet and much longer than the leaves. Peduncle up to 1.5 cm long, finely pubescent along with the rachis. Raceme up to 11 cm long, flowers quite widely spaced, white to pale mauve, pedicels finely pubescent, bracts lanceolate, acute, ciliolate, longer than the pedicels. Calyx lobes 1.5–2 mm long, shorter than the corolla tube, obtuse to subacute, ciliolate. Corolla lobes tending to be rather pointed.

DISTRIBUTION: South Island. Mainly found in the Nelson area from near Farewell Spit and the Richmond Range southwards to near Ross in Westland. Found mostly west of the main divide, usually in damp, shady forest and sometimes in swampy places, from sea level to 600 m.

Hebe gracillima 'Slate River Gold' (PLATE 39).

An attractive cultivar with soft, golden-yellow foliage that retains its colour for most of the year. It is smaller in all of its

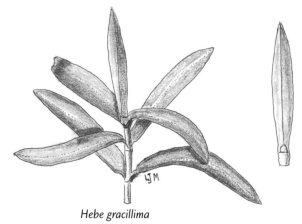

Hebe gracillima

parts than the typical form, and its leaves tend to be more acute. If anything, its smaller, more pointed leaves give it a daintier appearance. This cultivar was discovered by Simon Walls along the Slate River, a tributary of the Aorere River, in north-western Nelson.

Hebe haastii

This species is related to *Hebe macrocalyx* and *H. epacridea* but is distinguished by its leaves being elliptic to obovate or ovate rather than spathulate or elliptic to rhomboidal as in *H. macrocalyx*, and not hard and rigid to form a distinctly square-shaped stem as in *H. epacridea*. Its leaves tend to lie in the one plane instead of being placed all around the branchlet as with *H. epacridea*. Formerly, *H. macrocalyx* var. *macrocalyx* and *H. macrocalyx* var. *humilis* were considered to be varieties of *H. haastii*. It is a trailing or sprawling sub-shrub that usually grows to about 20 cm tall and forms clumps or patches up to 30 cm in diameter. It is named in honour of Julius Haast, who from 1861 until 1887 was provincial geologist and explorer for the province of Canterbury. He discovered *H. haastii* on several Canterbury mountains in 1862.

DESCRIPTION: A subshrub to 20 cm tall by about 30 cm in diameter. Branches ascending, green when young, internodes 2.5–7 cm long. Leaves sessile, decussate, 8.2–13 mm long by 5.5–9.3 mm wide, more or less spreading, elliptic to obovate or ovate, green and sometimes tinged with dark red, apex rounded to subacute, coriaceous to fleshy, flat, bases connate, midrib thickened beneath, margin not thickened, rounded, glabrous, entire and sometimes bluntly incised and/or obscurely erose, red or green. Inflorescences terminal and lateral, the reduced spikes arranged in a dense, terminal flowering head, 1.3–3.3 cm long; lowermost pair of bracts on a spike, opposite and connate, subopposite or alternate above, oblong to deltoid or lanceolate, acute to subacute or rarely obtuse, ciliolate and sometimes the insides also glandular-hairy; pedicels absent. Calyx 4–5 mm long, oblong to elliptic to lanceolate, subacute to obtuse, minutely ciliolate with the insides glandular-hairy, margins green but often tinged with red near their apexes. Corolla white; anthers held in the corolla throat. Flowers on individual plants either hermaphrodite or female.

DISTRIBUTION: Usually grows in open rocky sites on shattered rock, rock debris, and stable screes, extending from the Craigieburn Range in Canterbury, to Mount Hutt, the Winterslow Range, the Rangitata River catchment, Two Thumbs Range, Mount Dobson, and to Mount Nimrod on the Hunters Hills in South Canterbury. Grows at 1400–2100 m. Records of this species for outside of the Canterbury area all relate to *Hebe macrocalyx*.

Hebe haastii 'Mount Dobson'. A form collected by Graham Hutchins from Mount Dobson, South Canterbury, in 1981. According to Hutchins (1997), it was collected from a sprawling plant at about 1980 m. Although he describes it as the easiest form to grow, he also points out that his own specimen has never flowered. Similar to *H. haastii* 'Princess' but with purplish internodes and slightly smaller, red-margined leaves that are seldom if ever incised.

Hebe haastii 'Princess'. Hutchins collected this cultivar on Mount Princess, on the St. James Range near Lake Tennyson, and describes it as having red-margined, distinctly incised leaves. The flowers are white in showy clusters of short spikes.

Hebe hectori

Hebe hectori is an assemblage of various whipcord hebes formerly regarded as distinct species (Wagstaff and Wardle 1999). The group is characterised by occurring mainly in wetter districts and by the plants having ascending or erect main stems, with few lateral branchlets on each growth stage. Their colour ranges from yellow-green to olive-green, and the connate leaf bases are often partly covered by the leaves below each scale leaf. In addition, their calyx lobes are fused only at their bases. Of the various subspecies, the main differences appear to be the thicknesses of their branchlets and the stature of some compared with what used to be considered typical *H. hectori*.

Hebe hectori subsp. hectori

Hebe hectori subsp. *hectori* is a rather variable plant that may be recognised by its rather stout, erect stems, which are a distinctive yellowish-brown, presenting a richness of colour not usually found in whipcord hebes. It is very good in the garden when grown with the brighter and more golden members of the whipcord group as well as some of the grey-foliaged *Hebe* species. It is generally small enough for a rock garden, growing to about 45 cm tall on average, and is generally quite hardy, although care must be taken that it does not become too dry at the root. Discovered on Mount Alta in western Otago by geologist and explorer James Hector in 1863.

DESCRIPTION: A small but robust, much-branched shrub 15–75 cm tall. Branches stout and erect or sometimes spreading and ringed with the old leaf scars. Branchlets erect, terete to obscurely angled, 3–4 mm in diameter, yellow-green to brownish-yellow, internodes very close and usually hidden. Leaves very closely appressed to the branchlets, overlapping, 2.5–3 mm long and joined together for about half their length, broadly ovate-triangular, apex obtuse to more or less acute, thick and rounded on their backs and somewhat polished. Inflorescences axillary, crowded near the tips of the branchlets, 1–1.2 cm long, up to about 15-flowered. Flowers white, more or less erect, bracts about 3 mm long, broad-ovate, obtuse to acute or mucronate; calyx lobes linear-oblong, obtuse, as long as or slightly longer than the bracts; corolla tube equalling or slightly longer than the calyx lobes, corolla lobes spreading, obtuse. Capsule 3–4 mm long, oval to oblong, obtuse or subacute, longer than the calyx.

DISTRIBUTION: South Island. Found from the mountains of South Canterbury to

Otago and Southland as far south as the Takitimu Range. Grows at 1060–1800 m in mixed snow tussock–scrub and snow tussock–herbfield, and also extending into shallow snowbanks, moist depressions in fellfield, and in cushion vegetation. It is quite abundant in Fiordland and western Otago.

Hebe hectori subsp. *coarctata* (PLATE 40)

Formerly classified as a separate species, this plant is now part of the *Hebe hectori* group. Compared with *H. hectori* subsp. *hectori*, its branchlets are rather thin, usually only 1.5–2 mm in diameter. The branches are either not four-angled or are scarcely four-angled, slender and usually arching, usually glossy and on their upper sides bearing branchlets up to 5 cm long. This hebe is rather similar to *H. hectori* subsp. *laingii*, but its main branches tend to be more prostrate and have a greater density of lateral branchlets that tends to give them an arching or plume-like appearance. It also differs in its thickened leaf tips, which give the branchlets a slightly square appearance. The subspecific epithet *coarctata* comes from the Latin participle *coarctare* ("compressed"), which comes from *co* ("with" or "together") and *arcus* ("a bow"); it may refer to the rather tightly grouped branchlets on the upper sides of the branches but more likely refers to the arching or bow-shaped branchlets. This plant is thought to have been discovered by Thomas Frederick Cheeseman on the Mount Arthur Plateau in 1886.

DISTRIBUTION: South Island. Common in the mountains of Nelson Province and extending as far eastwards as the St. Arnaud Range. Commonly grows in damp snow tussock–herbfield, occasionally in somewhat drier sites, at 1200–1700 m.

Hebe hectori subsp. *demissa*

Formerly listed as a variety of *Hebe hectori*, this plant has been elevated to the rank of subspecies. It is a low, spreading plant seldom more than 15 cm tall, with branchlets about 2 mm in diameter. It is distinguished not only by its low stature but also by its convex leaves, which are appressed and rounded at their apexes, which have minute mucronate tips no more than 0.2 mm long. *Hebe hectori* subsp. *demissa* grades into the typical form of *H. hectori* and is about as hardy as this form. All cultivated plants apparently come from the original collection made by George Simpson, who discovered this plant on the Rock and Pillar Range, North Otago, prior to 1945. The subspecific name *demissa* means "hanging down" or "lowered" and refers to its low habit of growth.

DISTRIBUTION: South Island. Known only from the Rock and Pillar Range in North Otago, where it occurs on moist, grassy banks near small streams.

Hebe hectori subsp. *laingii*

This is a low shrub, up to 25 cm tall, with squarish branchlets only 2–2.5 mm in diameter. Its leaves are similar in shape to but smaller than those of *Hebe hectori* subsp. *hectori*.

Its internodes are also a little longer. This appears to be a variable subspecies, in some localities grading into subsp. *hectori*. Named after botanist and author R. M. Laing, who explored many parts of Canterbury Province and Banks Peninsula. Discovered on Mount Anglem, Stewart Island, by Leonard Cockayne early in the 20th century.

DISTRIBUTION: South Island. Confined to Fiordland and Stewart Island, where it grows in damp, grassy meadows on valley floors and on the summit of Stewart Island's Mount Anglem. Specimens from South Westland appear to be closer to *Hebe hectori* subsp. *hectori* than to subsp. *laingii*.

Hebe hectori subsp. *subsimilis*

This bushy shrub grows to about 30 cm tall, occasionally more. In its general dimensions it is similar to *Hebe hectori* subsp. *laingii* but differs in its subacute, thickened leaf tips, which tend to give the branchlet a squarish appearance when viewed in cross section. The leaves are also only faintly keeled and not unlike those of *H. hectori* subsp. *coarctata*. This hebe has certain similarities to *H. tetragona*, although the smaller flower heads of *H. hectori* subsp. *subsimilis* have fewer flowers. It is one of only two whipcord hebes that occur in the North Island. In the United Kingdom it is apparently not completely hardy. The specific name *subsimilis* refers to this plant being somewhat similar to *H. tetragona*. It was discovered on the Ruahine Range in February 1898 by H. Hill.

DISTRIBUTION: North Island. Occurs only on the Pouakai Range of Mount Taranaki and on the Ruahine and Tararua ranges. Usually grows in subalpine scrub, mixed snow tussock–scrub, and snow tussock–herbfield, up to about 1500 m.

Hebe hectori subsp. *subulata*

Hebe hectori subsp. *subulata* is a shrub from the eastern mountains of Central Otago and is generally more slender than *H. hectori* subsp. *demissa*, which grades into subsp. *subulata*. One of the main differences between the two subspecies is that the small mucro on the tips of the leaves of subsp. *subulata* may have a squarish appearance when viewed in cross section. *Hebe hectori* subsp. *subulata* bears some similarities to *H. imbricata* subsp. *poppel-wellii* and *H. lycopodioides*. It was discovered by Owen Fletcher in the 1940s on the Old Man Range in Central Otago. The subspecific name *subulata* means "awl-shaped" and refers to the leaves.

DISTRIBUTION: South Island. Confined to the ranges of Central Otago, where it occurs on the Old Man Range, Umbrella Mountains, and possibly one or two other nearby ranges. May be common in open, low-alpine snow tussock–grassland and on early snowbanks. Grows at 900–1300 m.

Hebe imbricata

A small to medium species of whipcord hebe that, for many years, was regarded as possibly being of doubtful status, having been collected only once from a wild habitat. It has erect growth and apparently has some affinities with *Hebe lycopodioides*. This species comprises *H. imbricata* subsp. *imbricata*, the typical form, and *H. imbricata* subsp. *poppelwellii*. Both forms occur on the South Island of New Zealand, mainly in Otago and Fiordland.

Hebe imbricata subsp. *imbricata* *

A small, much-branched shrub that is rather erect and seldom grows to more than 40–60 cm tall. It does not appear to be in cultivation overseas and is almost certainly not cultivated in New Zealand unless it survives in some gardens in the Otago area. It was discovered on Mount Cleughearn by J. Crosby-Smith during the early part of the 20th century. According to Lucy Moore (Allan 1961, p. 934), Donald Petrie wrote of this species: "This plant appears to have been in cultivation for a number of years but its wild habitat was, till recently, unknown." Moore further stated that only material from Mount Cleughearn had been seen.

This plant is closely allied to *Hebe lycopodioides* and *H. imbricata* subsp. *poppelwellii* (formerly *H. poppelwellii*); all three plants have keeled leaves and four-angled branchlets. On *H. imbricata* subsp. *imbricata* the leaf tips are rounded to subacute. Starting around 1926 it was suggested that this hebe may be of hybrid origin, especially since there were no further discoveries of the species. Of more recent years it has been discovered in one or two other localities. The name *imbricata* is the Latin participle of *imbricare*, meaning "to form like a tile," and refers to the leaves being closely appressed to the stems.

DESCRIPTION: A small, erect, much-branched shrub 40–60 cm tall. Branchlets 2–2.5 mm in diameter, more or less rounded, rather rigid and glossy; internodes about 1 m long, entirely hidden, nodal joint well marked. Leaves about 1.5 mm long, broadovate, connate for up to about half their length, thick and closely appressed, ribbed and more or less keeled, tip rounded and incurved. Bracts 2 mm long, ovate, obtuse, ribbed. Calyx about 2 mm long, anterior lobes oblong, obtuse, ribbed, free for about half to a third of their length. Corolla tube more or less equalling the calyx. Capsule about 3 mm long, oval, obtuse, equalling or slightly longer than the calyx.

DISTRIBUTION: South Island. Occurs in Fiordland on Mount Burns and one or two other ridge crests between Lakes Manapouri and Monowai at 800–1400 m.

Hebe imbricata subsp. *poppelwellii* *

This low, slender, much-branched shrub forms small yellowish-green clumps 5–15 cm tall. It is very similar to *Hebe imbricata* subsp. *imbricata* except that its branchlets are thinner and it is of slightly smaller stature. In addition, subsp. *poppelwellii* occurs on the drier mountains of Central Otago and not in the wetter mountain regions to the west. There is not enough difference between the two entities to warrant retaining subsp. *poppelwellii* as a separate species. Named after D. L. Poppelwell, a botanist who visited many parts of Otago, Southland, and Stewart Island. Discovered on Mount Tennyson, in the Garvie Mountains, by Leonard Cockayne during the early part of the 20th century.

DISTRIBUTION: South Island. Mainly found on the mountains of Central Otago, especially the Garvie Mountains, Mount Dick, the Rock and Pillar Range, and Mount Benger. Grows in low- to high-alpine areas at 1200–1700 m in sheltered, moist sites, depressions in cushion vegetation, and may descend into herbfield or snow tussock–grassland on exposed sites.

Hebe insularis

Hebe insularis is confined to the Three Kings Islands, which lie off the northern tip of the North Island about 53 km north-west of Cape Maria van Diemen. It was discovered here by Thomas Frederick Cheeseman in 1889. At one time it was restricted to sites inaccessible to the goats that were introduced to the islands during the 19th century to provide food for shipwrecked mariners. Since the goats have been exterminated, the species has been able to extend its range.

In cultivation it is a smallish shrub, generally about 30–40 cm tall, although in the wild it may grow to about 1 m tall. It is quite frost-tender and in colder climates must be grown under protection. The leaves are close-set and tend to have an almost succulent appearance. Its inflorescences are thrice- to five-branched and form a corymbose head of bluish flowers. The specific name *insularis* means "growing on islands."

This is apparently a rather variable species, especially with regard to the pubescence on its stems and the presence or absence of a leaf bud sinus. Its flowers soon fade to white after opening. The corolla tube is white; only the lobes are coloured.

DESCRIPTION: A small, erect or decumbent shrub 40 cm–1 m tall. Branchlets stout, hairy-pubescent, length of internodes about equalling the diameter. Leaf bud usually with a small, narrow sinus. Leaves more or less erect to spreading, 2–3 cm long by 1 cm wide, elliptic-oblong, more or less coriaceous and often glaucous, usually glabrous, subacute to shortly, bluntly mucronate, margins entire, cartilaginous to their bases. Inflorescences each usually thrice- to five-branched, about 4 cm long, forming a corymbose head that projects above the uppermost leaves; peduncle about 1.5 cm long, pubescent; bracts about 3 mm long, triangular, ciliolate; pedicels lengthening at fruiting time. Calyx lobes about 2 mm long, broadly ovate, subacute, ciliolate. Corolla pale bluish, tube about 3 mm long, rather wide, lobes about 3 by 2–2.5 mm, obtuse. Capsule erect, 4–5 by 3 mm, glabrous, usually twice as long as the calyx.

DISTRIBUTION: Confined to the Three Kings Islands on Great Island and South West Island, where it grows on rocky places.

Hebe ligustrifolia (PLATE 41)

This uncommonly grown hebe is probably in only a few collections. The most frequently grown form in New Zealand may be the one that grows in the far north on the Surville Cliffs. It is a loosely branched, smaller shrub, usually less than a metre tall. It is not particularly hardy, which may account for its rarity in gardens. It has distinctive leaves of pale green with a characteristic orange or yellow midrib. Its racemes of pale lavender to white flowers are up to 12 cm long. The specific name refers to the leaves, which resemble those of the privet (*Ligustrum*). *Hebe ligustrifolia* was discovered in the Bay of Islands by Richard Cunningham in 1833.

DESCRIPTION: A bushy shrub to 1 m tall. Branchlets greyish-brown, finely pubescent, length of internodes about three times the diameter. Leaf bud without a sinus. Leaves spreading, 2–5 cm long by 5 mm–1.5 cm wide, often quite variable on the one plant, ovate-oblong to narrow-lanceolate, usually a rather light yellowish-green with the midrib and base yellow, rather thin, glabrous except for some minute pubescence at their extreme bases, apex subacute, margins entire. Inflorescences slender, lateral, simple, up to twice the leaf length, peduncle about 1 cm long. Flowers rather loosely placed, pedicels about 2–3 mm long, mostly longer than the narrow, ciliolate bracts; calyx lobes about 2 mm long, narrow, acute, ciliolate. Corolla pale lavender fading to white, tube very short, about 1 mm long, lobes about 2.5 mm long, the broadest acute. Capsule about 3 by 2.5 mm, glabrous, erect to spreading, less than two times the length of the calyx.

DISTRIBUTION: North Island. In Northland, from about the North Cape area southwards to about Bream Bay on the east and Dargaville on the west. Usually grows in open scrub and around forest margins.

Hebe lycopodioides (PLATE 42)

In general form, this whipcord species shares some of the characters of the *H. hectori* group, with the difference that the lateral veins of the scale leaves lie close to their undersurfaces and are linked with the midribs at both the apexes and their bases. It is these veins that give the leaves their distinctively striated appearance. This is typically a shrub of the drier eastern areas of the northern two-thirds of the South Island. It is represented by subsp. *lycopodioides*, the typical form, and subsp. *patula* (formerly var. *patula*).

Hebe lycopodioides subsp. *lycopodioides*

This is a somewhat variable species, some forms of which have at times been recorded as *Hebe hectori*. In general it is easily identified by its distinctively yellowish or yellowish-green stems that have an obviously squared appearance. Its leaves are also suddenly narrowed into a thickened, blunt cusp or spine and have short ribs or stripes on their yellow margins, although this latter character is not always as distinct as it might be. This is one of the commonest whipcord hebes, found in drier eastern tussock grassland and herbfield, down the eastern side of the South Island. It was discovered in the Cameron Valley, Lake Heron, mid Canterbury, in 1864 by Julius Haast. The name *lycopodioides* alludes to this plant's resemblance to *Lycopodium* (club-moss), possibly to the strobili of some of the species.

In cultivation it is an accommodating little shrub, especially for a rock garden or container garden. It prefers to be grown in full sun, and this will bring out the lovely colour of its stems, but as with most whipcords, care should be taken that it does not become too dry at the root. It is very hardy. In the northern hemisphere, growers often experience problems with its leaves reverting to their juvenile form. This does not generally happen in New Zealand gardens and may be due to softer growing conditions such as too much humidity and lack of strong sunlight.

DESCRIPTION: A usually stout, erect, much-branched shrub 30–90 cm tall. Branches rigid, erect or sometimes decumbent at their bases. Branchlets distinctly four-angled, 2.5–4 mm in diameter, including the leaves, yellowish-green; internodes very close together and hidden. Leaves tightly appressed to the branchlets, 2–2.5 mm long, joined together for up to a third of their length, broadly delta-shaped to somewhat circular, keeled or rounded on their backs and shortly ribbed or striped from their yellow, cartilaginous margins, rather suddenly narrowed to a stout, blunt tip. Inflorescences terminal, 3- to 12-flowered. Flowers white, rather crowded, more or less erect, bracts ovate, rhomboid with a distinct point, furrowed and fused together for about a third of their length; corolla tube about equalling the calyx lobes, corolla lobes spreading. Capsule 3–4 mm long, broad-oblong, more or less acute, much longer than the calyx lobes.

DISTRIBUTION: South Island. In the ranges east of the main divide from the Raglan Range, Marlborough, to about the Kakanui Mountains in eastern Otago. In several places it even extends as far west as the main divide. Common in subalpine scrub and tussock grassland at 900–1700 m.

Hebe lycopodioides subsp. *lycopodioides* 'Clarence'. According to Graham Hutchins (1997, p. 192) this is the most typical of the cultivated forms. He describes it as growing up to 50 cm tall with yellow-green, squared branchlets, the final ones up to 10 cm long by 2 mm in diameter. The leaves have slightly spreading tips, a distinct yellowish cusp, and about seven vertical yellow ribs running down from the margins. Hutchins collected this plant from Clarence Pass in the Seaward Kaikoura Range.

Hebe lycopodioides subsp. *lycopodioides* 'Mount Harkness'. Another form collected by Hutchins, who described it as similar to the 'Clarence' form. A rather small, stiff bush about 8 cm tall, with final branchlets about 3 cm long. Leaves with a distinct ribbing. Flowers white, freely produced, similar to the 'Clarence' form. Capsules 3 by 2 mm, obtuse; seeds light brown, 1.5 by 1 mm.

Hebe lycopodioides subsp. *lycopodioides* 'Mount Princess'. Collected from Mount Princess on the St. James Range by Hutchins, who mentions that two forms have been collected from this location and that both are probably *H. lycopodioides* subsp. *patula* because of their smaller size, narrower branchlets, and smaller, narrower leaves, which are gradually narrowed into a thickened, acute tip that is scarcely cuspidate, and only weakly ribbed near their upper margins. Considering where they were collected, this is probably unlikely, because subsp. *patula* does not extend as far eastwards; therefore they are probably just small forms of subsp. *lycopodioides*. This cultivar forms bushy plants, only a few centimetres tall, with short, stiff branchlets. Their broad leaves are less distinctly ribbed.

Hebe lycopodioides subsp. *lycopodioides* 'Peter Pan'. This cultivar forms a small, dome-shaped plant with soft, feathery leaves of various shapes and sizes, from spear-shaped to pinnate with three to five divisions. It often remains in its juvenile stage for quite a number of years. According to Hutchins, young plants of 'Peter Pan' often die during hard winters. Therefore this cultivar is best grown in an alpine house, where it will form a well-shaped, compact plant about 10 cm tall by 15 cm in diameter.

Hebe lycopodioides subsp. *patula*

This smaller variety of *Hebe lycopodioides* forms low patches no more than 10 cm in height. Its branchlets and leaves are also narrower. It is rather similar in habit to *H. imbricata* subsp. *poppelwellii*. The name *patula* means "slightly spreading." Discovered during the 1940s on Mount Technical, in the Lewis Pass area, by George Simpson and John Scott Thomson.

DESCRIPTION: A smaller shrub with decumbent, rooting stems that form low patches 5–10 cm tall. Branchlets 1.5–2 mm in diameter. Leaves smaller and narrower, about 1–2 mm long, gradually narrowed into a thickened, acute tip that is scarcely cuspidate, only weakly ribbed near their upper margins.

DISTRIBUTION: North Canterbury, from near the Amuri Pass to the Victoria Range in southern Nelson.

Hebe macrantha

This species is very easily recognised by its erect habit of growth, its thick and rigid leaves with bluntly and regularly toothed margins, and its large white flowers—the largest of any in the genus. The species comprises two varieties: var. *macrantha*, the typical form, and var. *brachyphylla*. Var. *macrantha* occurs in the wetter regions of the central Southern Alps southwards to Fiordland. On the eastern side it grows mainly closer to the main divide, while along the western side it extends farther out from the divide. Var. *brachyphylla* is found only in the northern part of the range, from north-western Nelson to north-western Canterbury.

Hebe macrantha var. *macrantha* (PLATE 43)

The flowers of this hebe are up to 3 cm in diameter (hence the name *macrantha*, meaning "large-flowered"), and while its habit is not as attractive as many other species, a bush in full flower is a marvellous sight. When clustered around the tips of the branchlets, its flowers resemble nothing so much as gorgeous white cups or chalices. Flowering is usually between November (early summer) and March (autumn). In order to encourage good growth and a well-branched shrub, this bush should be lightly pruned immediately after flowering. It should be grown in a sunny position but should not be allowed to become dry at the root. It was discovered in the Canterbury Alps by Julius Haast during the middle of the 19th century.

DESCRIPTION: A short, stout to rather straggling shrub 30–60 cm tall. Branches usually erect or sometimes spreading, rigid, branchlets glabrous or with fine pubescence near the tips. Leaves thick, coriaceous, 1.2–2.5 cm long by 7–12 mm wide, more or less spreading on short, erect petioles, elliptic, apex obtuse to subacute, base cuneate, pale green to yellowish-green, upper surface shining, margins thickened, bluntly and regularly toothed. Inflorescences lateral, simple, the flowers extending above the leaves, two- to six-flowered, peduncle short, minutely puberulous. Flowers closely placed, more or less erect; pedicels erect, shorter than the linear-oblong bracts. Calyx glabrous, lobes very narrow-triangular, up to 1 cm long, acuminate, margins thin, pale, finely ciliate with glandular hairs; corolla up to 2.2 cm long, 2.5–3 cm wide, tube short, lobes up to 1.6 cm long by 1.5 cm wide, more or less rounded, the anterior lobe slightly smaller. Stamens about half as long as the corolla. Capsule 1 cm long by 7 mm wide, broad-ovoid, acute, glabrous.

DISTRIBUTION: South Island. Usually found on grassy slopes and in short, subalpine scrub on steep, rocky sites from the central Southern Alps southwards to Fiordland. Grows at 760–1500 m.

Hebe macrantha var. *brachyphylla*

This variety is similar to var. *macrantha* but differs in its red-margined leaves, which are broad-elliptic to almost orbicular. The name *brachyphylla* means "short-leaved," but the leaves are only fractionally shorter than those of the typical form. The flowers are also slightly smaller. This variety was discovered on Mount Arthur in January 1886 by Thomas Frederick Cheeseman.

DISTRIBUTION: South Island. Found in the northern part of the island in the wetter mountains of Nelson, the Wairau area, in Marlborough, and in the Amuri District of north Canterbury. Grows in damp, often rocky sites in mixed snow tussock–scrub and herbfield at 1000–1500 m.

Hebe macrocalyx

This species is an aggregate comprising the typical form, var. *macrocalyx*, and var. *humilis*. It belongs to the informal group "Connatae" and is related to *Hebe haastii*, under which species it was formerly included. When first collected by Joseph Beattie Armstrong, in 1881, this species was known as *Veronica macrocalyx*. In 1906 Thomas Frederick Cheeseman placed it as a variety of *V. haastii*, and it then became *V. haastii* var. *macrocalyx*, where it remained until 1926, when Leonard Cockayne and H. H. Allan transferred it to the recently recognized genus of *Hebe*. Following the publication of the *Flora of New Zealand* (Allan 1961), Lucy Moore listed it as *H. haastii* var. *macrocalyx*, along with *H. haastii* var. *humilis*, a variety first recognized by George Simpson in 1952, who at that time also recognized *H. macrocalyx* as a distinct species. To further complicate this nomenclatural tangle, in 1987 Michael J. Heads created the genus *Leonohebe*, which included both *H. macrocalyx* and its variety *humilis*. As the genus *Leonohebe* is not currently recognized, both *H. macrocalyx* and its variety *humilis* remain as originally proposed by Simpson.

Hebe macrocalyx is distinguished from *H. haastii* by its sprawling, mat-forming habit, its bright green, fleshy, and petiolate leaves that are often subdistichous, and its sometimes lax flowering heads and usually linear calyx lobes, whereas the leaves of *H. haastii* are dark green and coriaceous or rigid, and not or only slightly narrowed into a petiole. Their calyces are also usually elliptic to lanceolate, as opposed to those of *H. macrocalyx*, which are usually linear. The name *macrocalyx* means "large calyx" and refers to its calyx being larger than those of other species of the "Connatae."

Hebe macrocalyx var. macrocalyx

This form may be distinguished by its leaves, which are spathulate and not keeled, and by its leaf margins, which are green or colourless, cartilaginous, and smooth. The calyx lobes are green, linear, and 5–9 mm long. It is not a difficult plant to grow if given the correct conditions. It prefers a gritty soil with excellent drainage, and while it will tolerate a reasonable amount of sun, it does best where it can be shaded by a large rock, particularly during the middle of the day. It needs good drainage but must be kept moist around its roots at all times. This is an ideal hebe for growing in pots or trough gardens. It was discovered on the Black Range and Mount Armstrong in 1867 by Joseph Beattie Armstrong.

DESCRIPTION: A subshrub to 20 cm tall and forming quite large mats or patches up to a metre in diameter. Branches prostrate to decumbent, green when young, internodes 1–5.5 mm long. Leaves petiolate, decussate to subdistichous, 6–11 mm long by 3–8 mm wide, more or less spreading, elliptic to obovate, to spathulate, elliptic, ovate, or rhomboid, bright green, apex obtuse to rounded or slightly retuse, coriaceous to fleshy, flat, bases connate, midrib thickened beneath and slightly depressed to grooved above, margin cartilaginous or rounded, or minutely papillate-glabrous or glandular-ciliate, usually entire and/or obscurely erose, red or green near the tips, petiole 2–5 mm long, hairy along the margins. Inflorescences terminal and lateral, the reduced spikes arranged in a terminal flowering head, 1–3 cm long; lowermost pair of bracts on a spike opposite and connate, then above subopposite or alternate, lanceolate to linear or sometimes deltoid, usually subacute to obtuse, glabrous or minutely ciliolate and sometimes sparingly hairy inside; pedicels absent. Calyx 4.5–7 mm long, usually linear to linear-lanceolate, or rarely oblong or deltoid, subacute to obtuse or occasionally acute, minutely ciliolate with the insides glandular-hairy, margins green or tinged with red near their apexes. Corolla white; anthers held at the corolla throat. Flowers on individual plants either hermaphrodite or female.

DISTRIBUTION: South Island. Restricted to the main divide around the Arthur's Pass region, from Mount Alexander to the north, around the surrounding mountains of Arthur's Pass itself, including the upper Waimakariri River and the upper Bealey Valley to the south. Usually grows on rock debris or scree slopes at 1150–1900 m.

Hebe macrocalyx var. *humilis*

Of the two varieties of this species, var. *humilis* has by far the widest distribution, although it does not occur in Canterbury. It is distinguished from var. *macrocalyx* mainly by morphological characters, such as the shape of its leaves, which are elliptic to rhomboid, compared with the spathulate leaves of var. *macrocalyx*, and often smaller and more keeled; its leaf margins are papillose or rounded and usually red near the shoot apex, compared with the cartilaginous, green leaf margins of var. *macrocalyx*; and its calyx lobes are red-tipped. The varietal name *humilis* means "low-growing." This plant was discovered by George Simpson and John Scott Thomson on the slopes of Mount French, near Hector's Col, probably in the early 1950s.

DISTRIBUTION: South Island. Occurs from the Anatoki Range to Mount Owen in north-western Nelson, then across to Mount Richmond in Marlborough, and southwards to the Spenser Mountains in southern Nelson. It has also been recorded from Mount French, near Hector's Col, in western Otago, and from Mount Elliot, McKinnon Pass, in Fiordland (both recordings from plants collected and cultivated by Simpson in his Dunedin garden in 1952). Usually grows on rock debris or stable scree in rocky, alpine herbfield at about 1200–1900 m.

Hebe macrocarpa

This somewhat variable species may usually be recognised by its erect habit of growth, its rather thick, fleshy leaves, and its leaf bud, which has no sinus. It has rather large flowers, and its racemes may be unusually long. Another character that helps to identify it is its corolla tube, which may be quite wide. Because of the variability of this species, only the best forms should be selected for bringing into cultivation. There are two varieties: var. *macrocarpa*, the typical form, and var. *latisepala*. The plant formerly classified as *Hebe macrocarpa* var. *brevifolia* is now recognised as a distinct species: *H. brevifolia*.

Hebe macrocarpa var. *macrocarpa* (PLATE 44)

While the flowers of this variety are usually white, those of some forms have a most attractive greenish hue, making them very worthwhile garden plants. Generally, the flower racemes are much longer than the narrow-elliptic leaves. Another distinguishing character is that the sepals are obtuse to subacute. The name *macrocarpa* means "large-seeded."

Hebe macrocarpa var. *macrocarpa* is hardy throughout most of New Zealand but is somewhat tender in the colder climates of the northern hemisphere. It flowers from May (late autumn) till December (summer). In the northern hemisphere it will also produce flowers during winter if grown in a greenhouse.

DESCRIPTION: An erect, stiffly branched or somewhat straggly shrub to 2.4 m tall. Branchlets stout, glabrous or finely pubescent, pale brownish-green to yellow-green, length of internodes four to eight times the diameter or more. Leaf bud without a sinus. Leaves spreading, 7.5–13.7 cm long by 1.2–2.5 cm wide, narrow-elliptic to elliptic-oblong, green to dark green, upper surface with a dull sheen, paler beneath, coriaceous and often somewhat fleshy, sessile or on short petioles, apex subacute, glabrous or puberulous on the upper surface of the lower half of the midrib, margins entire, sometimes finely ciliolate, especially towards the base. Inflorescences lateral, simple, about 6.2–16.2 cm long, usually much exceeding the leaves; peduncle 1.2–3.2 cm long, puberulous. Flowers white, closely or somewhat loosely placed and not completely hiding the rachis, pedicels spreading, 1.5–7 mm long, puberulous, exceeding the lanceolate, ciliolate bracts. Calyx lobes up to 3 mm long, ovate-lanceolate or oblong, obtuse, ciliolate; corolla lobes about 4–7 mm long, broad and rounded, little spreading. Stamens little or much exserted. Capsules large, 7–8 mm long, ovate, acute, greatly exceeding the calyx lobes.

DISTRIBUTION: North Island. Occurs in Auckland Province from Hokianga and Mangonui southwards and extending to Poverty Bay on the east and Taranaki on the west. More common in the northern part of its range. Grows from sea level to 600 m.

Hebe macrocarpa var. *latisepala* (PLATE 45)

This most handsome variety has the typically erect habit of *Hebe macrocarpa* var. *macrocarpa*. Its flowers are a lovely deep violet-blue, a colour not duplicated in any other *Hebe* species. In very warm conditions, flower colour may fade just slightly. This variety is hardy throughout New Zealand but in the northern hemisphere may be somewhat tender in districts that experience severe winters. The varietal name *latisepala* alludes to its large sepals. Originally collected on Great Barrier Island by Thomas Kirk, possibly in the early 1890s.

DESCRIPTION: Generally similar to the typical form but with narrow-oblong leaves, not or very sparsely ciliolate leaf margins, and dull upper leaf surfaces. Racemes usually shorter than the leaves, up to about 10 cm long, peduncle about 2.5 cm long, dark purplish. Flowers bluish-purple, rather closely placed, rachis and pedicels dark purplish, pedicels little longer than the bracts. Calyx purplish, lobes ovate, obtuse to acute; corolla tube broad, white, lobes ascending. Filaments purple.

DISTRIBUTION: Great Barrier Island, Little Barrier Island, and Coromandel Peninsula.

Hebe masoniae (PLATE 46)

Formerly included as a variety of *Hebe pauciramosa*, this plant is now recognised as a distinct species. In fact, at first glance it appears to be so different from typical forms of *H. pauciramosa* that there should be no question of it being a separate species. It is a rather erect plant, up to 40 cm tall, with larger leaves than *H. pauciramosa*, and the flowers of plants growing in the wild are usually tinged with violet. Whereas the keel on the leaves of *H. pauciramosa* is distinctively flattened just below the leaf tips, the keel of *H. masoniae* is sharp throughout. Another distinctive feature is that the leafy branches are often quadrangular. Its inflorescences are all terminal and simple, with the new growth being continued by lateral shoots. It is not difficult to grow and may be less demanding of a moist soil than *H. pauciramosa*. It is named after Ruth Mason, who first recognised it as a distinct taxon, and who originally collected it from near the head of the Cobb Valley, Nelson, in 1946.

DESCRIPTION: A rather erect shrub to 50 cm tall or more. Branches stout and leafy, mainly only in their upper portions. Branchlets bifariously pubescent, length of internodes about equalling the diameter. Leaf bud with a heart-shaped sinus. Inflorescences all terminal and simple, with new growth continued by lateral shoots. Lowest bracts about equalling the adjacent leaves but generally more membranous, broad at their tops, margins ciliolate all around. Calyx lobes hidden by the bracts, up to 5 mm long, the two anterior ones not fused. Corolla tube broadly funnel-shaped, not longer than the calyx, lobes to about 5 by 5 mm broad. Capsule broadly ovate, very flat, little longer than the calyx.

DISTRIBUTION: South Island. Appears to be rather widely distributed in the mountains of north-western Nelson. Grows in subalpine to low-alpine areas in grassland, scrub, flushes, and other wet sites.

Hebe mooreae *

This relatively recently recognised species was not formally described until 1978. It is in the same group as *Hebe odora* but differs in its more robust growth and larger leaves, which have crenulate margins and do not narrow as abruptly to their petioles. Its inflorescences are consistently lateral and have larger flowers, broader corolla lobes, and golden rather than pink or magenta stamens. It is named in honour of Lucy Moore, who completed the section on *Hebe* in *Flora of New Zealand* (Allan 1961).

DISTRIBUTION: South Island. Found from north-western Nelson south-west to Mount Rochfort, southwards to South Westland, and from there to the Hump Ridge in Fiordland and the Longwood Range in Southland.

Hebe murrellii *

This is another species mainly from Fiordland, but it also occurs outside of that region. It belongs to the informal group "Occlusae" and was formerly classified as a variety of *Hebe petriei*. Research conducted in 1994 resulted in its reinstatement to the rank of a separate species. It has bright green foliage and terminal inflorescences of white flowers. It does not appear to be in cultivation, although some enthusiastic grower in the Otago region may have it in cultivation. *Hebe murrellii* is named after Robert Murrell, an explorer of Fiordland. It was discovered in 1942 by George Simpson and John Scott Thomson at the sources of the Freeman River in the Kepler Mountains.

DESCRIPTION: A spreading or trailing subshrub with ascending to erect branchlets to 20 cm tall. Old stems grey or brown. Branchlets greenish to pale brown with a red band at the nodes, bifariously pubescent, length of internodes one to two times the diameter. Leaf bud with a narrow, acuminate sinus. Leaves spreading, very shortly connate, elliptic to obovate, 3.5–9 mm long by 2–5 mm wide, more or less coriaceous, upper and lower surfaces bright green, usually with sparse, very short, tapering hairs on the midrib above and below, and on the margins, apex broadly rounded, base cuneately narrowed to a short, broad, flat petiole, margins entire, yellowish, rounded. Inflorescences terminal, racemose, 1–3 cm long, flowers crowded. Peduncle and rachis puberulent, peduncle very short, bracts linear-lanceolate to narrow-elliptic, obtuse to acute, minutely ciliolate, slightly shorter than the calyx lobes; pedicels more or less spreading, 0.5–2 mm long. Flowers white, female or hermaphrodite on separate plants, sweetly scented; calyx lobes four, oblong to elliptic, obtuse, subacute, 2.5–3 mm long by 1–1.5 mm wide, margins minutely ciliolate; corolla tube 1.5–2 mm long, glabrous, lobes recurved, elliptic to broadly elliptic, obtuse. Filaments white and long, exserted. Capsule flattened, 3.5–4 mm long by about 3 mm wide, ovate, acute.

DISTRIBUTION: South Island. Found in the Kepler Mountains, at the sources of the Freeman River and near Fowler Pass, Lake Manapouri, and the Murchison Mountains in Fiordland, and thence to the Takitimu Mountains in western Southland. Usually grows on alpine screes, talus slopes, and rock outcrops at 1100–1500 m.

Hebe obtusata (PLATE 47)

This handsome shrub is not widely known in gardens, and yet, being prostrate or semi-prostrate, it has a number of uses, particularly for growing over banks and walls or for use as a ground cover. It has attractive foliage and generally displays its flowers well. In many northern hemisphere areas it is not completely hardy and is really suited mainly for coastal gardens or areas with mild climates. Where conditions are suitable, it has quite a long flowering season, generally from January (mid summer) to June (early winter), but some intermittent flowering may also occur throughout the remainder of the winter. It can be recognised by its rather short, blunt-tipped leaves, which tend to lie in the one plane, and by its reddish to purplish branchlets. Although basically prostrate, in more sheltered situations it may eventually mound up to 60 cm tall and has a spread of up to 2 m or more. Its specific name refers to the blunt tips of its leaves. This species was discovered on the sea cliffs north of Manukau Harbour by Thomas Frederick Cheeseman prior to 1916.

DESCRIPTION: A prostrate or semi-prostrate, spreading shrub to 60 cm tall by 2 m or more in diameter. Branchlets reddish to purplish, puberulous, length of internodes three to nine times the diameter. Leaf bud without a sinus. Leaves spreading, lying more or less in the one plane, 2.5–5 cm long by 1.2–2.5 cm wide, broad-oblong to obovate-oblong, obtuse, rounded at the base and suddenly narrowed to a short petiole, upper surface green or yellowish-green, paler beneath, more or less coriaceous to almost fleshy, glabrous except for the upper surface of the midrib and petiole being puberulous, margins conspicuously and densely puberulous, entire or sometimes with a pair of very shallow notches. Inflorescences lateral, simple, usually much exceeding the leaves, 6.2–10 cm long, peduncle up to 2.5 cm long, puberulous with whitish hairs. Flowers mauve, rather closely placed and more or less hiding the rachis, pedicels spreading to ascending, 1.5–3 mm long, puberulous, bracts lanceolate, pubescent, conspicuously ciliolate, equalling the pedicels. Calyx puberulous, lobes about 4 mm long, ovate, acute, ciliolate; corolla tube equalling or slightly longer than the calyx lobes, corolla lobes equalling the tube, spreading, obtuse, minutely ciliolate. Stamens exserted, filaments mauve. Capsule 4 mm long, ovate, acute, glabrous, less than twice the length of the calyx lobes.

DISTRIBUTION: North Island. Occurs in coastal scrub along the west coast of Auckland Province, from the Manukau Heads to Muriwai.

Hebe ochracea

Hebe ochracea has to rate as one of the best whipcord species. It is also quite distinctive because of its rather strong, brown or ochre-coloured, firm, shining branchlets. It has rather thick leaves and, in cultivation, a dense, spreading habit of growth. Cultivated plants are usually quite wide-spreading, with a flattish top. A well-grown plant may be up to about 45 cm tall and 90–100 cm across. In the wild its growth is usually rather more open, and it does not have the dense growth that usually characterises cultivated plants. *Hebe ochracea* is very effective when used as an individual specimen or in group plantings. It is usually quite free-flowering. It also appears to be a little more tolerant of drought than some of the other whipcord species, although care should still be taken to ensure that it does not unduly suffer from lack of water. The name *ochracea* means "ochre-coloured" in allusion to the distinctive colour of the branchlets. It was discovered in the Cobb Valley by F. G. Gibbs, probably in the latter part of the 19th century.

The cultivar commonly grown under the name *Hebe ochracea* 'James Stirling' has nothing to distinguish it from typical *H. ochracea*. It was grown as an unnamed hebe in the grounds of the old government buildings in Wellington. When the gardener, James Stirling, was asked its name, he replied that he did not know, whereon the enquirer suggested that it be called 'James Stirling'. The name stuck, and this hebe is now widely grown as 'James Stirling'.

DESCRIPTION: A low-growing, spreading shrub 15–45 cm tall. Branches stout, rigid, arching, the branchlets arising mainly from their upper sides. Ultimate branchlets numerous and close-set, usually terete or sometimes appearing four-angled, 1.5–2 mm in diameter, olive-green to a brownish-ochre colour, the colour usually more intense towards the tips, shining. Internodes 1.5–2 mm long and partly exposed. Leaves tightly appressed, 1–1.5 mm long and joined together for about a third of their length, more or less deltoid, thick and strongly concavo-convex, keeled and projecting on their backs, narrowed to a more or less keeled, obtuse or subacute, incurved tip. Inflorescences terminal, up to about ten-flowered. Flowers white, sessile, bracts about 1.5 mm long, ovate, keeled and more or less subacute or obtuse. Calyx 2–2.5 mm long, anterior lobes fused into a single, obtuse or slightly emarginate, ovate-oblong segment, sometimes shortly, secondarily split. Corolla tube equalling or longer than the calyx. Capsule 3–3.5 mm long, oval or narrow-oval, obtuse or subacute, longer than the calyx.

DISTRIBUTION: South Island. Confined to low-alpine regions in the mountains of western Nelson at 1200–1700 m. Usually occurs in damp snow tussock–herbfield and fellfield. Not infrequently grows where there is underlying limestone and often occurs with *Hebe hectori* subsp. *coarctata*.

Hebe odora (PLATES 1 AND 48)
boxwood

In the garden this species is usually represented by just one or two clones, but in the wild it can be quite variable. It will also hybridise quite freely with species such as *Hebe traversii*, sometimes producing hybrid swarms that intergrade from one species to the other. It is generally an easily recognised shrub, distinguished by its rounded, ball-like shape; small, deep green leaves with glossy upper surfaces; and shield-shaped sinus on the leaf bud. Its *Buxus*-like foliage has given rise to this plant's common name, boxwood. Generally it will grow to about a metre tall but in good conditions may reach about 1.5 m or more. Other distinguishing characters are the distinctly bevelled edges to the margins of the leaves, the midrib usually being more pronounced on the lower surface of the leaves, and bases of the leaf blade being distinctly shouldered.

Although fairly common in cultivation, this species remains a handsome, useful shrub and should not be despised. When it flowers it can be quite showy, with flowering usually occurring from October (mid spring) to late November (early summer). The specific name suggests that the flowers should be scented, but various observers have failed to detect any trace of scent. *Hebe odora* can give the impression that it should be rather drought-tolerant, but it really prefers reasonably moist soil conditions and, if conditions become too dry, soon shows its intolerance. Mainly it grows in permanently moist sites, especially river valleys and on river terraces, but also in flushes. It generally flowers from October (mid spring) to March (early autumn). *Hebe odora* was discovered on the Auckland Islands by J. D. Hooker in 1840. A certain amount of confusion later arose following its collection on mainland New Zealand by Ernst Dieffenbach and its naming as *H. buxifolia* by George Bentham. Even overseas, *H. odora* is still not infrequently known as *H. buxifolia*.

DESCRIPTION: A shrub of varying habit and usually forming a rounded, ball-shaped bush up to 1.5 m tall. Branchlets bifariously pubescent, length of internodes approximately equalling or slightly greater than their diameter, young branchlets green to yellowish-green. Leaf bud with a distinctive heart-shaped or shield-shaped sinus. Leaves overlapping to more or less spreading, 1–2 cm (occasionally to 3.2 cm) long by 4–10 mm wide, elliptic-ovate, coriaceous and glabrous, more or less concave, subacute, upper surface dark green and shining, dull and paler beneath, stomata distinct and numerous, base somewhat rounded and forming more or less of a shoulder, margins entire, thick and cartilaginous or more or less bevelled. Inflorescences usually terminal and with one or two pairs of lateral spikes (sometimes with only one spike, which may be either terminal or lateral), peduncles short and hidden by the leaves, bifariously pubescent. Flowers white, erect, sessile in opposite pairs, together with leaf-like bracts hiding the rachis. Bracts equalling or shorter than the calyx, ciliolate. Calyx lobes 3–4 mm long, more or less keeled, ciliolate; corolla tube narrow-cylindric, equalling or slightly longer than the calyx lobes; corolla lobes narrow, subacute, spreading, equalling or longer than the tube. Capsule about twice as long as the calyx lobes, erect, glabrous.

DISTRIBUTION: North, South, Stewart, and Auckland islands. Common in sub-alpine to low-alpine areas in mountain regions from Mount Hikurangi southwards. Usually found in short, subalpine scrub and mixed snow tussock–scrub but may also extend into snow tussock–grassland or herbfield. Often found on permanently wet ground in flushes, river flats, and terraces at 600–1400 m.

Hebe odora 'Greenstone'. A small shrublet, no more than 20 cm tall, that forms a dense dome up to 30 cm across. Otherwise its characters are as for *H. odora* but on a smaller scale. Collected as a wild seedling on Mount Watson by D. Rooney.

Hebe odora 'New Zealand Gold'. Similar to typical *H. odora*, but its leaves are a slightly deeper green and those at the tips of the branchlets are golden. The golden colour of the leaves is not a constant character and may disappear for a time according to seasonal growing conditions. Collected by Kenneth Beckett in the Arthur's Pass National Park.

Hebe odora 'Prostrata' (PLATE 49). A form of *H. odora* that was collected on the Pouakai Range, Taranaki. It is quite prostrate as well as small in its growth, seldom spreading more than several centimetres in each direction. An attractive and useful little plant for a rock garden or container garden. Its deep green leaves stand out well against plants of a different colour. Similar plants may also be found on Mount Anglem, Stewart Island.

Hebe odora 'Purpurea'. This hebe was, in the 19th century, given species status as *H. anomala*; more recently it has been included with *H. odora*. It is now considered to be synonymous with *H. odora* and is mainly represented in cultivation by one clone that is quite distinct and easily recognised. This clone was probably that discovered by Joseph Beattie Armstrong in 1865 in the Rakaia Valley. In the *Manual of the New Zealand Flora* (1925, p. 809), Thomas Frederick Cheeseman states that this hebe is a "very handsome and attractive species, quite common as a garden plant but very rare in the wild state." It has similarities with *H. odora*, but its leaves are narrower and linear-oblong, rather than obovate-oblong, as with most *H. odora*. The plants in cultivation are quite possibly descendents of some of Armstrong's original collection from the Rakaia Valley. This material has been in cultivation for a long time and has been maintained in cultivation since at least the beginning of the 20th century. It has been cultivated under the names *H. anomala*, *H. anomala* 'Purpurea', and occasionally *H. anomala* 'Rubra'. Since the name 'Purpurea' has some thirteen years' priority over 'Rubra', and since *H. anomala* is now regarded as a synonym of *H. odora*, this cultivar must be known as *H. odora* 'Purpurea'.

    Hebe odora 'Purpurea' has handsome, dark green, shining leaves and is particularly distinguished by its young growing tips, which are quite purplish-red and especially striking on a well-grown plant. If the bush is regularly pruned to maintain its shape, the colour of the young growths will be further enhanced. This plant is very floriferous, covering itself with flowers, which typical *H. odora* seldom does. It is fairly hardy and is best when planted in a very open situation where it receives plenty of sun. With age it tends to become rather leggy, but that can be prevented by regular pruning.

Hebe odora 'Ruahine'. Described as a small, neat form that is similar to *H. odora* 'Stewart' but shorter, with a bushier habit and rich, green foliage. It was collected in 1985 on the Ruahine Range by Graham Hutchins.

Hebe odora 'Stewart'. Rather similar to the typical form but with smaller leaves than most other forms. It was collected on Stewart Island by Kenneth Beckett.

Hebe paludosa *

Leonard Cockayne originally described this hebe, in 1916, as a new variety of *Veronica salicifolia*, which he proposed to name var. *paludosa*. In 1926 he formally transferred the plant to *Hebe*, and it became *H. salicifolia* var. *paludosa*. In *Flora of New Zealand* (Allan 1961, p. 902), Lucy Moore made no comment concerning the status of this hebe, apart from noting that it resembled *H. gracillima* and could be a hybrid between this and *H. salicifolia*. In 1993 Michael J. Heads considered it worthy of recognition, as a distinct taxon, and provided a map of its distribution. Finally, as a result of fieldwork in South Westland, David Norton and Peter de Lange decided that it was evident that what until then had been known as *H. salicifolia* var. *paludosa* was distinct from *H. salicifolia* in the strict sense and should be recognised as a distinct species.

By all accounts *H. paludosa* is not the most garden-worthy shrub and will probably only appeal to avid collectors. The specific name *paludosa* means "swamp-growing" and refers to the plant's usual habitat.

DESCRIPTION: An erect, sparingly branched shrub to 5 m tall. Branches light red to reddish-brown. Branchlets slender, greenish-yellow tinged red, pubescent, internodes one to ten times the diameter. Leaf bud with a lanceolate sinus. Leaves 5–7 cm long by 9 mm–1 cm wide, usually mostly towards the tips of the branchlets, narrowly to broadly lanceolate, tapering with an often long, twisted point, upper surface dull and yellow-green or dark green, lower surface paler and usually faintly glaucous, membranous, apex acute, base broad-attenuate, margins sparsely toothed in the upper two-thirds and rarely entire, pubescent. Inflorescences lateral, simple, 5–7 cm long, usually decurved, flowers loosely spiralled on the rachis, usually with some aborted, pedicellate; peduncle and rachis uniformly yellow-green, conspicuously pubescent, peduncle 1.2–1.8 cm long, bracts 2–3 mm long, lanceolate, margins ciliolate, pedicels 3–4 mm long, often spotted brown with densely, prominent hyaline hairs. Flowers hermaphrodite, faintly scented, calyx lobes 2–3 mm long, overlapping at the edges, dull green, narrowly lanceolate, acute, bases glandular-hairy otherwise glabrous; corolla pure white, 3–4 mm long, lobes 4–5 mm long, projecting forwards, acute. Filaments white, anthers dark blue turning orange, pollen cream. Capsules 5 mm long by 3 mm wide, light brown, narrow-oblong to obovate.

DISTRIBUTION: South Island. Endemic to Westland from a little north of Greymouth to Jackson Bay in the south. More common between Lake Ianthe and the Cook River. Typically a shrub of wetlands, at the edges of lagoons, especially where there is a ready flow of fresh water.

Hebe pareora (PLATE 50)

This species is related to *Hebe amplexicaulis* and occurs in broadly the same area of South Canterbury. It is a member of the informal group "Subcarnosae." *Hebe pareora* forms a spreading to more or less prostrate shrub that in cultivation may grow to about 90 cm tall with a spread of 1.2–1.5 m. Wild plants may have even longer branches. Its grey or glaucous leaves are rather broadly oblong, with obtuse tips, and are quite strongly amplexicaul at their bases. The leaf margins are usually green or slightly yellowish. The inflorescences are on peduncles about 2–3 cm long, and the racemes are of a similar length. *Hebe pareora* is distinguished by its leaves being glabrous, by the peduncle of its inflorescences being glabrous, and by its flowers being on pedicels that are glandular-hairy or more or less glabrous. Although similar to *H. amplexicaulis*, *H. pareora* is generally a larger plant, with longer stems and racemose inflorescences on glabrous peduncles. It also has glabrous capsules. It is easily grown and very handsome, although with age it does tend to lose the leaves attached to the lower parts of its branches. This tendency is quite marked on wild plants.

DESCRIPTION: A low, rather spreading shrub, branched from its base, often with hanging or trailing stems. Stems glabrous, often bare of foliage except near their tips. Branchlets stout, length of internodes two to three times the diameter of the branchlets. Leaf bud without a sinus. Leaves 2–3 cm long by 1.5–1.8 cm wide, spreading, oblong, glaucous or grey, glabrous, strongly amplexicaul or subauriculate, apex broad, obtuse. Inflorescences lateral, simple, racemose, peduncle glabrous. Flowers pedicellate, pedicels glandular-hairy or glandless, 2–5 mm long. Bracts and calyx glabrous or minutely ciliolate, about 2 mm long. Flowers white, corolla lobes narrow, tube longer than the calyx. Anthers purple. Capsule glabrous, dark brown.

DISTRIBUTION: South Island. Confined to a small area of south-eastern Canterbury around the headwaters of the Pareora River and the Hunters Hills. Usually occurs on cliffs and steep rock bluffs in river gorges and similar shady sites. Grows at 300–1000 m.

Hebe parviflora

This species was formerly classified by John Buchanan in 1874 as *Veronica arborea*, then as *V. parviflora* var. *arborea* by Thomas Kirk in 1896, and finally as *Hebe parviflora* var. *arborea* by Lucy Moore in 1961. Recent research has shown that it was firstly named *V. parviflora* by a Norwegian botanist M. Vahl in 1794. Therefore, this name must take priority over its later synonyms.

Hebe parviflora is little known in gardens, possibly because of its potentially large size. Left alone it will grow to several metres tall, but it can be grown as a large shrub if kept pruned. Where space permits it can grow into a rather attractive small tree, particularly if its lower branches are pruned off so as to show the handsomeness of its main trunks. In the wild it generally grows in scrub along hillsides and around forest margins, particularly along streams and creeks. It occurs in coastal to lowland areas, but in the central North Island it can also occur in montane areas. Its specific name means "small-flowered."

DESCRIPTION: Large shrub or small tree to 7.5 m tall. Branches erect, bark of older stems pale grey. Branchlets varying from olive-green to brown or reddish-brown, usually with bifarious pubescence, internodes quite short and varying from little longer than the stem diameter to about eight times the diameter. Leaf bud without a sinus. Leaves more or less spreading to somewhat recurved, usually about 2.5–6 cm long by 1.5–7 mm wide, apex whitish, acute to shortly acuminate, base cuneate, upper surface light green, dull, lower surface paler with dense stomata, midrib depressed to grooved above and thickened beneath, margin not thickened, scabrous or minutely pubescent, entire. Inflorescences lateral, simple, racemose, 4–10 cm long, longer than the leaves, peduncle 5–19 mm long, pubescent, bracts ovate to deltoid, acute to obtuse, ciliolate, pedicels longer or shorter than the bracts, pubescent or sometimes glabrous. Flowers on individual plants either hermaphrodite or female; calyx terete, four-lobed, lobes ovate to elliptic, obtuse to acute, margins membranous, ciliate. Corolla white or with the lobes sometimes pinkish to mauve, fading to white after pollination, inside of tube hairy, calyx lobes glabrous or with a few hairs towards the base on the inner surface, corolla lobes obtuse, more or less erect to spreading. Stamens magenta, filaments white. Capsule ovoid, obtuse to subacute, glabrous, 2.5–3.5 mm long.

DISTRIBUTION: North and South islands. Found in the North Island from near Whangarei to the East Cape District, in the central montane areas, and in the southern part of the island to Wellington. Found in the South Island in a few localities in the Marlborough Sounds and at Kekerengu in eastern coastal Marlborough.

Hebe pauciflora

This small shrub rather resembles a miniature version of *Hebe odora*. It grows to no more than 20 cm tall, with flowers that seem to be rather large for its size. It comes from some remote mountain areas of Fiordland, especially those bordering Doubtful Sound. I had it in cultivation for several years before finally losing it, but it is probably no longer in cultivation in either hemisphere. It was not a particularly difficult plant to grow, and it flowered quite well, its large white flowers being well displayed at the tips of the branchlets. If it could be again brought into cultivation it would make a lovely plant for a rock garden or container culture. Its specific name means "few-flowered" and refers to the fact that it has only two flowers on each spikelet. It was discovered in 1942 by George Simpson near Fowler Pass at the head of the Freeman River near Lake Manapouri.

DESCRIPTION: A closely branched, small shrub no more than 20 cm tall. Branches tending to be prostrate and ascending at their tips. Branchlets glabrous, shining; those with the leaves on are about 1 cm in diameter. Leaf bud with an open sinus. Leaves imbricating to spreading, occasionally deflexed, 5–7 mm long by 3–5 mm wide, ovate-spathulate and usually rather broadly trowel-shaped, slightly concave, apex subacute, quite strongly coriaceous with both surfaces glossy, the base narrowed into a broad petiole, glabrous except for fine white cilia around the thick, cartilaginous, entire margins, midrib keeled. Inflorescences lateral, simple, usually only one pair in the leaf axils just behind the growing tip, each sessile spikelet about 1 cm long with two sessile flowers. Bracts opposite, about 3 mm long, subacute, ciliolate. Calyx lobes four, each about 5 by 2 mm, obtuse to subacute, slightly keeled, ciliolate. Corolla white, tube slightly shorter than the calyx, broad-cylindric, lobes usually four or occasionally five, about 4.5 by 3.5 mm, broadly ovate. Capsule erect, about 4 by 3 mm, broadly oblong, glabrous, about equalling the calyx.

DISTRIBUTION: South Island. Found on the mountains of Fiordland from the Kepler Mountains to the Wilmot Pass, near Fowler Pass above Lake Manapouri, and on Hamley Peak above Thompson Sound. Said to grow in open, grassy places but also grows on rocky places, around the summits, where it may be partially shaded. Found at 1100–1500 m.

Hebe pauciramosa

This species is closely allied to *Hebe odora* and generally appears as though it may be a small form of that species. It is smaller in all of its parts, however, its branchlets are not as pubescent, and its leaves do not have the same sheen. It is a useful small shrub either for ground cover or for low edgings around garden plots. With its neat habit and deep green foliage it can look particularly effective when planted with one of the smaller, glaucous-leaved hebes such as *H. pinguifolia* 'Sutherlandii'. While it flowers mainly between October (mid spring) and February (late summer), it is not unusual for it to produce occasional flowers throughout the year. Being a species that normally grows in wet ground, it is happiest when grown in a soil that does not dry out too much during dry weather. It will withstand some dry conditions, but excessive dryness will result in the loss of some of the lower leaves. This is a very hardy species. The specific name *pauciramosa* means "few-branched" and refers to the fact that in the wild this plant is relatively sparsely branched. *Hebe pauciramosa* was originally collected by Leonard Cockayne in 1921 in the Routeburn Valley, who described its habitat as "wet ground up to Lake Harris, 4000 feet or less."

The main differences between this species and *Hebe odora* are that on *H. odora* the upper surfaces of the leaves are comparatively glossy, the stomata are almost or quite confined to the undersurface, and the bevelled margins are glabrous, whereas the upper surfaces of the leaves of *H. pauciramosa* are not glossier than the undersurfaces, the stomata are numerous on both surfaces, and the rounded margins are minutely ciliolate when young.

DESCRIPTION: A small, rounded or straggling shrub of rather loose habit, up to 90 cm tall but generally shorter. Branches rather straight and erect although sometimes prostrate at their bases, leafy but with age the leaves are confined mainly to the upper portion of the branch. Branchlets bifariously pubescent, length of internodes approximately equalling the diameter. Leaf bud with a broad, heart-shaped sinus. Leaves overlapping to spreading, 4–7 mm long by 8–11 mm wide, broad-oblong to almost square, concave, upper surface dark green, lower surface somewhat paler, both surfaces dull with many large stomata evident, thick and coriaceous, glabrous, base truncate or shouldered before narrowing to a very short petiole, margins thickened, minutely ciliolate near the apexes, midrib obvious only on the underside, keeled and flattened just below the apex. Inflorescences usually lateral, simple, about 2 cm long, peduncle short and usually hidden by the leaves, with a few scattered hairs. Flowers white, crowded, erect, sessile in opposite pairs, hiding the rachis. Bracts triangular, acute, keeled, shorter than the calyx, ciliolate only towards the base. Calyx lobes 3–4 mm long, ciliolate, the two anterior lobes usually joined except for their tips, corolla lobes spreading, ovate, obtuse, about equalling the tube. Capsule about twice as long as the calyx, narrow-oblong.

DISTRIBUTION: South Island. Widespread in subalpine to low-alpine areas from north Canterbury to Southland at 600–1500 m. Mainly grows in the wetter regions, usually preferring seepage areas or flushes in grassland or herbfield, but sometimes on moraine and gravel riverbeds.

Hebe pauciramosa 'MacCabe'. An erect form that originated from Mount MacCabe, just above Lake Tennyson, north Canterbury. It is said to have distinctly narrower leaves measuring 7 mm long by 3–4 mm wide.

Hebe pauciramosa "Prostrate Form." Described as having spreading to decumbent, twisted branches. It grows to about 30 cm tall and often has purplish branchlets but is otherwise similar to the typical form of the species.

Hebe pauciramosa 'Tennyson'. Described as a bushy shrub with erect branches to about 40 cm tall. Older plants are usually leafy only on the upper halves of the branches. Collected from near Lake Tennyson, north Canterbury.

Hebe perbella (PLATE 51)

This species was discovered in 1980 by K. Bartlett in the Ahipara gumlands of the far north of the North Island. Bartlett did not collect any specimens of his find, and it was not until 1987 that the plant was re-discovered by A. P. Druce, another active field botanist, who collected herbarium (and presumably cutting) material of it. Initially it became widely known as *Hebe* "Bartlett." In the late 1980s it was also found in one or two other locations in the far north. The name *perbella* refers to the very attractive, colourful flowers of this species.

It has some similarities with *Hebe brevifolia* but is generally a little larger. Certainly, in cultivation it is a larger-growing species than *H. brevifolia*. Its recorded habitats are rocky or stony ground, and it is usually surrounded by kauri (*Agathis australis*) forest and associated gumland scrub. Its preferred sites are open cliff and rock outcrops, young slip scars, and slumps on unstable precipitous ridgetops. It is therefore a lithophyte or shrub that likes to grow on rocks or in rocky places. It also shows a preference for sites where moisture is generally present; in some areas it most frequently grows adjacent to waterfalls, in or near cliff seepages, and on boulders within narrow stream gorges. In one locality, Maungaraho Rock, it is virtually confined to the moister, south-facing, more vegetated slopes, where the largest specimens grow among dense, moisture-carrying swards of *Astelia* and *Collospermum*, or in the joints of the columnar andesite dyke, which usually contain much water. This particular site is considered to be rather anomalous because it is surrounded by intensively farmed land.

Hebe perbella usually grows to a larger size in cultivation than it does in the wild, to about 1.5–2 m, and generally forms quite a bushy shrub. Its handsome green to deep green leaves are further enhanced by a sheen or gloss on their upper surfaces. Although the flowers are said to vary from violet-red to violet or even pink, the only cultivated plant that I have seen had pale violet flowers. Nonetheless it was a very pretty plant. Considering that this hebe is from the far north of New Zealand, it would be wise to treat it as somewhat tender and to give it some protection in harsher climates. In milder climates it generally flowers throughout much of the winter and then into the spring months.

DESCRIPTION: A compact shrub usually to 1 m tall but occasionally as much as 2 m tall. Branches purple-grey, becoming grey as they age. Branchlets greenish-yellow, internodes one to ten times the diameter. Leaf bud without a sinus. Leaves 4–9 cm long by 1.4–1.8 cm wide, more or less spreading to spreading, lanceolate, oblanceolate, or elliptic, upper surface olive-green or dark green, with a sheen or more or less glossy, midrib pale yellow, glabrous except for some sparse, minute pubescence at the leaf base, undersurface pale green, apex obtuse to subacute, gradually tapering to the base, margins entire, glabrous. Inflorescences lateral, simple or occasionally twice-branched from the basal bracts, 4–10 cm long, flowers closely placed on the rachis; peduncle and rachis with minute, spreading, reddish-brown hairs, peduncle 4–10 cm long, basal bracts leaf-like, olive-green, usually falcate, lanceolate, 7–19 mm long, upper bracts 3–4 mm long, linear, acute, margins minutely puberulent, pedicels 2–5 mm long, reddish-brown, calyx lobes 2–3 mm long, violet fading to lilac, narrowly lanceolate, ciliolate. Flowers hermaphrodite, faintly sweet-scented, violet-red to violet or occasionally pink and with age fading to off-white, tube 1.5–2 mm long, narrow, usually included within the calyx lobes, corolla lobes 5–6 by 4–5 mm, erect to suberect, narrowly lanceolate to ovate, acute.

Filaments pink or violet-red, anthers sky-blue. Capsule 7–8 by 5–6 mm, rhombic to ovate, apex sharply acute, amber to amber-brown.

DISTRIBUTION: North Island. Endemic to western Northland from the Ahipara gumlands and Herekino and Warawara ranges and then to the Waima Forest, followed by a 75 km gap southwards to Maungaraho Rock, near Tokatoka on the Wairoa River.

Hebe petriei *

Hebe petriei is a small, prostrate to sprawling, much-branched, woody shrub to about 10–15 cm high with stems up to 50 cm long. It has entire, petiolate leaves and terminal inflorescences of white flowers. Its leaves are bright green to slightly glaucous. It usually occurs in high, rocky places of Otago and Southland. As is true of a number of the rarer and smaller species of *Hebe*, it is most likely not in cultivation or exists only in the collection of a specialist grower. It is named in honour of Donald Petrie, chief inspector of schools for Otago, who actively botanised the Otago area from 1875 onwards and discovered *H. petriei* on Mount Bonpland in 1881.

DESCRIPTION: A much-branched, small, trailing or straggling shrub with stems up to 50 cm long. Branchlets glabrous to minutely bifariously pubescent, internodes one to two times the diameter and almost hidden by the leaves. Leaves more or less spreading 6–10 mm long by 2–5 mm wide, obovate-spathulate, more or less coriaceous, bright green to slightly glaucous, glabrous except for minute marginal pubescence near the base, slightly narrowed above their broad, more or less shortly connate bases, apex obtuse, margins entire. Inflorescences terminal, simple, relatively large, compact, forming a cylindrical spike to 5 cm long by 1.5 cm wide, bracts 5–7 mm long, usually numerous without flowers at the inflorescence bases, calyx lobes 3.5–5 mm long, narrow, more or less acute, usually uneven in size and with a more or less well-developed fifth lobe. Corolla white, 4.5–8 mm long, lobes about equalling the tube, narrow-elliptic. Capsule 4–5 mm long by 2 mm wide, narrow-pointed.

DISTRIBUTION: South Island. Grows in the mountains around Lake Wakatipu, including the Livingstone Mountains, Mount Repulse, the Harris Mountains, the Eyre Mountains, and then extending to south-western Otago, western Southland, and Fiordland. Occurs in low- to high-alpine areas, usually on shady rock ledges and in loose stony debris at 1300–2100 m.

Hebe pimeleoides

This has been a rather confusing species for quite a long time, and it is only through recent botanical research that the correct situation has been determined. Previously it was regarded as a complex species comprising the usually diminutive plant known as *Hebe pimeleoides* var. *minor*, from Marlborough to North Otago; a larger-growing plant from Central Otago formerly known as *H. pimeleoides* var. *rupestris*; and a further upright plant known as *H. pimeleoides* var. *glauca-caerulea*. It has now been determined that *H. pimeleoides* comprises *H. pimeleoides* subsp. *pimeleoides* and *H. pimeleoides* subsp. *faucicola*. Subsp. *pimeleoides* is the generally diminutive plant that occurs from Marlborough to North Otago, and unfortunately, many northern hemisphere gardeners still refer to it as *H. pimeleoides* var. *minor*. Subsp. *faucicola* now includes the larger, more erect plants that occur mainly in Central Otago. These two subspecies are the only recognised members of the *H. pimeleoides* complex. The status of the plant known as *H. pimeleoides* var. *glauca-caerulea* (*Veronica glauca-caerulea*) is unresolved, largely because it has never again been collected since its first collection in 1869 in the upper Rangitata River by Joseph Beattie Armstrong; it is now known only as a cultivated plant.

Hebe pimeleoides subsp. pimeleoides

This diminutive but charming species is really only suitable for a rock garden or trough garden, or as a container specimen in an alpine house. It is usually prostrate or sprawling and seldom more than 5–9 cm tall. In its natural habitat it may be quite inconspicuous among low grasses and small shrubs. One of its characteristic features is its black or purplish-black branchlets, which are distinctively hairy. Its leaves are generally grey or glaucous, usually with reddish margins, and during winter they often turn quite a strong purplish-red. Considering the size of the plant, the flowers are quite large, and they are usually a strong bluish-purple, though sometimes they may be a pale mauve. When well grown, this can be quite a showy little shrub. The name *pimeleoides* refers to the fact that this hebe resembles a species of *Pimelea*.

Hebe pimeleoides was discovered at Port Cooper (now Lyttelton Harbour) by botanist and naturalist David Lyall prior to 1853. His specimens are lodged in the herbarium of the Royal Botanic Gardens, Kew, United Kingdom. Interestingly, *H. pimeleoides* has never again been collected from around Lyttelton Harbour, and it has been suggested that, at the same time, Lyall and others made a journey across the Canterbury Plains to near Culverden, and this might be where he collected specimens of *H. pimeleoides*.

DESCRIPTION: A low, sprawling or creeping shrub usually no more than 3–4 cm tall. Branchlets usually less than 1 mm in diameter, black to dark purplish-black with pubescent hairs, often rooting. Leaf bud without a sinus or sinus small and acute. Leaves more or less spreading to spreading, about 5–12 mm long by 2–5 mm wide, free at their bases, narrow to broadly elliptic, flat to slightly concave, apex acute to subacute or occasionally obtuse, glabrous or minutely ciliolate, upper surface glaucous and light green, lower surface similar. Inflorescences usually with 4–12 flowers, lateral, simple, 1.5–5.5 cm long, peduncle 0.4–2 cm long, pedicels usually absent or shorter than the bracts; flowers on individual plants all hermaphrodite. Calyces tapered at their bases, four-lobed and equally divided, lobes ovate to lanceolate or elliptic, acute to subacute, ciliate or hairy-ciliate. Corolla violet or blue to pale mauve, sometimes fading to pale pink or almost white, tube glabrous, funnel-shaped, lobes longer than the tube, corolla tube mauve to white. Stamen filaments mauve (sometimes fading to almost white), anthers pale pink or mauve. Capsules usually acute or subacute or obtuse, pale to dark brown.

DISTRIBUTION: South Island. Found in Marlborough from the Inland Kaikoura Range to Lake Sedgemere, the Acheron River, and thence to Canterbury, the Hawdon River, then to Lake Pukaki, and southwards to Queenstown Hill and Moke Lake near Queenstown. May occur around lake margins, river terraces, or in tussock grassland in dry inland basins. Often favours dry stony places. Grows at 500–1060 m.

Hebe pimeleoides subsp. *pimeleoides* 'Elf'. Described as a tiny, decumbent, creeping and rooting plant. Graham Hutchins named both 'Elf' and 'Imp' to distinguish them from other forms with which they could be confused.

Hebe pimeleoides subsp. *pimeleoides* 'Imp'. Similar to 'Elf' but stronger-growing and with larger leaves that are said to be a lighter, glaucous grey-green and more acutely pointed.

Hebe pimeleoides subsp. *faucicola*

This subspecies differs from subsp. *pimeleoides* mainly in its erect to ascending habit and mauve to pale pink flowers. The flower colour may vary somewhat but generally ranges within the mid to pale violet-blue group and mainly fades to pinkish only as the flowers age. It generally grows up to 70 cm tall and is primarily a rock dweller found on rock outcrops and cliff faces in river valleys and gorges. In fact the name *faucicola*, meaning "gorge dweller," refers to its usual habitat.

Hebe pimeleoides subsp. *faucicola* includes what was formerly known as *H. pimeleoides* var. *rupestris*, a plant that inhabits rocky places in the Manuherekia, Clutha, and Kawarau river valleys in Central Otago. It was originally collected from the Dunstan Mountains by Leonard Cockayne in the early part of the 20th century. The holotype on which its current name is based was collected from Lookout Point, near the Clyde Dam on the Clutha River.

This attractive shrub can be quite wide-spreading depending on which form is grown, although I have seen some quite erect plants in northern Central Otago that do not spread greatly. This hebe has quite glaucous foliage that is greatly complemented by its blackish or dark-coloured stems. It is not too difficult to grow and prefers a sunny situation and a well-drained soil.

DESCRIPTION: A rather spreading shrub of a more erect habit, 45–50 cm tall but occasionally up to 70 cm or more. Branches more or less spreading to quite upright and erect, rather stout, glabrous, dark to rather blackish, internodes rather longer than the leaves. Leaf bud without a sinus. Leaves 7.5–15 mm long by 3.1–8.7 mm wide, elliptic to broad-elliptic to rounded, very glaucous on both surfaces. Inflorescences with 4–12 (or occasionally as many as 24) flowers on short racemes, peduncles inclined to be glabrous; corolla usually mauve to pale mauve, tube white, fading to pale pink or almost white, lobes about 4 by 3 mm. Style, ovary, and capsule pubescent, calyces and bracts ciliolate or ciliate only.

DISTRIBUTION: South Island. Found in Central Otago and northern Otago from about the Dunstan Mountains to the Kawarau River gorge and the Manuherekia River gorge near Ophir. Usually grows on rocks or rock bluffs but may also grow among rocks. Found at 200–500 m.

Hebe pinguifolia

Hebe pinguifolia is a rather variable species that occurs throughout the drier mountains along much of the eastern side of the South Island. In just about every locality, it produces plants that may differ slightly from those of other areas. Variations may include height, with some shrubs growing to 80 or 90 cm tall, while others may be decumbent and no more than 20 cm, or even 10 cm, tall; leaf shape and size, and even degree of glaucousness; and margin colour, whether they are red, yellowish, or no distinct colour. The best forms have handsome, very glaucous leaves with distinct reddish margins. Most cultivated forms are of lower growth, and the taller forms are seldom grown.

Generally, regardless of what form is grown, this species flowers well, and its white flowers contrast very effectively against the glaucous foliage. It usually flowers from October (mid spring) to March (early autumn). It is easily grown and appears to be fairly hardy in most northern hemisphere climates. The lower forms are useful for growing in a rock garden, as a ground cover, or as an informal edging along the front of a border. While this hebe prefers a sunny situation, it also grows quite well where there is indirect shade, such as from a fence or building. It is also a good plant for dry soils. Its specific name means "thick-leaved," from *pinguis* ("fat") and *folium* ("a leaf"). It was discovered and collected from a number of localities before 1864, by W. T. L. Travers and Julius Haast. Both Travers and Haast collected it from various localities from Nelson to Canterbury.

DESCRIPTION: Varies from a small, decumbent shrub 15–23 cm tall to a more erect, bushy shrub to 90 cm tall. Branches usually rather stout, old leaf scars prominent. Branchlets sparsely bifariously pubescent, purplish or brownish, internodes quite short. Leaf bud usually without a sinus. Leaves more or less spreading and often overlapping, 1–1.4 cm long by 4–10 mm wide, sessile, broad-ovate, more or less concave, obtuse to subacute, tapering to a broad base, thick and coriaceous, glabrous, glaucous on both surfaces, margins entire, often reddish but also sometimes yellowish. Inflorescences lateral, simple, crowded near the tips of the branchlets and sometimes hiding the growing tips although little exceeding the leaves, up to about 1.2 cm long, peduncle up to 1.2 cm long, sparingly pubescent. Flowers white, densely placed and hiding the rachis, somewhat erect, sessile; bracts ovate, subacute, ciliolate, very similar to and about equalling the calyx lobes. Corolla tube not exceeding the calyx lobes, narrow-cylindric; corolla lobes spreading, narrow-ovate, subacute, longer than the tube, the anterior lobe the largest. Stamens exserted, about equalling the corolla lobes, anthers purple becoming brownish. Capsule erect, rounded, little longer than the calyx lobes, pubescent.

DISTRIBUTION: South Island, from Marlborough to South Canterbury. Occurs in subalpine scrub and rocky places in the drier mountain districts east of the main divide. Grows at 760–1370 m.

Hebe pinguifolia 'Black Birch' (PLATE 52). In the north of the South Island, particularly on some of the Marlborough mountains, some very diminutive forms of *H. pinguifolia* may be found. One in particular comes from the Black Birch Range in Marlborough. It usually grows to no more than about 6 cm or 8 cm tall, and its ovate leaves measure about 4 by 3 mm and have pale margins. Its racemes are about 1.5 cm long and the flowers are about 5–7 mm in diameter. They have violet anthers. Their leaf buds also have a minute sinus, which has led some botanists to mistakenly identify these diminutive forms as *H. carnosula*. This latter species, however, can be distinguished by its always prominent sinus, its usually more erect habit of growth, and its darker green leaves (under a glaucous bloom). These small forms of *H. pinguifolia*, some of which have a very compact habit, are ideal for growing in a rock garden or trough garden. This cultivar from the Black Birch Range in Marlborough is in cultivation but not yet very common. It is a very fine little cultivar.

Hebe pinguifolia 'Dobson'. Described by Graham Hutchins (1997, p. 110) as a small and compact bush that was collected on Mount Dobson at 1525 m altitude. He states that it is the smallest form of the species that he knows, growing to about 15 cm tall by 25 cm wide. Branchlets purplish-green; leaves 7–10 mm long by 4–6 mm wide, margins pale or slightly reddish.

Hebe pinguifolia 'Hutt'. Another form collected by Hutchins, from Mount Hutt, at 1525 m altitude. He describes it as a decumbent, low bush about 20 cm tall by 90 cm wide. Branchlets green to purplish; leaves 1–1.4 cm long by 7–9 mm wide, margins more or less reddish.

Hebe pinguifolia 'Pagei' (PLATE 53). This well-known, very hardy form originated in the Dunedin Botanic Garden sometime before 1922. It is named after Edward Page, who at that time was a subforeman in the garden. In cultivation it forms a low shrub to about 30 cm tall, with usually dark purplish branchlets. Leaves are 9–12 mm long, very glaucous, and margined with reddish-purple. It forms low mounds smothered with white flowers that are sessile, except for the lower ones, which are sometimes pedicellate. It is male-sterile. A worthwhile garden plant, especially for ground cover. In the United Kingdom it is widely used for ground cover plantings.

Hebe pinguifolia 'Sutherlandii'. Another older cultivar that originated in New Zealand sometime before 1925. An excellent ground cover plant, it may grow to about 40 cm tall but will eventually spread out to a metre or more. Its leaves are a little smaller than those of *H. pinguifolia* 'Pagei', about 8 by 7 mm, broadly ovate to somewhat rounded, and not quite as glaucous. Their margins are also pale yellowish. Nothing appears to be known of its origin.

Hebe propinqua (PLATE 54)

This is a somewhat variable species, especially regarding height. Plants vary from decumbent shrubs about 30 cm high to bushier shrubs up to 90 cm tall. Because of their more attractive appearance, the lower-growing forms are probably more commonly seen in gardens. As is common with whipcord hebes, this species has often been confused with other species such as *Hebe salicornioides*. The specific name *propinqua* means "related" or "neighbouring" and implies that it has a close resemblance to another species, probably *H. armstrongii*. *Hebe propinqua* was originally collected from Mount Maungatua, eastern Otago, by Donald Petrie, probably in the early part of the 20th century.

Horticulturally, the small, compact form of this species is often referred to as *Hebe propinqua* 'Minor', while the tall form is referred to as *H. propinqua* 'Major'. 'Minor' is considered the typical form of the species. Over a number of years this plant will gradually spread to form a lovely, light green, hummocky mass with a sculpted appearance. It will grow to a metre or more wide and about 30 cm tall. It is a most useful plant for the rock garden and prefers a soil that does not dry out very much. It should be planted where its distinctive habit can be readily admired. In cultivation it appears to be rather shy of flowering, although, rather strangely, its taller relation is not so shy. Even if it never flowered it would be a most attractive plant. The taller-growing form is often a rather openly branched shrub and is not nearly as attractive as the smaller, more compact plant.

DESCRIPTION: Usually a small, much-branched, decumbent or erect shrub 30–90 cm tall. Branches spreading and rather tortuous. Branchlets short, rather slender, about 1–1.5 mm in diameter including the leaves, light green to yellow-green, internodes one to two times the diameter, usually partly exposed, joints well marked. Leaves tightly appressed to the branchlet, 1–1.5 mm long, joined together for about a third to half their length, obscurely triangular, thick and coriaceous. Inflorescences of spikes with up to 12 flowers near the tips of the branchlets. Flowers white, more or less erect, bracts about 1.5 mm long, ovate-rhomboid, acute, the calyx lobes narrowly ovate-oblong, obtuse, free for about one-half to two-thirds their length; corolla tube more or less equalling the calyx. Capsule about 3 mm long, oval, obtuse, about equalling or twice as long as the calyx.

DISTRIBUTION: South Island. Apart from one record in the valley of the Rangitata River in Canterbury, it appears to be confined from eastern areas of Otago to the Lakes District. Usually grows in poorly drained, often peaty areas in mixed snow tussock–scrub at 800–1400 m.

Hebe pubescens *

This composite species comprises the typical form, which occurs on the mainland, and two subspecies, which occur on islands to the north of the Coromandel Peninsula and to the north of the Hauraki Gulf.

Hebe pubescens subsp. *pubescens*

This hebe is distinguished from other species by its leaves, their margins, midribs, and often their whole undersurfaces being fringed with soft, pilose hairs. Hairs also often cover the sinus of the leaf bud. *Hebe pubescens* subsp. *pubescens* was discovered by Joseph Banks and Daniel Solander in 1769 at Purangi, near Cook's Beach, Mercury Bay. It does not appear to be at all common in cultivation.

DESCRIPTION: A shrub to about 2 m tall. Branchlets varying from green to bronze on their lower surfaces, more or less with long pubescence; length of internodes three to six times the diameter. Leaf bud with a sinus often obscured by hairs from the leaf margins. Leaves spreading, 3.5–9 cm long by 6 mm–2.4 cm wide, oblong-lanceolate, not very coriaceous, petiole short and base sometimes almost auricled, apex obtuse, whole of the undersurface sometimes clad with soft, villous hairs, margins and underside of midrib with longer hairs. Inflorescences lateral, simple, sometimes much longer than the leaves. Peduncle closely and minutely villous. Flowers rather closely placed, pedicels 2–3 mm long, calyx lobes about 2 mm long, narrow, acute and villous overall. Corolla white to lavender, usually hairy on the outside, tube narrow and about equalling the calyx lobes. Capsule rounded, usually glabrous, about twice the length of the calyx.

DISTRIBUTION: Primarily an endemic of the Coromandel Peninsula, from about its northern extremity southwards to about the Kauaeranga Valley, and also on some of the immediately surrounding offshore islands. Distributed mainly in coastal areas, usually in open forest, where it is common under pohutukawa (*Metrosideros excelsa*), but also on steep cliff faces.

Hebe pubescens subsp. *rehuarum*

This subspecies differs mainly on account of its lanceolate or linear-lanceolate leaves, which are glabrous underneath; the undersides of the midribs are either glabrous or hairy. The epithet *rehuarum* commemorates the Ngati Rehua tribe of Great Barrier Island.

DISTRIBUTION: Endemic to Great Barrier Island and its immediately surrounding islands, including Broken Island. Usually grows in coastal habitats.

PLATE 1. The distinctive hemispherical shape of *Hebe odora* growing on a flush, on the Island Saddle, upper Wairau River

PLATE 2. *Hebe brachysiphon* in the valley of the upper Wairau River, Marlborough

PLATE 3. *Hebe* 'Hartii' grafted onto *H. barkeri* and trained as a standard

PLATE 4. The frothy, spittle-like excretion that indicates the presence of the meadow spittle bug

PLATE 5. Typical damage caused by leaf-rolling or leaf-tying moths

PLATE 6. *Hebe topiaria* quite severely affected by an attack of *Phytophthora*

PLATE 7. *Hebe* foliage severely attacked by septoria leaf spot

PLATE 8. The yellowing lower leaves of *Hebe albicans* 'Sussex Carpet' are the first indication that the plant is beginning to suffer from drought

PLATE 9. *Hebe acutiflora*

PLATE 10. *Hebe adamsii*

PLATE 11. *Hebe albicans*

PLATE 12. *Hebe albicans* 'Silver Dollar'

PLATE 13. *Hebe amplexicaulis*

PLATE 14. *Hebe amplexicaulis* f. *hirta*

PLATE 15. *Hebe annulata*

PLATE 16. *Hebe barkeri*

PLATE 17. *Hebe benthamii*

PLATE 18. *Hebe biggarii*

PLATE 19. *Hebe bishopiana*

PLATE 20. *Hebe bollonsii*

PLATE 21. *Hebe brachysiphon*

PLATE 22. *Hebe brevifolia*

PLATE 23. *Hebe buchananii*

PLATE 24. *Hebe canterburiensis*

PLATE 25. *Hebe chathamica*

PLATE 26. *Hebe cheesemanii*

PLATE 27. *Hebe cockayneana*

PLATE 28. *Hebe cupressoides*

PLATE 29. *Hebe decumbens*

PLATE 30. *Hebe dieffenbachii*

PLATE 31. *Hebe elliptica*

PLATE 33. *Hebe elliptica* var. *crassifolia*

PLATE 32. *Hebe elliptica* 'Donaldii'

PLATE 34. *Hebe epacridea*

PLATE 35. *Hebe evenosa*

PLATE 36. *Hebe gibbsii*

PLATE 37. *Hebe glaucophylla*

PLATE 39. *Hebe gracillima* 'Slate River Gold'

PLATE 38. *Hebe gracillima*

PLATE 40. *Hebe hectori* subsp. *coarctata*

PLATE 41. *Hebe ligustrifolia*, Surville Cliffs form

PLATE 42. *Hebe lycopodioides*

PLATE 43. *Hebe macrantha* var. *macrantha*

PLATE 45. *Hebe macrocarpa* var. *latisepala*

PLATE 44. *Hebe macrocarpa* var. *macrocarpa*

PLATE 46. *Hebe masoniae*

PLATE 48. *Hebe odora*

PLATE 47. *Hebe obtusata*

PLATE 49. *Hebe odora* 'Prostrata'

PLATE 50. *Hebe pareora*

PLATE 51. *Hebe perbella*

PLATE 52. *Hebe pinguifolia* 'Black Birch'

PLATE 53. *Hebe pinguifolia* 'Pagei'

PLATE 54. *Hebe propinqua*

PLATE 55. *Hebe ramosissima*. Photo by Joe Cartman

PLATE 56. *Hebe recurva*

PLATE 57. *Hebe rigidula*

PLATE 58. *Hebe rupicola*

PLATE 59. *Hebe salicifolia*

PLATE 60. *Hebe salicornioides*

PLATE 61. *Hebe speciosa*

PLATE 62. *Hebe stenophylla*

PLATE 63. *Hebe stricta* var. *atkinsonii*

PLATE 64. *Hebe stricta* var. *egmontiana*

PLATE 65. *Hebe stricta* var. *macroura*

PLATE 66. *Hebe strictissima*

PLATE 67. *Hebe subalpina*

PLATE 68. *Hebe* "Swamp"

PLATE 69. *Hebe tairawhiti*

PLATE 70. *Hebe tetrasticha*

PLATE 71. *Hebe topiaria*

PLATE 72. *Hebe townsonii*

PLATE 73. *Hebe treadwellii*

PLATE 74. *Hebe tumida*

PLATE 75. *Hebe urvilleana*

PLATE 76. *Hebe venustula*

PLATE 77. *Hebe vernicosa*

PLATE 78. *Hebe* 'Alicia Amherst'

PLATE 79. *Hebe* 'Amy'

PLATE 80. *Hebe* ×*andersonii* 'Andersonii'

PLATE 81. *Hebe* ×*andersonii* 'Andersonii Aurea'

PLATE 82. *Hebe* ×*andersonii* 'Andersonii Variegata'

PLATE 83. *Hebe* 'Champagne'

PLATE 84. *Hebe* 'Christensenii'

PLATE 85. *Hebe* 'Combe Royal'

PLATE 86. *Hebe* 'County Park'

PLATE 87. *Hebe* 'Eugénie Ombler'

PLATE 88. *Hebe* 'Eveline'

PLATE 89. *Hebe* 'First Light'

PLATE 90. *Hebe* ×*franciscana* 'Lobelioides'

PLATE 91. *Hebe* 'Glengarriff'

PLATE 92. *Hebe* 'Greensleeves'

PLATE 93. *Hebe* 'Hartii'

PLATE 94. *Hebe* 'Headfortii'

PLATE 95. *Hebe* 'Hinerua'

PLATE 96. *Hebe* 'Icing Sugar'

PLATE 97. *Hebe* 'Imposter'

PLATE 98. *Hebe* 'Inspiration'

PLATE 99. *Hebe* 'Inverey'

PLATE 100. *Hebe* 'Karo Golden Esk'

PLATE 101. *Hebe* 'Lavender Lace'

PLATE 102. *Hebe* 'Lopen'

PLATE 104. *Hebe* 'Miss Fittall'

PLATE 103. *Hebe* 'McEwanii'

PLATE 107. *Hebe* 'Oratia Gala'

PLATE 105. *Hebe* 'Nantyderry'

PLATE 106. *Hebe* 'Oratia Beauty'

PLATE 108. *Hebe* 'Orphan Annie'

PLATE 109. *Hebe* 'Otari Delight'

PLATE 110. *Hebe* 'Purple Tips'

PLATE 111. *Hebe* 'Quicksilver'

PLATE 112. *Hebe* 'Red Edge'

PLATE 113. *Hebe* 'Sandra Joy'

PLATE 114. *Hebe* 'Silver Queen'

PLATE 115. *Hebe* 'Snowdrift'

PLATE 116. *Hebe* 'Sunstreak'

PLATE 117. *Hebe* 'Walter Buccleugh'

PLATE 118. *Hebe* 'Wiri Charm'

PLATE 119. *Hebe* 'Wiri Dawn'

PLATE 120. *Hebe* 'Wiri Grace'

PLATE 121. *Hebe* 'Wiri Spears'

PLATE 122. *Hebe* 'Wiri Splash'

PLATE 123. *Hebe* 'Wiri Vision'

PLATE 124. *Heliohebe hulkeana*

PLATE 125. *Heliohebe raoulii* subsp. *raoulii*

PLATE 126. *Heliohebe raoulii* subsp. *maccaskillii*

PLATE 128. ×*Heohebe hortensis* 'Waikanae'

PLATE 127. ×*Heohebe hortensis* 'Spring Monarch'

PLATE 129. *Parahebe catarractae* 'Snow Cap'

PLATE 130. *Parahebe cheesemanii* subsp. *cheesemanii*

PLATE 131. *Parahebe hookeriana* 'Olsenii'

PLATE 132. *Parahebe linifolia* 'Blue Skies'

PLATE 133. *Parahebe lyallii*

PLATE 134. *Parahebe trifida*

PLATE 135. *Chionohebe thomsonii*

Hebe pubescens subsp. *sejuncta*

Subsp. *sejuncta* is distinguished by its obovate, oblanceolate, or narrowly elliptic leaves, the undersides of which are glabrous, with their midribs either glabrous or hairy. The epithet *sejuncta* means "isolated" and refers to its habitat.

DISTRIBUTION: Endemic to the larger islands of the Mokohinau group, Little Barrier Island, and one location on Great Barrier Island. Characteristic of flaxlands and petrel scrub.

Hebe rakaiensis

This species forms a rounded, ball-like shrub to 1 m or occasionally 2 m tall. It has bright green foliage and is commonly grown in the United Kingdom, where it is quite popular with gardeners. It is closely related to *Hebe glaucophylla*, from which it is distinguished by having very glossy green (rather than glaucous) leaves and an ovary that is pubescent with numerous, very fine, short (rather than scattered, stiff) hairs.

In cultivation *Hebe rakaiensis* generally grows to 75 cm–1 m tall but does not appear to reach 2 m, as has been recorded for some wild specimens. It will spread to 1.5 m across. It apparently flowers well and is useful for massed ground cover plantings and low hedging. Its shining, bright green leaves and ball-like habit of growth make it very useful and attractive, and it is also hardy. Flowering generally occurs from about mid summer to autumn. This species was discovered in the valley of the Rakaia River in 1868 by Joseph Beattie Armstrong. For quite some years there was doubt concerning its validity as a species; it was considered that it might be *H. traversii* var. *elegans* or even *H. scott-thomsonii*, a species described in 1938 but later deemed to be identical with *H. rakaiensis*.

More recently, in England there has been some attempt to apply the name 'Gold Dome' to a form of this species that is said to have golden young foliage. This colour, which is slightly yellowish but certainly not golden, is not a constant character and may vary from season to season and situation to situation. The tendency for young foliage to assume this colour may be more physiological than anything else. Plants of *Hebe rakaiensis* that I have seen in the United Kingdom appear to have nothing about them that would distinguish them from typical *H. rakaiensis*, which in any case, depending on cultural factors, tends to have bright green to yellowish-green foliage.

DESCRIPTION: A rather densely bushy shrub 1–2 m tall in cultivation and up to 2 m tall in the wild. Branchlets slender, finely bifariously pubescent, length of internodes usually about two to six times the diameter, leaf scars remaining rather rough. Leaf bud without a sinus. Leaves spreading, bright green, glossy or shining, about 2 cm long by 6 mm wide, obovate-oblong to elliptic-oblong, glabrous, more or less coriaceous, base narrow, apex subacute, margins entire but opaque with microscopic hair-like cilia. Inflorescences lateral, simple, 3–4 cm long when in flower but elongating in fruit. Flowers not very crowded, pedicels usually obvious; peduncle about half the length of the subtending leaf, very finely pubescent. Bracts very small, ciliolate, obtuse to acute, much shorter than the pedicels. Calyx lobes 1–1.5 mm long, some or all subacute on each flower, ciliolate, membranous, border very narrow. Corolla white, tube wide, scarcely equalling the calyx lobes, lobes about 2 mm long, rounded. Ovary with fine, close pubescence that sometimes extends to the style. Capsule 3 by 2 mm to 4 by 2.5 mm, narrow and pointed, drying to a rather light brown, two to three times the length of the calyx lobes.

DISTRIBUTION: South Island. Found on the eastern side of the main divide from mid Canterbury southwards to about south-eastern Otago, descending to sea level in the Catlins area. Generally grows along streamsides and on rocky outcrops.

Hebe ramosissima (PLATE 55)

Another species known only from a few very restricted habitats, from Mount Tapuae-o-Uenuku on the Inland Kaikoura Range, where it was originally collected, to north Canterbury. It is a small, prostrate or decumbent, closely branched shrub up to 20 cm tall that forms mats or patches 20–30 cm in diameter and up to about 5–7 cm high. Its small, green to dark green leaves are shortly joined at their bases, elliptic to elliptic-oblong, and somewhat fleshy, the margins often red but not thickened. The inflorescences are terminal, simple, and usually pedunculate. The white flowers, on individual plants, are either hermaphrodite or female. This species is part of the informal group "Connatae." It was discovered by George Simpson during the early 1940s on Mount Tapuae-o-Uenuku. It is found only in the collections of a few specialist gardeners. As suggested by its habitat, in cultivation it is happiest in a moist situation, preferably with light shade for part of the day, although the cultivated specimen that I have seen was actually collected from a rather dry and sunny situation, at a very high altitude in its type habitat. The specific name *ramosissima* means "much-branched" and refers to the plant's habit of growth.

DISTRIBUTION: South Island. Found on the mountains of eastern Marlborough and north Canterbury, from Mount Tapuae-o-Uenuku on the Inland Kaikoura Range to the Seaward Kaikoura Range thence to Mounts Terako and Lyford. There is also one record for south-eastern Nelson near Mount Weld. Usually grows on scree, rock bluffs, and in crevices, typically in moist places, at 1200–2100 m.

Hebe rapensis *

This is the only species of *Hebe* to be confined wholly and solely outside the New Zealand botanical region. It occurs on the volcanic island of Rapa (or Rapa Iti) some 1200 km south-east of Tahiti. It has affinities with *H. barkeri* of the Chatham Islands as well the other species of those islands. *Hebe rapensis* is endemic to Rapa and occurs on the peaks at altitudes of 180–315 m. It is uncommon and is very likely not in cultivation. It was discovered in 1921.

Hebe recurva (PLATE 56)

An interesting species that occurs only in north-western Nelson. It may be distinguished by its generally low, compact habit of growth and rather narrow, glaucous leaves that are sessile and stem-clasping at their bases. The leaves are more or less recurved (hence the specific name) and further help to identify it. It is a handsome species that does not grow too tall and is most useful for group plantings. Its compact shape combined with its height, usually to about 60 cm, means that it tends to require very little pruning, while the handsome white flowers contrast prettily against the glaucous foliage. In bud, the calyx lobes have a more or less pinkish colour that tends to give the impression that the corollas might be pinkish. As with other glaucous-leaved hebes, *Hebe recurva* is probably best in a sunny position, although it will tolerate a certain amount of shade providing the shade is not too dense. A well-drained soil suits it best. Flowering usually occurs from about mid December (summer) until late January (mid summer).

This species was first introduced into cultivation in England, as an unnamed species, shortly before or about 1923, and was first mentioned in the Aldenham Gardens catalogue during that year under the name *Hebe* "Aoira." "Aoira" is a corruption of "Aorere," the river where this hebe grows. It was not until 1940 that George Simpson and John Scott Thomson formally described it as a species. Later, in 1962, the Christchurch Botanic Gardens, New Zealand, received specimens of *H.* "Aoira" from England, and its resemblance to *H. recurva* was immediately noted. In 1963 this was confirmed by J. Souster of the Royal Botanic Gardens, Kew, who determined that *H.* "Aoira" was actually *H. recurva* and that "Aoira" was an obvious corruption of "Aorere." To illustrate how easily plant names can become corrupted, it's useful to note that over a period of 20 years the originally corrupted name of this species became further corrupted to "Aione" and "Aora," both epithets from quite reputable nurseries in the United Kingdom.

At various times, some growers have raised *Hebe recurva* from seed and claimed that the resulting progeny have green foliage of varying degrees with no signs of glaucousness. This is usually the result of hybridising with other garden hebes. Graham Hutchins has raised seedlings from wild-collected seed of *H. recurva* and observed that there was little difference except that the foliage of some seedlings was slightly less glaucous—something that would be likely to occur naturally, in any case.

DESCRIPTION: A much-branched, low-growing, spreading shrub to 90 cm tall, although generally smaller in cultivation. Branchlets green when young, sparsely pubescent, usually in bifarious bands but sometimes all around, length of internodes rather short, two to three times the diameter. Leaf bud without a sinus. Leaves spreading and deflexed or recurved, 3.2–5 cm long, 4–8 mm wide, sessile by a broad and stem-clasping base, narrow-lanceolate, coriaceous, glabrous, rather glaucous on both surfaces, margins entire and more or less cartilaginous, apex subacute. Inflorescences lateral, simple, not much exceeding the leaves, up to about 5.7 cm long, peduncle up to 1.5 cm long, pubescent with long, stiff hairs. Flowers white, closely placed and hiding the rachis; pedicels ascending, about 3 mm long, pubescent, exceeding the more or less ciliolate bracts. Calyx glabrous, lobes about 1.5 mm long, narrow and subacute to acute, ciliolate; corolla tube narrow-cylindric, almost twice as long as the calyx lobes, corolla lobes spreading, ovate, obtuse, margins somewhat in-rolled. Stamens exserted and exceeding the lobes, anthers purple. Capsule about 4 mm long, erect, ovate, acute, glabrous.

DISTRIBUTION: South Island. A plant of streams and rocky places, found along the banks of the Aorere River in north-western Nelson, typically growing on rock platforms. Apparently plentiful.

Hebe recurva 'Aoira'. This is the original clone of *H. recurva* that was first grown by Aldenham Gardens in England. It was initially known simply as *Veronica* "Aoira" and was said to be named after a Mount Aoira in New Zealand, but no mountain of that name has ever been known. Once it was finally identified as *H. recurva*, it became obvious that "Aoira" was a corruption of the name of the Aorere River, its type locality. Apart from the fact that its branchlets are pubescent all around, instead of in bifarious bands, it is identical with other more typical forms of *H. recurva*.

Hebe recurva 'White Torrent'. This seedling was raised from wild-collected seed and selected and named by Graham Hutchins (1997), who describes it as having less glaucous leaves and branchlets that are pubescent all around. Anthers are pale pinkish-purple. According to Hutchins, 'White Torrent' is a translation of the Maori *aorere*; however, that is not quite correct, as *aorere* is usually translated as *ao* ("clouds") and *rere* ("to fly"), possibly in allusion to the clouds observed by the original inhabitants of the area.

Hebe rigidula (PLATE 57)

Hebe rigidula comprises two varieties: var. *rigidula*, the typical form, and var. *sulcata*. Both occur on the South Island of New Zealand. Var. *rigidula* is confined to parts of Marlborough and Nelson provinces, while var. *sulcata* is found on D'Urville Island in the outer Marlborough Sounds and on one or two adjoining mainland locations.

Hebe rigidula var. *rigidula*

Although it lacks the bright colour of many cultivars, *Hebe rigidula* var. *rigidula* must rank as one of the finest hebes for general garden purposes. It is especially valued for its very neat, compact habit and is among the most floriferous hebes, generally smothering itself with masses of white flowers that more than compensate for any lack of colour. In fact, the flowers are so profuse that they quite hide the foliage. Immediately after flowering, this hebe should be given a light pruning in order to maintain its compactness. It generally grows to 60 cm tall but may grow taller if left unpruned. Flowering is from December (summer) to February (late summer).

In general appearance this shrub is rather similar to *Hebe divaricata*, differing principally in its inflorescences, which are seldom more than tripartite and often simple. It is further distinguished by its yellowish-green branchlets and by the usually somewhat glaucous undersurfaces of its leaves. The leaf bud has a long, narrow sinus. Although quite a straggly little plant in its natural habitat, in cultivation this hebe forms a well-shaped shrub to about 60 cm tall and at times may even reach 90 cm or more. *Rigidula* means "slightly or nearly rigid" and probably refers to the appearance of this plant in its natural habitat, where it seldom appears to be upright. *Hebe rigidula* was discovered in the Pelorus River valley in the early part of the 20th century by J. H. McMahon.

DESCRIPTION: A usually small, much-branched, erect to spreading shrub often no more than 15–60 cm tall. Branchlets bifariously pubescent, length of internodes two to three times the diameter and yellow-green when young. Leaf bud with a long, narrow sinus. Leaves slightly ascending to spreading, 1.2–2.5 cm long by 7–8 mm wide, on petioles up to 4 mm long, elliptic-oblong to linear-obovate, acute to subacute, coriaceous, upper surface green with a rather dull sheen, paler or somewhat glaucous beneath, margins entire, thickened. Inflorescences lateral, usually with two or more branches of the first order, crowded towards the tips of the branchlets, equalling or slightly overtopping the leaves, peduncle shorter than the leaves, hairy. Flowers white, closely placed and hiding the rachis, almost sessile, more or less erect, bracts ovate, obtuse, ciliolate, approximately equalling the calyx. Calyx glabrous, lobes about 1.5 mm long, margins translucent, ciliolate; corolla tube cylindric, about twice as long as the calyx lobes, corolla lobes spreading, ovate, obtuse, not quite as long as the tube. Stamens exserted, longer than the lobes, anthers creamy. Capsule small, about 3–4 mm long, acute to subacute, glabrous, less than twice as long as the calyx lobes.

DISTRIBUTION: South Island. Confined to the northern parts of Marlborough and Nelson provinces, where it occurs in the Pelorus and Maitai valleys, the Bryant and Richmond ranges, and on Serpentine Hill in the Lee Valley area. In particular it may be found along the Pelorus River and adjoining river valleys, usually on rocks and along streamsides from sea level to 1300 m.

Hebe rigidula var. *sulcata*

This variety differs from the typical form in having leaves that are somewhat M-shaped in their transverse section (although this is not always so noticeable) and that are often wider and more broadly elliptic. As a relatively recently recognised variety, it has not yet become available in general cultivation and is likely to be found only in the collections of one or two institutional gardens or connoisseurs. Cultivated material appears to have a slightly more compact habit of growth than typical *Hebe rigidula*, and the leaves are a deeper green. The varietal name *sulcata* means "furrowed" or "grooved" and refers to the furrowed appearance of the leaves, although this character is not initially obvious.

DESCRIPTION: Leaves usually M-shaped in transverse section, more broadly elliptic than those of var. *rigidula*, usually 1.35–2.5 cm long by 5–7.5 mm wide. Flower pedicels 0.4–2 mm long.

DISTRIBUTION: South Island. Occurs on D'Urville Island in the outer Marlborough Sounds and has also been recorded on one or two adjoining mainland locations such as Editor Hill, above Croiselles Harbour, and Lookout Peak. Like var. *rigidula* it appears to favour rocky habitats and short scrub, growing at 500–900 m. On D'Urville Island it may grow on exposed serpentine tors.

Hebe rupicola (PLATE 58)

This attractive species, formerly known as *Hebe lapidosa*, is confined to Marlborough and north Canterbury. It is seldom cultivated and is likely to be found only in the collections of a few enthusiasts. It is an accommodating hebe that does not grow overly large in cultivation, although it may grow to about 1.5 m in the wild and can be rather wide-spreading. The leaves are somewhat shining on their upper surfaces and may be rather glaucous beneath. White flowers are produced on usually simple, shortish inflorescences, although the lowermost may be thrice-branched. A plant of rocky places, along rivers and streams, *H. rupicola* prefers a rather moist but well-drained soil, and while it is best in full sun, it will tolerate some shade. Its specific name means "growing on rocks" and refers to its preferred habitat. This species was discovered in the Conway River gorge in the early part of the 20th century by Leonard Cockayne.

DESCRIPTION: An erect, branching shrub of rounded habit, to 1.5 m tall. Branchlets with well-defined pubescent bands above each leaf insertion, bark dark when dry, length of internodes two to four times the diameter. Leaf bud with a long, narrow sinus. Leaves more or less erect to somewhat spreading, 1.5–2.5 cm long by 5–7 mm wide, elliptic or ovate-oblong, coriaceous, upper surfaces yellowish-green to medium green, occasionally glaucous beneath, glabrous, apex obtuse to subacute, margins entire and cartilaginous. Inflorescences lateral, the lowermost often tripartly branched, the uppermost simple, longer than the leaves but not exceeding the leafy tips of the branchlets, peduncle short, almost glabrous. Flowers almost sessile, more or less opposite; bracts 4–5 mm long, broad-ovate, subacute, margins membranous, very finely ciliolate. Calyces hidden within the bracts, lobes about 3.5 by 1.5 mm, similar to the bracts. Corolla white, tube little longer than the calyx, lobes equalling the tube, narrow, subacute. Capsule erect, broadly oblong, obtuse, glabrous, little longer than the calyx and often shorter than the bracts.

DISTRIBUTION: South Island, from Marlborough to north Canterbury. Mainly occurs in rocky places, especially along streams and river gorges in subalpine scrub and on the stony debris of rocky benches.

Hebe salicifolia (PLATE 59)
koromiko

Because of its large size and spreading habit, *Hebe salicifolia* may not be as widely grown as some of the lower-growing hebes. It is encountered throughout the South and Stewart islands. In the 19th century there was a certain amount of confusion between this and the North Island *H. stricta*, which is quite similar but lacks the distinct leaf bud sinus of *H. salicifolia*. It is easily recognised among the South Island species by its willow-like foliage and its often long, more or less drooping flower racemes, which on some forms can be quite graceful. The flower racemes of some forms can be up to 24 cm long or even longer. Their colour can also vary, with some being rather pale and others an attractive medium violet. This can be a rather variable species, and it is possible that some of the best forms are not yet in cultivation. *Hebe salicifolia* also occurs on the coast of southern Chile at about the same latitude as its New Zealand counterpart. It is one of only three species of *Hebe* that occur outside the New Zealand botanical region. The specific name *salicifolia* refers to the leaves, which resemble those of *Salix* (willow). It was most likely discovered in Dusky Sound in 1773 by Johann or Georg Forster (father and son), who were on the *Resolution* during Captain James Cook's second voyage to New Zealand.

In the garden this hebe can form a rather spreading shrub to 2.4 m tall and is hardy enough to grow in a variety of situations. In northern hemisphere gardens it is considered to be fairly hardy and flowers over quite a long period. After flowering it is much improved if given a light pruning to remove all of the old flowers and to encourage more compact growth. The flowers of some forms are delicately and sweetly fragrant and on a warm day will quite strongly scent the surrounding air; in fact, this species is among the few hebes known to have quite strongly scented flowers. Flowering normally occurs from January (mid summer) to February (late summer) or even April (mid autumn). A well-flowered bush of *Hebe salicifolia* is a fine sight.

DESCRIPTION: A much-branched, erect to spreading shrub 1.5–4.6 m tall in the wild. Branchlets glabrous, length of internodes two to five times the diameter, pale green or yellowish-green. Leaf bud with a distinct sinus. Leaves slightly ascending to spreading. Leaf blade long-lanceolate to oblong-lanceolate, 8–12 cm long by 1.5–1.8 cm wide, narrowed to the long, acuminate apex, glabrous except for both surfaces of the midrib, which are puberulous; upper surface dark green to yellowish-green, paler

Hebe salicifolia

beneath; margins entire or obscurely and distantly denticulate. Inflorescence lateral, simple, usually much exceeding the leaves, sometimes up to 20 cm long or more. Peduncle 3.2–4 cm long, glabrous or sometimes minutely puberulous. Flowers closely placed but not completely hiding the rachis, pedicels more or less spreading, up to 3 mm long, puberulous, equalling or exceeding the narrow, ciliolate bracts. Calyx glabrous, lobes about 1.5 mm long, narrow, acute, ciliolate. Corolla tube white, about equalling the calyx lobes, corolla lobes white to violet, narrow-ovate and not very wide-spreading, more or less acute. Stamens shortly exserted, anthers violet. Capsule 3–5 mm long, ovoid, acute, glabrous, less than twice as long as the calyx.

DISTRIBUTION: Common throughout the South and Stewart islands except near the coast in the Marlborough Sounds, where its place is taken by *Hebe stricta* var. *atkinsonii*. Usually found around forest margins, along stream and lake banks, and in open forest, scrub, or subalpine scrub. Grows from sea level to 1060 m. Also found on the coast of southern Chile.

Hebe salicornioides (PLATE 60)

Another whipcord hebe. In the garden it usually forms a rather low shrub to 50 cm tall, although in the wild it sometimes grows taller. It is distinguished by its usually green or yellow-green branchlets being rather erect and tending to arise from the upper sides of the principal branches, giving it a rather distinct appearance from most other whipcord species. Its branchlets are soft and flexible, unlike some other hebes in this group. It is a very hardy plant and because of its lower and more compact growth is ideal for small gardens. In the wild it only inhabits quite wet sites and so should not be expected to endure particularly dry conditions in the garden. The specific name *salicornioides* alludes to its supposed resemblance to *Salicornia* (now *Sarcocornia*), glasswort; however, it would require some stretch of the imagination to see the similarity. It was discovered in the mountains of Nelson by a Captain Rough sometime in the mid 1800s.

DESCRIPTION: A low, spreading, much-branched shrub 30 cm–1 m tall. Branches erect, rather stout, with the old leaf scars prominent. Branchlets usually rather crowded, terete, 2–2.5 mm in diameter including the leaves, bright green to yellowish-green, dull, internodes close together but exposed for most of their length. Leaves tightly appressed to the branchlets, up to 1.5 mm long, joined together for at least half their length to form a short, sheathing tube, thinly fleshy and rather delicate when fresh, apex obtusely rounded or rarely subacute, sometimes slightly convex and incurved, margins pale and membranous, usually ciliate. Inflorescences terminal, two- to four-flowered. Flowers white, closely placed, sessile, erect, bracts broad-ovate, obtuse to truncate, ciliate, up to about 1.5 mm long. Calyx 1.5–2 mm long, anterior lobes fused together for about two-thirds of their length or completely so to the apex; corolla tube slightly less than or equalling the calyx, corolla lobes spreading, longer than the tube, ovate, obtuse. Stamens exserted, approximately equalling the lobes. Capsule 3–4 mm long, rhomboid-ovate, subacute to acute, longer than the calyx lobes.

DISTRIBUTION: South Island. Found in mountain districts from Nelson and Marlborough to north Canterbury and then to the Humboldt Mountains near Lake Wakatipu and to the Routeburn area. Occurs in subalpine scrub, mainly in rather moist or very wet ground. Often quite local in its occurrence. Ascends to 1060 m or more.

*Hebe scopulorum**

Hebe scopulorum is another recently described species. It has similarities with *H. rigidula* and *H. colensoi* but differs from the former in having leaf buds that are strongly squarish, pedicels that are usually 1.5–3 mm long, and leaves that are 2–4 cm long by 5–9 mm wide, and from the latter in having upper leaf surfaces that are not glaucous, corolla tubes that are longer than the calyces, and in having hairs on branches and calyx margins. As with several other recently described species, *H. scopulorum* is either not in cultivation or is only in one or two specialised collections. It is confined to the North Island, where it occurs near the west coast of south Auckland near Kawhia. The specific name *scopulorum* means "of the crags" and refers to the preferred habitat of this species.

DESCRIPTION: A low shrub to about 70 cm tall with erect or ascending branches. Old branches black or grey, bark becoming quite corky with age. Branchlets green to brown, internodes 2–5 mm long, leaf scars prominent, bifariously or uniformly pubescent. Leaf bud with a narrow, acute sinus. Leaves decussate to subdistichous, more or less erect to spreading, linear-elliptic or elliptic to oblanceolate, 2–4.4 cm long by 6–11 mm wide, upper surface green to dark green, glossy, lower surface glaucous and dull, more or less coriaceous, M-shaped, apex plicate and subacute or more or less apiculate, base cuneate, petioles 2–4 mm long, margins cartilaginous, thickened, rounded and minutely papillate. Inflorescences lateral, usually with one or two branches at their bases (though some simple inflorescences may also be present), usually 2–3.5 cm long, peduncle 8 mm–1.5 cm long, pubescent, rachis 1–1.8 cm long, pubescent, lower bracts usually opposite and decussate, becoming alternate above, acute to acuminate or rarely obtuse, sparsely ciliolate, pedicels equalling or shorter than the bracts. Flowers pale mauve becoming white, tube glabrous, 3–4 mm long, lower half expanded and contracted at the base, longer than the calyx, corolla lobes elliptic and subacute. Stamen filaments white, anthers pale mauve, violet, or white. Capsule 3.2–4.5 mm long by 2–3 mm wide, pale to dark brown.

DISTRIBUTION: North Island. Found south-east of Kawhia in south Auckland Province. Largely confined to exposed remnant limestone tors and a rock mesa that outcrop on either side of the upper Awaroa Valley, the eastern and southern portions of the Taumatatotara Range, Ngawhakatara (The Lady), Omaramanui (Rock Peak), Otuatakahi (Else Rock), and Osbourne's Bluff. It shows a marked preference for growing on limestone and is shade-tolerant, seemingly preferring south-facing exposures.

Hebe societatis

A rare species so far known only to occur on Mount Murchison in the Braeburn Range, situated between Lake Rotoroa and Murchison township. *Hebe societatis* was discovered by members of the Nelson Botanical Society on a field trip to the mountain in February 2002 and was accordingly named to commemorate the occasion.

This species is allied to *Hebe vernicosa* but has a number of different characters, including a low-growing habit, glaucous or glaucescent leaves, and purple anthers. Importantly, whereas *H. vernicosa* normally grows mainly in or at the margins of beech forests, *H. societatis* appears to grow mainly in the short *Chionochloa australis* grassland just near the summit of Mount Murchison. It is a rather inconspicuous plant; often only short portions of the branchlets are visible from among the dense turf of *Chionochloa*. If it is in cultivation, this hebe will only be in one or two specialised collections.

DESCRIPTION: A decumbent, small shrub usually to about 30 cm tall. Branches decumbent or ascending and often unbranched or sparsely branched. Branchlets green or red-brown, internodes 3.5–6.5 mm long, leaf scars evident, bifariously pubescent. Leaf bud with a broad and acute sinus. Leaves more or less distichous, erect to more or less spreading, 9 mm–2.4 cm long by 4–8.5 mm wide, elliptic to obovate, glaucous or glaucescent, upper surface dull, coriaceous and concave, margins not thickened, rounded to slightly bevelled, glabrous or minutely ciliolate, petiole 1–2 mm long. Inflorescences lateral, simple, 1.5–3.5 cm long, longer than the leaves immediately below; peduncle 0.45–0.7 cm long, pubescent, lowermost pair of bracts opposite, then more or less opposite or alternate above, obtuse to subacute, ciliate, suborbicular to deltoid, pedicels shorter than the bracts. Flowers white, on individual plants all hermaphrodite. Calyx tapered at the base, 2.5–3.5 mm long, four-lobed, lobes elliptic, subacute to obtuse, ciliate, margins membranous and sometimes tinged pink, tube glabrous, corolla lobes slightly longer than the tube. Stamen filaments white, anthers purple. Capsule subacute or acute, 3.7–5 mm long by 2.4–3.2 wide, pale brown.

DISTRIBUTION: South Island. Known only from Mount Murchison in the Braeburn Range. Usually grows on the steep, north-east-facing slope just below the summit in low- to subalpine herbfield, mainly in carpet grass or *Chionochloa australis*, at 1450 m.

Hebe speciosa (PLATE 61)
napuka, titirangi

This distinct species is unlikely to be confused with any other. Its broad, rather fleshy, blunt leaves and distinctive flowers readily identify it. Although its showy beetroot-purple flowers are outstanding, it rarely covers itself with flowers, but rather, it has a prolonged display of fewer flowers over many months of the year. It is undeniably a handsome plant, especially as its leaf margins, midribs, and petioles are often coloured red, contrasting well with its dark green leaves. Its flowers are also shown off very well against its foliage. Unfortunately, because of its northern and maritime habitat, this plant is rather frost-tender and will not withstand severe frosts. In the garden it grows equally well in sun or light shade. While it will also tolerate dry conditions quite well, particularly in seaside localities, it is much happier in a moister soil. It has been much used as a parent for the breeding of new cultivars, but its progeny frequently inherit some of its frost tenderness.

In his *Manual of the New Zealand Flora* (1925), Thomas Frederick Cheeseman observed that "all the wild plants that I have seen have the flowers a dark reddish-purple, but in cultivation they frequently become violet-purple." I have also cultivated this species for many years but have never observed any alteration to flower colour. It is very likely that some hybridisation had occurred with the plants Cheeseman observed. The specific name *speciosa* means "beautiful" and refers to the flowers.

Hebe speciosa has apparently always been an uncommon species with a restricted distribution. In fact, it is now regarded as both restricted and endangered. It naturally occurs in scattered localities along the western coast of the North Island and was discovered on the South Hokianga Head by Richard Cunningham in 1834. In 1999 two fieldworkers, E. Ganley and L. Collins, discovered a new population on the Waikato coast to the north of Aotea Harbour. This new population was found at the mouth of the Rengaren (possibly a local mispronunciation of Rengarenga) Stream. The description of the habitat given by its two discoverers provides a valuable insight into the kind of situation where this hebe grows and the conditions that best suit it. They describe the stream as forming a steep-sided gully, extending inland for perhaps 300 m. The hebe plants grow on both sides of the stream, towards its western end. Just to the north of the stream is a coastal cliff that has eroded back to form a steep-sided amphitheatre. *Hebe speciosa* plants are also growing on its steep faces, with a west to south-west aspect and also in the base of the amphitheatre. Both the gully and the amphitheatre are moist due to seepage coming from higher ground. On one side of the stream the hebe grows under an open canopy of *Metrosideros excelsa*, along with various sedges, ferns, and small shrubs. On the other side it grows among *Phormium*, *Pteridium*, *Metrosideros excelsa*, and a variety of other trees. In the amphitheatre the hebe plants grow either in isolation on the steep face or among shrubs and low-growing plants. They also grow along the margins of a small seepage.

DESCRIPTION: A rounded, bushy shrub 60 cm–1.5 m tall. Branches and branchlets leafy, stout, glabrous, length of internodes usually several times the diameter, young branchlets more or less compressed and angled. Leaf bud with a distinct sinus. Leaves 5–10 cm long by 2.5–4.7 cm wide, broad-elliptic to obovate-oblong, on short, thick petioles, apex obtuse, upper surface dark green, usually with a dull sheen, occasionally glossy, coriaceous to rather fleshy, midrib glabrous or pubescent on its upper surface when young, base cuneately narrowed to the petiole or with distinct shoulders, pubes-

Hebe speciosa

cent-edged, margin cartilaginous. Inflorescences lateral, simple, usually exceeding although not much longer than the leaves, up to 4 cm in diameter; peduncle long, stout, finely puberulous. Flowers reddish-purple, tightly placed, pedicels spreading, 1.5–4 mm long, puberulous, exceeding the narrow, ciliolate bracts. Calyx lobes ovate, subacute, ciliolate; corolla tube about 3 mm long and wide, somewhat longer than the calyx, corolla lobes up to 7 mm long, obtuse, finely ciliolate, little spreading. Stamens much exserted, filaments reddish-purple. Capsule up to 8 mm long by 4 mm wide, ovate, acute or subacute, more than twice as long as the calyx lobes.

DISTRIBUTION: North Island. Usually found on sea cliffs or similar sites. The only localities where it is now known to occur are from the south of Hokianga Head, Maunganui Bluff, the Awhitu Peninsula on the north Waikato coast, just to the north of Aotea Harbour, Tongaporutu, Mokau, and Urenui. It is believed that a population at Titirangi Bay in the Marlborough Sounds may have been obtained from the North Island and planted by some of the early Maori residents. A Kapiti Island population probably has a similar origin.

Hebe speciosa 'Variegata'. Exactly like the typical form but with leaves heavily variegated with grey-green and pale grey-green, and margins broadly and irregularly variegated with cream. During colder months the younger leaves become suffused with a deep rosy-pink. One reference book (Harrison 1960) states that this cultivar was recently introduced into New Zealand from England, but this is incorrect, because it appeared in the nursery catalogue of Duncan and Davies as early as 1926. The first reference to it appeared in 1854 when it was mentioned in *The Floricultural Cabinet and Florist's Magazine*. In the nursery trade it is sometimes listed as *H. speciosa* 'Tricolour', but that name has no validity.

Hebe stenophylla (PLATE 62)
kokomuka-taranga, koromiko-taranga
This hebe has been a continual source of puzzlement, particularly for growers, because it is a complex species that includes a number of different forms, ranging from shrubs about a metre tall to those up to 2 m tall or more. For many years it was well known as *Hebe parviflora*, although in earlier times it had also been known as *H. angustifolia* and *H. parviflora* var. *angustifolia*. Later, for a relatively brief period in the 1980s and 1990s, some

botanists claimed it should be called *H. squalida*, a name bestowed by Thomas Kirk in 1896. However, in 1841 it had been named *Veronica stenophylla* by E. C. Steudel, a German botanist. The discovery that the name *H. parviflora* should correctly be applied to another plant altogether (what had been known as *H. parviflora* var. *arborea*) meant that the next most suitable name, *H. stenophylla*, would have to be used. This matter has now been resolved, and so the very narrow-leaved hebe that occurs in central and eastern areas of the North Island, and in Nelson and Marlborough on the South Island, is correctly called *H. stenophylla*, a name which appropriately means "narrow-leaved."

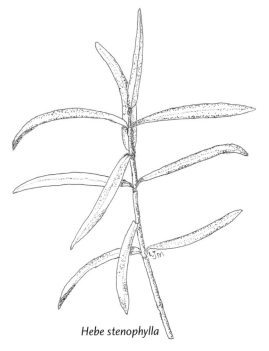

Hebe stenophylla

Hebe stenophylla var. *stenophylla* is the typical form, and there are two other varieties: var. *hesperia*, confined to north-western Nelson, and var. *oliveri*, known only from Stephens Island in Cook Strait. Var. *hesperia* is distinguished by its branchlets being bifariously to uniformly puberulent and by its corolla tube being hairy within; it occurs in near-coastal areas, usually on limestone. Var. *oliveri* is distinguished by its leaves being three to six times as long as broad and by the upper leaf surface having few stomata. It is possible that neither variety is in cultivation.

With its very narrow leaves, usually 3–4 mm wide by up to 5 cm long, *Hebe stenophylla* is a very distinct species that may easily be recognised. Because of its accustomed habitat, it frequently has yellow-green foliage, but cultivated plants are more likely to be medium green. *Hebe stenophylla* flowers at the latter end of the season, usually from late January (mid summer) to February (late summer). During this period, banks and rock faces are adorned with its masses of flowers, especially along roadsides and river valleys in Nelson and parts of Marlborough. Flower colour varies from white to mauve, with flowers fading to white as they age. Some of the mauve forms are quite pretty. Seedlings grown from seed collected from a wild plant that grew in isolation, without any opportunity to hybridise with other species, gave rise to plants having quite a wide range of flower colour, from white, through various shades of mauve, to one or two shades of quite a good light violet. With their violet anthers, the flowers present a very pretty sight. *H. stenophylla* flowers are either hermaphrodite or all female.

DESCRIPTION: A shrub up to 2 m tall or more. Branches generally erect, old stems grey. Branchlets olive-green to reddish-brown, length of internodes eight to fifteen times the width, glabrous or with bifarious pubescence. Leaf bud without a sinus. Leaves 4–8 cm long by 2.5–6.5 mm wide, occasionally wider, spreading to slightly recurved, linear to linear-lanceolate or lanceolate to elliptic, flat or slightly folded; apex acute, base evenly tapered, sessile. Inflorescence simple, peduncle up to 2.1 cm long; raceme 3.5–13 cm long, generally but not always longer than the leaves. Bracts acute or obtuse, ciliate, ovate to deltoid, pedicels varying from much longer than the bracts to about equalling them. Calyx 1.5–2.5 mm long, lobes all similar, obtuse to acute, margins membranous, occasionally tinged pink; corolla lobes usually tinged mauve but fading to white after pollination, obtuse, tube glabrous, white. Anthers red-purple. Capsules acute or obtuse, dark brown.

DISTRIBUTION: In the North Island it occurs particularly in central areas from near Gisborne to Wanganui and the Wairarapa. There is also one isolated occurrence on the northern Waikato River at the Narrows Bridge. In the South Island it occurs in Marlborough and Nelson from Cloudy Bay and the Pelorus River into eastern Nelson and the Buller River to about 33 km above Westport. It also occurs in various locations around the Marlborough Sounds and on D'Urville Island and the Chetwode Islands. It usually grows on cliffs, terraces, or rocky areas, particularly along streams and roadsides. This is mostly a lowland hebe but is found up to about 1200 m in some North Island localities.

Hebe stricta
koromiko

Hebe stricta is a compound species comprising *H. stricta* var. *stricta*, the typical form, and four other varieties. Superficially it resembles *H. salicifolia*, and in the past there was some confusion between the two species. *Hebe salicifolia* is confined to the South Island, and *H. stricta* is confined to the North Island, with the exception of *H. stricta* var. *atkinsonii*, which occurs in not only the southern North Island but also the South Island in the Marlborough Sounds and part of the Marlborough coast. The easiest way of distinguishing between *H. salicifolia* and *H. stricta* is to examine their leaf buds. The leaf bud of *H. salicifolia* has a distinct sinus, whereas with *H. stricta* and its varieties there is no sinus. *Hebe stricta* was probably collected by Joseph Banks and Daniel Solander from one or two localities around the North Island coast during Captain James Cook's first voyage to New Zealand, between 1769 and 1771. At the time they probably gave it the provisional manuscript name of *salicifolia*, because what was later known as *H. salicifolia* was then believed to occur around both the North and South islands. *Hebe stricta* and *H. salicifolia* are both known by the Maori name of koromiko.

Hebe stricta var. stricta

A shrub 2–4 m tall with willow-like leaves and racemes of white flowers in long, drooping racemes 10–24 cm long. It is not reliably hardy in some of the harsher climates of the northern hemisphere, even though it does ascend into montane areas of the North Island; accordingly, it should be grown in a sheltered situation. The growth habit of this species is reflected in its name, *stricta*, which means "erect and very straight."

DESCRIPTION: A rather erect shrub 2–4 m tall. Branchlets green, glabrous, with some purplish colour at the nodal joints. Leaf bud without a sinus. Leaves 5–12 cm long by 1–1.5 cm wide, lanceolate to linear-lanceolate. Inflorescences lateral, simple, 10–24 cm long, peduncle minutely pubescent, pedicels 2–4 mm long, pubescent, bracts narrow, 1–3 mm long, pubescent, ciliolate, acute; calyx green, 2–3 mm long, lobes pubescent, acute. Flowers white, not very densely placed and not hiding the rachis, tube about 4 by 1.5 mm, pubescent inside, corolla about 7 mm in diameter, lobes slightly spreading, obtuse, concave. Filaments about 6 mm long, anthers violet before dehiscing, pollen white. Capsule drooping, 5 by 2.5 mm, subacute.

DISTRIBUTION: North Island. Found in lowland and submontane areas from about the Ruahine Range northwards, commonly on the banks of streams and adjoining areas.

Hebe stricta var. *atkinsonii* (PLATE 63)

Of the varieties of *Hebe stricta* this is the only one to cross Cook Strait and to also grow in the South Island, where it is quite common around the Marlborough Sounds area. Originally it was thought to be a variety of *H. salicifolia*; it was not until 1961 that Lucy Moore finally determined that it was a variety of *H. stricta*. It is distinguished from the other varieties of *H. stricta* by its leaves rarely being acuminate, with only the margins of the calyx lobes and bracts being ciliolate, and by its often more or less erect capsules being glabrous.

Hebe stricta var. *atkinsonii*

DESCRIPTION: An openly branched, quite heavily wooded shrub to 2 m tall or more. Leaves about 5–10 cm long by 1–1.5 cm wide, narrow-elliptic to linear-lanceolate, not usually acuminate, bracts and calyx lobes ciliolate only. Capsules glabrous, often erect.

DISTRIBUTION: In the North Island it grows from about the southern Ruahine Range and Dannevirke southwards, where it is common, especially on banks. In the South Island it grows around the Marlborough Sounds and southwards to the mouth of the Awatere River, where it is often common on road banks.

Hebe stricta var. *egmontiana* (PLATE 64)

This variety occurs on Mount Taranaki (Egmont), after which it is named, and possibly extends eastwards to the East Cape ranges and Ruahine Range. It may be recognised by

Hebe stricta var. *egmontiana*

its closely branched, compact habit and by its linear-lanceolate leaves, which are not glossy on their upper surfaces. Its inflorescences are up to 20 cm long, rather erect, and may stand well clear of the foliage. The flowers are a lovely pure white, and flowering lasts from late summer well into autumn. This variety is not infrequently sold, in New Zealand, under the cultivar name 'Snowcap'; however, there is nothing to suggest that these plants in any way differ from typical *Hebe stricta* var. *egmontiana*. It is more likely that nurserymen did not know its correct identity and coined a cultivar name for it.

DESCRIPTION: A compact, round-headed shrub to 2 or 3 m tall. Branchlets stout, with usually short internodes. Leaves about 6–7 cm long by 8–10 mm wide, linear-lanceolate, tapering evenly from below the middle to a narrow tip, very shortly petioled, petiole yellowish at the base and the colour extending for a short distance up the midrib, firm-textured and smooth, barely shining. Bracts and calyx lobes ciliolate only. Capsule glabrous, erect to spreading.

DISTRIBUTION: North Island, from Mount Taranaki and possibly extending eastwards as far as the Raukumara and Ruahine ranges. Usually grows in subalpine scrub.

Hebe stricta var. *lata*

This mountain species is confined to the ranges of the East Cape area. It differs principally in its lower stature, usually less than one metre tall, being broader than high, and by its short, elliptic, usually glossy leaves. The name is derived either from this plant's broad habit of growth, compared with other varieties of *Hebe stricta*, or possibly (though less likely) from its leaves being broader.

DESCRIPTION: A compact, broad, low-growing shrub mainly less than 1 m tall and usually wider than high. Branchlets stout, with short internodes. Leaves about 5 cm long by 1.5 cm wide, elliptic, firm-textured, glossy. Inflorescences much longer than the leaves. Bracts and calyx lobes ciliolate only. Capsule glabrous, more or less erect.

DISTRIBUTION: North Island. Grows in tall tussock grassland in the Raukumara, Kaweka, and Kaimanawa ranges at 1000–1500 m.

Hebe stricta var. *macroura* (PLATE 65)

Var. *macroura* is quite different from the other varieties of *H. stricta* in having distinctly broader, deep green leaves and in being only a coastal plant. The long, drooping racemes of this handsome, quite wide-spreading hebe are much longer than the leaves and give the plant a fairly distinct appearance. *Hebe stricta* var. *macroura* is relatively hardy but in some areas may be damaged by severe frosts; therefore, it should preferably be grown in a sheltered situation. It is ideal for seaside planting and will withstand dry conditions quite well. The varietal name *macroura* means "long-tailed" and apparently refers to the racemes.

DESCRIPTION: A spreading, much-branched shrub 1–1.4 m tall. Branchlets rather stout, spreading, pale green to yellowish-green, glabrous. Leaf bud without a sinus. Leaves 5–10 cm long by 3–4.5 wide, deep green, spreading, broadly obovate-oblong to obovate-lanceolate or linear-oblong, sessile to more or less sessile, barely coriaceous, apex obtuse to acute, glabrous or with minutely pubescent margins. Inflorescences lateral, simple, longer than the leaves, 5–10 cm long, densely flowered, rachis and pedicels finely pubescent, calyx lobes oblong, obtuse. Flowers small, densely compacted, about 4 mm long, white or pale mauve. Capsule nodding, scarcely twice the length of the calyx.

DISTRIBUTION: North Island from about Hicks Bay, around East Cape, and southwards to about the Mahia Peninsula. Appears to occur mainly along the eastern coast and is usually found on coastal cliffs.

Hebe strictissima (PLATE 66)

This hebe appears to be somewhat similar to shorter-leaved forms of *Hebe stenophylla* but may be distinguished by its corolla tube, which is very short, barely equalling the short, obtuse calyx lobes. It grows to 2 m tall or more and forms quite a wide-spreading shrub. The flowers are white on racemes that are about twice as long as the length of the leaves. *Hebe strictissima* was formerly classified as *H. parviflora* var. *strictissima* and also as *H. leiophylla*. To further confuse the issue, it shows some resemblance to *H. traversii*, to which it is related, but has proved to be quite distinct from that species, as well as from *H. stenophylla*, which it superficially resembles. Since the 1920s it has been known by the name *H. leiophylla*, but specimens collected by Thomas Frederick Cheeseman labelled as *H. leiophylla* cover some 25 herbarium sheets that obviously represent a complex number of specimens that have been collected from a wide range of sources, thus demonstrating that *H. strictissima* is quite a distinct species, while the name *H. leiophylla* should probably be regarded as a synonym of *H. traversii*. *Hebe strictissima* is easily grown, quite hardy, and rather drought-tolerant. The specific name means "very straight" and may refer to the leaves or inflorescences.

DESCRIPTION: A laxly branched to rather stiffly branched shrub to 2 m tall or more. Branchlets rather stiff, glabrous or quite minutely bifariously pubescent, often reddish, length of internodes usually several times the diameter. Leaf bud without a sinus. Leaves erect to spreading, 2–4.5 cm long by 6–8 mm wide, narrow-oblong, more or less coriaceous, light to deep green, upper surface not shining, narrowing more or less abruptly to the apex, margins entire but minutely pubescent. Inflorescence lateral, simple, about twice the length of the leaves; bracts very small, ciliolate, shorter than the pedicels; calyx lobes about 1.5 mm long, obtuse, with a membranous, ciliolate margin. Corolla white, tube wide, equalling or very little longer than the calyx, lobes longer than the tube, rounded. Capsule erect, rather acute, usually glabrous, brown when mature, up to about three times the length of the calyx lobes.

DISTRIBUTION: South Island, where it is confined to Banks Peninsula. Usually grows around the margins of forest or occasionally within the forest itself.

Hebe subalpina (PLATE 67)

This species is common in subalpine scrub in the wetter mountain districts of the South Island. It is closely related to *Hebe traversii*, which differs in its branchlets being glabrous or pubescent but not bifariously so, its stems being smooth and not roughened by the old leaf scars, the leaves being dull and not shining, and its corolla tube being glabrous within. *Hebe subalpina* was discovered on Mount Rangi-Taipo, Westland, by Leonard Cockayne in 1896.

This is a handsome shrub, and it is worth finding a spot for it in the garden. It is reasonably hardy, easily grown, and flowers well in cultivation—in fact, even quite young plants flower freely. Flowering generally occurs from December (summer) to February (late summer). *Hebe subalpina* has the added advantage of growing well in sun or indirect shade. The foliage is shining and deep green, while the flowers are produced in short, crowded racemes towards the tips of the branchlets. It generally grows to about 90 cm tall but in favourable conditions may attain up to 1.5 m. After flowering it should be given a light pruning to maintain its compactness. The specific epithet refers to its subalpine habitat.

DESCRIPTION: Usually a much-branched, rounded shrub, 90 cm–1.5 m tall. Branchlets rather stout, with narrow lines of bifarious pubescence, length of internodes two to three times the diameter, green to purplish. Leaf bud without a sinus. Leaves usually spreading, about 2.5 cm long by 4–8 mm wide (on sheltered plants up to 4 cm long and broader), lanceolate to narrow-elliptic, coriaceous, upper surface shining, pale to deep green, rather dull beneath, apex subacute, only slightly narrowed to their broad bases and more or less sessile, margins smooth and with a very narrow, cartilaginous border. Inflorescences lateral, simple, 2.5–5 cm long, exceeding the leaves, peduncle up to 2.2 cm long, puberulous. Flowers white, crowded and hiding the rachis, pedicels more or less erect, puberulous, more or less equalling or shorter than the narrow, ciliolate bracts. Calyx lobes about 1.5 mm long, narrow, acute and ciliolate, corolla lobes spreading, about 3 mm long, rounded to broad-ovate. Stamens not or little exceeding the tube. Style and ovary glabrous. Capsule about 3 mm long, narrow-ovate, about two and a half times as long as the calyx lobes.

DISTRIBUTION: South Island. Found in the mountains of Westland and those of

Canterbury, which lie within the westerly rainfall, and then extending southwards to Fiordland. Occurs along the banks of streams and in subalpine scrub at 150–1060 m.

Hebe "Swamp" (PLATE 68)

This erect shrub occurs in the Hikurangi Swamp near Whangarei. Because of extensive land drainage and cattle grazing, only a few plants remain in what is left of the swamp scrub-vegetation. This hebe has some affinities with *Hebe stricta* but appears to be a quite distinct species and may have affinities with *H. bishopiana*. Until its proper status has been determined, it will continue to be known by the tag name *H.* "Swamp." It has rather narrow, lanceolate leaves that appear to be almost sessile, and the leaf bud is rather purplish. The flowers open mauve but soon fade to white, giving the raceme an attractive bicoloured effect. Flowering occurs in late summer (January–February). The flowers are faintly scented but cannot be compared with those of *H. salicifolia*. Being a plant of swampy places, *H.* "Swamp" will tolerate quite moist soil conditions, although it will also grow perfectly well in ordinary soils. It appears to be fairly hardy and because of its rather erect habit does not take up an excessive amount of room in the garden.

DESCRIPTION: Erect shrub up to 2–3 m tall. Branchlets minutely and finely pubescent, brownish-green to purplish-green, length of internodes four to six times the diameter. Leaf bud purplish-red, without a sinus. Leaves 6.8–10 cm long by 1–1.5 cm wide, spreading and often quite strongly arcuate, shortly petiolate, lanceolate to linear-lanceolate, upper surface deep green, paler beneath; margins entire, sometimes slightly sinuate, minutely pubescent, apex acute to subacute. Inflorescences lateral, simple, 9–11(–15) cm long including the peduncle, peduncle about 1.5 cm long, rachis and peduncle both finely pubescent, bracts small and much shorter than the pedicels, ciliolate. Flowers closely placed and hiding the rachis, pedicels and calyx pubescent; calyx lobes broad-lanceolate, acute, margins translucent, ciliolate; corolla tube pubescent inside, white, corolla lobes not wide-spreading, obtuse, pale mauve. Style magenta. Filaments pale violet.

DISTRIBUTION: North Island. Appears to be confined to the Hikurangi Swamp in Northland, where it occurs in low swamp scrub-forest. Only a few plants remain in its original habitat.

Hebe tairawhiti (PLATE 69)

This is a relatively newly described species from the eastern coast of the North Island. It was first recognised as a possible new species in the 1940s by Mrs. E. A. Hodgson from Wairoa, near Gisborne, but it was not until 1977 that A. P. Druce provided the first written justification towards recognising it as such. It became known by the tag name *Hebe* "Ahimanu" and was also referred to as *H.* "Wairoa." In 1996 B. D. Clarkson and Phil Garnock-Jones formally described it as a species and gave it the name *tairawhiti*, which is the Maori name for the region where this hebe predominantly occurs.

Hebe tairawhiti is mainly a coastal and lowland shrub occurring principally in coastal, shrub-dominated vegetation on mudstone ridges. It also occurs inland and on a limestone outcrop. It has similarities with the *H. stricta* complex and is found in lowland areas, whereas *H. stricta* var. *lata* and *H. stricta* var. *egmontiana*, which both occur in the eastern coastal region, are separated altitudinally. Possibly the most characteristic feature of this species is the broad yellowish stripe that marks the midribs, making the whole bush very attractive. A further point of note is the minute denticles that occur around the leaf margins. *Hebe tairawhiti* generally flowers from February (late summer) to April (mid autumn), its pale violet flowers soon fading to white. It has become a popular ornamental shrub, especially on account of its distinctive leaf colouration.

DESCRIPTION: A shrub of rather spreading habit, up to about 4.5 m tall. Branchlets yellowish-green, glabrous, length of internodes about 1.5–2.5 cm. Leaves 4–8 cm long by 7–10 mm wide, linear-lanceolate to lanceolate, apex almost acuminate, base abruptly narrowed and almost sessile, upper surface green to yellowish-green, midrib broadly defined by a yellowish stripe, margins with minute denticles. Inflorescences lateral, simple, up to 12 cm long, flowers not densely placed, pale violet soon fading to white, corolla tube long, lobes small and narrow, not wide-spreading, erect to suberect. Capsules dark brown.

DISTRIBUTION: North Island. Known only from the East Cape area from Wairoa to Waihau Bay and inland to the Motu River. Mainly found in coastal areas among shrub-dominated vegetation on mudstone slopes, but also occurs on riverbanks, road cuttings, and a limestone outcrop.

Hebe tetragona

This small-branching shrub generally forms a rounded, flat-topped bush from 30 to 90 cm tall but may be less than 30 cm depending on where it is growing. Its rather stout, erect branches are densely clad with closely appressed, scale-like leaves, thus giving the appearance of a small conifer. The leaves are in opposite pairs and give the branchlets a distinctly four-angled appearance. Consequently, *Hebe tetragona* is rather distinct among the whipcord hebes. It is a fine little shrub, especially for the front of a border or similar situation. As with most other whipcord species, in cultivation it prefers a soil that does not become too dry, although it will withstand some dryness for limited periods. It is not commonly cultivated in New Zealand, the United Kingdom, or Europe. Graham Hutchins (1997) considers it to be the least hardy of the whipcord hebes in the United Kingdom.

Hebe tetragona is confined to the North Island from Mount Hikurangi southwards to the northern end of the Ruahine Range, and along with *H. hectori* subsp. *subsimilis* is one of only two whipcord hebes to occur in the North Island. In recent years some botanists have tended to lump some of the South Island whipcord hebes in with *H. tetragona*, a view which may yet prevail, although the jury is still out on that particular verdict.

Interestingly, when John Carne Bidwill ascended Mount Ngauruhoe in 1839 he collected specimens of *Hebe tetragona*, believing it to be a species of conifer and little knowing that it actually belonged to *Hebe* (or *Veronica*, as the genus was then called). The story of its discovery is detailed under "The Discovery of Hebes" in Chapter 1. The specific name *tetragona* means "four-angled" and refers to the shape of its branchlets.

DESCRIPTION: A small, erect, much-branched shrub 15–90 cm tall. Branches stout, rigid, erect and bluntly four-angled. Branchlets 2.5–4 mm in diameter, yellow-green to deep green, internodes short and hidden, leaf tips usually much overlapping, nodal joint well marked. Leaves 2–2.5 mm long, joined at their bases, deltoid to deltoid-ovate, thick and coriaceous, backs keeled, apexes bluntly pointed, smooth and shining, margins ciliolate. Inflorescences of up to 12 flowers, forming a terminal head or spike, flowers white, sessile, bracts about 3 mm long, ovate to ovate-lanceolate, acute, ribbed or furrowed. Calyx to 3 mm long, lobes unequal, ovate-oblong, obtuse or subacute, ribbed; corolla tube shorter than the calyx lobes, corolla lobes spreading. Capsule about 3 mm long, obtuse to subacute, oval, longer than the calyx lobes.

DISTRIBUTION: North Island. Found from Mount Hikurangi south to Mounts Tongariro and Ruapehu, and from there southwards to the northern end of the Ruahine Range. Generally occurs in subalpine scrub and tussock grassland at 600–1500 m.

Hebe tetrasticha (PLATE 70)

This little gem of a species is mostly found on alpine rocks in the drier regions of the Southern Alps. In its natural habitat it usually wedges itself into a rock crevice where its roots can descend deeply and remain cool under all conditions. It is rather similar to *Hebe cheesemanii* but differs mainly in its branchlets, which are more cross-shaped than square when viewed from the growing tip or in cross section. In addition, the profile of the branchlet angles is not nearly as smooth as with *H. cheesemanii*. *Hebe tetrasticha* is one of four species belonging to the informal group "Semiflagriformes." While it is hardy, it is not always regarded as a satisfactory garden plant, possibly because of how it reacts to excessive summer warmth. However, it is excellent as a container-grown specimen, with greater control maintained over its growing conditions, and gardeners in cooler parts of the northern hemisphere may find it more satisfactory. It prefers growing conditions similar to those required for *H. cheesemanii*. The specific name *tetrasticha* means "arranged in four rows," referring to the tightly compacted leaves and branchlets with their four-angled appearance. Julius Haast first collected this species in 1862 in the Canterbury Alps, very likely on the Torlesse Range, and he may well have been accompanied by either John Francis Armstrong or Joseph Beattie Armstrong.

DESCRIPTION: A small, compact, usually rounded shrub to 20 cm tall and 20–30 cm across. Branchlets about 2.5 mm in diameter, grooved or concave down each face of the branchlet. Leaves densely crowded, about 1.5 by 1 mm, triangular about their broad bases, tips sharp but not acute, margins with short, stiff cilia. Inflorescences about 5 mm long, often hiding the tips of the branchlets, flowers white, male and female on separate plants or occasionally perfect.

DISTRIBUTION: South Island. Confined to the drier eastern ranges of Canterbury, where it is found in subalpine to high-alpine regions at 800–1800 m. Usually grows on rock faces and bluffs. Occasionally also found on ledges and in loose, stony debris.

Hebe topiaria (PLATE 71)

This is one of the most popular of the smaller-leaved hebes. It has a very neat, ball-shaped habit of growth, often rather flattish on top, which gives it the appearance of having been clipped—hence the name *topiaria*, which refers to its topiary-like appearance. In cultivation it maintains its appearance even if regular pruning has been neglected, and only begins to lose its neatness when it becomes fairly old. Its glaucous or blue-grey leaves are another of its good features. It does not appear to flower well until it is relatively old, and very young plants seldom flower at all, while older bushes produce only a few flowers; in spite of that, however, most gardeners value this hebe. Though valuable as a single specimen, it is even more effective when planted in a group of several plants. It usually flowers during November (early summer) and December (summer).

Hebe topiaria has rather variable foliage as regards shape, size, and colour, some forms being far more glaucous than others. Gardeners have not yet exploited these variations, however, and so far only about two variants (both similar) are commonly cultivated. One form that I have collected from the Arthur Range has very glaucous leaves that are larger than is usual for other cultivated forms of this species. It is a very good garden plant. *Hebe topiaria* was originally collected from the Mount Arthur Tableland, Nelson, by F. G. Gibbs in the early part of the 20th century.

DESCRIPTION: A much-branched, compact shrub of rounded habit, 70 cm–1.2 m tall. Branchlets bifariously and rather coarsely pubescent, greyish, length of internodes one to two times the diameter. Leaf bud without a sinus. Leaves more or less spreading, tending to overlap and hide the upper part of the stem, about 1.2 cm long by 6–8 mm wide, broad-elliptic to almost obovate, more or less concave, apex subacute, shortly petiolate and gradually tapering to a broad base, fleshy and coriaceous, glaucous on both surfaces, margins entire. Inflorescences lateral, simple, crowded near the tips of the branchlets and little exceeding them, 1.5–2 cm long, peduncle up to 1.5 cm long, hidden, shortly hairy. Flowers usually white, densely placed and hiding the rachis, more or less erect; bracts 1–1.5 mm long, ciliolate and usually about equal to the pedicels; calyx lobes 1.5–2 mm long, rather broad, obtuse to subacute, membranous, border very narrow, ciliolate. Corolla tube broad, longer than the calyx, lobes about equalling the tube, rounded. Capsule erect, subacute, glabrous, about twice as long as the calyx.

DISTRIBUTION: South Island. From the mountains of Nelson to the Amuri Pass in north Canterbury. Occurs in subalpine scrub, shrubland, and tussock grassland at 1000–1450 m.

Hebe townsonii (PLATE 72)

This very distinct and easily recognised species is probably not as well known in gardens as it could be. It has a rather erect habit of growth but is mainly distinguished by the two lines of slit-shaped or oblique domatia that are clearly visible on the undersides of the leaves, fairly close to the leaf margins. This character, which can be seen quite easily with the naked eye, is not found in any other hebe, and so there can be no mistaking this species for another. In the garden it will grow to about 1–1.2 m tall and thrives in either full sun or partial shade. The flowers are rather loosely arranged on the inflorescence, which tends to give this species a more graceful appearance than some others. With their sharply pointed corolla lobes, the flowers also have a very dainty appearance. They are pale mauve but quickly fade to white. Generally, flowering occurs from mid September (spring) to early November (early summer). In the colder parts of the northern hemisphere, this hebe is not fully hardy and may need to be grown in a slightly sheltered position. After flowering it should be given a light pruning to remove the old flower heads and encourage the production of new growth. A well-grown bush in full flower is really a fine sight. *Hebe townsonii* is named after W. Townson, a botanist who was quite active in the Westport region of southern Nelson during the latter part of the 19th century.

DESCRIPTION: An erect, bushy shrub 90 cm–2.1 m tall or more. Branchlets glabrous, length of internodes three to four times the diameter, yellowish-green. Leaf bud with a distinct sinus. Leaves more or less spreading to ascending, 3.2–7.8 cm long by 4–10 mm wide, linear-lanceolate, apex acute to subacute, dark to bright green, upper surface shining, paler beneath and with a single row of short, oblique domatia just within the margin, coriaceous, petioles short and up to about 3 mm long, margins entire and slightly revolute. Inflorescences lateral, simple, exceeding the leaves, up to 11.2 cm long; peduncle 1.2–2.5 cm long, glabrous or slightly puberulous. Flowers white to pale mauve soon fading to white, loosely placed and not hiding the rachis, pedicels ascending to more or less spreading, up to 7 mm long, slightly puberulous, usually shorter than the narrow, ciliolate bracts; calyx glabrous, lobes to 4 mm long, ciliolate; corolla tube about 3 mm long, shorter than the calyx lobes, corolla lobes wide-spreading, about 8 mm long, oblong or ovate-oblong, acute. Stamens much exserted but not longer than the corolla lobes. Capsule erect, about 4 mm long by 3 mm wide, acute, usually less than twice the length of the calyx.

DISTRIBUTION: In the North Island, occurs on Mount Messenger in North Taranaki. In the South Island, occurs from Mount Burnett, near Collingwood, to the rocky hills between the little Whanganui and Mokohinui rivers north of Westport, and southwards from there to the Fox River near Tiromoana. Usually grows on limestone rocks.

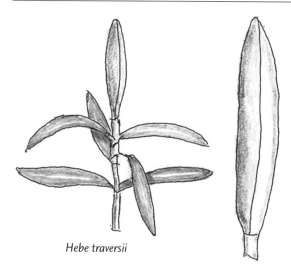

Hebe traversii

Hebe traversii

Another somewhat smaller-leaved species that has affinities with *Hebe stenophylla* and *H. strictissima*. It differs from the former in its narrow-oblong (not linear-lanceolate) leaves, which are more than 5 mm wide, and from the latter in its corolla tube, which is longer than both the calyx and corolla lobes. It is quite a hardy species and able to withstand fairly cold conditions, although soft late growth may be injured by early frosts. It has lightish green leaves, and its inflorescences of white flowers are about 4 cm long or more. It commonly grows along banks and streamsides and in the garden will prefer a moist soil. This species was named by J. D. Hooker in honour of W. T. L. Travers, who extensively botanised the alpine vegetation of the South Island, particularly of its northern half. He collected *H. traversii* in the Hurunui Mountains, probably sometime in the late 1850s.

DESCRIPTION: A loosely branched shrub to about 2 m tall. Branchlets rather slender, glabrous to finely pubescent, length of internodes two to six times the diameter, leaf scars becoming inconspicuous with age, older branches usually being smooth and grey. Leaf bud without a sinus. Leaves spreading, about 2–2.5 cm long by 4–7 mm wide, narrow-oblong, more or less coriaceous, yellowish-green, glabrous except for some minute pubescence near the base of the upper surface and on the upper margins, apex narrowing rather abruptly to a subacute tip but narrowing only slightly to the base, margins entire. Inflorescences lateral, simple, about twice as long as the leaves, peduncle short, finely pubescent; bracts less than 1 mm long, ciliolate and usually much shorter than the pedicels. Calyx lobes 1–1.5 mm long, broad, obtuse, ciliolate on their pale, membranous borders. Corolla white, tube about 3 mm long, narrow, hairy within, lobes rounded, shorter than the tube. Capsule more or less erect, 4–5 mm long, narrowly oval, flat and pale brown when mature, up to four times as long as the calyx lobes.

DISTRIBUTION: South Island, from Marlborough to mid Canterbury. Usually grows along streams and on banks at 150–1000 m.

Hebe treadwellii (PLATE 73)

This is a most distinct species that appears to be quite dissimilar to any other species, and certainly as applied to cultivated material. It is quite prostrate and, as a garden plant, will soon spread to cover a metre or more. The medium green leaves are elliptic and slightly pointed, and in their younger stages are rather concave. At first the young leaves are more or less erect and cupped around each other, but as they age they gradually become much more spreading. On older stems the leaf scars are quite distinct. The rather dumpy inflorescences tend to be hidden by the foliage, and the white flowers appear in late spring with occasional flowers continuing well into the summer. *Hebe treadwellii* is very drought-tolerant and will endure very dry conditions without appearing to show any distress. With its prostrate habit and

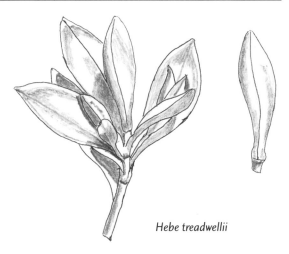

Hebe treadwellii

lively medium green foliage, it makes an excellent ground cover and is well worth growing. It was originally collected in the Mount Cook area and is named in honour of a Mr. Treadwell of Wellington.

Though now recognised as a valid species, *Hebe treadwellii* was for many years regarded as a doubtful species (*incertae sedis*) and as a consequence did not appear in cultivated collections. Then, in the late 1990s, a party of botanists discovered an interesting plant on Bald Knob Ridge, north-western Nelson, that they believed to be *H. matthewsii*, a species from the Humboldt Mountains of Otago. *Hebe matthewsii* had not again been collected since it was discovered around the beginning of the 20th century. This plant from Bald Knob Ridge was subsequently identified as *H. treadwellii*. Material from the Nelson plant is quite common in cultivation under its tag name, *H.* "Bald Knob Ridge," but growers now must accustom themselves to referring to it as *H. treadwellii*.

DESCRIPTION: A prostrate little shrub eventually spreading to 1 m or more across and occasionally mounding up to about 15 cm. Branchlets rather stout, internodes one to two times the diameter, green with bifarious pubescence. Leaf bud without a sinus. Leaves closely placed, 2.0–2.8 cm long by 10–13 mm wide, tapering to a broad base, upper surface medium to deep green and somewhat shining, a little paler beneath, apex obtuse to subacute. Inflorescences about 3 cm long including the peduncle of up to 12 mm. Flowers white, corolla tube longer than the calyx lobes (about twice as long), corolla lobes wide-spreading, obtuse to subacute, corolla about 7–8 mm in diameter. Anthers yellow. Style longer than the stamens. Capsules ovoid, about 6 mm long, acute.

DISTRIBUTION: South Island. Found from the Victoria Range in southern Nelson, the Doubtful River and north Canterbury, the Sealy Range, Mount Cook, and the ranges of southern Westland, from about the Wilberg Range to about the Olivine Range. Usually occurs in stony ground in subalpine shrubland and tussock grassland.

Hebe truncatula

This species is confined to the mountains of western Hawkes Bay, where it grows around forest margins. It is a tallish shrub, up to about 2.5 m tall, although generally less than that. In cultivation it has rather narrow leaves, usually no more than 4 cm long. It is quite uncommon in cultivation, especially outside New Zealand. In the garden it tends to have a flattish top, and its inflorescences of white flowers are not greatly longer than the leaves. *Hebe truncatula* is somewhat similar to *H. evenosa* but differs in its subacute leaves being elliptic rather than obovate to oval and broadly obtuse. The leaves of *H. truncatula* are also mostly longer than 2 cm, whereas those of *H. evenosa* are generally less than 2 cm long. The specific name refers to the minutely truncated or abruptly ended apexes of the leaves. This species was discovered on the eastern side of the Ruahine Range sometime during the latter part of the 19th century.

DESCRIPTION: A flat-topped shrub to 2.5 m tall, usually much-branched from the base. Branchlets completely and minutely pubescent, length of internodes one to three times their diameter. Leaves more or less spreading, 2–4 cm long by 5–10 mm wide, elliptic-oblong, upper surface shining, paler beneath, glabrous except for some very minute pubescence on the upper side of the midrib and in a narrow band along the margins, apex minutely truncated. Inflorescences lateral, simple, slender, 5–6 cm long, and when in flower not much longer than the leaves but elongating in fruit, peduncles about 1 cm long. Bracts ciliolate, equalling or shorter than the pedicels; calyx lobes 1.5–2 mm long, obtuse to subacute, ciliolate on their pale borders. Corolla white, tube about equalling the calyx, lobes about 2.5 by 1.5 mm, rounded. Capsule erect, about 4 by 2.5 mm, more or less pointed.

DISTRIBUTION: North Island, where it is confined to the Ruahine Range. Usually occurs at or just within forest margins.

Hebe tumida (PLATE 74)

Hebe tumida is the fourth species in the informal group "Semiflagriformes." In cultivation it is a most attractive little shrub for a rock garden or for growing in a container in an alpine house. In general appearance it is similar to *H. tetrasticha* and *H. cheesemanii* but differs in its branchlets being almost square, rather than cross-shaped, when viewed in cross section. It also differs from *H. tetrasticha* in its projecting leaf tips being blunt and swollen rather than thin and flattened, and its branchlets are generally a brighter green. As a garden plant *H. tumida* forms a very neat, compact, bun-shaped shrub about 10 cm tall, with old plants as much as about 30 cm wide. The older leaves are a deep green, while those at the growing tips are brighter, giving the plant quite a lively appearance. It is easily grown in a gritty, well-drained soil and prefers a sunny or slightly shaded situation. In a good season its white flowers liberally stud the bush. As with the other members of this group, male and female flowers are on separate plants. The specific name *tumida* means "swollen" and refers to the leaf tips.

DESCRIPTION: A prostrate or trailing little shrub forming compact patches up to about 10 cm tall and 10–25 cm wide or more. Branchlets leafy, 1.5–2 mm in diameter, tetragonous, but serrate rather than smooth in profile because of its projecting leaf tips. Leaves closely and densely imbricated, 1.5 by 1.5–2 mm, shortly and bluntly deltoid above their rather narrow bases, tumid and rounded particularly towards their tips, upper surface of the blade concave where it fits against the back of the next leaf, margins with blunt, inconspicuous cilia. Inflorescences emerge from just below the growing tips and overtopping them, up to about 12 mm long; peduncle about 2 mm long; flowers in rather loose heads, white, pedicels about 1 mm long; calyx lobes 2.5–3 mm long; corolla tube equalling the calyx, narrow, lobes 3 by 2 mm, male and female flowers sometimes less distinct than those of *Hebe cheesemanii* and *H. tetrasticha*. Capsules 3.5 by 2 mm, narrowed towards their tips.

DISTRIBUTION: Confined to the drier mountains of eastern Nelson as well as western and southern Marlborough. Usually grows on rock ledges and in crevices in snow tussock–herbfield and fellfield in low- to high-alpine habitats, 1100–1700 m. Also occasionally found in stabilised, fine debris.

Hebe urvilleana (PLATE 75)

This species is related to *Hebe subalpina*, *H. fruticeti*, *H. evenosa*, and *H. traversii* and bears some similarities to them. In the garden it forms a rounded shrub to 1 or 1.5 m tall with smallish, elliptic or elliptic-oblong leaves usually to about 2–2.5 cm long. When in flower it is quite attractive, as the flowers are a very pale mauve fading to white and give the inflorescences a bicoloured appearance. It is easily grown, very drought-tolerant, and hardy. Its specific name derives from the fact that it was originally found on D'Urville Island in the Marlborough Sounds. It was first collected there by W. R. B. Oliver in 1943 and named a distinct species in 1944. It has since been found on the adjoining mainland near the island.

DESCRIPTION: A loosely branched to more compact shrub to 1.5 m tall. Branchlets slender to rather stout, green to yellowish-green, bifariously pubescent with dark hairs especially when young, leaf scars remaining obvious for some time, length of internodes about three times the diameter. Leaf bud without a sinus or with only a small, roundish sinus. Leaves elliptic to elliptic-oblong, 1–2.5 cm long by 4–9 mm wide, upper surface yellowish-green, dull or with a slight sheen, lower surface only slightly paler, apex subacute, base abruptly narrowed to a short petiole, margins entire, bevelled and cartilaginous. Inflorescences lateral, simple, up to 4 cm long, usually about twice the length of the leaves, peduncle about 1.5 cm long; bracts shorter than the pedicels. Calyx lobes about 1–1.5 mm long, obtuse to subacute. Corolla tube rather narrow, about one and a half times the length of the calyx and about equalling the lobes. Capsule erect, glabrous, broadly ovate, about twice the length of the calyx.

DISTRIBUTION: South Island. Originally confined to D'Urville Island but more recently found on some adjoining parts of the mainland of Marlborough Sounds.

Hebe venustula (PLATE 76)

This is one of the "box-leaved" species. In foliage it rather resembles *Hebe odora* (called boxwood for its resemblance to *Buxus*), and its rounded, ball-like habit of growth heightens that illusion. However, botanically the two species are actually quite widely separated. The leaf bud of *H. venustula* has a long, narrow sinus instead of the shield-shaped sinus so typical of the leaf bud of *H. odora*. Sometimes its inflorescences may be branched and have one to two pairs of side branches. It can be an extremely floriferous shrub and is well worth a place in the garden, particularly if one of the forms with mauve flowers can be obtained. It usually flowers between December (summer) and February (late summer). It may grow to a height of 1.5–1.8 m but can be kept to a smaller size if pruned immediately after flowering. *Hebe venustula* is quite hardy and not difficult to grow. The specific name means "handsome" or "charming" and is a diminutive from *venustus*, which has similar meanings and is derived from the Greek goddess Venus. It was discovered on the eastern side of the Ruahine Range by A. Olson in 1893. Several cultivars have been named and described, but it is difficult to state just how distinct they are from each other and how garden-worthy they might be.

DESCRIPTION: An erect, bushy shrub 90 cm–1.5 m tall or more. Branchlets yellowish-green, bifariously puberulous, length of internodes one to two times the diameter. Leaf bud with a long, narrow sinus. Leaves spreading or sometimes more or less arranged in the one plane, 8–17 mm long by 5–8 mm wide, elliptic-oblong to obovate-oblong or ovate-oblong, apex acute to slightly apiculate, petioles short and thick, glabrous, upper surface bright green and somewhat shining, paler beneath, margins entire, somewhat bevelled and with minute hairs. Inflorescences lateral, simple or with one or two pairs of branches, crowded towards the tips of the branchlets and hiding the terminal growth, peduncle shorter than the leaves, sparingly pubescent. Flowers white or pale violet, closely placed and more or less hiding the rachis, pedicels ascending, up to 2 mm long, sparingly puberulous to almost glabrous, equalling or slightly exceeding the narrow, ciliolate bracts; calyx glabrous, lobes about 2.5 mm long, narrow-ovate, more or less acute to obtuse, margins white, ciliolate; corolla tube rather broad, pubescent inside, much longer than the calyx lobes, corolla lobes spreading, about equalling the tube, ovate, obtuse. Stamens exserted, longer than the corolla lobes. Capsule about 4 mm long, ovate or ovate-oblong.

DISTRIBUTION: North Island. Found in mountain areas from Mount Hikurangi, near the East Cape, to the Volcanic Plateau and then southwards to Cape Palliser, but not known from the Tararua Range. Usually grows in subalpine scrub at 760–1500 m. It has been recorded from the Nelson mountains, but that has not been verified.

Hebe venustula '**Mount Hikurangi**'. Described as a form with rather larger leaves and pale blue flowers, usually with five petals. Selected by Graham Hutchins from material originally collected from Mount Hikurangi.

Hebe venustula '**Patricia Davies**'. Named by Hutchins. It was originally known as *H. venustula* 'Pale Blue', but after one or two other cultivars of this species were brought into cultivation, Hutchins decided the plant should have a distinguishing name and called it 'Patricia Davies' after the botanical artist who illustrated his book on hebes. The flowers are very pale lilac-blue to almost white.

Hebe venustula '**Ruapehu**'. Named from a form of this species collected from Mount Ruapehu by Hutchins in 1990. White-flowered and about 1 m tall.

Hebe venustula '**Sky Blue**'. Discovered on the Ruahine Range prior to 1974 by S. White of Parva Plants Tauranga. It appears to be fairly typical of *H. venustula*, its flowers a slightly deeper pale violet-blue. Young plants do not appear to flower quite as freely as those of some other forms of this species.

Hebe venustula '**Violet Profusion**'. Similar to the typical form of the species, with quite good violet-blue flowers. It was named from an old plant of unknown provenance growing in the Christchurch Botanic Gardens, New Zealand. A very good cultivar.

Hebe vernicosa (PLATE 77)

Hebe vernicosa is easily recognised because of its usually open, rather spreading habit of growth; its shining, bright green leaves that are generally inclined in the one plane; its leaf bud, with its long, narrow sinus; and its lateral inflorescences, which are crowded towards the tips of the branchlets so as to give the impression that they are terminal. Its growth habit can be somewhat variable, as can the height to which it grows. With its graceful, spreading form and bright green foliage, this hebe can be a most attractive garden plant. As an added bonus it generally flowers very well, even at a young age. It is a hardy species and, if one of the smaller-growing forms is available, makes a most useful shrub for gardens with limited space. It usually flowers between mid October (mid spring) and mid November (early summer), and sometimes to mid February (mid to late summer). It is most often found within *Nothofagus* forests and will grow in full sun or light shade. The specific epithet *vernicosa* means "polished" or "varnished," quite an appropriate name considering this plant's shining leaves. *Hebe vernicosa* was discovered in the upper Wairau River valley, Nelson, by a Dr. Munro in 1854.

DESCRIPTION: A usually erect or sometimes low-growing shrub 90 cm–2 m tall. In open situations its main branches grow more or less horizontally, but in forest situations they are generally more erect. Branchlets greenish to purplish, bifariously or fully pubescent, length of internodes one to two times the diameter. Leaf bud with a long, narrow sinus. Leaves spreading, those on the undersides of the branchlets usually twisted on their petioles so that they all appear to lie in the one plane, 1.1–1.6 cm long by 7–8 mm wide, elliptic to obovate, upper surface bright green and shining or glossy, lower surface bright green but not glossy, glabrous, rather coriaceous, glabrous, apex subacute, margins entire and sometimes ciliolate towards the base. Inflorescences lateral, simple, 2.8–5 cm long, much exceeding the leaves and sometimes hiding the growing tip; peduncle short, puberulous. Flowers white, fairly closely placed and almost hiding the rachis, pedicels very short, in the axils of the lanceolate, ciliolate bracts. Calyx lobes up to about 1.5 mm long, usually obtuse, ciliolate. Corolla lobes spreading, up to about 4 mm long, ovate, obtuse. Capsule erect, about three times the length of the calyx lobes, glabrous, not very acuminate.

DISTRIBUTION: South Island. Occurs in Marlborough and eastern Nelson provinces and the western Amuri District of north Canterbury. Found commonly on the floors of *Nothofagus* forests where it grows as an understory shrub. Occasionally grows on rocky banks in more open situations. Sea level to the timber line.

8

Hebe Cultivars

This chapter covers most of the horticulturally valuable hybrids and cultivars not directly assigned to a species. Flowering times and months given apply to the southern hemisphere unless otherwise stated. Seasonal equivalents are provided where there may be doubt. For example, a plant that blooms in December in New Zealand is said to bloom in early summer.

Hebe 'Alicia Amherst' (PLATE 78)
This older cultivar dates back to the early days of the 20th century. It is a hybrid from *Hebe speciosa* but its other parent is unknown. It is known for its broad (up to 5 cm wide), handsome, deep green leaves and bold racemes of deep purple flowers. It forms a robust bush 1–1.5 m tall and as much across. Its main disadvantage is that it is not particularly hardy and may be damaged by severe frosts, which can cause the bark of the stems to split. The flower racemes are quite plump and up to 16 cm long. Flowering occurs from May (late autumn) to October (mid spring), with a second flowering usually occurring during late summer and early autumn. This cultivar is named after Alicia Amherst (1865–1941), author and collector of plants from various countries, and wife of Sir Evelyn Cecil (Baron Rockley).

Hebe 'Amanda Cook'
A branch sport from *Hebe* 'Autumn Glory'. The foliage is variegated, with variable yellow margins, and flushed with pink when young. In all other respects this cultivar is similar to its parent and has the same rather deep violet flowers. It is inclined to produce green reversion shoots, which should be removed as soon as they appear. It has been described as an eye-catching plant for fans of variegated shrubs. Sometimes incorrectly called *H.* 'Amanda'.

Hebe 'Amy' (PLATE 79)
This fairly erect shrub grows to 90 cm tall or more and is valued for its dark purple stems and shining foliage, which is flushed with purple when young, especially during colder weather. Its flowers are also a rich violet-blue. Flowering is from about mid summer to autumn. This hebe is not completely hardy. *Hebe* 'Amy' was apparently introduced by

Treseder's Nursery in Truro, Cornwall, United Kingdom, sometime during the 1960s. It has had a variety of names, including "Lady Ardilaun," "Lady Amy," and "Ruth." Its origin has been attributed to Ireland, and it is believed to have been named after Lady Ardilaun. Unfortunately, Lady Ardilaun's first name was not Amy, and there is no evidence to indicate that this cultivar actually originated from her home at St. Anne's Gardens, Dublin. Although not completely hardy, I have seen it actually flourishing and obviously undamaged in an ordinary suburban garden in Edinburgh, Scotland.

Hebe ×*andersonii* 'Andersonii' (PLATE 80)

An old favourite that has been around for many years and remains a very good large hebe for the garden. It was probably the first artificial hybrid between two native New Zealand plants and was raised by Isaac Anderson-Henry of Maryfield, near Edinburgh, Scotland, sometime prior to 1849. The male parent is *Hebe speciosa*. The female parent, formerly known as *Veronica lindleyana*, was at one time thought to be the South Island *H. salicifolia* but is now known to be the North Island *H. stricta*. In suitable climates there is hardly a time of year when flowers cannot be seen on this hebe, with the main flowering occurring in mid summer. Like so many of the larger hebes, however, *H.* ×*andersonii* 'Andersonii' does not give its best flowering until it has attained some degree of maturity.

Hebe ×*andersonii* 'Andersonii' has been a long-time favourite with gardeners and nurserymen, and inevitably, over the years, seedlings from it have been raised in various establishments and given names. Mostly they resemble the parent but differ in various ways. They are all quite tolerant of seaside conditions, usually have a long flowering period, and are quite attractive large shrubs. Some of the main offspring are *H.* 'Anne Pimm', *H.* 'Gran's Favourite', *H.* 'Mauvena', *H.* 'Midsummer Beauty', and *H.* 'Miss Fittall'.

DESCRIPTION: A wide-spreading shrub when mature, grows to about 2.5 m tall. Branchlets puberulous when young, length of internodes four to five times the diameter. Leaves deep green, up to 11 cm long by 2–3.5 cm wide, ovate-lanceolate to oblong-lanceolate, apex subacute to more or less obtuse, glabrous except for the midrib and petiole, both of which are puberulous on both surfaces. Leaf bud with a small sinus. Inflorescence lateral, simple and exceeding the leaves, 11–17 cm long by about 2.8 cm in diameter, peduncle puberulous, 2–3.2 cm long, flowers violet, fading with age and almost hiding the rachis. Pedicels 2–4 mm long, spreading, puberulous, calyx lobes ciliolate; corolla tube about 2 mm long, little exceeding the calyx lobes, corolla lobes 3–4 mm long, oblong, obtuse, spreading. Stamens exserted, filaments violet.

Hebe ×*andersonii* 'Andersonii Aurea' (PLATE 81)

This cultivar has the general characters and dimensions of *Hebe* ×*andersonii* 'Andersonii Variegata', but the margins of the leaves are irregularly variegated with a brighter cream to yellow, and the central portion of the leaf is mainly green. It is said to be a little more hardy than 'Andersonii Variegata'.

Hebe ×*andersonii* 'Andersonii Variegata' (PLATE 82)

A variegated version of the typical form. Because of its variegation, it is perhaps not as vigorous, but otherwise its general dimensions and flower colour are like those of *Hebe* ×*andersonii* 'Andersonii'. Its leaves are variegated with dark green and shades of grey-green with a creamy-white margin. It is a handsome shrub and does not lose its attractiveness even when in a flush of growth. Occasionally it can be a little prone to producing plain green reversion shoots, which should be pruned off as soon as they appear. This cultivar originated quite early and was mentioned in *The Gardeners' Chronicle* at least as early as 1856.

Hebe 'Autumn Glory'

Although quite an old cultivar, 'Autumn Glory' has, unfortunately, suffered a certain amount of misnaming from nurserymen. It is sometimes called "Autumn Gem," and in New Zealand some nurseries insist on calling it "Autumn Beauty." It originated at Tobacorran, Whiteabbey, in County Antrim, Northern Ireland, where it was found as a seedling when the grounds were being renovated during the early part of the 19th century. *Hebe* 'Autumn Glory' is distinguished by its low habit of growth, being no more than 45–60 cm tall, by its dark purplish stems with leaves that vary from green to a mixture of greyish-green, and by its short, crowded racemes of violet flowers. It flowers from mid December (summer) till mid January (mid summer) and then usually intermittently until April (mid autumn). It is reasonably hardy, although it may sometimes be damaged by severe frost, and in certain conditions the young growths may be attacked by downy mildew.

Hebe 'Baby Marie'

A small hebe to about 40 cm tall with green to purplish stems and small leaves that are usually about 6–8 by 3–4 mm. The leaf bud has a narrow sinus. Its flowers are produced in short racemes, 1–2 cm long, arising from just below the terminal growth. They are pale lilac and quite showy. This cultivar was for many years known as *H. buxifolia* 'Nana', and once it was realised that it was of hybrid origin it became necessary to give it a suitable name. Accordingly, it was given the name of 'Baby Marie'. Its pale lilac flowers immediately suggest its hybrid origin.

Hebe 'Barnettii'

A very satisfactory hebe for the garden. Its ball-like habit of growth and attractive, very glaucous foliage make it a particularly striking shrub, especially when grown with something of a contrasting colour. It usually flowers abundantly, which further adds to its attractions. Flowering usually commences about mid summer.

Hebe 'Barnettii' is of unknown origin. It is perhaps closest to *H. albicans* and indeed may prove to be a form of that species. It bears some resemblance to plants of *H. albicans* that grow on Takaka Hill (Nelson) but is quite distinct from them. It also comes true from seed. This cultivar is named after M. J. Barnett, a former director of parks in Christchurch, New Zealand. Barnett was known to have collected in north Canterbury, southern Marlborough, as well as other parts of the South Island with plant collectors such as Leonard Cockayne, and this cultivar very likely originated from one of the areas where they collected. Should it prove to be a form of *H. albicans*, it would then have to be known as *H. albicans* 'Barnettii'.

DESCRIPTION: A much-branched, rounded shrub 60–90 cm tall. Branchlets minutely puberulous, length of internodes two to two and a half times the diameter. Leaf bud without a sinus. Leaves spreading, 1.4–2 cm long by 5–9 mm wide, sessile. Leaf blade narrow-elliptic to elliptic-oblong, gradually narrowed to a rather broad base, apex subacute, upper surface strongly glaucous, lower surface slightly less so. Inflorescence lateral, simple, 2–5 cm long and 2–2.5 cm wide, crowded at the tips of the branchlets, flowers white, densely placed. Stamens much exserted.

Hebe 'Beatrice'

This hebe grows to about 60 cm tall, with glabrous, greenish stems that are purplish around the nodes. The leaf bud sinus is small and indistinct. Leaves are green and about 3 cm long by 7 mm wide. Inflorescences are 6–10 cm long, occasionally branched. Flowers are white to pale lilac with obtuse corolla lobes. This cultivar originated at County Park Nursery, Essex, United Kingdom, from a seedling grown from *Hebe* 'Bowles's Hybrid'. It is said to flower fairly continuously from summer to autumn and is hardy.

Hebe 'Beverley Hills'

A very good garden plant for the front of a border or in smaller gardens. Flowering commences around the beginning of summer and continues until after mid summer, the bluish-purple flowers contrasting well with the dark green leaves. This is a chance seedling that originated in the Cambridge, New Zealand, garden of an employee of Annton Nursery in 1997. It was discovered in the vicinity of *Hebe diosmifolia* and *H.* 'Inspiration', and it is assumed that these may be its parents. Like its presumed parents, it has excellent disease resistance.

DESCRIPTION: A rather small hebe to about 50–60 cm tall. Branchlets green to light reddish-brown, finely bifariously pubescent. Leaf bud with a distinct sinus. Leaves 1.8–2.5 cm long by 7–8 mm wide, obovate-elliptic to oblong-elliptic, upper surface deep green, somewhat shining, petiole 2–3 mm long, apex subacute, margins entire or sometimes with one or two pairs of minute incisions. Inflorescences crowded near the branchlet tips, lateral, simple to several-branched; peduncle and rachis pubescent.

Flowers bluish-purple, pedicellate, corolla tube white, short, less than the calyx lobes. Anthers violet, pollen whitish.

Hebe 'Blue Clouds'

This somewhat larger-growing cultivar grows to about 1 m tall. Its green and purplish stems are clothed with green leaves, 3–4 cm long by 7–10 mm wide, which turn a deep purple in winter. A seedling raised at County Park Nursery in Essex, United Kingdom, in 1974 with *H.* 'Mrs. Winder' as one parent. It flowers for quite a long period over the summer.

Hebe 'Bowles's Hybrid'

A distinct and easily recognised shrub that has probably been around for at least sixty years. It has been variously known as *Hebe diosmifolia* 'Bowles's Variety', *H.* 'Bowles's Variety', *H. parviflora* 'Bowles's Variety', and *H.* 'Eversley Seedling'. *Hebe* 'Eversley Seedling' is quite similar to 'Bowles's Hybrid' but has been accepted as a separate and distinct entity.

'Bowles's Hybrid' is a very good cultivar that has out-performed some of the newer cultivars in the United Kingdom, especially because of its size, flowering habit, and disease resistance. It has a rather open habit of growth and is very free-flowering, with branched inflorescences of light bluish-mauve flowers that fade to white. Flowering usually occurs in summer, with a second flowering in autumn. This hebe will form a rather spreading bush up to 50 or 70 cm tall. It is not entirely hardy and may need some shelter. Its name commemorates E. A. Bowles, well-known author, plant collector, and gardener of Myddleton House, Enfield, United Kingdom.

Hebe 'Caledonia'

Another cultivar that has been given a variety of names by overenthusiastic gardeners. It has been called 'E. B. Anderson', 'Knightshayes', 'Percy Picton', and 'Porlock'. According to Graham Hutchins (1997), who first encountered it in a Scottish nursery in 1975, this cultivar has been around for more than 30 years. Its cultivar name may indicate its Scottish origin. Little else is known of its origin. It is a low-growing shrub, about 60 cm or more in height, and is noted for its reddish-purple stems and slightly grey-green leaves with red margins and midribs. The leaves are 1.5–2.4 cm long by 6–8 mm wide. During the colder months, the leaves often become completely suffused with a purplish colour. The flowers are violet-purple.

Hebe 'Candy'

A seedling from *Hebe albicans* 'Snow Mound' that was raised at County Park Nursery, Essex, United Kingdom, in 1978. Its broad, pinkish-purple racemes of flowers are said to be rather reminiscent of candyfloss. It is hardy and easy to grow.

Hebe ×*carnea* 'Carnea'

An early New Zealand cultivar, unusual among early cultivars for its rosy-purple flowers, because at that time, few others had a similar flower colour. It was probably a spontaneous hybrid that arose in cultivation sometime during the middle of the 19th century, but no details are known of its origin. In fact, it was at one time considered to be a species, with its origin being attributed to various improbable localities.

It grows into a shrub up to 1 or 1.5 m tall with long, narrow leaves 4–8.2 cm long by 7–11 mm wide. They are more or less sessile and acute or subacute. Its flowers are produced on racemes up to 8.7 cm long and are pinkish-purple with a white corolla tube. Flowering is usually during December (summer) and January (mid summer), possibly with a later period from May (late autumn) until July (mid winter). In the colder parts of New Zealand it may be rather frost-tender, with bark splitting during severe frosts; however, in warmer areas it makes a good garden shrub and flowers well. If it has one fault it is its susceptibility to downy mildew.

Hebe ×*carnea* 'Carnea Variegata'

As for the typical form but with its leaves variegated with grey-green and pale, creamy grey-green, and usually broadly margined with cream. During autumn and winter its young foliage becomes heavily suffused with rose. When well grown, it is a very fine hebe, its main disadvantages being its susceptibility to frost damage and downy mildew. In the past, nurseries have sold it as *Hebe* 'Carnea Tricolour', *H.* 'Tricolour', *H.* 'Variegata', and one or two other appellations. It appears to be most commonly cultivated under the name *H.* 'Tricolour', both in New Zealand and overseas; however, its correct name, *H.* ×*carnea* 'Carnea Variegata', dates back to 1945, whereas *H.* 'Tricolour' only dates back to 1960.

Hebe 'Champagne' (PLATE 83)

A low, spreading shrub with small, dark green leaves that may be flushed with purple, especially when young. White flowers, often with a touch of violet, are produced on rather short racemes. It flowers prolifically during February (late summer) and March (early autumn) and may produce occasional flowers at other times. This cultivar arose as a spontaneous seedling at Naturally Native New Zealand Plants, Tauranga, possibly sometime during the early 1990s. The seedling appeared alongside a plant of *Hebe bishopiana* and appeared to be a cross between that species and a small-leaved hebe that was growing nearby.

Hebe 'Christabel'

A whipcord hybrid collected by Graham Hutchins from above Lake Christabel in the Spenser Mountains. It makes a compact shrub to about 20 cm tall by 30 cm across, with its ultimate branchlets about 5 mm in diameter. It leaves are bright green, close-set, and erect to slightly recurved. According to Hutchins (1997), it may be a hybrid between *Hebe lycopodioides* and *H. pauciramosa*. He likens it to *H*. 'Emerald Gem'.

Hebe 'Christensenii' (PLATE 84)

This hebe is probably more commonly cultivated in the South Island than it is further north. It is also cultivated in the United Kingdom, although often under an incorrect name (likewise, a completely different plant may be grown under the name 'Christensenii'). It is probably derived from a whipcord species, perhaps *Hebe cupressoides*, possibly crossed with *H. odora*. It is very shy of flowering—in more than 50 years, I have never known it to flower—but in any case it is a handsome shrub. Strangely, similar plants sent to me, possibly with similar parentage, do flower quite well. 'Christensenii' was named after C. E. Christensen of Hanmer Springs, who was known to have accompanied Leonard Cockayne on some of his collecting trips in that area.

This much-branched shrub grows to 90 cm or 1.5 m tall and usually forms a rounded shape. The bright green to deep green leaves are erect to more or less spreading and more or less overlapping. They are about 3–4 mm long by 1.5–3 mm wide, oblong-ovate to ovate, subacute to obtuse, and sessile. Both leaf surfaces are dotted with stomata. As a garden shrub this cultivar is not only very handsome but also very useful for associating with other hebes. Since it probably originated from a cross between *Hebe odora* and a whipcord species, both of which prefer moist situations, *H*. 'Christensenii' needs to be planted in a soil that does not dry out too easily.

Hebe 'Combe Royal' (PLATE 85)

The nomenclature of this very useful old favourite has been quite chequered. It was formerly known as a cultivar of *Hebe ×franciscana*, and even now, nurseries and gardeners persist in referring to it as *H*. 'Blue Gem' or *H. ×franciscana* 'Blue Gem', plus one or two other epithets.

The situation was clarified by Peter Heenan in 1994 when he researched the origins of this and other similar cultivars. *Hebe* 'Combe Royal' was bred in 1856 by John Luscombe of "Combe Royal," Kingsbridge, Devon, United Kingdom, when he crossed *H. elliptica* with *H. speciosa*. For years this plant was incorrectly known as *H*. 'Blue Gem', and later as *H. ×franciscana* 'Blue Gem', when the epithet *×franciscana* was coined for hybrids between those two species. When not in flower, *H*. 'Combe Royal' and *H. ×franciscana* 'Lobelioides' are difficult to distinguish, but 'Combe Royal' has stouter branching, a larger flower, a broader corolla tube, and a larger bud before the corolla lobes open out. There is also a greater diameter between the lateral corolla lobes on fully opened flowers. The flower colour is a reddish violet-purple (appearing rather pinkish) compared to the violet-blue of *H. ×franciscana* 'Lobelioides'. In his 1994 paper on *Hebe ×franciscana*, Heenan details the reasons for not accepting the epithet 'Blue Gem' for 'Combe Royal'; likewise, he states that 'Combe Royal' does not belong to *H.* ×*franciscana* because he considers 'Combe Royal' to have resulted from a cross of not only *H. elliptica* and *H. speciosa* but also another parent as well.

Hebe 'Combe Royal' is a very fine cultivar, especially for coastal locations, and grows into an excellent shrub to 2 m tall and perhaps 2 m or more in diameter. It will flower during the latter part of the summer and, depending on the season, often again in autumn and winter; it may also produce occasional flowers at other times. It has become naturalised in the United Kingdom around parts of coastal Cornwall and on some of the Scottish islands.

Hebe 'County Park' (PLATE 86)

This cultivar was raised by Graham Hutchins at County Park Nursery, Essex, United Kingdom, and is said to have been a seedling from *Hebe* 'Glauca-caerulea'. It is a popular, prostrate to decumbent shrub with spreading branches to about 60 cm across. It seldom grows to more than 15 cm tall. Its branchlets are pubescent and dark purplish, and its leaves are 1.2–1.8 cm long by 5–7 mm wide and grey-green with red margins. During winter the young leaves and leaf bud become purplish. Its inflorescences are up to 3 cm long, branched, and crowded with violet-purple flowers during summer. Quite hardy and easy to grow.

Hebe 'Edinensis'

Hebe 'Edinensis' is a low-growing whipcord hybrid that makes a pleasant ground cover shrub. It eventually grows to about 15 or 30 cm tall and up to about 60 cm across and has attractive green foliage. Its branchlets have a somewhat similar appearance to those of *H.* 'Christensenii' except that they are larger and wider-spreading, with broad bands of bifarious pubescence of long white hairs on its internodal spaces. Its leaves are erect and appressed to the branchlets for about half their length before more or less spreading. They are dark green and shining on their upper surfaces and a little paler beneath. I have never seen it flower, but the flowers are said to be pale blue. According to Graham Hutchins (1997), inflorescences are occasionally produced in June (early winter) or July (mid winter), and the flowers are white with a light mauve tinge; his own plants apparently went a few years without flowering. *Hebe* 'Edinensis' was produced in Edinburgh, Scotland, during the early years of the 20th century. It is said to be a cross between *H. hectori* and *H. pimeleoides*. It is hardy and easily grown.

Hebe 'Edington'

A bushy cross between *Hebe* 'Autumn Glory' and *H.* 'Midsummer Beauty' that will grow to about 1 m tall. It is noted for its bronzed leaves and stems, and for its purplish young leaves and leaf bud. Its inflorescences are about 12 cm long, and its flowers are a rich violet-purple. It flowers from mid summer to autumn. It was raised in 1975 by Douglas Chalk, the former hebe grower and owner at Polden Acres Gardens, Bridgwater, Somerset, England. He named it after the Somerset village of the same name.

Hebe 'Emerald Gem'

This rather small hebe has been burdened by no fewer than 11 synonyms in its 34-year history, including 'McKean', 'McKeanii', 'Milmont Emerald', 'Emerald Green', 'Emerald Queen', 'Emerald Cushion', 'Green Globe', 'Green Carpet', and 'Emerald Dome'. It is a very attractive, very easily grown cultivar, most useful for a rock garden or the front of a border. It makes a small, bun-like shrub with bright green foliage rather after the nature of *Hebe* 'Christensenii' or *H.* 'Edinensis'. Ultimately it will grow to about 30 cm tall by about 45 cm in diameter. It was collected by A. W. McKean prior to 1970 on the Ruahine Range, growing in company with its presumed parents, *H. odora* and *H. hectori* subsp. *subsimilis*.

Hebe 'Eugénie Ombler' (PLATE 87)

This attractive ground cover shrub deserves to be better known. It obviously has *Hebe decumbens* as one parent, and its wide leaf bases and long peduncles indicate that *H. amplexicaulis* may be the other. Its red-margined leaves, which show the influence of *H. decumbens*, are rather larger than that species, and in addition to being concave are broadest towards their tips. It has the dark stems of *H. decumbens*, which add to its attractiveness. It flowers well, and although its inflorescences are rather short and dumpy, they thrust out from the leaves on longish peduncles so that the white flowers are quite prominent. It is fairly drought-tolerant and grows well in an open, sunny situation. It is named after the nurseryperson from whom this plant was obtained.

DESCRIPTION: A decumbent shrub to 15 cm that may spread to about 1 m in diameter, with branchlet tips ascending. Glabrous branchlets reddish-brown, internodes three to five times the diameter. Leaf bud is without a sinus. Leaves 1.5–2.3 cm long by 8–12 mm wide, tapering to a broad base, apex obtuse to almost subacute, upper surface medium green to yellowish-green and dull. Margins prominently red. Inflorescences few, near to the tips of the branchlets, short and dumpy, up to 3.5 cm long, peduncle to about 1.5 cm long, flowers shortly pedicelled, bracts ovate, obtuse, flower buds showing pink when they first develop. Flowers white, very close-set, corolla tube 3–4 mm long, lobes wide-spreading, obtuse.

Hebe 'Eveline' (PLATE 88)

A fine cultivar that goes back to at least the 1890s. Like so many other early cultivars, its nomenclature has had a chequered history, and it still occurs in nurseries and garden centres under one or another of its synonyms. Over the years it has been variously known as *Hebe* 'Gauntlettii', *H.* 'Pink Payne', *H.* 'Payne's Pink', *H.* 'Rainer's Beauty', and *H.* 'Pink Pearl'. The name 'Eveline' first appeared in *The Garden* in 1893, giving it considerable priority over later names. It is a showy hybrid that obviously has a great deal of *H. speciosa* in its make-up. Bold racemes, up to 16 cm long, of bright rose-pink flowers are produced over a long period, with flowering also occurring more or less intermittently throughout winter in mild areas. Even in colder districts this plant will produce an occasional winter flower if planted in a suitable situation. It has quite bold foliage, with leaves up to 15 cm long by 2.5 cm wide. With age it will grow to about 1.5 m tall and make quite a substantial bush.

Hebe 'Fairlane'

This is a hybrid from *Hebe pinguifolia*, possibly with *H.* 'Youngii' being the pollen parent. It was raised at County Park Nursery, Essex, United Kingdom, by Graham Hutchins in 1970. *Hebe* 'Fairlane' grows into a low, spreading shrub to about 30 cm tall with a spread of about 60 cm or more. Its small, slightly concave leaves are green to more or less glaucous, and the margins of the young leaves are purplish. The inflorescences are dense, 3–5 cm long, and the flowers are pale violet. According to Hutchins (1997) it is very hardy, free-flowering, and useful where low ground cover plantings are required.

Hebe 'First Light' (PLATE 89)

The flowers on this cultivar's compact inflorescences open a pinkish colour (75b in the purple group of the RHS Colour Chart) and contrast well with the slightly grey-green foliage. Flowering occurs during summer and again in autumn. Bred in New Zealand and named to commemorate the dawn of the new millennium.

DESCRIPTION: Low, spreading shrub 40–50 cm tall. Branchlets green, glabrous except for a few scattered hairs, length of internodes one to two times the diameter. Leaf bud without a sinus. Leaves 1.5–2.2 cm long by 7–10 mm wide, elliptic, greyish-green, sessile. Inflorescences up to 6 cm long; rachis, pedicels, and bracts pubescent. Flowers close-set, corolla tube white, lobes opening pink and fading to white.

Hebe 'Flame'

This cultivar grows to about 1 m tall and has a semi-erect habit. Its shining, oblanceolate leaves are deep green during summer and a strong bronze-purple during winter. Rosy-pink flowers are produced on short racemes about 5 cm long, and while they first appear during summer, the most prolific flowering occurs in autumn. This New Zealand cultivar is commonly sold under the name *Hebe speciosa* 'Flame'. It is most likely a secondary or tertiary hybrid and may have some *H. speciosa* in its make-up, but it is certainly not a cultivar of that species; in fact, it has been suggested that *H.* ×*carnea* 'Carnea' may have been involved in its parentage.

Hebe ×*franciscana* 'Lobelioides' (PLATE 90)

Another cultivar whose name has been the subject of considerable confusion among gardeners, nurseries, and garden centres. The name *Hebe* ×*franciscana* is applied to culti-vars belonging to the hybrid group of *H. elliptica* × *H. speciosa* and was first used for an unnamed plant of this cross growing in Golden Gate Park, San Francisco, California. Sometime prior to 1862, well-known hebe breeder Isaac Anderson-Henry of Maryfield, near Edinburgh, Scotland, hybridised the Falkland Islands form of *H. elliptica* (then known as *H. decussata*) with *H. speciosa* to produce what he called *Veronica* 'Lobelioides'. This cultivar, as was not uncommon at the time, soon became confused with John Luscombe's cultivar (now known as *H.* 'Combe Royal') and the similar *H.* 'Blue Gem'. From then on nobody appeared to know what was what, and the various cultivars became well and truly confused. *Veronica* 'Lobelioides' was imported into New Zealand prior to 1868, just a few years after it was introduced into cultivation, and most New Zealand stock of this cultivar is likely to have come from that original importation. The situation in New Zealand is no different from that of other countries, and there remains confusion as to which plant should correctly be known as *H.* ×*franciscana* 'Lobelioides'.

This is a very good plant, especially for coastal areas, where it withstands persistent and cutting salt-laden winds without showing any signs of wind burn or other damage. It is also useful for growing where there is shade from adjoining trees, and in dry places. Apart from its flower colour, which is violet-blue, it is superficially quite similar to *Hebe* 'Combe Royal', which has reddish violet-purple flowers. However, it appears to be more resistant to downy mildew than *H.* 'Combe Royal'.

Hebe 'Geoff Turnbull'

A somewhat unusual cultivar in that it commences as an almost decumbent shrub but gradually increases in size until it eventually attains a height of 80–90 cm. Its deep green foliage is quite handsome and it flowers well. It originated at Talisman Nursery, Otaki, New Zealand, prior to 1990. Its parentage is not known, and it is named after the son of the proprietor, Alastair Turnbull.

DESCRIPTION: A shrub at first, almost prostrate to decumbent, becoming larger with age, up to 90 cm tall by 1 m wide. Branchlets reddish-brown and finely bifariously puberulous. Leaf bud with a narrow sinus. Leaves 14–20 mm long by 7–8 mm wide, oblong-lanceolate to elliptic-obovate, on short petioles, margins entire or with a pair of small incisions about a third of the way down from the apex. Inflorescence simple or tripartite, up to 4 cm long. Corolla to 8 mm in diameter, mauve to light rosy-purple fad-ing to whitish with age. Anthers medium purple changing to creamy-white as they dehisce.

Hebe 'Gibby'

Another cultivar that originated from County Park Nursery, Essex, United Kingdom. It is the result of crossing *Hebe gibbsii* with *H. pimeleoides* subsp. *pimeleoides*. Several seedlings were produced, but the one that was eventually named is an openly branched shrub with glaucous blue-grey leaves and short racemes of pale lilac-blue flowers. Its stems are bifariously pubescent and its leaves are margined with white hairs. According to Graham Hutchins (1997), it is hardy and easily grown. Flowering occurs during summer.

Hebe 'Glaucophylla Variegata'

The correct determination of this cultivar remains a mystery. It was formerly known as *Hebe darwiniana* 'Variegata' and then, at a later date, the name was changed to *H. glaucophylla* 'Variegata'. The status of *H. darwiniana* as a species is doubtful, but in any case the descriptions of this and *H. glaucophylla* appear to be quite similar. As this cultivar has racemes of pale lilac-blue flowers, it is clearly of hybrid origin and not *H. darwiniana* or *H. glaucophylla*, both of which have white flowers. It is a shrub up to 1 m tall. The leaves are 1.2–1.6 cm long by 3–5 mm wide, variegated with pale green and creamy-white, and their margins are minutely pubescent. The slender flower racemes are 4–6 cm long, and the flowers are rather loosely placed. Regardless of what it might correctly be called, it is a rather popular cultivar in the United Kingdom.

Hebe 'Glengarriff' (PLATE 91)

This cultivar is also something of a mystery, as nothing much appears to be known of it. One catalogue describes it as "a handsome, intense glaucous-blue variety of compact habit with neat, pointed leaves and white flowers in July." Its leaves are oval and slightly concave, the upper surfaces being covered with fine hairs. Graham Hutchins suggests it may belong to *Hebe albicans* or *H. pareora*; however, the hairiness of the leaves suggests that *H. amplexicaulis* f. *hirta* might have something to do with its origin. It is a good garden plant, being easy to grow and enjoying a good well-drained soil in a sunny situation. It is said to have been introduced by N. Treseder of Truro, Cornwall, United Kingdom, but that has not been confirmed.

Hebe 'Gran's Favourite'

A seedling from *Hebe* 'Midsummer Beauty' that was raised in 1974 by Graham Hutchins of County Park Nursery, Essex, United Kingdom. This compact shrub grows to about 90 cm tall and has lanceolate leaves about 6.5 cm long by 1.25 wide. The young leaves have purplish undersurfaces, as does the leaf bud. Pale mauve flowers are produced on racemes up to 10 cm long. It has a long flowering period and will flower through the latter part of the summer and well into the autumn.

Hebe 'Great Orme'

Hebe 'Great Orme' is rather similar to *H.* ×*carnea* 'Carnea', and according to Douglas Chalk it is a hybrid from that cultivar. It forms a much-branched, rounded shrub to about 1.3 m tall. Its oblong-lanceolate leaves are up to 6 cm long by about 1.25 cm wide. Their upper surfaces are yellow-green and shining. The flowers are bright pink and produced on 5–10 cm racemes from late summer into the autumn. It is very attractive but is inclined to be a little frost-tender.

Hebe 'Greensleeves' (PLATE 92)

An erect, bushy shrub that grows to about 60 cm tall. Its whipcord-like branchlets are green, and the leaves are inclined to spread slightly from just below their tips. They are not glossy, about 3–4 mm long, and keeled on their outer surfaces, with ciliolate margins. According to Graham Hutchins (1997), who bred this cultivar, it is hardy, easily grown, and among the few free-flowering whipcord hebes. As many as 12 white flowers are produced on terminal spikes about 4.5 cm long. *Hebe* 'Greensleeves' was a seedling from *H. ochracea*, but its other parent is unknown. Originated in 1973.

Hebe 'Hartii' (PLATES 3 AND 93)

A prostrate shrub very useful for rock gardens, where it can be used for trailing over walls or edgings, or as a ground cover at the front of a border. It usually will not exceed about 10 cm in height and spreads to about 75 cm across. The leaf bud has a small, narrow sinus. Its medium green leaves are about 1.2–1.6 cm long by 4–7 mm wide and all lie in the one plane, which heightens its prostrate appearance. Mid violet-blue flowers are produced from early November (early summer) until early December (summer) on simple or branched, lateral racemes 2.5–4 cm long. With age the flowers fade to white. 'Hartii' is easily grown and is happiest in a sunny situation. It is named after L. B. Hart of Weatherstones, Lawrence, Otago, who was an avid collector and cultivator of New Zealand's native plants, especially hebes.

Hebe 'Havering Green'

This quite small cultivar originated as a chance seedling in County Park Nursery, Essex, United Kingdom. It is a rather low, spreading plant that trails on the ground and grows to no more than a few centimetres in height. Its small green leaves are 1–1.5 cm long by 5–7 mm wide and virtually glabrous. The leaf bud has no sinus. This is another hebe that does not appear to flower. According to Graham Hutchins (1997), his own specimen has never produced a flower in the 20 years that he has grown it. It is useful for rock gardens or as a ground cover plant at the front of a border.

Hebe 'Headfortii' (PLATE 94)

Except for its much deeper flower colour, in foliage and form *Hebe* 'Headfortii' is quite similar to *H.* 'Inspiration'. It is an older cultivar that originated at Headfort House, near Kells, County Meath, Ireland, probably in the late 1920s or early 1930s. It grows into a spreading shrub ultimately up to about 75 cm tall and more than 1 m in diameter. The leaf bud has quite a large sinus. Its leaves are oblanceolate, about 2.5–4 cm long by 1–1.2 cm wide. Their margins are entire or with one or two small incisions near their apexes. The inflorescences are lateral, branched, and about 4–6 cm long. Flowers are a deep violet-purple and are usually produced in early summer. Although hardy in New Zealand, this hebe is rated as being rather tender in the United Kingdom.

Hebe 'Heidi'

A cultivar of unknown origin. It is an upright and well-branched shrub with narrow, elliptic to oblanceolate leaves 2.5–3 cm long by 8–10 mm wide. During cooler weather its young leaves turn purplish. The flower racemes are 6–7 cm long, and its flowers are bluish-mauve, fading with age. This cultivar could be a selection from *Hebe* 'Waikiki' or may have *H. bishopiana* as one parent.

Hebe 'Heilan Lassie'

This is another cultivar about which nothing appears to be known. It first appeared in the nursery catalogue of Messrs. Hillier and Sons, United Kingdom, in 1950. It grows as a bushy, fairly wide-spreading shrub to 1 m tall and is relatively hardy, although it is probably safest to give it a sheltered situation. Its branchlets are purplish, and the leaves are 3–5 cm long by 1.5–2 cm wide. The leaf bud has a distinct sinus. The undersurfaces of the youngest leaves are purplish, while the margins and midribs are also purplish. Its flowers are violet-purple on racemes 6.5 cm long during summer. According to Douglas Chalk (1988), this plant may have *Hebe speciosa* as part of its parentage, which may account for its slightly tender nature.

Hebe 'Hinerua' (PLATE 95)

Hebe 'Hinerua' is a whipcord cultivar that was collected on the Hinerua Ridge of the Ruahine Range by Graham Hutchins in 1985. According to Hutchins (1997), it is most likely a hybrid between *H. odora* and *H. hectori* subsp. *subsimilis*, both of which occurred in the area. It is hardy and he likens it to *H.* 'Christensenii' or *H.* 'Greensleeves'. It has yellow-green foliage and forms a much-branched shrub to about 60 cm tall. Its leaves are 4–5 mm long by about 2 mm wide and gradually taper to a subacute apex that recurves slightly from the branchlet. Its flowers are produced in short, terminal spikes 1–2 cm long. The white flowers are about 8 mm in diameter.

Hebe 'Icing Sugar' (PLATE 96)

An attractive cultivar. Its leaves are 5–5.5 cm long by 1–1.2 cm wide and have a slight sheen. Rose-pink flower buds on lovely 7–11.5 cm racemes open to a similar colour and then quickly fade to white, giving the whole raceme a most attractive effect. The stamen filaments are also pink and fade to white as the flowers age. It flowers during mid to late summer and peaks in early autumn. *Hebe* 'Icing Sugar' originated in New Zealand, possibly in the 1980s, but little else is known of its origin.

Hebe 'Imposter' (PLATE 97)

An unnamed cultivar that originally masqueraded in the United Kingdom as *Hebe anomala* or *H.* 'Anomala' but proved to be neither and was subsequently named 'Imposter' by Graham Hutchins of County Park Nursery, Essex, United Kingdom. It forms a densely bushy shrub up to a metre or more in height with erect, slender branches. Its branchlets are bifariously pubescent. The leaf bud has a narrow sinus. Leaves are 8–10 by 3–4 mm, shiny above, dull beneath, and very shortly petiolate, with a subacute apex. White flowers are produced in lateral racemes up to about 4 cm long and are similar to those of *H. odora*. This cultivar does not appear to be much grown outside the United Kingdom.

Hebe 'Inspiration' (PLATE 98)

Apart from its flower colour, this cultivar is almost identical to *Hebe* 'Headfortii'. Interestingly, *H.* 'Inspiration' originated in New Zealand, probably in the 1950s, while *H.* 'Headfortii' originated in Ireland, probably in the 1920s or 1930s. *Hebe* 'Inspiration' is the result of *H. speciosa* hybridising with *H. diosmifolia* and is believed to have arisen in Bruce Given's Nelson garden sometime before 1957. It forms a neat, compact shrub and because of its *H. speciosa* parentage is well suited for coastal conditions. The leaf bud has a distinct sinus. As with *H.* 'Headfortii', its leaves are broadest near their apexes and have a pair of small incisions along the margins of their upper part. The flowers are petunia-purple, and the inflorescences are either simple or with one or two lateral branches. The flowers are usually closely placed and hiding the rachis. Flowering is from early November (early summer) till mid December (summer), and there may also be later intermittent flowering from late July (mid winter) until November (early summer). According to Graham Hutchins (1997) this plant is not hardy enough to survive in most gardens in the United Kingdom but is worth trying in the warmer and coastal areas.

Hebe 'Inverey' (PLATE 99)

This cultivar originated at Inverey Nursery in Signal Hill, Dunedin, New Zealand, around 1974. Its parents are speculated as being *Hebe decumbens* and *H.* 'Glauca-caerulea', but its very pubescent branchlets indicate that its parents are more likely to be *H.* 'Glauca-caerulea' and *H. amplexicaulis* f. *hirta*. This is a very fine little shrub either for a rock garden or for the front of a border, where it can be used as a ground cover. It is very drought-tolerant and quite hardy. Flowers are produced over quite a long period during late spring and summer, and sometimes there is a second flowering in autumn.

DESCRIPTION: A small, decumbent, slightly spreading shrub to 10 cm tall by 75 cm in diameter. Branchlets dark blackish-purple, quite densely pubescent, length of internodes two to three times the diameter. Leaf bud without a sinus. Leaves 10–12 mm long by 5–7 mm wide, margins yellowish. Young leaves and leaf bud flushed with purplish-red during winter and early spring. Flowers bluish-mauve, borne on short racemes, about 2.5–3 cm long.

Hebe 'Jack's Surprise'

A cultivar of unknown parentage. It is a smallish to medium-sized shrub to about 60 cm tall by about 90 cm across. Its growth is more or less erect and with a somewhat spreading habit. Its leaf bud has quite a small sinus. The leaves are about 5 cm long by 1.5 cm wide, broad-elliptic to elliptic-oblong, the upper surface yellowish-green, margins usually entire but sometimes with one or two small incisions. Flowers are violet-purple on inflorescences up to 10 cm long. This is a hardy plant and often has a few inflorescences up to mid winter. It was raised by K. W. Harker of Bourne, Buckinghamshire, United Kingdom, in 1981.

Hebe 'James Platt'

Another small cultivar that may have some affinities with *Hebe* 'Youngii'. It grows to about 60 cm tall and has dark purplish branchlets. The leaf bud has a small sinus. Its leaves are about 1–1.5 cm long by 5–7 mm wide, slightly concave, with red margins. Violet-blue flowers are on lateral (sometimes terminal) racemes that may occasionally be branched. This cultivar is free-flowering, with flowers produced during the summer. It was raised by Graham Hutchins (1997) of County Park Nursery, Essex, United Kingdom, and according to Hutchins it is easily grown.

Hebe 'Jasper'

This low shrub has a bun-like habit and grows to about 30 cm tall by about 40 cm across. Its attractive green foliage is similar to that of *Hebe odora* but smaller. During the autumn and winter it develops a purplish-red flush near the tips of the branchlets and has a yellowish-green band around the margins of the leaves. It has lateral and terminal, branched racemes, with about six white flowers per raceme. It is ideal for a rock garden or planted as a group at the front of a border. It was discovered before 1980 at the Forest Research Nursery, Rangiora, Canterbury, where it originated among some seedlings raised from some wild-collected seed from the Craigieburn Range. It was named 'Jasper' for its winter colour, which resembles the colour of the jasper stone frequently found in north Canterbury riverbeds.

Hebe 'Joan Lewis'

This medium-sized shrub grows to about 80 cm tall and is openly branched. Its branchlets are rather coarsely pubescent all around, and the leaf bud has no sinus. The leaves are sessile, grey-green, and 1.6–2.4 cm long by 1–1.2 cm wide. They are rather spreading to slightly reflexed and have pale or slightly reddish margins. Its flowers are whitish with a pinkish tinge and are borne on short, dense racemes about 1.5 cm long. This hebe appears to be reasonably hardy and is quite floriferous. It originated as a spontaneous seedling in the garden of Joan Lewis, secretary of the Essex Hardy Plant Society.

Hebe 'Joyce Parker'

Although not very tall, this cultivar is useful for ground cover purposes. It grows to about 40 cm tall and spreads to a metre or so in diameter. Its branchlets are green and covered with fine lines of bifarious pubescence. The leaf bud has a very small sinus. Leaves are 3–4 cm long by 1–1.2 cm wide, pale green, and slightly twisted on their petioles so that they tend to lie in the one plane. Leaf margins are entire and pubescent, and there is also some pubescence on the undersurface of the midrib. Flowers are a pale lilac-blue, fading to white with age, and are produced on lateral racemes 5–8 cm long; they are densely placed and almost hide the rachis. As well as being hardy, *Hebe* 'Joyce Parker' is relatively quick in its growth. It occurred as a chance seedling in County Park Nursery, Essex, United Kingdom, sometime during the 1970s.

Hebe 'Karo Golden Esk' (PLATE 100)

A hybrid between *Hebe armstrongii* and *H. odora* that originated as a wild-collected plant in 1988. It is valuable as a garden plant for both its form and its foliage colour, normally yellow-green but turning a most attractive golden green with the onset of colder winter weather. After three years or so in the garden it reaches about 40 cm tall by about 80 cm in diameter. Its branchlets are about 1 mm in diameter. Leaves are generally 2–3 mm long, sessile, and appressed when young, becoming more spreading when mature, and have acute apexes. Unlike some whipcord hybrids, 'Karo Golden Esk' does flower, producing up to eight white flowers on a terminal inflorescence. It was discovered by Brian Molloy when undertaking a botanical survey of the upper Esk Valley in the Waimakariri River catchment area, growing among a population of *H. odora* on the margin of a tarn along the Nigger Stream, a tributary of the Esk River. Molloy concluded that the other parent was *H. armstrongii*, the only other hebe present. "Karo" is an acronym that stands for "known and recorded origin."

Hebe ×*kirkii*

This rounded shrub grows to about 1.5–2 m tall. The leaf bud has no sinus. Its shining green leaves are about 2.5–4 cm long by about 1 cm wide and of a rather thick texture. White flowers are produced on slender racemes 5–10 cm long. *Hebe* ×*kirkii* is a hybrid probably between *H. salicifolia* and a small-leaved species, most likely *H. rakaiensis*. It was originally collected by Joseph Beattie Armstrong in the valley of the upper Rangitata River, Canterbury, and is named after Thomas Kirk, a prominent botanist from the 1860s until the late 1890s. It is not widely cultivated overseas and is not cultivated in New Zealand. In the United Kingdom it is considered to be a good background shrub.

Hebe 'La Séduisante'

An old cultivar with *Hebe speciosa* as one of its parents. It will grow into a shrub 1–1.8 m tall and has dark foliage with purplish colouration on its stems and young leaves. Its leaf bud has a distinct sinus. The leaves are 7–11.2 cm long by 2–4 cm wide, more or less elliptic, the upper surface dark green and shining, the lower surface paler and purplish when young. Leaf margins are purplish. Inflorescences are lateral, simple, and 7.5–11.2 cm long, with violet-purple flowers closely placed and hiding the rachis. Because of the influence of *H. speciosa*, 'La Séduisante' can be rather frost-tender. In districts that experience severe frosts, it should be given a sheltered situation; otherwise the bark may split, leading to severe damage. Its main flowering period is from late December (summer) until late January (mid summer), with some intermittent flowering from then until about June (early winter). Nothing appears to be known of its origin. Because of its name, it is assumed to have originated in France; however, the first available mention of it appears to be in an English nursery catalogue in 1906.

Hebe 'Lavender Lace' (PLATE 101)

Ultimately forming a rather loose shrub to 2 m tall by about 2.5 m in diameter, this cultivar has very narrow leaves, similar to those of *Hebe stenophylla*, and produces shortish spikes, up to 7 cm long, of mauve flowers. This hebe is almost never without a flower. It has quite a long flowering period, sometimes lasting about three months, and sometimes has another flowering period in autumn that can last right through winter to early spring. This altogether rather pretty shrub appears to be quite hardy and responds well to clipping, which enables it to be kept small. It originated in New Zealand, but nothing else is known of its origin.

DESCRIPTION: A shrub to 2 m tall by 2.5 m across. Branchlets yellow-green and minutely bifariously puberulous, internodes two and a half to three times the diameter. Leaf bud without a sinus. Leaves 3.5–4.5 cm long by 4–6 mm wide, lanceolate to linear, narrowing to a short petiole, apex acute, medium to deep green above and similar beneath. Inflorescence simple to tripartite, in several pairs from the nodal joints just below the growing tip. Peduncle to 2 cm long. Rachis to 7 cm long, flowers pedicellate, corolla to 8 mm in diameter, mauve fading to white with age.

Hebe ×*lewisii* 'Lewisii'

Hebe ×*lewisii* 'Lewisii' is a very fine shrub, especially for coastal gardens, since it is so well adapted to withstand the continual buffeting of salt-laden breezes. In addition to this it is a fine flowering shrub. Growing to about 1.2–2.4 m tall with a more or less erect habit, this hebe is very useful for background plantings. It is a good winter-flowering shrub, its main flowering period occurring from May (late autumn) until October (mid spring), with another short period from mid December (summer) to early January (mid summer).

This is an old cultivar that was discovered by Joseph Beattie Armstrong in the vicinity of Timaru, South Island, New Zealand, sometime before 1881. It is believed to have been named after a Mr. Lewis, who had a nursery in Timaru at that time. *Hebe* ×*lewisii* 'Lewisii' has been shown to be a hybrid between *H. salicifolia* and *H. elliptica*.

DESCRIPTION: Branchlets stout, covered with fine, greyish-white pubescence. Leaf bud with a small sinus. Leaves 3.5–6.2 cm long by 1.4–2.5 cm wide, oblong or elliptic-oblong, upper surface dark green, dull or with a slight sheen, midrib and petiole puberulous, margins finely ciliolate. Inflorescences lateral, simple, 4–6.2 cm long. Flowers violet fading to white, producing a bicoloured effect.

Hebe 'Lindsayi'

An erect, rounded shrub to about 75 cm tall. Its rounded, obovate leaves are about 2.5 cm long by 1.25 cm wide and distinctly concave, their upper surfaces mid green and with a slight sheen. The inflorescences are about 5 cm long, often branched, and tightly covered with pale pinkish flowers in summer. This cultivar is considered to be quite hardy, and it flowers profusely. It originated prior to 1898 with Robert Lindsay, curator of the Edinburgh Botanic Garden, Scotland; it was raised from seed collected from *Hebe amplexicaulis* that may have hybridised with *H. pimeleoides*. It is still in cultivation.

Hebe 'Loganioides'

This whipcord hybrid is apparently no longer grown in New Zealand, although it does seem to remain fairly common in the United Kingdom. It forms a low, spreading shrub to about 25 cm tall. It has yellow-green, hairy branchlets, with the ultimate branchlets about 4 cm in diameter, including the bright green leaves. The leaves are appressed against the stem for about half their length and then become slightly spreading. They are 3–5 mm long by about 4 mm wide and sometimes have one or two pairs of incisions on their margins. The flowers are white with fine pinkish veins and are borne on lateral racemes about 2–3 cm long. According to Leonard Cockayne and H. H. Allan (1934), it has the habit of a whipcord *Hebe* cross and the capsule and flower of a *Parahebe*. They considered it to be a remarkable hybrid between a whipcord *Hebe* and *Parahebe* (*Veronica*) *lyallii*. Flowering usually occurs in summer. Because of its small size, this hebe is suitable for growing in a scree garden or trough garden.

    Hebe 'Loganioides' was discovered by John Francis Armstrong in 1869 in the upper Rangitata River valley, Canterbury. Material from the original collection was propagated in the Christchurch Botanic Gardens by the discoverer's son, Joseph Beattie Armstrong, who is known to have widely distributed it to other gardens. It is quite possible that material now grown in the United Kingdom originated from this source.

Hebe 'Longacre Variety'

As with so many other *Hebe* cultivars, nothing seems to be known of the origin of 'Longacre Variety', although it is presumed to have originated at "Longacre," a house near Newcastle, United Kingdom. It first appeared in nursery catalogues in the early 1950s. Over the years there has been a certain amount of confusion concerning its name, which is often incorrectly written as 'Longacre' or 'Long Acre Variety'. It is similar to *H.* 'Autumn Glory' but more erect in its growth, and may be a seedling from it. It grows to about 90 cm tall. Its leaves are rounded, obovate or elliptic, up to 3 cm long by 1.25 cm wide, and generally green above, while the younger leaves are shining. Flowers are reddish-purple on occasionally branched racemes up to 6 or 9 cm long. This hebe does not appear to be as hardy as *H.* 'Autumn Glory' and should be planted in a more sheltered situation.

Hebe 'Lopen' (PLATE 102)

This cultivar arose as a variegated branch sport that appeared on a plant of *Hebe* 'Midsummer Beauty'. It is like the parent in all ways but that its leaves are irregularly variegated with grey-green, yellow, and cream. It is also similar to *H.* ×*andersonii* 'Andersonii Aurea', except that its leaves are paler and the midribs of the young leaves are purplish. It was discovered in 1976 growing in the garden of the Malt House, Hinton St. George, Somerset, United Kingdom, and was propagated by E. J. Goddard, a nurseryman from Lopen Head, Somerset, who named it after the village where he had his nursery.

Hebe 'Margret'

Hebe 'Margret' forms a low, compact, rounded shrub usually no more than about 60 cm tall. It has green branchlets with minute bifarious pubescence, and its leaves are 1.2–1.4 cm long by 6–7 mm wide. The leaf bud has an indistinct sinus. Upper leaf surfaces are shining, the apex subacute and based narrowed to a short petiole. Inflorescences are 4–6 cm long, with rather densely arranged sky-blue flowers that fade to white as they age. Flowering is from late spring to early summer, with several additional flushes in late summer. This cultivar is said to be hardy. It originated at Rocklands Nurseries, Pickering, North Yorkshire, United Kingdom, and is named after co-owner Margret Potter. The name is frequently misspelt 'Margaret', an orthographic error that should be corrected.

Hebe 'Marjorie'

This hebe of unknown origin is rated as very free-flowering and, according to the 1941 nursery catalogue of Messrs. Hillier and Sons, United Kingdom, was the only hebe to survive the harsh winter of 1940. It forms a shrub to 1.4 m tall and about as much in diameter. It has green to purplish branchlets with bifarious lines of minute pubescence. The leaf bud has a small, inconspicuous sinus. Its leaves are elliptic, 3–4 cm long by 1–1.4 cm wide, yellow-green, with a shining upper surface, and tend to be suberect to spreading. The pale, mauve-blue flowers are produced on rather dense racemes about 5–10 cm long. The flowers fade to white as they age, giving the racemes a bicoloured appearance. This cultivar has been in existence for at least 60 years, and it is strange that so little appears to be known of it.

Hebe 'Mary Antoinette'

Hebe 'Mary Antoinette' is a low shrub to about 75 cm tall and a bit wider, although it may ultimately grow to about 1 by 1 m. Its branchlets are glabrous and purplish, becoming green as they age. The leaf bud has no sinus and is purplish. The leaves are about 3.5–4 cm long by about 1 cm wide, linear-oblong, the upper surface deep green and rather dull, paler beneath. Inflorescences are lateral, simple, and usually crowded towards the tips of the branchlets. The peduncle is about 2 cm long, the raceme 3.5–4 cm long. The red-purple flowers fade to white, the corolla tube is white, the lobes are narrow and ovate, and the margins are quite strongly red-purple. This cultivar originated in Annton Nursery of Cambridge, New Zealand, sometime prior to 1986, where it was discovered by Ann Burton. It resembles *H.* ×*carnea* 'Carnea' in a number of ways and may be a seedling from that cultivar.

Hebe 'Mauve Fingers'

This cultivar originated in the Otari Native Botanic Garden, Wellington, as a spontaneous seedling during the early 1970s or 1980s. It is quite wind-hardy but is inclined to be frost-tender and should be grown in a sheltered situation. It would appear that one of its parents may be *Hebe macrocarpa* var. *latisepala* or, more likely, *H. brevifolia*. However, the other parent is completely unknown.

DESCRIPTION: A rather low-growing shrub to about 80 cm tall and 1 m or so in diameter. Branchlets green with fine bifarious pubescence. Leaf bud without a sinus. Leaves long, narrow, 7–10 cm long by 1.4–1.7 cm wide, lanceolate to linear-lanceolate, upper surfaces medium green and with a sheen, paler beneath, apex subacute, base narrowed to a very short petiole, margins entire. Inflorescences 7.5–10 cm long, including peduncles about 2 cm long. Flowers medium rosy-purple, corolla tube whitish.

Hebe 'Mauvena'

Hebe 'Mauvena' forms a rounded, much-branched shrub to about 1.5 m tall or more. Its branchlets are green, ageing to brownish, and slightly pubescent. It belongs to the group that includes *H. ×andersonii* 'Andersonii', but its leaves are narrower and usually have duller upper surfaces. They are up to 7.5 cm long by 2.5 cm wide, oblong-lanceolate, the base narrowing to form small shoulders just before the short petiole, and the leaf margin sometimes with a few obscure teeth near the apex. Inflorescences are 9–10 cm long, and the arrangement of the flowers is more open than other cultivars in the group. The flowers are quite a deep purple but fade to white with age, and the corolla tube is white. *Hebe* 'Mauvena' is said to be hardier than most other cultivars in its group. Flowering occurs during summer. This cultivar originated sometime before 1915, but there is no information concerning its origin.

Hebe 'McEwanii' (PLATE 103)

This grey-leaved shrub is fairly compact and rather erect, growing to a height of 45–50 cm. Its branchlets are dark purplish and contrast attractively with its rather small, glaucous leaves. The leaves are about 1.5 cm long by 5 mm wide, oblong-lanceolate, and glaucous on both surfaces. The inflorescences have one to several branches, and the flowers are mauve or pale violet. *Hebe* 'McEwanii' is a hardy cultivar and is also quite drought-tolerant. It first appeared in the 1925 nursery catalogue of Duncan and Davies, New Plymouth, New Zealand. It flowers during December (summer). The foliage is suggestive of *H. pimeleoides,* but the origin of the branched inflorescences is puzzling. In many publications the name is misspelt as 'MacEwanii'. Its origin has often been attributed to the United Kingdom, but it is clearly of New Zealand origin.

Hebe 'Megan'

A hebe of prostrate growth that originated in County Park Nursery, Essex, United Kingdom, in 1990. According to Graham Hutchins (1997) it was a seedling that came from the plant known in cultivation in the United Kingdom as *Hebe barkeri,* from which it differs in having slightly smaller leaves and a prostrate habit. It more closely resembles *H. chathamica,* although it is easily distinguished from this species by its dark purple, glabrous branches. Its leaves are 2.5–4 cm long by 8–12 mm wide, rather thick, sessile, and glabrous. Its flowers are pale lilac with a white centre, and borne on rather dense, lateral racemes 3–5 cm long. It is described as an attractive hebe that is reasonably hardy and free-flowering, with flowers appearing during the summer. *Hebe* 'Megan' was named after the daughter of Patricia Davies, the botanical artist who illustrated Hutchins's book on hebes.

Hebe 'Midsummer Beauty'

This hebe belongs to the group of cultivars that includes *Hebe* ×*andersonii* 'Andersonii' but is distinguished from the other cultivars in that group by the reddish colour on the undersides of its young leaves. It forms an erect, much-branched, rounded shrub to 1.5 or 2 m tall. Its branchlets are green to slightly purplish and glabrous, and its purplish leaf bud has a small, rounded sinus. The leaves are oblong-lanceolate, 9–11.5 cm long by up to 2 cm wide, bright green above, paler beneath, while the undersides of the young leaves in particular are reddish or plum-coloured. Inflorescences are 12.5–15 cm long, though occasionally much longer. Flowers are a quite dark violet and do not fade much with age. This cultivar is fairly hardy and flowers well from summer until autumn. It is good for coastal gardens. It was raised prior to 1945 at Seaford, East Sussex, United Kingdom, and distributed by J. Cheal and Sons of Crawley, West Sussex, but it is not known whether it was actually raised by Cheals. The parents are said to be *H.* 'Miss Fittall' and *H. speciosa*.

Hebe 'Miss Fittall' (PLATE 104)

A robust shrub of upright growth and attaining about 1.5 m or more. Its branchlets are green, turning brownish with age, with very fine bifarious pubescence. The leaf bud has a distinct oval sinus. Leaves are lanceolate to oblong, wide-spreading, 7.5–10 cm long by about 2.5 cm wide, the upper surfaces medium green with a slight sheen, the undersurfaces paler, apexes subacute, and bases rounded. Flowers are cobalt-violet in dense, narrow racemes up to 15 cm long and do not fade much as they age. This cultivar is reasonably hardy and, as with other members of the *Hebe* ×*andersonii* 'Andersonii' group, is a good plant for coastal gardens. 'Miss Fittall' is said to have been bred by A. Andrews, superintendent of parks for the Plymouth City Council during the first quarter of the 20th century. It was named after the daughter of the then town clerk. The name began as 'Miss Fittall', but then during the 1960s somebody decided to include her initial, and the name became 'Miss E. Fittall'. Later it was decided to expand the name to 'Miss Eleanor Fittall'. Both versions, particularly 'Miss E. Fittall', are commonly used, but because the original cultivar name (given by Treseder's Nursery, Cornwall, United Kingdom, between 1910 and 1920) was simply 'Miss Fittall', all subsequent versions are incorrect.

Hebe 'Mist Maiden'

Hebe 'Mist Maiden' is a seedling that was raised from a plant of *H.* 'Bowles's Hybrid'. It is similar to its parent but differs in having pale lilac to nearly white flowers. *Hebe* 'Mist Maiden' grows to about 40 or 50 cm tall and up to 60 cm or more in diameter. The branchlets are brownish-purple with fine bifarious pubescence, and its leaf bud does not usually have a sinus. The medium green leaves are spreading to recurved or reflexed and 2–2.5 cm long by 5–8 mm wide, with a dull upper surface. Inflorescences are lateral, simple, and about 5 cm long, while the flowers are a very pale lilac, fading to white with age. This is a hardy shrub. It usually flowers during the summer and may have a later flowering from early to late autumn. It was bred by Graham Hutchins of County Park Nursery, Essex, United Kingdom, who raised it sometime around 1976.

Hebe 'Monica'

A low-growing cultivar raised from *Hebe* 'Glauca-caerulea' possibly crossed with *H.* 'Youngii'. It grows to about 50 cm tall and has an erect habit. Its branchlets are dark purple and pubescent all around. The leaf bud has a narrow sinus. Leaves are about 1.5 cm long by 6 mm wide, more or less elliptic, and lightly glaucous, with reddish margins. Inflorescences are lateral, simple, and 3–5 cm long. Flowers are pinkish-purple, with white corolla tubes. *Hebe* 'Monica' is hardy and flowers during the summer. It originated at County Park Nursery, Essex, United Kingdom, in 1974.

Hebe 'Mrs. Winder'

This early cultivar remains popular, being especially valued for its foliage, which takes on dark purplish or bronze tints during the colder months of the year. It is also very hardy. Its growth is fairly compact and rounded, and it will grow to about 90 cm tall. Branchlets are brownish or dark purple and have sparse, bifarious hairs. This cultivar does not form a true leaf bud, which is one way of distinguishing it from spurious lookalikes. The dark green leaves are about 4.5 cm long by 1 cm wide, oblong-elliptic, and slightly concave, with reddish-purple margins. Inflorescences are 6.5–10 cm long. Violet-blue flowers appear during autumn. Although the origin of *Hebe* 'Mrs. Winder' cannot be traced with any certainty, it has been traced back to T. Smith's Daisy Hill nursery catalogue of 1933–1934, which suggests that it might have an Irish origin.

Hebe 'Nantyderry' (PLATE 105)

This is a hebe of more recent origin, having been discovered in the late 1970s, when it was noticed in a private garden in the United Kingdom. It forms a loosely rounded shrub to about 75 cm tall with a diameter of about 75 cm. The leaves are about 3 cm long, with a mid green upper surface and margin of dark purplish-brown during the growing season, becoming a shining, reddish-purple during winter. Its inflorescences are about 3 cm long, and the flowers are violet fading to white. Flowering occurs during summer. *Hebe* 'Nantyderry' appeared as a small seedling in the garden of Rose Clay, who later registered it with the International Registration Authority for *Hebe*.

Hebe 'Neil's Choice'

One of the taller cultivars, *Hebe* 'Neil's Choice' will grow to about 1.5 or 2 m tall. It is quite hardy and is worth growing for it foliage, which takes on a reddish colour during the winter. It originated in County Park Nursery, Essex, United Kingdom, in 1976. According to Graham Hutchins (1997) it is very hardy and will flower from summer until the middle of winter, when, even after severe frosts, it will still have flowers on it.

DESCRIPTION: Branchlets dark reddish-purple, glabrous, sometimes with indefinite bifarious pubescence. Leaf bud rather small and without a sinus. Leaves 5–8 cm long by 1–2 cm wide, narrow-elliptic to ovate-oblong, apex subacute, abruptly narrowed to an almost sessile base, margins and midribs reddish-purple. Inflorescences lateral, simple, 7–12 cm long; flowers rather densely placed, deep violet-purple, corolla tube white.

Hebe 'Netta Dick'

Hebe 'Netta Dick' is a lower-growing hebe that only attains a height of about 50 cm. Its branchlets are green to brownish and bifariously pubescent. It does not have a distinct leaf bud and therefore has no sinus. The leaves are 2–3 cm long by 7–10 mm wide, elliptic to ovate-elliptic, the upper surface a deep green, and the margins and young growth a reddish-purple. Inflorescences are lateral, simple, and 4–9 cm long, the flowers violet-purple and densely placed. This hebe is very hardy and flowers from about mid summer until winter. It originated as a chance seedling in County Park Nursery, Essex, United Kingdom, about 1990.

Hebe 'Nicola's Blush'

A low- to medium-growing plant that forms a rounded bush 60 cm–1 m tall. Its green to slightly purplish branchlets are pubescent all around. It does not form a tight leaf bud and consequently has no sinus. The narrow-elliptic to elliptic-lanceolate leaves are 2.5–4.5 cm long by 10–12 mm wide, the upper surface green, and the margins reddish and finely pubescent. Inflorescences are lateral, simple, and 4–8 cm long, the flowers almost hiding the rachis. The flowers are a very pleasant colour, pink at first but fading to white, producing a bicoloured effect. This cultivar originated in County Park Nursery, Essex, United Kingdom, in 1980. According to Graham Hutchins (1997) it has a very long flowering period, commencing in mid summer and often continuing until late autumn or, if the season is mild, even until mid winter.

Hebe 'Ohakea'

A cultivar with a rounded habit of growth, up to perhaps 80 cm tall by 1 m in diameter. The faintly red-margined leaves are about 1.9 cm long by 4 mm wide and are olive-green overlaid with tones of bronze. It has pinkish-lavender flowers that are produced on openly branched inflorescences during late spring or early summer.

Hebe 'Ohakea' was a spontaneous seedling that arose in the garden of nurseryman J. Allerdice of Sanson, Manawatu, around 1999. Because of Allerdice's proximity to the

Ohakea air base, the plant was named 'Ohakea'. The seedling appeared near a plant of *H. diosmifolia*, and it is assumed that this species may be one of the parents.

Hebe 'Oratia Beauty' (PLATE 106)

A very attractive cultivar that is quite floriferous. Its flower racemes provide an interesting effect: they are medium pink in the bud, but the flowers then open to a pure white, so that the raceme has a bicoloured appearance. This hebe is easily grown and quite drought-tolerant, but it may also be sufficiently frost-tender to require protection, particularly in parts of the northern hemisphere. Flowering is during mid summer.

This cultivar was introduced into cultivation by Hugh Redgrove of Oratia, Auckland, who grew it for a number of years. His plants originated from cutting material provided from an unknown source, and so nothing is known of its origin or parentage.

DESCRIPTION: A shrub to 75 cm tall. Leaf bud without a sinus. Leaves 4–6 cm long by about 2 cm wide, deep green and shining above, paler beneath, more or less elliptic. Flowers in short, compact racemes in mid summer, pink in bud and opening to white.

Hebe 'Oratia Gala' (PLATE 107)

This handsome shrub originated in the Oratia Native Plant Nursery, Auckland, in the early 1990s. It is possible that *Hebe* 'Oratia Beauty' had some influence on its parentage. Its shining leaves are attractive at all times, and it is quite drought-tolerant and easily grown.

DESCRIPTION: A shrub to 1.5 m tall by 1.5 m across. Branchlets green, glabrous. Leaves closely placed to rather widely spaced. Leaf blade 4–5.5 cm long by 1.4–2.3 cm wide, upper surface a bright shining green, very shortly petiolate. Flowers produced in compact racemes up to 6 cm long, excluding the peduncles, which are up to 3 cm long; flowers pedicellate, light beetroot-purple, posterior corolla lobe much longer than the rest.

Hebe 'Orphan Annie' (PLATE 108)

Discovered in 1995 as a branch sport of *Hebe* 'Mary Antoinette' by Ann Burton, proprietor of Annton Nursery, Cambridge, New Zealand. Its foliage is similar to that of its parent but with attractive cream and green variegation. Young leaves are a deep wine colour, and foliage is further enhanced during cold weather when the younger leaves take on a rosy flush. This cultivar is somewhat slower growing than its parent and forms a rounded shrub 40–50 cm tall with a diameter of about 50–60 cm. It grows well in full sun but will succeed quite well in direct shade that is not too intense. Prefers good drainage.

Hebe 'Otari Delight' (PLATE 109)

This cultivar originated in the Otari Native Plant Museum, Wellington, and is a hybrid between *Hebe townsonii* and *H. diosmifolia*. It arose as a spontaneous seedling. It appears to be reasonably hardy, although in many northern hemisphere gardens it may need to be given some protection over winter. It also appears to be fairly resistant to some of the more common problems afflicting hebes, such as downy mildew and septoria leaf spot. With its dark green, shining foliage and branched inflorescences of pale mauve flowers, it makes a handsome shrub, especially where something a little taller is required. It has fairly erect growth, and the inflorescences are crowded near the tips of the branchlets so that it is very showy when in full bloom. Its flowers have many of the characters of *H. townsonii* and are very dainty with their acutely pointed corolla lobes. Flowering is usually from late spring to early summer.

DESCRIPTION: A rather erect shrub to about 1.5 m tall. Branchlets glabrous, greenish to brownish, length of internodes two to three times the diameter. Leaf bud with a narrow sinus. Leaves 1.5–2.5 cm long by 4–6 mm wide, linear to linear-oblong or lanceolate, upper surface medium green to deep green, shining, paler beneath with domatia just in from the margin, margins with a number of small incisions or teeth that approximate the domatia; petiole short, about 4 mm, apex acute. Inflorescence simple or branched, peduncle to 8 mm long, rachis 1.8–2.5 cm, corolla tube longer than the calyx lobes, corolla 8–10 mm in diameter, lobes ovate, acute, pale mauve fading to white.

Hebe 'Petra's Pink'

This low-growing cultivar is usually no more than about 30 cm tall. It has a spreading habit and may be about 50 cm in diameter. The leaf bud has no sinus. Its leaves are obovate to elliptic-ovate, 1.2–1.8 cm long by 6–9 mm wide, spreading to recurved, green, gradually narrowed to a very short petiole, with purplish margins. Flowers are mauve-pink and loosely placed on 5–10 cm racemes. It originated at County Park Nursery, Essex, United Kingdom in 1982. According to Graham Hutchins (1997), this was the first small-leaved hebe cultivar with pink flowers. It is said to be quite hardy, and flowers are produced abundantly during summer.

Hebe 'Pewter Dome'

Although this cultivar was originally listed as belonging to *Hebe albicans*, the description of this cultivar leads one to suppose it is almost certainly of hybrid origin. It grows to about 90 cm tall, forming a densely rounded shrub, and spreads to cover about 1.5 m. Its leaves are generally smaller than those of typical *H. albicans* and their colour is not as glaucous. It produces white flowers in mid summer. This cultivar may have originated in the nursery of Jackman and Sons, Woking, Surrey, United Kingdom, probably before 1972.

Hebe 'Pimeba'

This cultivar grows to about 30 cm tall. Its whippy brown stems bear small, oval, attractively glaucous-grey leaves that become flushed with lavender in cooler months. The branchlets have lines of bifarious pubescence. Inflorescences are about 5 cm long, and flowers are violet-blue but fade to white with age. It originated at Blundells in Broadwell, Moreton-on-Marsh, Gloucestershire, United Kingdom, during the mid to late 1970s. According to J. Elliott, the originator, it was a self-sown seedling that originated in the stock beds of his nursery; he believes it to be the result of *Hebe* 'Glauca-caerulea' crossed with a plant of *H*. 'Caledonia' that was growing nearby.

Hebe 'Primley Gem'

Hebe 'Primley Gem' is reasonably common in cultivation. It grows to about 70 cm tall and is bushy and relatively hardy. Its green or brownish branchlets have minute bifarious pubescence. The leaf bud is small and has no sinus. Leaves are 2–3.5 cm long by 7–11 mm wide with dark green upper surfaces and entire, reddish, slightly sinuate margins; the midribs are reddish on young leaves. Flowers are purplish-blue, fading with age, and are densely placed on racemes 5–8 cm long. Flowering time is from early summer often until late autumn. *Hebe* 'Primley Gem' is said to have been raised at the Paignton Zoo, Devon, United Kingdom, possibly in the early 1960s or earlier. It is also known as *H*. 'Margery Fish', but that is a later name than 'Primley Gem'. One or two similar cultivars have been raised by other growers. 'Morning Glory', for example, was raised by a Mr. Sidford in 1972 and is said to be virtually indistinguishable from 'Primley Gem'.

Hebe 'Purple Tips' (PLATE 110)

This cultivar originated as a variegated branch sport on a plant of *Hebe* 'La Séduisante' that was growing in a private garden in New Plymouth, New Zealand. It was discovered before 1970. It is similar to 'La Séduisante', including its flowers, but its grey-green leaves are overlaid and variegated with cream. During the colder months of the year the leaves take on quite a strong rosy flush.

Hebe 'Quicksilver' (PLATE 111)

Graham Hutchins, the originator of this cultivar, considers it to be a seedling from what he refers to as the original form of *Hebe pimeleoides*; unfortunately, however, he does not indicate to which particular form he refers. Therefore, in the meantime and taking into account the nature and growth habit of this cultivar, it should not be regarded as a cultivar from either of the two subspecies of *H. pimeleoides* but rather as a hybrid that may have had one or the other subspecies in it. In habit and general appearance it is quite different from what would be expected of a cultivar of *H. pimeleoides* subsp. *pimeleoides*. Assuming that it may have been raised from what was formerly known as *H. pimeleoides* var. *rupestris* (now *H. pimeleoides* subsp. *faucicola*), there would still be doubt as to its veracity. Accordingly, it is preferable to regard it as a separate cultivar and not assign it to any particular species. It originated at County Park Nursery, Essex, United Kingdom, in 1965.

Hebe 'Quicksilver' has a rather stiff, wide-spreading habit of growth and may be up to 60 cm tall by as much across. It has dark purplish-black stems and smallish, glaucous, very grey leaves that usually measure about 4–8 mm long by 3–6 mm wide. The leaves contrast most effectively against the dark stems. Its violet-blue flowers are produced on short inflorescences 2–4 cm long. It usually flowers for quite a long period during the summer. It is best grown in a sunny situation.

Hebe 'Red Edge' (PLATE 112)
Although often referred to as belonging to *Hebe albicans*, this cultivar is really a hybrid from that species. It was raised as a seedling from a plant of *H. albicans* 'Snow Mound', and it was not until several years later, when it flowered and the flowers were violet, that it was concluded to be of hybrid origin. Its red-margined leaves also indicated its hybrid origin. It is a very handsome shrub, with lovely, red-margined, glaucous leaves and young shoots that assume a purplish-pink during winter months. Its mauve flowers are freely produced during mid summer, though only on older plants. It originated at County Park Nursery, Essex, United Kingdom, around 1974.

Hebe 'Rosie'
A rather dwarf hebe, 30–60 cm tall and usually as much across. It is said to be similar to *Hebe* 'Nicola's Blush', but its leaves are shorter, 2–2.5 cm long by 8–10 mm wide and more obovate. Its branched racemes are 4–8 cm long, and its flowers are quite a bright pink, but they typically fade to white with age. *Hebe* 'Rosie' originated in Bransford Nurseries, Worcester, United Kingdom, in 1985. It was discovered by the owner, John Tooby, who named it after his granddaughter. It flowers during mid summer but may also flower intermittently into the winter. *Hebe* 'Great Orme' may have been one of its parents.

Hebe 'Sandra Joy' (PLATE 113)
Hebe 'Sandra Joy' forms a rounded, bushy shrub to about 90 cm tall. The leaf bud has no sinus. Leaves are 6–10 cm long by 1.5–3 cm wide, elongate-elliptic to oblanceolate, the apex obtuse to subacute. Margins are pubescent and reddish. Flowers are a rich purple, fading with age, and borne on simple racemes up to 12 cm long. This hebe is a cross between what is said to be a bronze form of *H. speciosa* (most likely a hybrid) and *H. macrocarpa* var. *latisepala*. It originated in the Auckland Regional Botanic Gardens in 1988; the originator was Jack Hobbs.

Hebe 'Sapphire'
A cultivar of unknown origin that probably originated sometime before 1969. It is of medium to largish growth and may reach a metre tall or more. Its narrow, elliptic-oblong leaves are up to 6.5 cm long by about 1 cm wide and dark green. During winter, the

young leaves become suffused with a most attractive reddish colour. Bluish-purple flowers are produced on simple racemes 4–7 cm long, with flowering occurring over quite a long period during mid to late summer. *Hebe* 'Sapphire' is reasonably hardy, but if there is any doubt it should be planted where other shrubs may provide some protection.

Hebe 'Silver Queen' (PLATE 114)

Along with *Hebe* ×*franciscana* 'Lobelioides', this cultivar is much confused in horticulture and has numerous synonyms. This is the shrub that in the United Kingdom is commonly known as *H. elliptica* 'Variegata', *H.* 'Blue Gem Variegata', *H. (Veronica) elliptica* 'Latifolia Variegata', and *H.* ×*franciscana* 'Variegata', while in New Zealand and elsewhere it is incorrectly known as *H.* ×*franciscana* 'Waireka' and *H.* ×*franciscana* 'Variegata'. In one Danish pamphlet it has even been labelled *H.* 'Andersonii Variegata'. In his investigations into various cultivars of *Hebe*, Peter Heenan managed to trace the naming of this cultivar back to about 1911, when in the *Proceedings of the Royal Horticultural Society* (volume 37, p. 240) it was called *H.* 'Silver Queen' and was described as "dwarf shrub, pale yellow leaves, 1⅛ in. [2.8 cm] × 2⅛ in. [5.4 cm], central streak of pale green." In the same year it also appeared in London's *Garden Magazine* (volume 54, pp. 819–820) as *Veronica* 'Silver Queen'. Therefore, the plant that has long been known under a variety of synonyms should now be known as *H.* 'Silver Queen'.

In general growth and habit this cultivar is similar to *Hebe* ×*franciscana* 'Lobelioides', though usually smaller. Its deep green leaves are broadly variegated with creamy-yellow around their margins, and the foliage remains attractive at all times of the year, making this a useful shrub. According to Heenan, this cultivar is a variegated sport from *H.* 'Combe Royal'. Its flowers are a reddish violet-purple, similar to those of *H.* 'Combe Royal', and quite distinct from the violet-blue of *H.* ×*franciscana* 'Lobelioides'. The name *H.* ×*franciscana* 'Waireka', still commonly used in New Zealand, is attributable to Duncan and Davies, New Plymouth, New Zealand, who bestowed the name in 1963 believing the plant to be an unnamed cultivar. Unfortunately, the epithet 'Waireka' has persisted, and it is now very difficult to convince nurseries that this name should be abandoned and replaced with 'Silver Queen'.

Hebe 'Simon Délaux'

This cultivar is somewhat similar to *Hebe* 'La Séduisante', a cultivar that originated in the late 19th century. 'Simon Délaux' is a much-branched shrub to 1.2 m tall. Its deep green leaves are ovate to obovate, about 5 cm long by 2.5 cm wide, and have a purplish undersurface, as does the leaf bud. Its flowers are crimson and produced on racemes that may be 10 cm or more in length. In northern hemisphere countries it is not fully hardy and should be grown where it has a reasonable degree of protection during the winter. It is believed that 'Simon Délaux' is a hybrid from *H. speciosa* and was raised by Délaux of Toulouse, France, possibly during the latter part of the 19th century. The name of the originator is frequently misspelt as Deleaux.

Hebe 'Snowdrift' (PLATE 115)

This New Zealand–raised cultivar originated from a plant purchased by the Auckland Regional Botanic Gardens under the name *Hebe brachysiphon*; however, it proved to be quite different from that species and was given the name 'Snowdrift'. It may be derived from *H. stenophylla*.

DESCRIPTION: A shrub to 2 m tall by 2 m wide. Branchlets glabrous, brownish. Leaf bud with a small, very narrow sinus. Leaves linear to linear-lanceolate, 2.5–3.5 cm long by 4–5 mm wide, shortly petioled, apex acute. Inflorescences in several pairs, simple to occasionally tripartite, raceme about 5.4 cm long including peduncle. Flowers pedicellate, corolla 7–8 mm in diameter, initially white but later in the season may show a hint of pale mauve. Anthers deep purple.

Hebe 'Southern Burgundy'

A cross that has *Hebe speciosa* in its parentage. Its olive-green leaves are about 6.5 by 1.8 cm, their upper surfaces shining. Midribs are purple and, along with the purplish stems, darken during the winter months. Plum-purple flowers are produced on racemes about 6 cm long and generally appear from late summer to autumn. The bush has an erect habit of growth and will attain about 1 m by perhaps 80 cm in diameter. It was raised by Stephen Membrey of Southern Advanced Plants of Mornington, Victoria, Australia.

Hebe 'Southern Drift'

This smaller hebe forms a compact, rounded habit, growing to only about 60 cm tall with a diameter of about 70 cm. The upper surfaces of its lime-green leaves are shining, and the leaf blades are about 3 cm long by 6 mm wide. Its pink flowers are quite pale and appear on 3 cm long racemes through late summer and autumn. The stamen filaments are also pink. Raised by Southern Advanced Plants of Mornington, Victoria, Australia.

Hebe 'Southern Glory'

Apparently similar to *Hebe* 'Autumn Glory' but with a somewhat larger, more open habit of growth and not heavily branched. Its foliage is similar to but larger than that of 'Autumn Glory', and the leaves are a similar colour, although with reddish margins and midribs. The flowers are produced on racemes about 7 cm long and are a deep violet. Flowering is generally from late summer to autumn, and the whole bush makes a very fine display. Raised by Southern Advanced Plants of Mornington, Victoria, Australia.

Hebe 'Southern Seas'

This hebe grows to about 1.2 m high by about 1.5 m in diameter and has an open, often rather sprawling habit of growth. Its shining leaves are about 6 cm long by 1.8 cm wide and medium green with pale midribs. The racemes are about 5 cm long, and dark mauve flowers are produced from late spring to summer. Raised by Southern Advanced Plants of Mornington, Victoria, Australia.

Hebe 'Southern Skies'

This compact, bushy shrub may measure about 80 by 80 cm. Its leaves are pale green and have distinct reddish margins. The racemes are about 4.6 cm long, and the flowers are pale bluish-purple. The young tips of the new foliage are somewhat susceptible to downy mildew. Raised by Southern Advanced Plants of Mornington, Victoria, Australia.

Hebe 'Southern Snow'

Probably one of the smallest of the "Southern" series of hebes raised by Southern Advanced Plants of Mornington, Victoria, Australia. It will grow to about 45 cm tall and has a diameter of about 60 cm. Its leaves are deepish green and about 2.7 cm by 6 mm. Its white flowers are produced on racemes about 3.5 cm long. While it is reported as growing well in Canterbury, New Zealand, in some other areas the leaves may be quite severely attacked by downy mildew.

Hebe 'Southern Sunrise'

This medium-sized shrub grows to about 80 cm tall with a diameter of 1 m. Its medium green leaves have yellow-green midribs and its branchlets are a similar colour. Leaves vary in size on a single plant and may be from 3 cm by 9 mm to 6 by 1.5 cm. The rose-pink flowers are loosely placed along racemes up to 12 cm long. Flowering generally occurs from January (mid summer) to February (late summer), with some intermittent flowering at other times. As the name indicates, this is another cultivar raised by Southern Advanced Plants of Mornington, Victoria, Australia.

Hebe 'Spender's Seedling'

Hebe 'Spender's Seedling' is rated as being reliable, hardy, and very free-flowering. It grows to about a metre tall and has narrow, deep green leaves that are not shiny and about 5–7.5 cm long by 5–7 mm wide. The leaf bud has no sinus. Its racemes are slender, lateral, simple, and 7–10 cm long, with somewhat loosely placed flowers. The flowers are white with violet-purple anthers and are produced over several months. It is an ideal border plant and is very easily grown.

The plant that is often distributed under the name 'Spender's Seedling' is usually a form of *Hebe stenophylla*. There is also confusion with a similar or identical cultivar that is grown under the name 'C. P. Raffill', the suggestion being that the plant known as 'C. P. Raffill' is the true 'Spender's Seedling'. However, there will probably continue to be arguments as to which plant should be regarded as the true 'Spender's Seedling'.

Hebe 'Sunstreak' (PLATE 116)

Hebe 'Sunstreak' arose as a variegated branch sport on 'Wiri Image'. Its leaf margins are irregularly margined with cream, while the centre varies from grey-green to pale green and deep green with some greyish-green; otherwise its general dimensions are much the same as for 'Wiri Image'. It originated with Paul Hipkin of Napier, New Zealand.

Hebe 'Temptation'

This cultivar will attain about a metre in height and as much in diameter. Its rather olive-green leaves are about 3.5 cm long by about 1 cm wide. They tend to have a reddish margin when young and exhibit a distinctly bronze shading during colder weather. Delicate shell-pink flowers are produced on racemes about 4.5 cm in length, while the lower portions of the corollas fade to white as they age. Bred by Lowaters Nursery in England.

Hebe 'Tiny Tot'

A seedling raised from *Hebe* 'Youngii' in 1972 at County Park Nursery, Essex, United Kingdom. It makes a compact little shrublet up to about 10 cm tall, and Graham Hutchins (1997) regards it as the smallest of the many seedlings that he raised from *H.* 'Youngii'. It has very small leaves that are closely placed, and violet-blue flowers on short racemes. It is quite hardy and a useful plant for rock gardens or trough gardens. Flowering is from about mid to late summer.

Hebe 'Trixie'

This cultivar is a seedling that was raised from *Hebe albicans* 'Snow Mound' and produced at County Park Nursery, Essex, United Kingdom, in 1970. According to Graham Hutchins (1997), it is not very similar to its parent, which poses the question of what its other parent may be. It grows to about 60 cm tall and spreads to as much or more across. The leaf bud is small and has no sinus. Its rather closely placed leaves are dark green and, although not variegated, have distinctive yellowish margins. They measure about 1.2–1.8 cm long by 5–8 mm wide. Its white flowers are produced in simple, dense, lateral racemes up to 4 cm long. The anthers are purple before dehiscing. Flowering occurs from mid to late summer.

Hebe 'Violet Meikle'

This very distinctive cultivar is unlikely to be mistaken for any other. In growth and general appearance it has similarities with *Hebe speciosa*, but its flowers are much larger and in shape and size are more akin to those of *H. elliptica*. However, its most outstanding feature is the very deep purple of its flowers. Such depth of colour exists in extremely few *Hebe* cultivars. *Hebe* 'Violet Meikle' is quite frost-tender; severe frosts will cause stems to split, which may result in the death of the plant. Accordingly it should be grown only in sheltered situations and is more suited to a frost-free climate. This hebe was named by W. Meikle, a New Zealand nurseryman in the 1930s. Whether he had a wife named Violet or named the plant on account of its colour is open to question.

DESCRIPTION: A bushy shrub 90 cm–1.5 m tall. Leaf bud with a conspicuous sinus. Leaves are spreading, 6.2–7.5 cm long by 2.2–2.5 cm wide, oblanceolate to oblong-obovate, apex obtuse or occasionally subacute. Inflorescences lateral, simple, up to 9.5 cm long. Flowers dark purple and closely placed. Corolla lobes wide-spreading and about 7 mm long. Stamen filaments deep purple.

Hebe 'Waikiki'

This cultivar forms a wide-spreading shrub to about 1.5 m tall. During the growing season its leaves are medium green, but during the winter the younger leaves turn a most attractive purplish-bronze. Its leaf bud has no sinus. The leaves are oblong-lanceolate to narrow-elliptic and 2.5–3.5 cm long by 8–10 mm wide. Apexes are subacute. Inflorescences are lateral, simple, and much exceeding the leaves, up to 7 cm long. Violet flowers are closely placed but not completely hiding the leaves. This hebe is very hardy and well worth a place in the shrub garden. It first appeared in the 1941–1942 nursery catalogue of Messrs. Hillier and Sons, United Kingdom, but nothing is known of its origin or its name, which seems to refer to the famous Hawaiian beach, and which is certainly not a New Zealand place name.

Hebe 'Walter Buccleugh' (PLATE 117)

Another seedling from *Hebe* 'Youngii'. It originated at Boughton House, Northamptonshire, United Kingdom, possibly sometime in the early 1970s. It forms a low-growing, spreading shrub with rather erect branches up to about 45 cm tall. The branchlets are dark purplish. Leaves are about 1–1.2 cm long by about 5 mm wide, and although they are commonly described as slightly grey-green, they are in fact green or only a slightly greyed green. The margins are reddish. Flowers are a reddish-purple and densely produced on lateral racemes up to 3 or 4 cm long. Occasionally some racemes may be branched. This is quite a hardy cultivar and is suitable for a rock garden or the front of a border.

Hebe 'Walter Buccleugh' was originally known as 'Boughton Claret', but as its flowers were not claret, the raiser agreed to change the name. Accordingly it was named after the eighth Duke of Buccleuch, who had admired the plant when visiting his cousin's garden at Dower House. For unknown reasons, the older spelling of his name was adopted.

Hebe 'Wingletye'

Another cultivar that originated with Graham Hutchins in County Park Nursery, Essex, United Kingdom, in 1971. According to Hutchins (1997), it is a sister plant of *Hebe* 'County Park', both being raised from the same batch of seed that was collected from *H.* 'Glauca-caerulea'. It is a spreading or decumbent shrub to about 20 cm tall and may grow to a metre in diameter. The branchlets are green to purplish. Leaves are 1–1.5 cm long by 5–6 mm wide and glaucous, with pale or reddish margins. Inflorescences are 4–5 cm long and rather dense, with amethyst or lilac-blue flowers produced in early to mid summer. This plant is quite hardy and useful for rock gardens or trough gardens.

Hebe 'Wiri Blush'

Hebe 'Wiri Blush' forms a spreading bush that has shiny green leaves suffused with purple. It has purplish-red flowers during the summer that continue, on the bush, until the autumn. It can also have a second flowering during the spring. It was raised by Jack Hobbs in the Auckland Regional Botanic Gardens in 1986, but was not considered to be worthy of inclusion in the "Wiri" series. However, it was eventually released to Omahanui Nursery (now Naturally Native New Zealand Plants), who put it on the market under the name of 'Wiri Blush', with the approval of the originator.

Hebe 'Wiri Charm' (PLATE 118)

Raised from seed collected from *Hebe* 'Wiri Jewel' (a selected form of *H. speciosa*) pollinated by pink-flowered *H. diosmifolia*. It forms a shrub to 75 cm tall by 1.30 m across and is more compact and less upright than *H.* 'Wiri Gem'. Leaves are 3–4 cm long by 8–12 mm wide and oblanceolate, with slightly undulating margins and obtuse apexes. Branchlets are reddish. Flowers are a deep shade of rose-purple, on racemes that are 3–5.5 cm long and simple or often branched. Flowering is very prolific and occurs over a long period during summer, with a less pronounced flush sometimes occurring during winter. This cultivar was produced by Jack Hobbs of the Auckland Regional Botanic Gardens in 1986. It is quite disease-resistant.

Hebe 'Wiri Cloud'

This fairly hardy, small-leaved cultivar flowers quite early in the summer. Its flowers are a deep pink and cover the tips of the stems. It was bred at the Auckland Regional Botanic Gardens by Jack Hobbs, but Hobbs did not consider it good enough to be included in the "Wiri" series. However, material was released to Naturally Native New Zealand Plants, Tauranga, and was retailed as 'Wiri Cloud', a name subsequently approved by its breeder.

Hebe 'Wiri Dawn' (PLATE 119)

This small, much-branched shrub grows to about 45 cm tall with a diameter of about 75 cm or more. The leaf bud has a small sinus. The spreading leaves are 2–3 cm long by 5–6 mm wide and linear with acute apexes. Inflorescences are lateral, simple, and 3–4 cm long. Flowers are a pale pink with a white corolla tube. Flowering occurs over quite a long period during the summer months, with a second flowering occurring in autumn and winter. With its low, spreading habit, this plant is ideal for growing over a low wall where its stems will cascade down. It was bred at the Auckland Regional Botanic Gardens by Jack Hobbs in 1987. Its parents were *H.* 'Wiri Joy' and a prostrate form of *H. albicans*.

Hebe 'Wiri Desire'

This vigorous shrub is among the largest cultivars of the "Wiri" series, growing to 1.2 m tall or more, with quite a large spread. Its inflorescences are about 7 cm long and quite dense. The deep rose-pink flowers are most attractive when in bud and contrast quite nicely with the new foliage, which is flushed with bronze tints. This hebe was raised at the Auckland Regional Botanic Gardens by Jack Hobbs. One parent was *Hebe speciosa*; the other is unknown.

Hebe 'Wiri Gem'

Raised from seed collected from *Hebe* 'Wiri Jewel' pollinated by pink-flowered *H. diosmifolia*. It forms a rather upright shrub to 1 m tall and has a neat, symmetrical shape. Branchlets are reddish, becoming dark grey-purple with age. The leaf bud has a distinct sinus. Leaves are 2.5–4 cm long by 7–12 mm wide and oblong. The apex is acute, and the margins and part of the midrib are reddish. Inflorescences are lateral, simple, or sometimes with two branches, and crowded near the tips of the branchlets. Rose-purple flowers are produced intermittently over a period of about nine months, the main flowering occurring from April (mid autumn) to October (mid spring), with a brief flush in December (summer). Raised at the Auckland Regional Botanic Gardens in 1986 by Jack Hobbs.

Hebe 'Wiri Grace' (PLATE 120)

Hebe 'Wiri Grace' forms a much-branched shrub to 2 m tall or more. The leaf bud has an indistinct sinus. Its leaves are about 9 cm long by about 2.5 cm wide, yellowish-green, and glabrous, with entire margins. The inflorescences are lateral, simple, and 9–13 cm long. Flowers are pale mauve. It was raised in 1982 at the Auckland Regional Botanic Gardens by Jack Hobbs. Its parents are a mauve hybrid of *H. speciosa* and probably *H. bollonsii* × *H. stricta*, the latter hybrid being the pollen parent. In general appearance it resembles *H. stricta* but is more compact. It is disease-resistant and more ornamental than typical forms of *H. stricta*. Its long mauve inflorescences are abundantly produced during January (mid summer) and February (late summer), but sporadic flowering also occurs until winter. It should be pruned in order to maintain compactness.

Hebe 'Wiri Image'

This much-branched shrub grows to about 1 m tall and about 1.4 m in diameter. Its leaf bud has a very small sinus. The spreading to more or less ascending leaves are 2–5 cm long by 7 mm–2.5 cm wide and linear-lanceolate, with a dark green upper surface, obtuse to subacute apex, and entire, slightly revolute margins. Racemes are lateral, simple, and 7–10 cm long. Flowers are in the mid violet range, and flowering occurs during November (early summer), December (summer), and January (mid summer), with intermittent flowering occurring throughout winter. This cultivar was raised at the Auckland Regional Botanic Gardens in 1982 by Jack Hobbs. Its parents are *Hebe bollonsii* and possibly *H. venustula*.

Hebe 'Wiri Jewel'

A rounded shrub 1–1.5 m tall. In habit it is similar to *Hebe speciosa*. The leaf bud has a distinct sinus. Leaves are about 11 cm long by 3.5 cm wide, the upper surface deep green, the midrib reddish, the apex subacute, and the margins entire and undulating. Inflorescences are lateral, simple, and 7–10 cm long, the flowers a rich ruby-red. This cultivar was raised at the Auckland Regional Botanic Gardens in 1982 by Jack Hobbs. It was grown from seed collected from an open-pollinated plant of *H. speciosa*.

Hebe 'Wiri Joy'

This compact shrub reaches about 80 cm in height and up to about 1 m in diameter. The leaf bud has a distinct sinus. Leaves are about 5 cm long by 11 mm wide, deep green and shining above, with margins that are entire or with a pair of small incisions near their apexes. Inflorescences are lateral, simple, and about 5 cm long, the flowers a pinkish-purple. This cultivar was raised at the Auckland Regional Botanic Gardens in 1982 by Jack Hobbs. Its parents are *Hebe speciosa* and *H.* ×*carnea* 'Carnea'.

Hebe 'Wiri Mist'

Hebe 'Wiri Mist' is distinguished by its compact growth, which tends to be rather flattish on top, and by its very compact, almost dumpy inflorescences of white flowers. When in bud the sheathing calyces conceal the unopened corollas so that they appear to be greenish or slightly pinkish. It is very floriferous, the flowers almost completely hiding the plant. Flowering generally occurs from late spring to early summer and occasionally again in autumn. This cultivar originated prior to 1991 in the Auckland Regional Botanic Gardens as part of their hebe-breeding programme. It is a hybrid between *H. diosmifolia* and *H. albicans*. Its raiser, Jack Hobbs, considers it to be the best of the "Wiri" series that he bred.

DESCRIPTION: A spreading shrub to 60 cm tall by up to 75 cm wide. Branchlets minutely bifariously pubescent, internodes about one to two times the diameter. Leaf bud with a small sinus. Leaves quite close-set, 1.5–2 cm long by 5–8 mm wide, elliptic to oblong-elliptic, medium green above, slightly paler beneath. Peduncle of inflorescence to 1–1.5 cm long, minutely puberulous. Inflorescence up to 4 cm long by 2 cm in diameter, very compact, flowers pedicellate, white, about 8 mm in diameter, anthers pink.

Hebe 'Wiri Port'

Forms a rounded shrub to about 90 cm tall and about as much in diameter. It has large leaves with a tinge of purple. Its inflorescences are about 6 cm long and densely covered with distinctive pink to wine-red flowers. It usually flowers from late summer to autumn. *Hebe* 'Wiri Port' originated in the Auckland Regional Botanic Gardens as part of their hebe breeding programme. It is a hybrid from *H. speciosa*, but the other parent is not known.

Hebe 'Wiri Prince'

A shrub to 1.5 m tall of vigorous, upright habit. Inflorescences are lateral, simple, and about 11 cm long, the flowers a rich violet purple. Its main flowering is from May (late autumn) to August (late winter) with additional flushes during mid and late summer. This cultivar was raised in 1989 by Jack Hobbs at the Auckland Regional Botanic Gardens. It was bred from seed collected from a plant of 'Wiri Jewel'.

Hebe 'Wiri Spears' (PLATE 121)

Hebe 'Wiri Spears' is an erect shrub to 1.2–2 m tall. The leaf bud has a distinct sinus. Its leaves are 9–12 cm long by 1.5–2.5 cm wide and lanceolate, with deep green upper surfaces and distinctly red margins and midrib. The inflorescences are 12–16 cm long, and the bluish-purple flowers are fairly close-set. Where space permits, *H.* 'Wiri Spears' makes a fine background shrub or specimen plant. It usually flowers from mid to late summer and when in full bloom is a fine sight. It was bred in 1982 in the Auckland Regional Botanic Gardens by Jack Hobbs.

Hebe 'Wiri Splash' (PLATE 122)

Hebe 'Wiri Splash' is a pretty shrub, but others in the "Wiri" series are probably more desirable. It originated in the Auckland Regional Botanic Gardens in 1982 and was the result of seed collected from an open-pollinated plant of *H. brachysiphon* that may have crossed with a nearby plant of *H.* 'Lavender Lace'. It was raised by Jack Hobbs. It usually flowers from about mid summer.

DESCRIPTION: A compact shrub to about 90 cm tall with a spread of about 1 m. Branchlets green to brownish, glabrous, length of internodes two to three times the diameter. Leaf bud with a long, narrow sinus. Leaves 1.8–2.8 cm long by 4–7 mm wide, linear to oblanceolate, spreading to somewhat recurving, upper surface medium green to yellowish-green. Inflorescences 3.5–4.5 cm long. Flowers rather crowded, rosy-purple fading to white; calyx lobes shorter than the corolla lobes, tube white.

Hebe 'Wiri Vision' (PLATE 123)
This cross between 'Wiri Jewel' and 'Wiri Joy' grows to about 90 cm tall and may spread to about 1.2 m in diameter. Its leaf bud has a small sinus. The leaves are about 5–6.5 cm long by 1.2–2 cm wide and obovate-oblong to oblanceolate, the upper surface is a deep green, and the margins are entire, somewhat undulating, and tend to be somewhat revolute. The racemes are lateral and simple, the flowers purple-red. Generally it flowers over quite a long period, from autumn to winter, and has a secondary flowering during summer. It was bred in the Auckland Regional Botanic Gardens in 1987 and raised by Jack Hobbs.

Hebe 'Wiri Vogue'
A shrub to about 1 m with a good ball-like habit. Leaves are a dark, glossy green. Racemes are quite plump, 6–8 cm long; flowers are soft pink, filaments white. Flowers well in both summer and autumn. Bred in the Auckland Regional Botanic Gardens by Jack Hobbs. One parent was *Hebe speciosa*; the other is not known.

Hebe 'Youngii'
Hebe 'Youngii' dates back to before the 1920s, and since that time it has masqueraded under one or two synonyms and given rise to quite a number of similar cultivars. It was first grown in the Christchurch Botanic Gardens, New Zealand, as an unnamed seedling. Around the mid 1920s, L. B. Hart of Lawrence, Otago, visited the gardens in the company of curator James Young and much admired the plant in question. According to an eye-witness account, he drew a plant label from his pocket, wrote *Veronica youngii* on it, and stuck the label in the ground in front of what is now *H.* 'Youngii'.

At one stage this plant was incorrectly catalogued as *Veronica* (*Hebe*) *spedenii*, which is actually a whipcord hybrid, and later, in the early 1960s, it was sent to England as an unnamed hebe by North Otago nurseryman Carl Teschner. Valerie Finnis, to whom it was sent, decided to name the plant after its sender. Thereafter, *H.* 'Carl Teschner' became firmly entrenched in English gardens, and many years passed before English gardeners could be persuaded that *H.* 'Youngii' and *H.* 'Carl Teschner' were one and the same plant.

Hebe 'Youngii' is actually a hybrid between *H. pimeleoides* subsp. *pimeleoides* and *H. elliptica*. It probably arose in the Christchurch Botanic Gardens as a spontaneous hybrid.

Many years later, W. B. Brockie, who had been present when *H.* 'Youngii' was named by L. B. Hart, replicated the cross. To do so he used *H. pimeleoides* subsp. *pimeleoides* and the Stewart Island form of *H. elliptica*. This form of *H. elliptica* has white flowers without the touch of violet common among many other forms of the species, and so the flower colour of some of the resultant seedlings was a little lighter than that of *H.* 'Youngii'.

This cultivar is a neat plant of decumbent habit. Its dark purplish branchlets are clad with small, even leaves. The leaf bud has a small sinus. Leaves are 7–12 mm long by 3–5 mm wide, lanceolate to oblong-lanceolate or broad-ovate, medium green above, and coriaceous. Inflorescences are about 4 cm long and crowded near the tips of the branchlets. Flowers are violet and loosely placed, although more or less hiding the rachis. This hebe is easily grown and is a good choice for rock gardens or trough gardens.

9
Hebe Relatives

This chapter covers the many garden-worthy relatives of *Hebe*, including species and hybrids of *Heliohebe*, ×*Heohebe*, *Parahebe*, and *Chionohebe*. Flowering times and months given apply to the southern hemisphere unless otherwise stated. Seasonal equivalents are provided where there may be doubt. For example, a plant that blooms in December in New Zealand is said to bloom in summer. More newly recognised species that I have not yet seen or grown myself are marked by an asterisk (*).

Heliohebe

This genus includes species that were formerly in the *Hebe* informal group "Paniculatae." It comprises five species, a number of varieties, and two well-known cultivars. All members of the genus seem to be very susceptible to downy mildew, especially during the spring and early summer when conditions may be warm and humid. Once downy mildew attacks, it can be extremely difficult to control. In general, heliohebes appear to be more resistant to the attacks of this debilitating disease when they are grown in a dry climate. They usually prefer a well-drained soil and an open, sunny situation with plenty of air circulation. Being planted in a well-drained soil does not necessarily mean that they should be grown under drought conditions, however.

Heliohebe acuta *
This more recently discovered species (1990) has a very restricted distribution in Marlborough. It is generally similar to *Heliohebe raoulii* subsp. *raoulii* but can be distinguished by its narrower leaves, which are longitudinally folded and have more teeth around their margins. The leaf apexes are also more narrowly acute, and it has bright pink flowers. It is usually a small, twiggy shrub with thick, corky bark. After pollination the flowers become mauve. I am not certain whether this species is in cultivation, but if so, it will only be in the collections of one or two enthusiasts and institutions. Its specific name refers to its pointed leaves.

DESCRIPTION: A small, twiggy shrub no more than 5–20 cm tall with thick, corky bark. Branches ascending to erect, branchlets red-brown to grey, internodes 1–4 mm long. Leaves 5–15 mm long by 2–6 mm wide, lanceolate to oblanceolate, coriaceous, rigid and folded, apex acute, margins red, with three to eight pairs of crenate to serrate teeth, upper surface green to bronze-green, dull, undersurface paler and dull, petiole 1–5 mm long. Inflorescences 1–2 cm long, peduncle 3–6 mm long, rachis pubescent, bracts opposite and decussate, acute, ciliate and deltoid; pedicels shorter than the bracts, pubescent; calyx deeply divided, lobes ovate to deltoid. Corolla 4–5 mm in diameter, bright pink, tube 1.8–2 mm long by 1 mm wide, shorter than the calyx, glabrous, lobes glabrous. Stamen filaments coloured, anthers pale yellow. Style pink to mauve. Capsule dark brown, 2–2.5 mm long by 1–1.5 mm wide, truncate to emarginate.

DISTRIBUTION: South Island. Found in Marlborough Province in only two known localities: the George Stream at the northern end of the Seaward Kaikoura Range and at Palmer Stream in the Clarence Valley. There is also probably a third location at Kowhai Stream on the Seaward Kaikoura Range. Grows at 700–830 m.

Heliohebe ×*fairfieldensis* 'Fairfieldii'

This cultivar is not only among the most beautiful shrubs for the home garden but is also one of the most adaptable of the heliohebes. It eventually grows to about 90 cm tall and about 1.2 m wide. Its red-margined foliage is handsome at all times, and its large sprays of pinkish lavender-violet flowers are abundantly produced. It prefers a sunny situation and a well-drained soil. One of the secrets to successful maintenance is to prune off all spent flower spikes immediately after flowering. This not only keeps the plant tidy but also encourages the production of new growth, which is essential for keeping the bush healthy and compact. *Heliohebe* ×*fairfieldensis* 'Fairfieldii' originated in William Martin's Fairfield Nursery, near Dunedin, New Zealand, sometime during the latter part of the 19th century. Its parents are believed to be H. *hulkeana* and H. *lavaudiana*. It is widely cultivated in New Zealand and is often erroneously sold as H. *hulkeana*.

DESCRIPTION: A rather stout, erect, much-branched shrub 60 cm–1.2 m tall. Branchlets finely pubescent, purplish, length of internodes several to many times the diameter. Leaves more or less spreading, 2–3.2 cm long by 1.6–2 cm wide, broad-ovate to oblong-orbicular, obtuse to more or less subacute, rather abruptly to gradually narrowing to a broad, channelled petiole up to 1.2 cm long, glabrous, coriaceous, bright green to dark green, upper surface shining, paler beneath, margins reddish, coarsely crenate-dentate. Inflorescences rather broad, terminal panicles 15–23 cm long, the branches to 8.2 cm long with some of the basal ones again branched, peduncles and branches finely pubescent or puberulous. Flowers lavender-violet, erect, sessile, crowded, hiding the panicle branches; bracts about 2 mm long, ovate-lanceolate, acute, glabrous, margins ciliolate. Calyx glabrous to slightly puberulous, lobes acute, ciliolate, exceeding the bracts; corolla about 11 mm in diameter, tube slightly shorter than or equalling the calyx lobes, corolla lobes spreading, about twice as long as the tube, broad-ovate to more or less rounded, obtuse to subacute. Stamens a little exserted. Capsule about twice as long as the calyx.

Heliohebe 'Hagley Park'

A hybrid that originated in the Christchurch Botanic Gardens, New Zealand, during the 1940s, raised from open-pollinated seed collected from a plant of *Heliohebe raoulii* subsp. *raoulii* that is presumed to have crossed with a nearby plant of *H. hulkeana*. It was raised by W. B. Brockie, who was in charge of the New Zealand plant section at that time, and who named the plant after the location of the botanic gardens in Hagley Park. Some nurseries have misnamed it *H.* "Hagleyi" and *H.* "Lady Hagley." Like *H.* ×*fairfieldensis* 'Fairfieldii', this cultivar is far more amenable to cultivation than either of its parents. It grows to about 50 cm tall and is ideal for a small garden or rock garden. It has a very neat appearance and, as with *H.* ×*fairfieldensis* 'Fairfieldii', should be clipped over immediately after flowering in order to encourage the production of new growth and to keep it tidy. It grows best in a sunny situation and a well-drained soil. It has narrow, red-margined leaves, usually 4–5 cm long, and produces panicles, up to 30 cm long, of rosy-purple flowers.

DESCRIPTION: An erect to somewhat spreading shrub 30–50 cm tall. Branchlets pubescent with short, downward-pointing hairs, internodes three to four times the diameter. Leaves 2.8–5 cm long by 1–1.2 cm wide, tapering to a narrowly winged petiole, oblong-elliptic to slightly obovate, glabrous, coriaceous, upper surface shining, paler beneath, margins reddish, bluntly serrate. Inflorescences terminal panicles 11.2–30 cm long with secondary branching towards their bases. Flowers rosy-purple, sessile, bracts 2–3 mm long, rather broad, subacute, ciliate. Calyx lobes similar to the bracts but broadly ovate and more obtuse; corolla lobes about 3 mm long, longer than the tube, ovate. Capsule about 3 mm long, longer than the calyx lobes.

Heliohebe hulkeana (PLATE 124)
New Zealand lilac

This medium shrub is seldom more than 70 cm tall, although it may spread more widely. Its leaves are usually shining and red-margined, and when in flower it may be regarded as one of the gems of the Marlborough flora. Its inflorescences are 15–35 cm or even occasionally up to 48 cm long. The flower colour varies from pale violet to mauve or pale pinkish and may even occasionally be white. Two subspecies have been named. Subsp. *hulkeana*, the typical form, has puberulous young stems and petioles; the individual rachises of the inflorescence racemes are densely pubescent or glandular-puberulent, while the calyx lobes are usually obtuse, rarely subacute, and closely eglandular-ciliate. Subsp. *evestita* differs in its stems and petioles being glabrous; the individual rachises of the inflorescence racemes are either glabrous or sparsely eglandular-puberulent or glandular-puberulent, while the calyx lobes are acuminate or acute, distantly glandular-ciliolate, or with mixed glandular and eglandular cilia.

Heliohebe hulkeana subsp. *hulkeana*

Heliohebe hulkeana subsp. *hulkeana* is the more widely spread of the two subspecies, and it occurs from the Awatere Valley in northern Marlborough to north Canterbury. It is usually distinguished by its young stems being densely puberulent, by its leaves being more or less erect to spreading, with usually 5–10 or even 20 marginal teeth (occasionally to 35), and by its broader, more blunt calyx lobes. This subspecies is rather variable in a number of respects, from the size and shape of its foliage to its growth habit and flower colour. It was named in 1863 by botanist Ferdinand von Mueller, who mistakenly attributed it to having been found in Taranaki Province, well outside its native range in the South Island. The next botanist to find the species was Joseph Beattie Armstrong, who collected it from Mount Grey in north Canterbury. It is named in honour of the collector, Th. H. Hulke, Esq.

This species is one of the gems of the New Zealand flora. In the more coastal parts of Marlborough, it flowers in early summer, making rocky banks and similar sites very beautiful. It often grows in company with such plants as *Pachystegia insignis*, *Notospartium glabrescens* (*Carmichaelia glabrescens*), and *Sophora prostrata*. In the garden it is easily grown but should be planted in an open situation with full sun, plenty of air circulation, and a well-drained soil to counteract downy mildew. It usually flowers from late October (mid spring) to December (summer).

DESCRIPTION: An erect to spreading, laxly branched shrub 30–90 cm tall. Branchlets slender, finely pubescent, purplish-red, length of internodes usually many times the diameter. Leaves spreading, 2.5–5.7 cm long by 1.2–2.5 cm wide, oblong-elliptic to oblong to ovate or suborbicular, apex subacute to obtuse, base narrowed to a more or less winged and channelled petiole up to 1.2 cm long, glabrous and more or less coriaceous, upper surface bright green and glossy with minute glandular hairs on the midrib, paler beneath and glabrous or sparingly hairy on the midrib, margins reddish, evenly serrate-dentate to sharply serrate with 5–12 or even up to 20 pairs of teeth. Inflorescences rather broad, terminal panicles 15–23 cm long (sometimes longer), the branches up to 7.5 cm long, the lowest ones usually again branched, the peduncle and branches finely pubescent or puberulous. Flowers varying from pale violet to almost white, more or less erect to slightly spreading, rather crowded but not hiding the panicle branches, bracts about 1.5 mm long, broad-ovate, acute, glabrous, margins ciliolate. Calyx usually slightly pubescent at the base, lobes usually obtuse or rarely subacute and similar to the bracts but larger, closely ciliate with simple hairs. Corolla up to 1 cm in diameter, tube shorter than the calyx lobes, corolla lobes more or less spreading, up to 7 mm long, twice as long as the tube or more, broad-ovate to almost orbicular, usually obtuse. Stamens but little exserted. Capsule erect, about twice as long as the calyx lobes, narrow-oblong.

DISTRIBUTION: South Island. Found from near Taylor Pass, north of the Awatere Valley in Marlborough, on the coastal cliffs and gorges of the Seaward Kaikoura Range, to the Clarence River and Oaro, and then on to about the Leader River and Mount Grey in north Canterbury. Usually found in river gorges and on coastal cliffs, bluffs, rock outcrops, and banks. It grows on both limestone and greywacke as well as on conglomerate, from sea level to 915 m.

Heliohebe hulkeana subsp. *hulkeana* 'Averil'. Bred in 1973 at Graham Hutchins's County Park Nursery, Essex, United Kingdom, as a seedling from *H. hulkeana* subsp. *hulkeana*. Hutchins (1997) describes it as having green leaves with no red margin and a more compact inflorescence of blue flowers.

Heliohebe hulkeana subsp. *hulkeana* 'Havering'. Originated in Hutchins's County Park Nursery, Essex, United Kingdom. He describes it as being a rather lax-growing shrub with dark green, distinctly red-margined leaves. Panicles are broad and up to 20 cm long. Flowers are lilac-blue, and flowering occurs about three weeks later than other cultivars.

Heliohebe hulkeana subsp. *hulkeana* 'Lilac Hint'. This strong-growing form was raised from seed collected by Hutchins from the Clarence Pass track. It has rather small, light green leaves and lax branches. Its flowers are pale lilac.

Heliohebe hulkeana subsp. *hulkeana* 'Sally Blunt'. Another cultivar collected by Hutchins from near the Clarence Pass area. He describes it as a robust shrub with exceptionally large, bright green leaves and rather narrow, erect panicles up to 24 cm long. Flowers are said to be wisteria-blue.

Heliohebe hulkeana subsp. *hulkeana* 'Sea Spray'. A selected seedling from seed collected along the Kaikoura coast by D. Rooney in 1992. He describes it as having extra large flower panicles. May no longer be in cultivation.

Heliohebe hulkeana subsp. *hulkeana* 'White Falls'. Discovered at Cuckoo Creek, Marlborough, in 1981 by Hutchins, who describes it as a very lax form with pure white flowers. Hutchins distributed many plants of it but subsequently lost all of his stock.

Heliohebe hulkeana subsp. *evestita*

This subspecies has quite a restricted distribution. It is similar to subsp. *hulkeana* but usually differs in having glabrous stems that may be sparingly puberulent when young; leaves that are lanceolate, rhomboid, or rarely elliptic; an acute apex that is apiculate or rarely obtuse; and fewer marginal teeth (usually 5–10, sometimes 15). The rachises of its panicles are either glabrous, sparsely hairy, or glandular-puberulent. The calyx lobes are acuminate or acute (not obtuse or subacute) and glandular-ciliolate or with mixed glandular and simple hairs. The subspecific name refers to the glabrous stems.

DISTRIBUTION: South Island. Found only in Marlborough on Mount Benmore, Boundary Creek, Whernside Ridge, Kekerengu, at the gorge of Woodside Creek, and in the valley of the Waima (Ure) River. Occurs on rocks in shrubland and on limestone rocks and limestone cliffs. Grows from near sea level to 1100 m.

Heliohebe hulkeana subsp. *evestita* 'Lena'. This cultivar is distinguished by its pale green leaves, which have no trace of red at the margin, and by its pure white flowers. It has a rather lax habit of growth and is quite outstanding when in flower. This plant was found by myself on a high road bank in the valley of the Waima River, and it was named after my wife. The bank where it was found was almost covered with plants of *H. hulkeana* subsp. *evestita* in a whole range of colours, from very pale pinkish to pale violet. Near the top of the bank, in the midst of all of these colours, stood one solitary plant with pure white flowers. It just cried out to have cuttings taken from it, and so I did, the cuttings being taken back to the Christchurch Botanic Gardens. Sadly, when I revisited the area some years later, that same road bank was almost devoid of *Heliohebe* plants. Whether this was the result of roadside spraying or road works I am uncertain, but there was no trace of any progeny from the white-flowered form.

Heliohebe lavaudiana

Another species with a restricted distribution but not nearly as limited as *Heliohebe acuta*. *Heliohebe lavaudiana* occurs on Banks Peninsula, where it is usually found on bluffs and rock outcrops. While it usually grows on the shady sides of such situations, it also occurs on the northern sides, although usually in rock crevices where its roots are kept shaded and cool. *Heliohebe lavaudiana* is quite a small shrub, usually no more than about 20 cm tall, although larger plants may sometimes be found. It has small, red-margined, rounded leaves with three to ten pairs of teeth around the margin. When in flower it is very beautiful, with its pink flower buds intermingled with its white, fully opened flowers. Unfortunately, it is a rather difficult species to manage in cultivation because it so readily succumbs to downy mildew. It seems to be much happier in a sunny situation, although it should be planted in a rock crevice where it roots will be in the shade. As with other species of this genus, it needs plenty of air circulation around it and a well-drained soil. Flowering usually occurs from November (early summer) to December (summer), or earlier, when in cultivation, October (mid spring) to November (early summer). *Heliohebe lavaudiana* was named in honour of Commodore Lavaud, commander of the French corvette *L'Aube*, who was at Akaroa just after the arrival of the French settlers, in the Comte de Paris, in August 1840. It was discovered and described by Etienne

Raoul, naval surgeon and botanist on the ship. The *L'Aube* was later replaced by *L'Allier* until 1843.

DESCRIPTION: A small shrub 10–30 cm tall, occasionally to 40 cm. Branches prostrate to decumbent and ascending at their tips, internodes usually 4–8 mm long, uniformly glandular-pubescent. Leaves spreading, 2–3 cm long by 1.3–1.7 cm wide, obovate to suborbicular, coriaceous and rather fleshy, upper surface deep green to somewhat greyish-green, lower surface paler, margins with three to ten pairs of teeth, red, apex obtuse, narrowed to a short petiole about 5 mm long. Inflorescences branched, terminal, 3–4 cm long, composed of usually simple spikes of crowded, sessile flowers, rachises glandular-pubescent, calyx 4–5 mm long; flowers white (pink in the bud), 11–13 mm in diameter, corolla tube 1.5–2 mm long by 1.7–2 mm wide, shorter than the calyx, glabrous, corolla lobes glabrous, subacute. Stamen filaments white, anthers yellow. Capsule dark brown, usually 3.5–4 mm long by 2–2.5 mm wide.

DISTRIBUTION: South Island. Endemic to Banks Peninsula, where it grows on basalt bluffs, cliffs, and rock outcrops at 300–900 m. Records of it being found on the Canterbury Plains are believed to be in error.

Heliohebe pentasepala

Heliohebe pentasepala was discovered in 1949 by H. H. Allan at Gooseberry Gully on the Molesworth Station, Marlborough, and was originally classified as a variety of *H. raoulii*. It was not until 1993 that it was recognised as a distinct species and named as such by Phil Garnock-Jones. It may be distinguished from *H. raoulii* by its habit, which is more erect; its leaves, which are widest at or about their middles; and its five calyx lobes, which are free, with the posterior one usually only slightly smaller than the others. In addition, its leaves are distinctly partially folded so that they present a shallow V shape in cross section.

This distinct species usually grows to about 20 cm tall, with fairly small leaves and flowers that are pink in the bud but open to a very pale lilac or white. It is one of the first species to flower in spring. It is small enough to plant in a trough garden and is easily grown, but it is also susceptible to downy mildew. The specific name refers to the five free sepals.

DESCRIPTION: A small subshrub or shrub to 10–30 cm tall. Branches usually erect, branchlets red-brown ageing to grey-brown, internodes usually 4–10 mm long, stems uniformly pubescent with simple hairs or rarely glandular. Leaves more or less spreading, oblanceolate or narrowly elliptic, 1–3 cm long by 4–8 mm wide, coriaceous or rather fleshy and slightly folded along the midrib, apex usually subacute, acute or obtuse, base gradually tapered to a short winged petiole, margins red, rounded, smooth, serrate or rarely entire, upper surface green to bronze-green, glossy, undersurface glabrous, green to pale green, midrib not thickened, depressed to grooved above. Inflorescences 2–7 cm long, peduncle 5 mm–1 cm long (occasionally longer), rachis usually 1–3 cm long, pubescent, bracts more or less opposite to alternate or opposite and decussate below, becoming alternate above, ciliate with simple hairs, deltoid; pedicels very short or absent, calyx divisions equally deep, calyx 2.4–3.5 mm long, lobes five, not all similar. Corolla 7–8 mm in diameter, pink becoming paler after pollination, corolla tube 2–2.5 mm long, slightly swollen at the base, equalling or shorter than the calyx, glabrous, corolla lobes subacute, erect or spreading. Stamen filaments white, anthers pale yellow. Capsule dark brown, 3.5–4 mm long by 2.5 mm wide, glabrous.

DISTRIBUTION: South Island. Found in inland valleys of northern and central Marlborough from the Awatere River, the Clarence, Hodder, Leatham, and Acheron rivers, the Tarndale flats, and the upper reaches of the Wairau River. Usually grows on cliffs, rocky slopes, and steep grassland at 300–1450 m, often on limestone, though not exclusively.

Heliohebe raoulii

Heliohebe raoulii comprises two subspecies. The typical form, subsp. *raoulii*, is found from central and southern Marlborough down to about mid Canterbury. It is a small shrub to 30 cm tall with spatula-shaped leaves that have reddish margins and a few teeth towards their apexes. The inflorescences are branched, and flowers are lavender or pinkish. Subsp. *maccaskillii* is a rather small shrub, often only 10 cm tall, with very small leaves usually no more than 9 mm long. Its inflorescences are usually simple or have only one or two lateral spikes, and its flowers are often white. It is usually found on limestone and has a very restricted distribution in north Canterbury.

Heliohebe raoulii subsp. raoulii (PLATE 125)

This subspecies is readily distinguished by its small, spatula-shaped leaves, which are usually serrate towards their apexes and have reddish margins. It is a much-branched shrub and makes a more compact bush in the garden than it does in the wild. Wild plants exhibit a range of flower colour, from pinkish to mauve or even almost white. Its habit is also variable, with plants ranging from spreading to more erect and bushy.

Unfortunately, like other members of this genus, it can very susceptible to the dreaded downy mildew. At the first sign of infection, spray the plant with a recommended fungicide and repeat the process about every ten days until all signs of the fungus have disappeared. Before each spraying, pick off and destroy any infected leaves. Downy mildew is really the only problem with the cultivation of this plant, which is otherwise quite hardy. The species was named by J. D. Hooker to commemorate Etienne Raoul, the naval surgeon and botanist on board the French naval corvette *L'Aube* while it was stationed at Akaroa from August 1840 until November 1841, and on another ship, *L'Allier*, from November 1841 until January 1843. Its discovery has usually been attributed to Raoul, who botanised around the vicinity of Akaroa, but it is not known to occur on Banks Peninsula. About or later than that time it was subsequently collected in several localities from north Canterbury to the Wairau Valley. It was most likely discovered by David Lyall.

DESCRIPTION: A small, much-branched, erect or straggling shrub 10–30 cm tall. Branchlets pubescent with short, downward-pointing hairs, internodes short or long, young branchlets purplish. Leaves spreading or ascending, 1–2.5 cm long by 4–8 mm wide, tapering to a narrow but poorly defined petiole, upper surface medium to light green, undersurface similar, coriaceous, glabrous, margins reddish, upper portion serrate with usually two to four pairs of teeth. Inflorescences terminal, usually a panicle or corymb, the spikes subtended by progressively smaller leaves, 2–5.7 cm long, peduncles puberulous. Flowers lavender to pinkish or sometimes almost white, erect, crowded, almost sessile and hiding the rachis, bracts 1.5–3 mm long, lanceolate, obtuse or subacute, minutely ciliolate or sometimes glabrous; calyx glabrous, lobes but little exceeding the bracts, ciliolate; corolla tube equalling the calyx lobes, corolla lobes spreading, longer than the tube, ovate to suborbicular, obtuse. Stamens little exserted, not as long as the lobes. Capsule up to 4 mm long, oblong, obtuse, usually glabrous, exceeding the calyx.

DISTRIBUTION: South Island. Found in Marlborough from the Seaward Kaikoura Range and the Tarndale area to the Inland Kaikoura Range, to north Canterbury, and thence southwards to the Rakaia River gorge. Occurs mainly on rocks, in rocky places, and on rock outcrops in the drier mountains and hills, mainly in grassland, scrub, and in river gorges. Occasionally found on talus and stable scree slopes, but not on limestone. Grows at 150–1060 m.

Heliohebe raoulii subsp. *maccaskillii* (PLATE 126)

This very small shrub has such a unique appearance that observers can be forgiven for believing it to be a distinct species rather than a subspecies of *Heliohebe raoulii*. It is frequently less than 10 cm tall although at times may attain 30 cm. It is recognised by its twiggy habit and by its very small leaves, usually no more than 4–9 mm long by 2–5 mm wide. Some forms are quite variable. On Mount Brown in the Waipara River gorge area, for instance, I have seen plants with leaves no more than 4–6 mm long by about 2–3 mm wide, and swollen so as to be quite fleshy. The inflorescences are very short, often with only one spike bearing just three or four white to pale mauve flowers. Unlike *H. raoulii* subsp. *raoulii*, this plant has the distinction of being confined to limestone areas. It was discovered by L. W. McCaskill in October 1937 on limestone rock formations in the Weka Pass area of north Canterbury. It is named after McCaskill, with the different spelling of the subspecific epithet conforming to the rules of the *International Code of Botanical Nomenclature*.

DESCRIPTION: Often a very small, spreading shrub 5–30 cm tall. Branches prostrate to decumbent, more or less divaricating, branchlets brown to greyish, pubescence eglandular, internodes usually 1–5 mm long. Leaves more or less erect to spreading, oblanceolate to obovate or spathulate, usually 4–9 mm long by 2–5 mm wide, apex obtuse to rounded, margins smooth, entire or with zero to two pairs of crenations, upper surface green to bronze-green, dull, petiole 1–2 mm long. Inflorescences with 10–60 flowers or sometimes just a few, rachis densely pubescent with eglandular hairs and sparsely glandular-pubescent, bracts subopposite to alternate, ciliate with both glandular and eglandular hairs; pedicels absent or much shorter than the bracts, calyx lobes five, ciliate with eglandular hairs. Corolla mauve to white and pinkish in the bud. Stamen filaments 3–3.5 mm long. Capsule with a shallow notch at the apex or appearing to be twinned.

DISTRIBUTION: South Island. Confined to a rather small area of north Canterbury from Waipara and Rangiora to Pyramid Valley and the Waipara River gorge, Weka Pass, Whiterock, and Mount Cass. Common on limestone at 100–573 m.

×*Heohebe*

×*Heohebe* is presumed to be the result of a bigeneric cross between *Heliohebe hulkeana* subsp. *hulkeana* and *Hebe diosmifolia*. So far it appears to be the only cross between these two genera. It originated in New Zealand and is virtually unknown elsewhere. Both cultivars belonging to this hybrid genus appear to have originated during the late 1980s or early 1990s. Very little is known about their origin and who was responsible for making the original cross.

×*Heohebe hortensis* 'Spring Monarch' (PLATE 127)
This appears to be the first named cultivar of this hybrid genus. It probably originated during the mid to late 1980s, as evidenced by the sizable, obviously quite well established specimens observed in street plantings in the city of Napier in 1996. In 1991, Annton Nursery of Cambridge, New Zealand, received some plants of an unnamed hebe under the name *Hebe* (*Heliohebe*) *raoulii*. Realising that it was obviously not that species, they named it 'Misty Prince' in their 1993 catalogue. It seems reasonably clear that ×*Heohebe hortensis* 'Spring Monarch' was the first cultivar of this group to be formally named, and consequently that name is accepted as valid. Both 'Spring Monarch' and 'Misty Prince' may well be one and the same, in which case 'Misty Prince' would be reduced to synonymy; however, this has yet to be determined. ×*Heohebe hortensis* 'Spring Monarch' is actually a fine shrub and is quite drought-tolerant. It is even more easily cultivated than *Heliohebe hulkeana* subsp. *hulkeana*, one of its presumed parents, and is generally not as susceptible to downy mildew. It usually flowers around October (mid spring) and when in full flower is most attractive. Immediately after flowering the old flower heads should be pruned off, not only to make the bush tidy but also to encourage good new growth for the following season.

DESCRIPTION: A spreading shrub to about 60 cm tall by about 90 cm in diameter. Branchlets slender, reddish-purple, length of internodes four to six times the diameter, sparsely bifariously puberulous with pale hairs. Leaves spreading, 15–20 mm long by

7–8 mm wide, shortly petioled. Leaf blade elliptic to somewhat oblanceolate, apex acute, base cuneate; upper surface yellowish-green to medium green, paler beneath, margins yellowish, with five to eight small incisions or teeth along either side. Leaf bud with a small sinus. Inflorescence lateral, compound, crowded near to the tips of the branchlets and overtopping the leaves to form a somewhat loose head. Peduncles equalling or longer than the leaves, puberulous with pale hairs. Flowers pale lilac to mauve, fading to white with age, usually closely placed, bracts about equalling or slightly exceeding the pedicels, acute. Calyx lobes 2–2.5 mm long, ovate, acute. Corolla tube about 3 mm long, funnel-shaped, exceeding the calyx lobes. Corolla lobes 4–5 mm long, ovate, obtuse, wide-spreading. Stamens shorter than the corolla lobes, filaments white.

×*Heohebe hortensis* 'Waikanae' (PLATE 128)

This cultivar originated in Gus Evans Nurseries, Waikanae, New Zealand, around 1994. It appeared among a batch of seedlings of *Heliohebe hulkeana* and was selected because it seemed to be so different from the rest of the batch. It is a really fine flowering shrub and deserves to be better known. It is more robust than 'Spring Monarch' and probably makes a better garden plant. Its flowering season is quite long, usually from October (mid spring) to about December (summer), and as with *Heliohebe hulkeana*, spent inflorescences should be clipped off so as to keep the plant compact and encourage new growth.

DESCRIPTION: A spreading shrub to 1 m tall by 2 m or more in diameter. Branchlets rather slender, reddish-purple, length of internodes up to six times the diameter, bifariously puberulous with minute, pale hairs. Leaves spreading, 2–3 cm long by 8–10 mm wide, shortly petioled. Leaf blade elliptic to somewhat oblanceolate, apex acute, base cuneate, upper surface medium to deep green, paler beneath, midrib reddish. Margins slightly thickened, yellowish to reddish, with up to six small teeth or incisions along the upper half of either side. Leaf bud with a small, narrow sinus. Inflorescences lateral, compound, usually crowded near the tips of the branchlets and overtopping the leaves to form a loose, open head. Peduncles usually equalling or longer than the leaves, puberulous with pale hairs. Flowers pale heliotrope to mauve fading to white, loosely placed, pedicels pubescent, bracts about equalling the pedicels, acute to subacute. Calyx lobes about 2 mm long, ovate, obtuse. Corolla tube about 2 mm long, funnel-shaped, shorter than the calyx lobes. Corolla lobes 4–5 mm long, ovate, obtuse, wide-spreading. Stamens shorter than the lobes, filaments white.

Parahebe

Parahebe is mainly a New Zealand genus but does extend to Australia and New Guinea, although some species from those countries are now treated under *Derwentia* and *Detzneria*. There are about 17 indigenous species of *Parahebe*, most of which are prostrate to decumbent shrubs or subshrubs with woody or semi-woody stems, although one or two species tend to be more herbaceous in nature. Parahebes have opposite leaves that are mainly crenate or toothed and sessile or shortly petioled. Flowers are produced in long axillary racemes, or they may sometimes be quite reduced so that there are only solitary flowers. The flowers of most *Parahebe* species are generally larger than those of *Hebe* and often display more colour, mainly in the form of pink or purple veining. The corolla has a very short tube; its limb is broadly saucer-shaped, with four or five unequal lobes.

Most of the *Parahebe* species in general cultivation are relatively easy to grow, requiring only a well-drained, gritty soil in either a sunny situation or where there may be some direct or indirect light. About half the species are either not in cultivation or one or two are cultivated only by a few dedicated collectors. This especially applies to *P. densifolia* and *P. trifida*, which may have more specialised requirements. Propagation is easily effected by cuttings, division (of some species), or seed.

Parahebe 'Baby Blue'

Parahebe 'Baby Blue' is an attractive little subshrub that displays its lovely violet-blue flowers over quite a long period during the summer. The dark green foliage also acts as a good foil for the flowers. It prefers a moist soil and will grow in sun or light shade but is not as drought-tolerant as some other parahebes.

DESCRIPTION: A loosely branched shrub to 20–40 cm tall. Branchlets brownish-green, bifariously pubescent. Leaves quite widely spaced, shortly petiolate, 1.8–2.5 cm long by 9–14 mm wide, ovate to elliptic, coarsely and irregularly serrate, upper surface dark green, paler beneath. Racemes 11–12 cm long on peduncles up to 3.5 cm long; flowers numerous on pedicels 8–9 mm long; corolla saucer-shaped, about 8 mm in diameter, lobes rounded, medium violet with a pale yellow eye, surrounded by a red-purple ocular ring and veined with a similar colour.

Parahebe ×*bidwillii*

Before the 1960s there was a certain amount of confusion concerning the hybrid *Parahebe* ×*bidwillii* and *P. decora*, especially in New Zealand. What is now correctly known as *P. decora* was until then generally referred to incorrectly as *P. bidwillii*. Only with the publication of the first volume of *Flora of New Zealand* (Allan 1961) was the situation rectified. This case of mistaken identity apparently goes back to the time of J. D. Hooker, in 1864, when his *Handbook of the New Zealand Flora* was published. What is now known as *P.* ×*bidwillii* is most likely a hybrid between *P. decora* and *P. lyallii*. As a wild plant it does not appear to be overly common and is little cultivated in New Zealand, although it appears to more commonly cultivated in the United Kingdom. Superficially *P.* ×*bidwillii* seems to be more like *P. decora*, with its prostrate habit of growth, dark stems, very small, rounded leaves, and flowers that stand above the prostrate stems on rather delicate peduncles.

The flowers are pinkish with a purple-red ocular ring and veined with a similar colour. It is an easily cultivated, attractive little plant for a rock garden or trough garden. It was named after early botanist and explorer John Carne Bidwill.

Parahebe 'Gillian' is said to be a cross between *P. decora* and *P. lyallii* that was raised in the garden of K. Beckett of Stanhoe, Norfolk, United Kingdom. It is rather similar to *P.* ×*bidwillii* except that its flowers are white.

Parahebe birleyi *

A small, straggly subshrub up to about 10 cm tall or more, usually forming loose plants up to about 20 cm in diameter. Its spreading to somewhat erect leaves tend to be fleshy, obovate, and 5–7 mm long or more by 4–6 mm wide, with deep green and purplish or greyish, densely hairy upper surfaces and distinctively toothed leaf margins. The flowers are similar to those of *Parahebe trifida*. The specific name commemorates alpine guide Harry Birley.

DISTRIBUTION: South Island. Found along the main divide from southern Westland to northern Fiordland and extending out to the Eyre Mountains, Hector Mountains, and Remarkables, but absent from the Mount Aspiring region. Usually found in rock crevices, sometimes in loose debris, at 1800–2900 m. Recorded as one of the most high-altitude native flowering plants of New Zealand.

Parahebe brevistylis *

This species was once regarded as *Parahebe linifolia* subsp. *brevistylis* but has been elevated to specific rank. It is a low plant, 5–15 cm tall, and is usually decumbent to ascending. Its linear leaves are 8–12 mm long by 1.5–3 mm wide, with green, shining upper surfaces, a rounded or truncate apex, and margins that are ciliate, especially at their bases. The racemose inflorescences are not branched and vary from 1 to 2.5 cm long. Its flowers are white with an ocular ring and veins that are either pinkish or absent. I have not seen this species, but it would appear that it is similar to a fairly pale-flowered form of *P. linifolia*. The specific name refers to the fact that the style of the flower is shorter than that of *P. linifolia*.

DISTRIBUTION: South Island. Occurs in montane to subalpine areas on both sides of the main divide, from the Rangitata River in South Canterbury to Fiordland and the Hump Ridge. Grows on rock outcrops, cliffs, river gravels and banks, in grassland, and on moraine.

Parahebe canescens

This has to be the smallest of the *Parahebe* species and is certainly the smallest plant included in the broad group of *Hebe*. When not in flower it is extremely difficult to locate in its natural habitat. It inhabits lakeshores, particularly those in montane areas, and

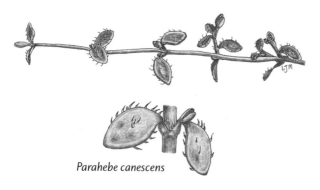

Parahebe canescens

sometimes can only be found when the water level drops late in the season to expose more of the shoreline; in between times it may often be underwater. It has sparse, very fine, thread-like, creeping stems with pairs of round, greyish leaves, often little larger than a pinhead, and it blends almost perfectly with the stones and silt of the lakeshore.

Its solitary sky-blue flowers are often the only indication that tiny scraps of this species are growing around a lakeshore. Although quite minute in its natural habitat, in the garden it may form a closely matted patch to 60 cm or more in diameter. When it blooms, virtually the whole plant may be covered with flowers, which are quite large for such a diminutive plant. It is easily grown and only requires a moist, gritty soil in full sun. It was discovered at Lake Lyndon, Canterbury, by Thomas Kirk in the 1870s. The specific name refers to the off-white hairs that occur on its leaves.

DESCRIPTION: A minute, creeping herb of prostrate and rooting habit, its stems frequently no more than 1–2 cm long. Stems filiform, few- or much-branched, sparsely white-hairy. Leaves 1–2.5 by 1–1.5 mm, broad-ovate, obtuse, entire, upper surface greyish, both surfaces clad with lax, flattened, greyish-white hairs, very shortly petiolate to almost sessile. Flowers solitary and axillary, blue, 5–8 mm in diameter, peduncles slender, 2–5 mm long, calyx about 3 mm long, densely greyish-white hairy; corolla tube short, shorter than or equalling the calyx, corolla lobes four, unequal, apexes shallowly notched. Capsule about 1.5 by 2 mm, compressed, glabrous.

DISTRIBUTION: South Island. Occurs east of the main divide from the Waiau River in north Canterbury to Lake Te Anau. Usually found at the margins of lakes and lagoons in muddy or stony-silty patches, especially where the marginal areas dry up in summer. Grows from sea level to 900 m.

Parahebe catarractae

Formerly thought to occur in the North, South, and Stewart islands, *Parahebe catarractae* is now regarded as being confined to Fiordland. Plants from other parts of New Zealand are now included as part of the *P. lanceolata* complex, which occurs in the North Island and the north of the South Island. The best forms of *P. catarractae* make very good garden plants, especially for the front of a border or in a rock garden. It is mainly a plant of damp or wet places, such as alongside streams or on damp rocks. In the garden it is best planted in a situation that does not receive full sun, especially during the middle of the day. It is easily propagated by cuttings, particularly if selected colour forms are to be grown.

Depending upon the situation where it grows, it forms a rounded bush to about 30 cm tall, and the older stems often root where they touch the ground. Its lanceolate or ovate-lanceolate leaves are up to 10 cm long or more, rather whitish beneath, and sharply pointed. Numerous flowers are borne on peduncles up to 23 cm long, and individual flowers are 7–12 cm in diameter. They vary from white to white veined with pink or magenta and often have a deeper magenta eye around the stamens. *Parahebe catarractae* has a long flowering season that may extend from October (mid spring) to about April (mid autumn). The specific name means "of waterfalls" and refers to its preferred habitat.

DESCRIPTION: A rather slender, decumbent to more or less erect shrub or subshrub to about 30 cm tall. Branchlets bifariously pubescent and occasionally almost completely pubescent. Leaves spreading, 3–10 cm long (occasionally longer) by 7–20 mm wide, lanceolate to ovate-lanceolate or elliptic, upper surface bright to deep green, undersurface having a somewhat whitish appearance, apex acute, base almost sessile, margins coarsely or shallowly serrate. Racemes usually long and many-flowered, peduncles 7.3–23 cm long; flowers white or white veined with pink or magenta, sometimes with an ocular ring of a deeper colour, 1.2–1.4 cm in diameter, on slender, pubescent pedicels up to 1.6 cm long; bracts narrow, ciliate, calyx lobes 2–3 mm long, narrow-ovate, acute to subacute; corolla bowl-shaped, pubescent and ciliate, with a very short tube, lobes four, spreading, not of equal size, rounded, obtuse. Capsule broadly oblong, turgid, somewhat two-lobed, about 3 mm long.

DISTRIBUTION: South Island. Confined to Fiordland, where it grows from lowland to mountain areas, sea level to 900 m, along streamsides, on cliffs, rock bluffs, rocky places, and in loose, moist debris.

Parahebe catarractae 'Delight'. Rather similar to *P. catarractae* 'Miss Willmott' but differentiated by its more highly coloured flowers, which are 1.2 cm in diameter and heliotrope overall, with darker veining and a central eye of chartreuse ringed with beetroot-purple. This cultivar originated from a long-cultivated plant in the Christchurch Botanic Gardens. It flowers from late November (early summer) until late January (mid summer). The United Kingdom cultivar *P. catarractae* 'Porlock Purple', which originated in the garden of a Dr. Hadden in Porlock, Somerset, is said to be similar to 'Delight'.

Parahebe catarractae 'Miss Willmott'. A cultivar presumed to have originated in the garden at Warley Place, Essex, United Kingdom, may be similar to *P. catarractae* 'Delight'. It is described thus: "Growth similar to *P. catarractae*, but flowers are veined mauve in colour, in summer" (Chalk 1988).

Parahebe catarractae 'Snow Cap' (PLATE 129). This cultivar comes within the larger size range of the species and has deep green leaves. Its prominent white flowers are veined with magenta and oculate with a deeper magenta eye. It is a very handsome plant and well worth a place in the garden. It is not known from where it was collected.

Parahebe cheesemanii

Parahebe cheesemanii comprises two subspecies: the typical form, subsp. *cheesemanii*, and subsp. *flabellata*.

Parahebe cheesemanii subsp. *cheesemanii* (PLATE 130)

This rather small species grows mainly from a single taproot but also develops a tendency to creep and root-in, although it often just forms small, single plants. It is sometimes regarded as a subshrub but could also be taken to be almost a herb. Its leaf colour and small size make it difficult to discern when growing in the stony debris of a shingle scree or similar area. The leaf blade is 2–3 by 2–3 mm, bronze-green to grey-green, ovate or deltoid, pinnatifid or bipinnatifid, and usually rather hairy. The white flowers are mainly solitary, in pairs or sometimes in threes, and about 5–7 mm in diameter. The name *cheesemanii* commemorates the early botanist Thomas Frederick Cheeseman, who first collected this plant in the Raglan Mountains, Nelson.

I have grown this species only once, and then lost it to some thief who was obviously a collector of such plants. It can be successfully cultivated if grown in a potting mixture that approximates the shingle screes in which it is commonly found.

DISTRIBUTION: South Island. Found in low- to high-alpine from the mountains of north-western Nelson, the Richmond Range, and the Raglan Range to the Nelson Lakes National Park. Usually grows in the finer stony mix of fairly stable screes at 1200–1800 m.

Parahebe cheesemanii subsp. *flabellata* *

This subspecies differs from subsp. *cheesemanii* mainly in its leaves being more shallowly lobed, the incisions going only to about halfway, whereas in subsp. *cheesemanii* they go about three-quarters of the way. The leaf blade is also elliptic to orbicular rather than ovate or deltoid, and there is a gap of several hundred kilometres between the southernmost limit of subsp. *cheesemanii* and the northernmost limit of subsp. *flabellata*.

DISTRIBUTION: South Island. Found in low- to high-alpine areas in the Arthur's Pass National Park, where it occurs on the Kelly Range, upper Otira Valley, upper Bealey Valley, Rough Creek, and Temple Basin. Grows at 1350–1800 m.

Parahebe decora

Parahebe decora is a common species, especially along mountain streams and riverbeds. It is fairly easily recognised by its dark stems and the pairs of rather minute leaves scattered along them. The leaves are deep green, often with a reddish colouration, and usually have one pair of small notches on their margins. It is most easily recognised when it flowers, because the flowering stems stand well above its prostrate growing stems and usually bear 10–15 bowl-shaped flowers, varying from white to pink to violet with darker lines.

This is an easily cultivated species, particularly for a rock garden or trough garden. It prefers a well-drained, gritty soil, preferably with some added humus, and a position in full sun or light shade. The soil should not be allowed to become too dry during summer. *Parahebe decora* is rather variable as regards depth of flower colour. It usually flowers from November (summer) to about February (late summer). It appears to have been first collected in the Hooker Valley, Mount Cook, by Thomas Frederick Cheeseman. Its specific name means "decorative" or "becoming comely."

DESCRIPTION: A prostrate, much-branched shrub or subshrub that forms loosely matted to dense patches 50 cm or more in diameter. Branches darkly coloured, slender and leafy but becoming woody with age, rooting at the nodes, uniformly and finely pubescent with white hairs. Leaves close-set or distant, blade 1.5–4 by 1–3 mm, ovate to more or less orbicular, more or less fleshy, deep green or often purplish-red and shining above, pale or reddish beneath, broadly rounded at the apex, margins with a pair (rarely two pairs) of deep notches towards the base; petiole 1–3 mm long. Racemes 6- to 10- to 15-flowered on wiry peduncles up to 15 cm tall; flowers white to pink to magenta, up to 1 cm in diameter, tube very short, lobes four, spreading and rounded. Capsule 4–5 mm long, much longer than the calyx, broad-oblong.

DISTRIBUTION: South Island. Occurs in montane to low-alpine areas, mainly east of the main divide, from Nelson and Marlborough to northern Southland. Usually grows on well-drained, stony sites such as gravel riverbeds and streambeds, moraine and stable screes, and sometimes on stony areas in grassland, at 300–1500 m.

Parahebe hookeriana

Parahebe hookeriana is a small but rather stout plant of prostrate habit, with stems up to about 25 cm long. Its leaves are thick and somewhat fleshy, and are rather crowded along the stems. In fact it is distinguished from *P. decora* and other related species by its tough, closely arranged leaves, which may be glabrous, glandular-hairy, or white-pubescent. It generally has fewer, rather large, usually purplish flowers.

It is easily cultivated, requiring only a moist, gritty, well-drained soil. Because its flowers are usually highly coloured and its growth quite compact, it makes a desirable garden plant. It will tolerate either sun or light shade and is useful in a rock garden. It was originally collected on Mount Tongariro by John Carne Bidwill and was named in honour of J. D. Hooker.

DESCRIPTION: A stout, trailing or creeping, much-branched species that roots into the ground. Branches crowded with thick, leathery, rounded leaves 4–12 by 3–8 mm and sparsely covered with hairs on both surfaces, petioles rather stout, margins deeply crenate to shallowly serrate. Flower stems about 2–6 cm long, usually with only a few

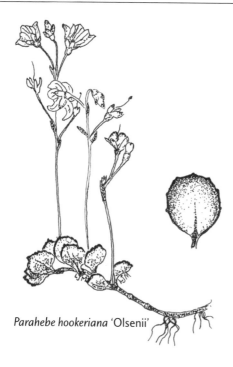

Parahebe hookeriana 'Olsenii'

(four to eight) flowers, densely glandular-hairy. Flowers quite large, up to 1 cm in diameter, pedicels about 1 cm long; calyx lobes 2–3 mm long, ovate-oblong, subacute, ciliolate. Corolla mostly lavender but may range to white, tube short, much shorter than the calyx; lobes four, unequal, ovate-oblong, obtuse. Capsule sometimes very large, 4–6 by 3–5 mm.

DISTRIBUTION: North Island. Found in subalpine to high-alpine regions of the Raukumara, Kaimanawa, Huiarau, Maungaharuru, and Ruahine ranges as well as the mountains of the Volcanic Plateau. Grows at 900–1800 m, usually on rocky sites, especially on exposed ridges in tussock grassland-herbfield or on loose, stony debris in fellfield.

Parahebe hookeriana 'Olsenii' (PLATE 131). This cultivar is distinguished from the typical form of *P. hookeriana* by having glabrous leaves with more pointed tips; they are usually sharp, but the teeth are shallower, while the petioles are distinctly flattened. The flower stems are also more slender. *Parahebe hookeriana* 'Olsenii' is easily cultivated and makes a fine rock garden plant. Though formerly known as *P. hookeriana* var. *olsenii*, it is not now recognised as being botanically distinct from *P. hookeriana*, although it is quite horticulturally distinct. In the wild it is confined to the Ruahine Range, where it occurs in habitats similar to those of the species.

Parahebe lanceolata

This complex species was formerly included with the related *Parahebe catarractae*, which accounts for earlier recordings of that species in the North Island. *Veronica lanceolata, V. irrigans, V. catarractae* var. *diffusa, P. catarractae* subsp. *lanceolata*, and *P. catarractae* var. *diffusa* are all synonyms of what is now referred to as *P. lanceolata*. The specific name refers to the narrow shape of the leaves, which are lanceolate or spear-shaped.

This parahebe mainly occurs in the North Island but is also present in the very north-western part of the South Island. A number of geographical variants occur, mainly in various parts of the North Island. It is easily cultivated (similar to *P. catarractae*) and mainly requires a gritty soil that does not become too dry. It will tolerate full sun, if given sufficient moisture, or light, indirect shade.

DESCRIPTION: A subshrub to about 30 cm tall or more. Branches prostrate to erect, brown or reddish-brown, stems bifariously pubescent. Leaves more or less erect to spreading, 1.5–3 cm long by 5 mm–1.5 cm wide, linear-lanceolate to oblanceolate to ovate, oblong to elliptic to suborbicular to deltoid or rhomboid, upper surface medium green to bronze-green or occasionally light green, margins serrate with two to ten pairs of teeth, apex acute, subacute, or acuminate. Inflorescences 10–20 cm long or more with 10–25 flowers, not branched. Flowers about 8–12 mm in diameter, white, yellow in the throat, ocular ring purplish or pinkish, veins similar. Capsules about 3–3.5 by 3–4 mm.

DISTRIBUTION: Found in the North Island from the Coromandel Peninsula and Waikato to Taranaki and the Mount Taranaki area, to the central mountain chain and the Volcanic Plateau, and from East Cape to Wellington. Found on the South Island on the Wakamarama Range in north-western Nelson. Grows from sea level to 900 m.

Parahebe laxa *

This small parahebe is little known or unknown in cultivation. It is described as a softly woody subshrub 2–7 cm tall with decumbent or ascending branches. Its more or less erect to spreading leaves are about 5–7 by 4–6 mm, bright green, shining, and elliptic to orbicular or spathulate. Its white flowers are about 5–6 mm in diameter, and the anthers are violet. The specific name *laxa* means "loose" or "open" and refers to the plant's habit.

DISTRIBUTION: South Island. Mainly found from northern to central Fiordland, from Mount Tutoko, north of Milford Sound, to Mount Burns, to the north of Lake Monowai. Usually grows in fine, sandy debris among boulders and on screes and moraine at 800–1500 m.

Parahebe linifolia

Parahebe linifolia is a delightful little species that is not difficult to manage in a rock garden or trough garden. It usually grows to no more than about 15 cm high, although in its natural habitat it may trail down a rock face for about 30 cm. Its narrow, deep green leaves seldom exceed 2 cm long by about 2.5–4 mm wide. The flowers are quite large for the size of the plant, generally about 1.2 cm in diameter, and vary from white to pinkish or bluish with darker oculate markings around the eye.

It usually grows in damp or moist habitats such as alongside mountain streams or waterfalls, on shady rock bluffs, and in loose debris such as that which may occur on moraine. In the wild it is often rather sprawling, but in the garden it is usually more compact. It is happiest when planted on the shady side of a rock and does not receive much in the way of direct sunlight. Flowering usually occurs during December (summer) and January (mid summer). The specific name *linifolia* refers to the very narrow leaves, which resemble those of *Linum*.

DESCRIPTION: A small, much-branched, softly woody shrub, usually of a rather sprawling nature, up to about 15 cm tall. Branchlets often rooting below, ascending at their tips, glabrous, internodes short. Leaves spreading to slightly ascending, close-set, sessile to shortly petiolate, 8 mm–2 cm long by 2.5–4 mm wide, linear to linear-lanceolate, subacute, bases sometimes slightly jointed. Leaf blade subacute to acute, upper surface dark green and shining, paler beneath, glabrous except for some cilia on the petiole, rather fleshy, midrib obscure. Racemes 1–3 towards the ends of the branchlets, two- to four-flowered (occasionally more), peduncles to about 2 cm long, glabrous. Flowers white to pinkish or bluish, 8 mm–2 cm in diameter, pedicels slender, glabrous, about 7 mm–2.5 cm long; bracts up to about 4 mm long. Calyx lobes up to about 4 mm long, linear-oblong, obtuse, glabrous or sparingly ciliolate; corolla shallowly bowl-shaped to almost flat, tube much shorter than the calyx lobes; corolla lobes four, unequal, broad-ovate to more or less orbicular or somewhat rhomboid, obtuse. Stamens exserted, shorter than the lobes, filaments flattened. Capsule broad-obcordate, shorter than or more or less equalling the calyx lobes, up to 4 mm long.

DISTRIBUTION: South Island. Found in subalpine to low-alpine areas from north-western Nelson to the Rangitata River. Occurs on both sides of the main divide. Grows in wet, rocky places in wet mountain areas, alongside and in streambeds, alongside waterfalls, on moist rock ledges and cliffs, in loose debris where there is ample moisture. Found at 450–1520 m.

Parahebe linifolia 'Blue Skies' (PLATE 132). A lovely form. The lobes of the lavender-violet flowers are citron-green at their bases, and the three upper lobes have beetroot-purple veining. In addition to having the best colour of any form of *P. linifolia*, its flowers are also larger, up to 2 cm in diameter. Flowering may commence in mid November (early summer) and continue until mid December (summer), recommencing in February (late summer) and running to about April (mid autumn). I collected this plant on Mount Owen, a large limestone massif in southern Nelson.

Parahebe lyallii (PLATE 133)

Parahebe lyallii is a fairly common, rather variable species that occurs in many areas of the South Island. It usually forms rather loosely branched plants, up to about 10 or 15 cm high, and its stems have a habit of rooting-in near their bases. Its small leaves are larger and broader than those of *P. decora* and may have up to three pairs of notches on their margins. Its flowering stems are not usually as stiff and erect as those of *P. decora*. The flowers of *P. lyallii* are larger, and their colour is similarly variable. Mostly they tend towards the paler tints, although they still have the purple or magenta veining and oculate eye. The flowering period is generally quite long.

This species is useful in a rock garden or trough garden and is quite easily grown, although it seems to prefer a moister soil than some other parahebes. Occasionally some very good pink-flowered forms may be found in the wild. Its specific epithet commemorates David Lyall, a botanist and naturalist who was assistant surgeon on the *HMS Terror* from 1839 to 1841 and on the *HMS Acheron* from 1847 to 1851. Lyall discovered *Parahebe lyallii* at Milford Sound during the voyage of the *Acheron*.

Parahebe lyallii

Southern and western Nelson are home to forms of *Parahebe lyallii* that in the past have been named *P. lyallii* var. *suberecta* and *P. lyallii* var. *angustata*. The former was originally found in the valley of the Wangapeka River, while the latter was found on rocks at the mouth of the Ngakawau River. Neither variety is now recognised as a separate botanical entity. Horticulturally, however, *P. lyallii* var. *suberecta* is a rather distinct and attractive plant that is well worth growing in a rock garden. It has slender wiry stems and narrow, ovate-oblong leaves about 1 cm long by about 3 mm wide with usually two pairs of incisions around their margins. The upper surfaces of the leaves are medium green with a suggestion of a sheen. Its flowers are white to a pale lilac-blue with pale greenish-yellow in the throat, a reddish-purple ocular ring, and veining of a similar colour.

DESCRIPTION: A low, much-branched, small subshrub about 10–15 cm tall when flowering. Stems slender, usually woody at their bases, prostrate to decumbent and rooting at the nodes, upper parts ascending. Leaves 5–10 by 4–8 mm, suborbicular to ovate to ovate-oblong or linear-obovate, sometimes more or less fleshy, glabrous, upper surfaces often reddish, lower surfaces pale, more or less deeply crenate or incised with two or three pairs of teeth, apex obtuse to subacute, base cuneately narrowed to a short petiole. Racemes many-flowered; peduncles slender, 3–8 cm long, glabrous to densely pubescent; flowers white to pink, about 1 cm in diameter; calyx lobes 2.3–4.5 mm long, acute, ciliolate; corolla tube about 1 mm long, lobes four, unequal.

DISTRIBUTION: South Island. Occurs almost throughout the island in lowland to montane and subalpine regions. Usually grows along streamsides, on stable riverbanks, moraine, rock bluffs, snow tussock–shrub herbfield, and in similar moist sites, ascending to about 1300 m.

Parahebe lyallii 'Rosea'. One of the finest pink-flowered forms of this species. Its growth is more compact than many other forms of the species, and it is particularly well suited for a rock garden. It was discovered in the Wairoa River gorge, Nelson, by W. B. Brockie, probably sometime during the early 1940s.

Parahebe martinii

This is another species formerly included within the *Parahebe catarractae* complex, when it was known as *P. catarractae* subsp. *martinii*. It has some similarities with certain forms of *P. lanceolata* but differs in its prostrate habit, stem colour, and the subacute or obtuse apexes of its leaves. The specific name commemorates William Martin, an early 20th-century botanist who specialised in botanising in the Marlborough area.

DESCRIPTION: A prostrate to decumbent shrub to about 20 cm tall. Branches reddish-brown to purplish, bifariously pubescent or glabrous. Leaves about 1–2 cm long by 4–10 mm wide, oblanceolate to ovate or elliptic, upper surface mid green, dull, paler beneath, apex subacute or obtuse, base cuneate, margins serrate, petioles 1–4 mm long. Inflorescences racemose, not branched, to 12–21 cm long, flowers 11–13 mm in diameter, white or sometimes pale mauve, yellow in the throat, ocular ring and veins purplish or pinkish. Capsules 3.5–4 mm long by 1.5–1.7 thick.

DISTRIBUTION: South Island. Confined to the Marlborough area, where it occurs on the Seaward Kaikoura Range from the Waima River to Mount Terako and the Mason River. Also occurs on the Inland Kaikoura Range and the Wairau Mountains. Usually found in river gorges, along streamsides, and on cliffs, on limestone and greywacke rocks, especially in shaded situations.

Parahebe planopetiolata *

One publication describes this species this way: "Its habit may be similar to *Parahebe linifolia* but plants are usually smaller and more compact" (Mark and Adams 1995). However, judging from an illustration, it does not appear to bear too much resemblance to *P. linifolia*. The specific name refers to its flattened petioles.

DESCRIPTION: Small, loose cushions to about 2–5 cm high. Branches reddish-brown and pubescent, glabrous, or sparingly bifariously pubescent. Leaves 4–7 by 2–4 mm, oblanceolate, oblong, elliptic, or rhomboid, upper surface a dark shining green, lower surface paler or sometimes purplish, apex obtuse to rounded, base cuneate, margins glabrous or ciliate and entire or sometimes shallowly crenate. Flowers solitary or occasionally paired, white or changing to pale mauve or pinkish with age, 7–9 mm in diameter.

DISTRIBUTION: South Island. Found from South Westland to western Otago, usually on damp, rocky sites along small streams, especially on scree, moraine, and fellfield, and on rock ledges of cliffs and so forth. Grows at 900–1800 m, seldom descending below the tree line.

Parahebe senex *

The specific name *senex* refers to the fact that many plants of this species have stubbly hairs that resemble the white whiskers of an old man. In New Zealand the term "old man" is also used to refer to large and aged plants of certain species, and hence, in this instance, refers to the size and woodiness of plants of this species. With its relatively broad, largish leaves, *Parahebe senex* may resemble some forms of *P. lanceolata*.

DESCRIPTION: A prostrate or decumbent shrub to about 35 cm tall. Branches brown to black or purplish, stems with either bifarious or uniform pubescence. Leaves lanceolate to oblanceolate, ovate, or elliptic, 3–4 cm long by 1–1.8 cm wide, upper surface mid green to dark green (occasionally pinkish), dull, undersurface paler, hairs numerous to sparse, margins pubescent or glabrous, serrate, apex acute to subacute. Inflorescences racemose, not branched, to 10–25 cm long, flowers 1–1.2 cm in diameter, white, yellowish or greenish in the throat, ocular ring and veins magenta. Capsules 3–4 by 3–3.5 mm.

DISTRIBUTION: South Island. Confined to north-western Nelson, where it is known from only three sites along the Anatori Stream, Raukawa Stream, and Ryan's Creek. Occurs on limestone and calcareous sandstone cliffs and talus slopes.

Parahebe spathulata *

A much-branched subshrub of prostrate habit that forms low patches up to about 5 cm high and 25 cm in diameter. Its branches are brown to reddish-brown and, along with the leaves and flowering stems, have a dense covering of white hairs.

DESCRIPTION: Leaves orbicular to rhomboid, 2–6 mm long by 2–6 mm wide, upper surface green to deep green, undersurface pale to purplish, apex subacute, obtuse or rounded, margins glabrous or ciliate or pubescent, crenate or lobed in usually two or three pairs. Inflorescences racemose, not branched, mostly 1–1.8 cm long, flowers two to six, white or sometimes pale mauve, 6–8 mm in diameter. Capsules 3–4 by 3–4 mm, strongly flattened.

DISTRIBUTION: North Island. Found on the mountains of the Central Volcanic Plateau and Kaimanawa, Kaweka, and Ruahine ranges. Usually confined to screes, loose, stony debris, and scoria in fellfield. Grows at 1100–1800 m.

Parahebe spectabilis *

This species has some affinities with *Parahebe birleyi* and apparently bears quite a strong resemblance to it. Its lobed leaves are a dull grey-green; the lobes are rounded and have reddish undersurfaces. *Parahebe spectabilis* grows to about 20 cm high and is a subshrub of decumbent or ascending habit. Its leaves are 6–13 mm long by 4.5–6 mm wide. The leaf hairs are scattered to rather numerous along the margins or on all parts of the leaf.

The white flowers are either solitary or in pairs and about 2 cm or more in diameter. Capsule 4–5 by 4–5 mm, strongly flattened.

DISTRIBUTION: South Island. Confined to the Takitimu Mountains in Southland, where it occurs only between Tower Peak and Excelsior Peak. Usually found on rock outcrops, in crevices, and on ledges among mosses at 1340–1460 m.

Parahebe trifida (PLATE 134)

This small, trailing or creeping species may be recognised by its almost fleshy, brownish-green leaves, which have one or two pairs of sharp incisions near their apexes. The flowers are large for the size of the plant and are produced on racemes of one to three at the tips of the branchlets. It is an attractive species, especially as its large, white flowers are carried well above the tips of the branchlets. It is not too difficult to cultivate and requires only a moist, though well-drained, humus-rich soil. In areas that experience hot summers it should be planted on the shady side of a large rock, but in cooler areas should succeed in a more open situation. On some forms of this species, the flowers are flushed with mauve, and the selection of one of these coloured forms would be well worthwhile. *Parahebe trifida* is easily propagated by cuttings, division, or seed. It normally flowers from December (summer) to February (late summer). The specific name refers to the fact that its leaves are commonly trifid, although the margins may vary from having no incisions to having up to seven incisions. This species was first collected in 1923 on the Titan Ridge, near the Blue Lake on the Garvie Mountains, by James Speden and Henry Darton.

DISTRIBUTION: South Island. Found mainly in the high-alpine areas of some of the ranges of Central Otago and Southland, such as the Eyre Mountains, Hector Mountains, Old Man Range, Garvie Mountains, and Umbrella Mountains. Usually grows in wet ground, mainly around the edges of snowdrifts and snowbanks where there are seepages and flushes of meltwater. Found at 1200–1700 m.

Parahebe 'Walter Brockie'

Possibly a hybrid between *Parahebe linifolia* 'Blue Skies' and *P. catarractae*, and may be one of a number of seedlings that originated in the Christchurch Botanic Gardens when those two species were artificially crossed in the mid 1960s. This rather free-flowering garden plant is useful for the front of a border or a rock garden and has the advantage of being reasonably drought-tolerant. It is named after W. B. Brockie, who was for many years in charge of the rock garden and native plant section of the Christchurch Botanic Gardens.

DESCRIPTION: A subshrub 50–80 cm in diameter by 20–30 cm high. Branchlets reddish-brown, pubescent with tawny to golden hairs. Leaves 1.7–2 cm long by 7–10 mm wide, upper surfaces medium green and more or less shining, ovate to ovate-oblong, margins with five or six pairs of teeth, petiole up to 5 mm long. Inflorescences simple, to

10 cm long, with up to 15 or more flowers. Flowers 7–9 mm in diameter, white flushed with pale pink, greenish-yellow in the throat, ocular ring magenta, veins similar.

Chionohebe

A small genus of but six species that are confined to the high mountains of the South Island of New Zealand, with two of those species also occurring in Australia. They differ from *Hebe* mainly in their seed capsules being in twin sections, with their partitions across the narrowest diameter. Most of the species are small, compact, cushion-like plants, and their flowers are solitary in the leaf axils near the tips of the branchlets. *Chionohebe* was once in the genus *Pygmea*, but that genus was considered to be no more than an orthographic variation of the name of the lichen genus *Pygmaea*; consequently, it became necessary to create the genus *Chionohebe* to accommodate these relations of *Hebe*.

The species of *Chionohebe* are not well known among horticulturists and are rarely cultivated even in their home country. The delightful *C. pulvinaris* is the most likely species to be available from specialist plant nurseries and cultivated by alpine enthusiasts. Chionohebes are mainly high alpines, usually occurring between 1400 and 2400 m, and most are small cushion plants, with the exception of *C. densifolia*, which is trailing or creeping. Most of the cushion species are not easily grown outdoors, particularly in areas that experience wet winters. Some form of winter protection, such as a square of glass overhead, may be necessary. Alternatively, cultivation in an alpine house may be a good option. Seed or division is the usual method of propagation.

Chionohebe ciliolata

This species forms pale green cushions and is similar to *Chionohebe pulvinaris*, although plants vary considerably depending upon where they are growing. Sometimes the cushions are so loose that they barely qualify as a cushion. The leaves are small, about 2.5–5 by 1–3.5 mm, obovate to linear-spathulate or narrow-ovate, with a broadly obtuse to subacute apex. The flowers are white and 6–7 mm long, with the tube shorter than the calyx, which has obtuse lobes. *Chionohebe ciliolata* comprises three varieties, which differ mainly in the size and rigidity of their cushions, leaf shape, size, and hairiness.

DISTRIBUTION: South Island in the higher-rainfall regions and just about exclusively west of the main divide. Occurs from Nelson to Fiordland and western Southland, as well as in Australia and Tasmania. Grows in low- to high-alpine areas, usually on rock outcrops or fine debris in exposed and sheltered fellfield habitats.

Chionohebe ciliolata var. *ciliolata* *

This variety has larger, softer cushions, usually about 2–5 cm high, while its leaves are more loosely imbricated. They are usually obovate-spathulate, broadly obtuse to subacute, and rather closely and evenly ciliate around their broad upper portion, but with usually few cilia near their bases. The name *ciliolata* refers to the fringed or ciliate leaves. This plant was first collected in the Hopkins River valley by Julius Haast.

DISTRIBUTION: South Island. West of the main divide from south of the Browning Pass to about Mount Aspiring.

Chionohebe ciliolata var. *fiordensis*

The cushions of this variety are usually more compacted and tend to be more rigid than those of the other two varieties. It also has more stiffly imbricated leaves that are narrow-ovate to ovate-spathulate, with subacute to acute apexes, and usually ciliate more or less to their bases with only a few cilia near the tips except for a prominent tuft at the apex. The name *fiordensis* refers to the area where this variety occurs. It was first collected in Takahe Valley, Fiordland, by W. R. B. Oliver.

DISTRIBUTION: South Island. Found in the mountains of Fiordland.

Chionohebe ciliolata var. *pumila*

This variety has small, rather soft cushions about 1–2 cm high. Its leaves are loosely imbricated, more or less spathulate, obtuse to subacute, and ciliate especially in the upper half. The varietal name *pumila* means "dwarf" and refers to its dwarf habit. First collected on the Discovery Peaks, Spenser Mountains, by W. T. L. Travers.

DISTRIBUTION: South Island. Occurs on the mountains of Nelson and northern Westland.

Chionohebe densifolia

This is a low, creeping species that forms loose patches 5–15 cm across. Its branches are short and square, with four rows of brownish-green leaves. The leaves are 3–6 by 1.5–3.5 mm and have a few hairs along their margins. Its flowers are quite large, about 1–1.5 cm across, and vary from white to pale mauve. They usually occur singly at the tips of the branchlets. The calyx and corolla are both five-lobed and deeply cut. The specific name *densifolia* refers to the leaves, which are densely arranged on the stems.

DISTRIBUTION: South Island. Low to high alpine on the higher mountains of the Lakes District in Central and North Otago. Also occurs in Australia in the Mount Kosciusko area. Mainly grows on open and exposed sites in snow tussock–grassland or in sheltered, moist sites in fellfield and cushion vegetation at 1100–1800 m.

Chionohebe glabra *

Formerly included as a variety of *Chionohebe thomsonii* (var. *glabra*), this chionohebe was accorded specific rank by Michael J. Heads. It differs from *C. thomsonii* in being glabrous or having only a few scattered hairs on the margins. In form it is between *C. thomsonii* and

C. myosotoides, to both of which it bears some resemblance. At times its inflorescence may also be quite elongated. This species was originally collected on Mount Pisa in Central Otago by Donald Petrie prior to 1906.

Chionohebe myosotoides *

This species is rather similar to *Chionohebe thomsonii* but differs in having more loosely set leaves with distinctive hairs. It also forms cushions that are similar to those of *C. pulvinaris*. Its leaves are 3–4.5 by 1.5–2.5 mm, linear to obovate-spathulate, with an obtuse to broadly subacute apex. The upper part of the outer surface is sparsely clad with slender, lax, tangled hairs. Its flowers are white and 4.5–5 mm long, with the tube more or less equalling the calyx lobes. The specific name *myosotoides* refers to this plant's resemblance to a species of *Myosotis*, possibly *M. pulvinaris*. Discovered on Mount Pisa by Donald Petrie.

DISTRIBUTION: South Island. A species so far found only on the summits of the Rock and Pillar Range and Pisa Range in Central Otago, where it occurs among the cushion vegetation at 1800 m.

Chionohebe pulvinaris

This is one of the commonest species occurring from the mountains of Nelson and Marlborough to Canterbury. It forms very distinctive, little, moss-like cushions of a dull greyish-green, usually 5–15 cm in diameter and as much as 4 cm high. Generally they are quite firm and dense. Its white flowers are 5–6 mm long and similar to those of other *Chionohebe* species; their anthers are bluish and after rain the flowers appear as though filled with diluted ink. Among chionohebes this plant is the easiest and most amenable to cultivation. It requires a gritty, well-drained soil and a sunny or partially shaded situation. It is also impatient of too much overhead moisture during the winter. The specific name *pulvinaris* refers to this plant's cushion-like habit of growth. Discovered on the Torlesse Range by Julius Haast.

DISTRIBUTION: South Island. Often widespread in the mountains of Nelson, Marlborough, and Canterbury. Occurs on exposed, rocky sites, such as eroding ridgetops in snow tussock–grassland and herbfield, and on loose debris or outcrops in fellfield. Grows at 1400–1900 m.

Chionohebe thomsonii (PLATE 135)

In colour and habit *Chionohebe thomsonii* is generally similar to *C. pulvinaris* except that its cushions are denser and firmer. Its leaves are also broader and more closely imbricated. They are 2.5–4 by 1–2 mm and linear-spathulate to rhomboid-ovate, their inner surfaces densely and finely hairy, with the hairs often forming a well-defined band just below their tips. The white flowers are 4–6 mm long and have bluish or purplish anthers. This species is named after a Mr. Thomson, probably G. M. Thomson, a school teacher who botanised Otago during the latter part of the 19th century. Discovered on Mount Alta, Otago, by Messrs. Buchanan and McKay.

DISTRIBUTION: South Island. Occurs in high-alpine areas on the higher mountains of Otago and northern Southland. Usually grows on windswept rocks and rock outcrops, loose debris in fellfield, and with other cushion vegetation, at 1400–2400 m.

Conversion Tables

INCHES	CENTIMETRES		FEET	METRES
¼	0.6		1	0.3
½	1.25		6	1.8
1	2.5		8	2.4
2	5.0		10	3.0
3	7.5		20	6.0
4	10		25	7.5
5	12.5		30	9.0
6	15		50	15
7	18		100	30
8	20		1000	300
9	23		2500	750
10	25		5000	1500
15	37		7500	2250
20	51		10,000	3000

TEMPERATURES

$$°C = \tfrac{5}{9} \times (°F - 32)$$
$$°F = (\tfrac{9}{5} \times °C) + 32$$

Glossary

acuminate: tapering to a gradually diminishing point

acute: sharply pointed but not drawn out; also applied to any organ having a sharp edge or margin

amplexicaul: clasping the stem

anterior: before or in front of

anther: the pollen-bearing part of a stamen

apex: the tip or free end of an organ or part

apiculate: abruptly ending in a short, sharp point

appressed: lying flat or pressed close for the whole length, as hairs to the surface of a leaf

approximate: close together

arcuate: curved like a bow

ascending: rising somewhat obliquely; not quite erect

attenuate: tapering gradually; drawn out

bench: a land form usually caused by rivers of glaciation where the action of water, or ice, cuts down the adjoining land in a series of steps or benches

bifarious: arranged in two opposite rows

bipartite: in two parts

blade: the expanded part, as of a leaf or petal

bloom: a white or glaucous powdery covering

bract: a modified leaf subtending a flower or cluster of flowers, placed in the space between the calyx and the true leaves

calyx: the outer series of floral envelopes

cartilaginous: resembling cartilage; firm and tough but flexible

ciliate: fringed with hairs (diminutive: *ciliolate*)

concave: hollow, as the inner surface of a saucer

conidiophore: a simple, unbranched fungal hypha that bears spores

connate: united, either congenitally or by subsequent growth

convex: having a more or less rounded surface

cordate: having two equal rounded lobes at the base

coriaceous: tough and leathery

corolla: the inner perianth, consisting of the petals, free or united

corymb: a flat-topped or convex open inflorescence with a short axis, flowering from the circumference inwards

corymbose: arranged in corymbs or resembling a corymb

crenate: cut into rounded notches; applied to a leaf margin

crenulate: finely crenate

cultivar: a plant originating and persisting under cultivation; the word is a combination of *cultivated* and *variety*

cuneate: wedge-shaped; gradually and evenly narrowed to the base

cusp: a sharp, rigid point

cuspidate: having a sharp, rigid point

decumbent: reclining or horizontal at the base but ascending at the tips or summit

decussate: in pairs crossing alternately at right angles, as the leaves of most species of *Hebe*

deflexed: bent abruptly downwards

dentate: toothed, with the teeth regular and pointing straight outwards

denticle: a minute tooth

depressed: flattened from above

dioecious: unisexual; having male and female flowers on different plants

distichous: to be in two opposite rows so as to lie in the one plane

distinct: separate; not united

domatia: small pits, as on the abaxial surface of the leaves of some species of plants, such as *Nothofagus* and *Coprosma*; located in the angle between a lateral vein and the midrib, and nearer the margin as in *Hebe townsonii*

eglandular: without glands

elliptic: having the form of an ellipse; oblong with regularly rounded ends

emarginate: having a notch at the end as if a piece had been taken out

endemic: confined to a particular country or region

entire: having an even margin without toothing or division of any kind

erose: jagged, as if irregularly gnawed or bitten off

exserted: thrust forth, or protruding or extending from surrounding organs

falcate: sickle-shaped, strongly curved

family: a group of related plants; a taxonomic category just above a genus

filament: (1) the stalk or support of an anther; (2) any thread-like body

filiform: thread-shaped or thread-like

forma (f.): a taxonomic unit inferior to a variety; differs from the type in certain constant characters of subordinate value

fulvous: tawny; dull yellow with a mixture of grey or brown

fused: united congenitally

genus: a clearly defined group of naturally applied species

glabrescent: becoming glabrous

glabrous: smooth, without hairs or pubescence

gland: an organ or part that secretes oil, resin, or another liquid

glandular: (1) bearing glands; (2) having the nature of a gland

glaucescent: slightly glaucous or becoming so

glaucous: having a distinctly bluish-green colour, not necessarily due to a bloom

hermaphrodite: having stamens and pistils on the same flower

hoary: greyish-white with a fine pubescence

holotype: the one specimen used by the author of a name or designated by the author as the nomenclatural type

hyaline: transparent or nearly so

hybrid: a cross between two species; obtained when the pollen of one species is placed upon the stigma of the other

imbricated: overlapping, as the tiles on a roof, or, in reference to leaves in bud, over-lapping at the edges only

incision: a small, sharp cut

incurved: bent inwards

indigenous: native; not introduced

inserted: attached to or growing upon

insolation: the degree of exposure to the sun's rays

internode: the part of a stem between the buds or nodes

lanceolate: shaped like a lance head; tapering upwards from a narrow, ovate base

lateral: produced from the side

lax: loose, distant

limb: the expanded part of a petal or sepal

linear: narrow and elongated, with parallel margins

lobe: any division, as of a leaf or corolla, especially if rounded

locule: a compartment or cavity of an organ, such as the ovary, seed capsule, and so forth

membranous: thin and more or less pliable

mucro: a sharp terminal point

mucronate: possessing a mucro

naked: bare; without the usual covering or appendages, as a stem without leaves or a flower without a perianth

node: the part of a stem from which leaves or branches are given off; the knots in the stems of grasses

oblique: (1) having unequal sides; (2) slanting, turned to one side

oblong: considerably longer than broad, with parallel sides and rounded ends

obovate: inversely ovate, with the broadest part towards the apex

obtuse: blunt or rounded at the end

ocular ring: the usually coloured ring on the inside of a corolla from which the nectary guides radiate

orbicular: having a circular outline; applied to a leaf or other body

ovate: shaped like the longitudinal section of an egg, with the broadest part towards the base

ovoid: of a solid body with an ovate outline

panicle: a loose, irregularly branched inflorescence usually containing many flowers; a branched raceme or corymb

papillate: having minute, pimple-like processes

pedicel: the stalk supporting a single flower in a compound inflorescence

peduncle: a general or primary flower stalk bearing one or many flowers

perfect: having both stamens and pistil; applied to a flower

perianth: the floral envelopes, including the calyx or the corolla, or both

persistent: not falling off; remaining attached to its support

petiolate: the adjectival form of *petiole*

petiole: the footstalk of a leaf

pilose: bearing soft, shaggy hairs

pinnate: compound, with the parts arranged along either side of an axis, as in a feather

pinnatifid: divided in a pinnate manner

plicate: folded lengthwise into plaits, like those of a fan

plumose: feather-like

posterior: following after or later; at the back

pubescent: clad in short, soft hairs (diminutive: *puberulent, puberulous*)

raceme: an inflorescence having several pedicellate flowers arranged on a prolonged axis, with the lower flowers opening first

racemose: bearing racemes or like a raceme

rachis: the axis of an inflorescence, compound leaf, or frond

recurved: curved backwards or downwards

reflexed: bent abruptly down or backwards

retuse: having a rounded apex with a shallow notch at the centre

revolute: having the margins or apex rolled backwards

rhombic: obliquely four-sided

scabrous: rough to the touch; furnished with minute points or asperities

scarious: thin, dry, and membranous, not green

sepal: each separate part or division of a calyx

serrate: sharply toothed, with the teeth pointing forwards like the teeth of a saw

sessile: sitting directly on the point of support without any intervening footstalk or petiole

simple: of one piece; not compound

sinus: an angular or rounded recess or depression separating lobes or segments, as found in many species of *Hebe*

species: a group of all those individuals possessing the same and distinctive characters; a taxonomic rank just below a genus

spike: an inflorescence having several or many sessile flowers arranged on a lengthened axis, with the lower flowers opening first

stamen: the pollen-bearing organ of the flower, consisting of an anther usually borne on a filament or stalk

stigma: the portion of the pistil that receives the pollen, usually situated at the tip of the style

stomata: distinctive pores through which gasses diffuse; from *stoma*, meaning "mouth" or "opening"

striated: marked with fine longitudinal lines

strict: upright and very straight

style: the upper attenuated part of a pistil or carpel, bearing the stigma at its top

subshrub: a small plant with stems more or less woody at the base; not quite a shrub

subspecies (subsp.): a subdivision of a species; differs from the type in certain constant characters of subordinate value

subtend: to stand below, usually close to another organ such as a bract

subulate: awl-shaped

synonym: a superseded or disused name

taxon: a taxonomic group of any rank, such as family, genus, species, or variety

terete: cylindrical or nearly so, not angled or grooved

tetragonous: four-angled

tortuous: twisted or winding

trifid: cut into three parts

tripartite: in three parts

tumid: swollen

type: the one specimen or element used by the author of a name or designated by the author as the nomenclatural type

typical: that which corresponds with or represents the type

ultramafic: composed of rocks, mostly plutonic, consisting primarily of ferromagnesian minerals and very low in silica and feldspar

unisexual: of one sex; applied to flowers having stamens only or pistils only

variety (var.): a subdivision of a species; differs from the type in certain constant characters of subordinate value

villous: clad in long, soft hairs not matted together

Bibliography

Albach, D. C., H. M. Meudt, and B. Oxelman. 2005. Piecing together the "new" Plantaginaceae. *American Journal of Botany* 92 (3): 297–315.

Allan, H. H. 1961. *Flora of New Zealand*. Volume 1. Government Printer: Wellington, New Zealand.

Armstrong, J. B. 1880. A synopsis of the New Zealand species of *Veronica* [*Hebe*]. *Transactions of the New Zealand Institute*.

Bailey, L. H. 1928. *The Standard Cyclopedia of Horticulture*. MacMillan: New York.

Bayly, M. J., P. J. Garnock-Jones, K. A. Mitchell, K. R. Markham, and P. J. Brownsey. 2000. A taxonomic revision of the *Hebe parviflora* complex (Scrophulariaceae), based on morphology and flavonoid chemistry. *New Zealand Journal of Botany* 38: 165–190.

Bayly, M. J., P. J. Garnock-Jones, K. A. Mitchell, K. R. Markham, and P. J. Brownsey. 2001. Description and flavonoid chemistry of *Hebe calcicola* (Scropulariaceae), a new species from north-western Nelson, New Zealand. *New Zealand Journal of Botany* 39: 55–67.

Bayly, M. J., A. V. Kellow, K. A. Mitchell, K. R. Markham, P. J. de Lange, G. E. Harper, P. J. Garnock-Jones, and P. J. Brownsey. 2002. Descriptions and flavonoid chemistry of new taxa in *Hebe* sect. *Subdistichae* (Scrophulariaceae). *New Zealand Journal of Botany* 40: 571–602.

Bean, W. J. 1925. *Trees and Shrubs Hardy in the British Isles*. 4th edition. Murray: London.

Bean, W. J. 1950. *Trees and Shrubs Hardy in the British Isles*. 7th edition. Murray: London.

Bean, W. J. 1973. *Trees and Shrubs Hardy in the British Isles*. 8th edition. Volume 2. Murray: London.

Bean, W. J. 1981. *Trees and Shrubs Hardy in the British Isles*. Supplement. Murray: London.

Brockie, W. B. 1945. *New Zealand Alpines in Field and Garden*. Caxton Press: Christchurch, New Zealand.

Cervelli, C. 1996. Flowering of *Hebe* in the Riviera di Ponte—Italy (in Italian). *Flortecnica* 3: 3–13.

Cervelli, C. 2003. *Hebe: Cultivation Guide in a Mediterranean Climate* (in Italian). Istituto Sperimentale per la Floricultura: Sanremo, Italy.

Cervelli, C., C. Mascarello, and C. Dalla Guda. 1998. Effect of propagation date on flowering of five *Hebe* cultivars. *Acta Horticulturae* 454: 281–288.

Cervelli, C., C. Mascarello, and M. Devecchi. 1997. Effect of different temperatures on flowering of two *Hebe* cultivars (in Italian, with abstract). *Italus Hortus* 4 (1): 42–48.

Chalk, D. 1988. *Hebes and Parahebes*. Christopher Helm: London.

Cheeseman, T. F. 1914. *Illustrations of the New Zealand Flora*. Government Printer: Wellington, New Zealand.

Cheeseman, T. F. 1925. *Manual of the New Zealand Flora*. Government Printer: Wellington, New Zealand.

Chittenden, F. J. 1951. *Dictionary of Gardening*. Royal Horticultural Society: London.

Clarkson, B. D., and P. J. Garnock-Jones. 1996. A new *Hebe* species: *Hebe tairawhiti*. *New Zealand Botanical Society Newsletter* 44 (June): 13–14.

Cockayne, L. 1924. *The Cultivation of New Zealand Plants*. Whitcombe and Tombs: Christchurch, New Zealand.

Cockayne, L. 1967. *New Zealand Plants and Their Story*. 4th edition. Government Printer: Wellington, New Zealand.

Cockayne, L., and H. H. Allan. 1934. An annotated list of groups of wild hybrids in the New Zealand flora. *Annals of Botany (London)* 48: 1–55.

de Lange, P. J. 1997. *Hebe brevifolia* (Scrophulariaceae)—an ultramafic endemic of the Surville Cliffs, North Cape, New Zealand. *New Zealand Journal of Botany* 35: 1–8.

de Lange, P. J. 1998. *Hebe perbella* (Scrophulariaceae)—a new and threatened species from Northland, North Island, New Zealand. *New Zealand Journal of Botany* 36: 399–406.

Eagle, A. 1975. *Eagle's Trees and Shrubs of New Zealand*. 2nd series. Collins: Auckland, New Zealand.

Fisher, M. E., E. Satchell, and J. M. Watkins. 1970. *Gardening with New Zealand Plants, Shrubs and Trees*. Collins: Auckland, New Zealand.

Ganley, E., and L. Collins. 1999. A new population of *Hebe speciosa* (titirangi) on the Waikato coast. *New Zealand Botanical Society Newsletter* 57 (September): 16–19.

Garnock-Jones, P. J. 1975. *Hebe rapensis* (F. Brown) Garnock-Jones comb. nov. and its relationships. *New Zealand Journal of Botany* 14: 79–83.

Garnock-Jones, P. J. 1976. Breeding systems and pollination in New Zealand *Parahebe* (Scrophulariaceae). *New Zealand Journal of Botany* 14: 291–298.

Garnock-Jones, P. J. 1976. Infraspecific taxonomy of *Parahebe linifolia* (Scrophulariaceae). *New Zealand Journal of Botany* 14: 285–289.

Garnock-Jones, P. J. 1980. *Parahebe catarractae* (Scrophulariaceae) infraspecific taxonomy. *New Zealand Journal of Botany* 18: 285–298.

Garnock-Jones, P. J. 1993. *Heliohebe* (Scrophulariaceae—Veroniceae), a new genus segregated from *Hebe*. *New Zealand Journal of Botany* 31: 323–339.

Garnock-Jones, P. J. 1993. Phylogeny of the *Hebe* complex (Scrophulariaceae: Veroniceae). *Australian Systematic Botany* 6: 457–479.

Garnock-Jones, P. J., M. J. Bayly, W. G. Lee, and B. D. Rance. 2000. *Hebe arganthera* (Scrophulariaceae), a new species from calcareous outcrops in Fiordland, New Zealand. *New Zealand Journal of Botany* 38: 379–388.

Garnock-Jones, P. J., and B. D. Clarkson. 1994. *Hebe adamsii* and *H. murrellii* (Scrophulariaceae) reinstated. *New Zealand Journal of Botany* 32: 11–15.

Garnock-Jones, P. J., and D. G. Lloyd. 2004. A taxonomic revision of *Parahebe* (Plantaginaceae) in New Zealand. *New Zealand Journal of Botany* 42: 181–232.

Garnock-Jones, P. J., and B. P. J. Molloy. 1982. Polymorphism and the taxonomic status of the *Hebe amplexicaulis* complex (Scrophulariaceae). *New Zealand Journal of Botany* 20: 391–399.

Garnock-Jones, P. J., and B. P. J. Molloy. 1982. Protandry and inbreeding depression in *Hebe amplexicaulis* (Scrophulariaceae). *New Zealand Journal of Botany* 20: 401–404.

Garnock-Jones, P. J., and S. J. Wagstaff. 2000. Patterns of diversication in *Chionohebe* and *Parahebe* (Scrophulariaceae) inferred from ITS sequences. *New Zealand Journal of Botany* 38: 389–407.

Given, D. R. 1981. *Rare and Endangered Plants*. Reed: Wellington, New Zealand.

Harrison, R. E. 1960. *Handbook of Trees and Shrubs for the Southern Hemisphere*. 2nd revised edition. Harrison: Palmerston North, New Zealand.

Harrison, R. E. 1967. *Handbook of Trees and Shrubs for the Southern Hemisphere*. 4th edition. Harrison: Palmerston North, New Zealand.

Heenan, P. B. 1992. *Hebe* 'Karo Golden Esk'—a new cultivar. *Journal of the Royal New Zealand Institute of Horticulture* 3 (2): 5–6.

Heenan, P. B. 1993. John Luscombe—a pioneer hybridiser of *Hebe* and *Rhododendron*. *Journal of the Royal New Zealand Institute of Horticulture* 4 (2): 23–27.

Heenan, P. B. 1994. The origin and identification of *Hebe* ×*andersonii* and its cultivars (Scrophulariaceae). *Journal of the Royal New Zealand Institute of Horticulture* 5 (1): 21–25.

Heenan, P. B. 1994. The origin and identification of *Hebe* ×*franciscana* and its cultivars (Scrophulariaceae). *Journal of the Royal New Zealand Institute of Horticulture* 5 (1): 15–20.

Heenan, P. B. 1994. The status of names in *Hebe* published by Professor Arnold Wall in 1929. *New Zealand Journal of Botany* 32: 521–522.

Hibbert, M. 2004. *Aussie Plant Finder*. Florilegium: Rozelle, New South Wales, Australia.

Hooker, J. D. 1864. *Handbook of the New Zealand Flora*. Lovell Reeve: London.

Hutchins, G. 1997. *Hebes Here and There*. Hutchins and Davies: United Kingdom.

Kellow, A. V., M. J. Bayly, K. A. Mitchell, K. R. Markham, and P. J. Brownsey. 2003. A taxonomic revision of *Hebe* informal group "Connatae" (Plantaginaceae), based on morphology and flavonoid chemistry. *New Zealand Journal of Botany* 41: 613–635.

Kellow, A. V., M. J. Bayly, K. A. Mitchell, K. R. Markham, and P. J. Garnock-Jones. 2003. Variation in morphology and flavonoid chemistry in *Hebe pimeleoides* (Scrophulariaceae), including a revised subspecific classification. *New Zealand Journal of Botany* 41: 233–253.

Laing, R. M., and E. W. Blackwell. 1906. *Plants of New Zealand*. Whitcombe and Tombs: Christchurch, New Zealand.

Laing, R. M., and E. W. Blackwell. 1927. *Plants of New Zealand*. Whitcombe and Tombs: Christchurch, New Zealand.

Mark, A. F., and N. M. Adams. 1995. *New Zealand Alpine Plants*. Revised edition. Godwit: Auckland, New Zealand.

Martin, W. 1929. *Flora of New Zealand*. Whitcombe and Tombs: Christchurch, New Zealand.

Metcalf, L. J. 1972. *The Cultivation of New Zealand Trees and Shrubs*. Reed: Wellington, New Zealand.

Metcalf, L. J. 2001. *International Register of Hebe Cultivars*. Royal New Zealand Institute of Horticulture: Canterbury, New Zealand.

Moore, L. B., and J. B. Irwin. 1978. *The Oxford Book of New Zealand Plants*. Oxford: Wellington, New Zealand.

Nicholson, G. 1887–1900. *Dictionary of Gardening*. Upcott Gill: London.

Noack, Linda. 1991. A thesis on the environmental control of flower induction in horticultural plants. Case study: *Hebe*. PhD thesis. Copenhagen, Denmark: The Royal Veterinary and Agricultural University.

Norton, D. A., and P. J. de Lange. 1998. *Hebe paludosa* (Scrophulariaceae)—a new combination for an endemic wetland *Hebe* from Westland, South Island, New Zealand. *New Zealand Journal of Botany* 36: 531–538.

Richards, E. C. 1947. *Our New Zealand Trees and Flowers*. Whitcombe and Tombs: Christchurch, New Zealand.

Wagstaff, S. J., M. J. Bayly, P. J. Garnock-Jones, and C. D. Albach. 2002. Classification, origin, and diversification of the New Zealand hebes (Scrophulariaceae). *Annals of the Missouri Botanical Garden* 89: 38–63.

Wagstaff, S. J., and P. Wardle. 1999. Whipcord hebes—systematics, distribution, ecology and evolution. *New Zealand Journal of Botany* 37: 17–39.

Wheeler, C., and V. Wheeler. 2002. *Gardening with Hebes*. Guild of Master Craftsman Publications: Lewes, United Kingdom.

Williams, G. R., and D. R. Given. 1981. *The Red Data Book of New Zealand*. Nature Conservation Council: Wellington, New Zealand.

Wilson, H., and T. Galloway. 1993. *Small-Leaved Shrubs of New Zealand*. Manuka Press: Christchurch, New Zealand.

Index

Boldface indicates a principal reference.